D0897787

NEW YORK

A Guide to the Metropolis

NEW YORK

A Guide to
the Metropolis

WALKING TOURS
OF ARCHITECTURE
AND HISTORY

by GERARD R. WOLFE

NEW YORK UNIVERSITY PRESS

PROJECT EDITOR: NAT LA MAR

DESIGNED BY PHILIP GRUSHKIN

MAPS BY HENRY SIWEK

Frontispiece photo courtesy Port Authority of N.Y. & N.J.

Copyright © 1975 by New York University

Library of Congress Catalog Card Number: 74-21706

Library of Congress Cataloging in Publication Data

Wolfe, Gerard R   1926–
    New York, a guide to the metropolis.

    Bibliography: p.
    1. New York (City)—Description—1951–   —Tours.
2. New York (City)—Buildings. I. Title.
F128.18.W58   917.47′1′044   74-21706
ISBN 0-8147-9160-3
ISBN 0-8147-9163-8 pbk.

Printed in the United States of America
by Quinn & Boden Company, Inc., Rahway, New Jersey

*To my students, whose keen enthusiasm
for New York's fascinating cityscape
was the inspiration for this book.*

Contents

Introduction

What a thrill is in store for the reader of this guide who is facing the adventure of a walking tour in New York City.

Our prominent landmarks are easily seen—Times Square, Central Park, the steel canyon of the Avenue of the Americas, the beauty and sparkle of Fifth Avenue, and the monumental twin towers of the World Trade Center.

You will have the privilege of seeing the magnificent Brooklyn Bridge, a 19th century wonder of construction and beauty that gives reason for Americans to feel they need yield nothing to the Gothic cathedrals of Europe. And be sure to see the Flatiron Building at 23rd Street and Fifth Avenue. At the turn of the century, it was New York's most unique skyscraper, a building of dignity which stands guard over the massive intersections of our unbelievably bustling city.

New York is a city of surprise and adventure, best seen on foot, where one can not only see but feel and hear its multitudes. There is color and vivacity and variety here among our New Yorkers and above all there is love of life.

Professor Wolfe's *New York: A Guide to the Metropolis* will help you experience all the history, beauty, and excitement New York City has to offer.

Jacob K. Javits

Foreword

The writing of this book evolved from a course I have been teaching at New York University, entitled *The Many Faces of Gotham*. Consisting of a series of lectures and walking tours to sections of New York City of architectural and historic interest, the content, which is changed each semester, has attracted a rather large number of students who take the course year after year. It was this coterie of enthusiastic and dedicated "New York building observers" who induced me to prepare this guide so that others might share in the exhilarating discovery of our city—and at what more appropriate moment than on the occasion of our nation's Bicentennial.

No walking-tour guidebook of New York City can be called complete and still be portable. Many agonizing compromises had to be made, and in the process, some neighborhoods and historic districts had to be omitted. From the dozens of walking tours offered in recent years I have selected 20 that seemed to generate the greatest interest, and which both I and my students agreed offered the broadest perspective of the city's many architectural styles as well as a general historical overview.

Obviously, no visitor to the city should omit such important landmarks as Lincoln Center, Rockefeller Center, the Empire State Building, the Metropolitan Museum of Art, the Guggenheim and Whitney museums, the Cloisters, the Bronx and Brooklyn Botanic Gardens, the Brooklyn Museum, the Jumel Mansion, among others; nor should he skip the spectacular Staten Island Ferry ride or a trip to the Statue of Liberty and its Museum of Immigration. These are individual points of interest for which a walking-tour guidebook serves no purpose. Excellent walking tours of Central and Prospect parks are available from the Greensward Foundation [*see* page 281], and the historic Richmondtown Restoration on Staten Island offers conducted tours on weekends. Any newsstand or bookstore, or the New York City Convention and Visitors Bureau, can supply a listing of the city's many tourist attractions; and a pocket listing of all designated landmarks and historic districts is distributed free by the New York City Landmarks Preservation Commission.

Through the years, many of our great landmarks have disappeared, either through natural catastrophes (such as the Great Fire of 1835, which eradicated every remaining Dutch Colonial building in Manhattan), or through

the man-made catastrophes of the wrecker's ball. Yet almost miraculously
an enormous number of beautiful old buildings still survive. No other city in
America can boast the quantity and variety of architecture that can be seen
in our public and private buildings, which span almost three centuries. However, a dark, menacing cloud has emerged in the form of a temporarily successful legal challenge to the ten-year-old Landmarks Preservation Law. At
this writing, we are about to lose the J. P. Morgan House, one of the last freestanding Italianate mansions in the city. Also threatened is that magnificent Beaux Arts architectural masterpiece, Grand Central Terminal, whose
owners, the Penn Central Corporation, plan its demolition and replacement
with an unneeded office tower. Perhaps logic will prevail in the higher courts,
and the *42nd Street Walking Tour* will not have to be corrected to include
an obituary for the landmark.

The walking tours vary in length from two to five hours, but can be
divided easily into shorter walks if desired. Each itinerary is clearly indicated
on the tour map. The tours are arranged chronologically in Manhattan, following the northward growth of the city. In Brooklyn, beginning with the
Brooklyn Heights tour, the pattern is essentially the same, although the *Park
Slope* and *Clinton Hill* sections developed at about the same time. *Historic
Flushing,* the only tour in Queens, covers much of the early Dutch Colonial
period, no evidence of which exists any longer in Manhattan. Some tours,
such as *Greenwich Village, Madison Square,* and *Gramercy Park* are more
"experiential" than architectural. Those tours whose points of interest are
at some distance from each other are numbered in the text and on the map.
A brief glossary of architectural terms will be found on page 159, following
the SoHo Cast-Iron District Walking Tour.

This guidebook is designed not only for the out-of-towner, but for the
usually blasé native New Yorker who customarily scarcely glances at buildings, and rarely if ever above the first floor. In short, its purpose is to help
provide insight into the tangible aspects of our city's history as represented
in its buildings. Hopefully, the reader will be encouraged to explore New
York City on foot, learning to look at buildings with a new and discriminat-
ing eye, deriving pleasure and satisfaction from the discovery of these vestiges
of our past . . . and perhaps becoming a vigorous advocate of their preservation.

GERARD R. WOLFE
November 1975

Acknowledgments

This book could not have been possible without the cooperation and assistance of many individuals and organizations.

I am particularly grateful to Beverly Moss Spatt, Chairman, New York City Landmarks Preservation Commission, who in the interest of having the public better informed about the architectural importance of New York City's buildings, gave me permission to quote from the Commission's copyrighted Designation Report of the SoHo Cast-Iron District, and made available the wealth of information contained in the designation reports of the Chelsea, Cobble Hill, Henderson Place, and Park Slope Historic Districts.

I am also indebted to Dr. Ellen Kramer of the Landmarks Commission for useful reference material, and for her many suggestions on the preparation of the manuscript; to Allan Burnham of the Landmarks Commission for reading a sample chapter and making helpful comments which served as guidelines for the rest of the book; to Charlotte La Rue of the Museum of the City of New York for many hours spent patiently helping me select appropriate photographs from the Museum's extensive collection; and to Roxanne Young of the Long Island Historical Society who unlocked a wealth of illustrative material in the Society's archives on my periodic visits.

For other photographs and prints, I am greatly obliged to Ernest Pawel, New York Life Insurance Company; William H. Hand, Brooklyn Union Gas Company; Henry J. DiRocco, Office of the Borough President of Queens; Susan C. Holahan, Consolidated Edison Company of New York; Eleanor C. Waters, Seamen's Bank for Savings; Dorothy C. Gates, Home Insurance Company; Margaret Knowles, Community Service Society of New York; Margaret I. Carman, Bowne House Historical Society; David G. Oats, *Flushing Tribune;* and to the librarians of the Metropolitan Life Insurance Company; the archivists of the American Telephone & Telegraph Company; the Religious Society of Friends of Flushing; the historians of the South Street Seaport Museum; the Equitable Life Assurance Society of the United States; the Fred F. French Investing Company; the Williamsburgh Savings Bank; the Brooklyn Savings Bank; the Singer Company; the Morgan Guaranty Trust Company; the Firefighting Museum of the Home Insurance Company; John

Stobart, artist, and the Kennedy Galleries, Inc.; the Picture Decorator, Inc.; and the United Nations Photo Service.

I acknowledge with thanks permission to quote from *Turn West on 23rd,* by Robert Baral, Copyright 1965, Fleet Press Corporation, New York; and also the generosity of Warner Brothers Music, Hollywood, for authorization to reproduce Al Dubin's lyrics to *Forty-Second Street.*

There were in addition, a number of people who extended themselves in a multitude of ways by opening doors to sources of information not generally available to the public, by lending me family scrapbooks, by allowing me entry to private archives, by sharing reminiscences, and by aiding with obscure but highly important bits of research. Among them were the staff of the Long Island Historical Society, the staff of the South Street Seaport Museum, members of the Queens Historical Society, Friends of Cast-Iron Architecture, Gruzen & Partners, the Brooklyn Heights Association, the Colonial Dames of America; as well as Alex Parker, One Times Square; John Virgil, Wurlitzer Music Company; Dr. George Litch Knight, Lafayette Avenue Presbyterian Church; Rev. David L. Slater, Cadman Memorial Church; Bob Gesslein, Long Island University; Harry Kirschbaum, architect; Judith Ann Yavarkovsky; Capt. Joseph Zito, New York City Police Department (retired); and my father, Samuel Wolfe, whose fascinating recollections of the Lower East Side were priceless.

I am especially grateful to Dr. Toby B. Bieber for her encouragement and support, and for her imperishable enthusiasm which helped sustain me through the project; and also to Prof. Mendor T. Brunetti, great teacher and friend, whose counsel and recommendations were invaluable.

Finally, to my editor Nat LaMar I owe special recognition and obligation for his tireless efforts steering the manuscript through the tribulations and traumata of publication, and for his skill in helping me solve the innumerable and frustrating problems a writer must face before his book becomes a reality.

G. R. W.

lovely brass floor medallions, in addition to a marble and bronze sculpture, *Service to the Nation,* by Chester Beach.

No. 192 Broadway, across the street, is an undistinguished survivor from the 1880s, somehow bypassed by the land developers. Interesting are the so-called Queen Anne cast-iron bay windows. A few feet around the corner was the **site of the John Street Theater,** from 1767 to 1798. During the British occupation of New York in the Revolutionary War, General Howe's army officers frequently would take part in the cast and production of plays. Later, Royall Tyler's play, *The Contrast,* opened as the first comedy work by a native author ever produced in America. George Washington was an often seen theatergoer here.

No. 175 Broadway, the Germania Building, an even older survivor, is typical of the commercial architecture of the 1860s—the Palladian Italian Renaissance style. This was the style so often copied by the cast-iron architects and later recopied in stone. That this 1865 building remains at all is a minor miracle.

Cross Broadway to the northeast corner of Maiden Lane.

Set in the sidewalk is a large glass clock. Dating from 1925, it replaced an earlier model installed by the same firm of William Barthman in 1896. The timepiece is adjusted from the basement, and the protective glass—1½-inches thick—must be changed three times a year because of the constant scuffing from millions of pedestrians' shoes. In 1911 a runaway horse smashed into the store window, splintering the showcase and scattering a quarter-of-a-

Busy Broadway in the mid-1880s, lined with horse-drawn traffic. All the buildings on the right side, to the corner of Cortlandt Street, are still standing; but only one, the narrow, white Germania Building, erected in 1865, has not undergone a "face-lifting." (American Telephone & Telegraph Company)

million dollars in jewelry across Broadway. Yet the street clock below the pavement remained undamaged.

Turn right (west) at Cortlandt Street.

Until the arrival of the World Trade Center, Cortlandt Street was the center of the amateur radio hobbyist. Rows of stores selling electronic gadgets, used parts, and an endless variety of radio hardware lined both Cortlandt Street and neighboring Church Street.

The East River Savings Bank, at the northeast corner of Cortlandt and Church streets, is an almost perfect example of the Art Deco style of the 1930s. This was the approximate **site of a large windmill** built c. 1686 that appears in many old prints of the early city. New York became an important flour-milling center, and two flour barrels appear as part of the city's Great Seal.

The World Trade Center, created by the Port Authority of New York and New Jersey, was planned as a center of world commerce, and took more than ten years to complete. Consisting of two 110-story towers rising 1350 feet and four low-rise Plaza Buildings on a 16-acre site, it is the world's largest commercial complex. The design of the towers involved some revolutionary concepts in skyscraper technology. The conventional skyscraper has been built as a skeleton of structural steel supports, with the outer walls as the "skin." In the World Trade Center towers, the exterior walls bear the load. It consists of closely spaced vertical columns, tied together by massive horizontal spandrel beams that girdle the tower at every floor. The only interior columns are in the core, which contains the elevators. Thus there is

The twin Hudson Terminal buildings were razed to make way for the 110-story World Trade Center. Underneath, was the terminal of the Hudson & Manhattan "Tubes," now called the PATH, and presently located about 100 yards west, beneath the twin Trade Center towers. (Port Authority of New York & New Jersey)

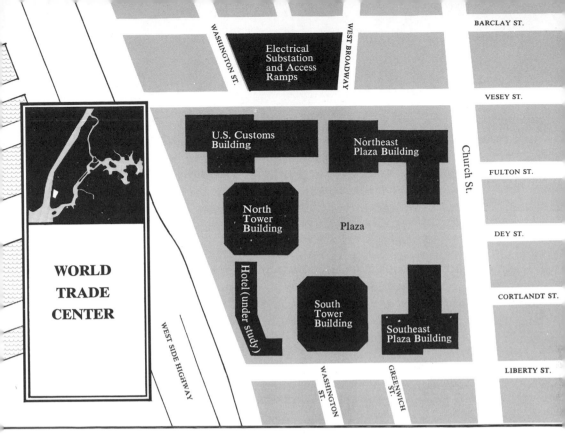

a maximum open, column-free floor space, but large "picture windows" had to be sacrificed. Because of their near-record height, the towers had to be erected from within. Four kangaroo cranes, nestled in the elevator shafts, lifted the tons of steel up the sides of the building; and when the walls rose to the height of the cranes, they were jacked up to a new position to begin again. When the top was finally reached, each crane was dismantled and lowered by a neighboring crane. The last one hoisted up a guy derrick that disassembled the remaining kangaroo crane, lowered its parts to the ground, and was in turn dismantled and brought down by freight elevator. A neat trick and a spectacular show for the thousands of lunchtime "sidewalk superintendents."

To provide efficient access to the upper floors of the towers, the elevator system is divided into three zones, each with its own lobby. Above the Concourse are "skylobbies" on the 44th and 78th floors. There are 23 express and 72 local elevators plus 4 large freight elevators in each tower.

The five-acre central plaza is dominated by an enormous bronze, sculptured globe. More than 1.2 million cubic yards of earth and rock were removed from the excavation to be used for landfill for the nearby Battery Park City project. The architects of this mammoth Center were Minoru Yamasaki and Emery Roth & Sons.

New York's skyline lost one of its great landmarks when U.S. Steel demolished the Singer Tower in 1968 to erect its own building on the site. Architect Ernest Flagg's crowning achievement, the tower was completed in 1908, and was once the world's tallest building. (The Singer Company)

Turn south on Church Street (now called Trinity Place) to Liberty Street and left (east) toward Broadway.

The United States Steel Building (1 Liberty Plaza), appropriately designed to emphasize the "steel I-beam look" occupies the site of the late lamented Singer (Sewing Machine Company) Building as well as the ornate City Investing Building. When the old Singer Tower was completed in 1908, it was the tallest building in the world, until eclipsed by the Metropolitan Life Tower 18 months later. Architect Ernest Flagg's liberal use of metal and glass, incorporated into a graceful shaft in Eclectic style, produced one of the most beautiful buildings ever to grace the New York skyline. Its replacement, built in 1968, adds nothing exciting to the cityscape, and only heightens the feeling of loss. The plaza area was built in accordance with the new zoning regulations, which impose a ratio of open space to a building's verticality. Stop in during working hours at Merrill Lynch's exhibit "The Money Tree," on the main floor.

The Westinghouse Building (150 Broadway), on the northeast corner of Liberty Street, has an attractive plaque marking the site of the founding of the National Board of Underwriters in 1866.

Continue east on Liberty Street.

The **New York Chamber of Commerce Building** (65 Liberty Street) is an attractive example of the French Beaux Arts style. Designed in 1901 by James Barnes Baker, it was built for the State Chamber of Commerce, which was founded in Fraunces Tavern in 1768. The solid Ionic columns seem to frame empty spaces. Originally, there were three large sculpture groups that did not survive New York's air pollution (and pigeons) and suffered so much decay that they were removed some years ago. The impressive white marble edifice was dedicated by President Theodore Roosevelt in an elaborate ceremony witnessed by former President Grover Cleveland and several foreign ambassadors.

The **Liberty Towers** (55 Liberty Street) is a good example of the neo-Gothic style applied to tall commercial buildings. It was designed by Henry Ives Cobb in 1909, but is now overwhelmed by its new neighbor across the street. Step back a few yards down narrow Liberty Place, and observe the fantasy of Gothic reflections in the glassy façade of the Marine Midland Building.

Return to the Plaza in front of 140 Broadway.

The **Marine Midland Building,** designed by Skidmore, Owings & Merrill in 1967, is one of the first New York skyscrapers to have its own plaza. The use of matte black spandrels between rows of glass gives an unexpected effect of sleekness, in sharp contrast to the ornamented façades of nearby buildings. The dark, smooth appearance is further offset by the orange, cube-shaped stabile in the plaza, by sculptor Isamu Noguchi. Before the Marine Midland Bank erected its tower, the site was occupied by the Guaranty Trust Company Building—a very impressive Classic "temple" designed by York & Sawyer in 1912 which had received the American Institute of Architects Medal for Distinguished Architecture two years after its completion.

Continue south on Broadway.

The **U.S. Realty Building** (115 Broadway) and its neighbor to the south, **The Trinity Building** (111 Broadway), are a delightful pair of early 20th-century skyscrapers. Both were designed in the year 1906 by architect Francis H. Kimball, in a modified Gothic style. There is an intimate quality about these narrow twins lacking in most modern buildings. Despite their height, they seem almost like charming residences. Look up at the catwalk connecting the two like a prop for a silent thriller movie. Diminutive Thames Street was originally an 18th-century carriageway leading to the DeLancey stables.

The **Equitable Building** (120 Broadway), designed by Ernest R. Graham in 1915, replaced an earlier Equitable Life Building that was destroyed by fire in 1912. Using every square inch of space, this blockbuster of a building rises 41 stories without setback for a total of 1,200,000 square feet of floor space on a site slightly under an acre! The result is a floor area of about 30 times the plot's. Present zoning laws allow less than 12. Upon completion of the building there arose such a tremendous clamor against the enormous building density, that in 1916 new zoning laws were introduced, establishing the setback requirements that have been progressively tightened through the years.

The Bank of Tokyo (100 Broadway) was formerly the American Surety Building, and was built in 1895 from plans by Bruce Price. The eight allegorical figures were sculpted by J. Massey Rhind.

Trinity Church, designed by Richard Upjohn in 1846, is the third church on the site. Its location at the head of Wall Street makes it one of the best known landmark churches in the city. The original church was established in 1697 by Royal Charter of King William III of England, but it remained for Queen Anne to grant the land in 1705. The first church was destroyed by the Great Fire of 1776, and the second was demolished because of structural failure. With its six chapels, the Trinity Parish is one of the largest of the Episcopal Church. (St. Paul's, St. Christopher's, St. Luke's, etc., are *chapels* of Trinity Parish.) Artistically, the most striking feature of Trinity Church is the three huge sets of bronze doors, designed by Richard Morris Hunt. They were a gift of William Waldorf Astor, and are patterned after the famous Ghiberti bronze doors of the Baptistery in Florence. The sculpture work for the main entrance doors was executed by Karl Bitter, the south doors

The classic Guaranty Trust Company Building, built in 1912, was awarded the AIA Medal for Distinguished Architecture. In its place at 140 Broadway stands the Marine Midland Building. (Morgan Guaranty Trust Company)

by Charles H. Niehaus, and the north doors by J. Massey Rhind. The splendid stained-glass chancel window was designed by Upjohn himself. The building exterior is of brownstone. The 280-foot spire was for years a prominent New York landmark until it was dwarfed by the surrounding skyscrapers. The "ring" of ten bells in the steeple is played before services, and adds a quieting note to the commotion of the neighborhood. The side wall buttresses, while inserting a touch of Gothic glamor, are false, as the ceiling vaults are made of plaster and are hung for decoration only. The interior, however, is somber and majestic. To the left of the sanctuary is the lovely All Saints Chapel, built in 1913.

Surrounding the church is the burial ground, shaded by trees of many species. In the north section is the ornate Gothic style Martyrs' Monument, a memorial to Continental soldiers who, during the American Revolution, died while imprisoned in a sugar house on Liberty (then Crown) Street. The various monuments read like a page from American History: Alexander Hamilton, Robert Fulton (whose steamboat *Clermont* set sail from the foot of Cortlandt Street), Captain James Lawrence (who, as commander of the ship *Chesapeake* in the War of 1812, immortalized himself with his dying command, "Don't Give Up the Ship!"), Albert Gallatin (twice Secretary of the Treasury under Thomas Jefferson, and a founder of New York University), Francis Lewis (signer of the Declaration of Independence), and William Bradford (early champion of freedom of the press, and editor of New York's first newspaper, the *New York Gazette*). The churchyard is a favorite lunch-hour retreat in warm weather for office workers in the surrounding financial district; and the Church presents noontime concerts every Wednesday. Trinity Church is a designated New York City Landmark and is listed in the National Register of Historic Places.

The Irving Trust Company Building (1 Wall Street) is a massive limestone pile of Art Deco. An interesting touch by architects Voorhees, Gmelin & Walker in this 1931 building are the fluted walls and chamfered corners. An addition to the building was built in 1965. The attractive lobby is decorated with a polychrome mosaic design that gives a startling flamelike appearance. When illuminated at night it literally glows in patterns of bright red and orange.

Wall Street is named for the original palisade fence or wall, built in 1653 on orders from Dutch Governor Peter Stuyvesant. It was supposedly intended as a defense against hostile Indians, but actually served as a bulwark against an invasion by British colonists from New England. The wall stood from river to river for about 50 years. [For a tour of the Wall Street area and neighboring streets, *see* Manhattan's Financial District walking tour.]

No. 71 Broadway, the Empire Building, at the southwest corner of Rector Street, still houses the main office of the United States Steel Corporation, in spite of a newer building at 165 Broadway.

The American Express Company Building (65 Broadway) is the New York headquarters of the worldwide firm that began as a one-man operation in 1839, when William F. Harnden made four trips by train to Boston every week to deliver parcels and make collections. In 1850 he merged with two other express companies, operating a fleet of delivery wagons. Under the leadership of president Henry Wells and secretary William G. Fargo, the American Express Company's new subsidiary, Wells Fargo, helped open the West. The novel "Traveler's Cheque" was introduced in 1891, and by 1918 express services were abandoned altogether, the company concentrating only on financial and travel services.

No. 50 Broadway marks the **site of New York's first skyscraper.** The Tower Building, designed by Bradford L. Gilbert, was an 11-story steel-skeleton building, completed in 1889. Gilbert had to occupy the topmost floor himself to dispel the fears of New Yorkers that the structure would collapse.

No. 39 Broadway has a plaque indicating the site of the Alexander McComb Mansion—George Washington's second presidential residence, occupied from February 23 to August 30, 1790.

No. 26 Broadway, the **former Standard Oil Building,** was the corporate headquarters of John D. Rockefeller's Standard Oil. Later, the company became SOCONY (*Standard Oil Co. of N.Y.*) when the government "trust busters" took action; then Socony-Mobil; and with a final simplification to Mobil Oil, the firm moved into its new headquarters on East 42nd Street (*see* 42nd Street, p. 257). A statue of the founding father oversees the lobby. The curved façade conforms to the principle of the "street wall"—so vital in good urban planning. Architects Carrère & Hastings (who designed the New York Public Library at Fifth Avenue and 42nd Street, among other fine buildings) and the firm of Shreve, Lamb & Blake planned this imposing building in 1922 with the skyline in mind. Although the lower section of the building conforms to the path of Broadway, the upper tower coincides with the geometry of the Manhattan street grid. Atop the tower, an appropriately symbolic oil-burning lantern (actually the chimney) crowns the massive structure. The building is best viewed from a distance. Before the rash of post-World War II boxlike skyscrapers, the Standard Oil Building formed an integral part of the lovely New York skyline, and was clearly visible from the harbor.

Across Bowling Green, the immense **Cunard Building** (25 Broadway) is a harmonious counterpart to the Standard Oil Building. Constructed in 1921 from plans by Benjamin Wistar Morris, when a transatlantic crossing by luxurious ocean liner was "the only way to travel," it is one of the finest office buildings in the world. The Cunard Line arrived in New York with the maiden voyage of Samuel Cunard's *Britannia* on July 4, 1840, and remained in the forefront in ocean travel until fairly recently. Merging with the White Star Line in the 1920s, it became the largest passenger ship company in the world. (The names of Cunard ships always ended in *-ia: Mauretania, Lusitania,* etc., White Star's in *-ic: Britannic, Titanic,* etc. Later exceptions were the great "Queens" including the *QE2.*) The building's ornate Renais-

sance façade is quite handsome with its three arched entranceways and second-story colonnade, but the charm of the impressive structure is in its vestibule and Great Hall—certainly one of the most beautiful interior spaces
anywhere. Passing through one of the central bronze doors, the visitor enters
the high vaulted vestibule whose ornament was created by artist Ezra Winter.
Beyond high wrought-iron gates (by Samuel Yellin) is the *pièce de résistance,*
the Great Hall. The octagonally shaped chamber measures 185 feet long by
74 feet wide, and the central section is surmounted by a dome 65 feet above
the floor. Study the magnificent murals and pendentives covered in fresco.
The walls and floor are covered with travertine with considerable detail,
and the artistic maps of the world were executed by Barry Faulkner. The
aesthetic climax of the great room is its groined, vaulted ceiling ornamented
with arabesques and a multitude of design motifs. Ezra Winter and most
of the artists who combined their talents here were winners of the Rome
Prize. The four supporting pendentives created by Winter represent the ships
of Christopher Columbus, John Cabot, Sir Francis Drake, and Leif Ericson.
In the heyday of steamship travel, the rooms were called the Freight Distribution Hall and the Bill of Lading Hall. Thomas Hastings (of the firm of
Carrère & Hastings) was a consultant to architect Morris, and is said to have
suggested the plan of the Great Hall based on Raphael's Villa Madama in
Rome. The Cunard Building is unquestionably one of the finest examples of
the American Renaissance, and, in the words of Henry Hope Reed, author
of *The Golden City* and Curator of Parks, "Great art is to be found not in a
glorified warehouse called a museum, but in such buildings as 25 Broadway."
The Great Hall now houses a branch of the U.S. Post Office.

Bowling Green was New York City's first park. It lay just beyond the
original fort, and was merely an open space leading into *De Heere Wegh*
(The Main Street, or Broadway). It served as a cattle market and also as
a parade ground. In 1733 it was rented privately for "one peppercorn per
year for the recreation and delight of the inhabitants of this city." An iron
fence ornamented with crowns was erected in 1771 to protect the little park
and its newly erected statue of King George III. A symbol of British tyranny,
the gilt-lead statue was pulled down by patriots after General Washington
ordered the Declaration of Independence read publicly on July 9, 1776. The
crowns that topped the fence posts also were destroyed. Curiously, parts of
the original statue still exist, and pieces later turned up near the town of
Wilton, Connecticut, where the pieces had been taken to be melted into
musket balls. The Park and fence will be restored after renovation of the
Bowling Green IRT Subway station just below. Abraham de Peyster, whose
statue will return to the lower end of the Park, was the son of a leading Dutch
burgher and served under the English as Treasurer and later Mayor of New
York from 1691 to 1695. His statue was sculpted by George Edwin Bissell
in 1896. **The Bowling Green fence** is a designated New York City Landmark.

No. 11 Broadway, on the west side of Bowling Green, is an amusing
hodgepodge of styles. Framing the entrances are "Egyptian" pylons, while

The Produce Exchange on Bowling Green, which was replaced in 1957 by No. 2 Broadway, was completed in 1884. One of George B. Post's most notable works, the enormous red brick structure had a true iron "skeleton" and a main hall measuring 220 by 144 feet. At the right foreground is the statue of Abraham de Peyster. (Museum of the City of New York)

above the third story the building takes on the bold look of the Chicago School of Architecture, with its glazed brick piers and articulated spandrels. It was designed in 1898 by W. G. Audsley. Adjacent **No. 9 Broadway,** the Bowling Green Offices, is a continuation of the "west wall."

No. 1 Broadway, the United States Lines–Panama Pacific Lines Building, also hearkens to the days of sea power, when our country had at least some semblance of a respectable merchant marine. Built in 1921 from plans by Walter B. Chambers, the enormous structure is more famous for what used to be there. This was almost the southern tip of Manhattan Island and site of the original Dutch fort that stood just a few yards to the south. During the late 18th century the Kennedy House was headquarters for Generals Washington and Lee. More recently, an ornate commercial structure named the Washington Building stood on the site until 1919.

No. 2 Broadway (to the left of the Custom House), built in 1959 by Emery Roth & Sons, marks the site of one of our most tragic building losses, the Produce Exchange. Designed in 1884 by noted architect George B. Post, it was a true iron skeleton building, faced with dark red brick, and several years ahead of its time. The façade was adorned with terra-cotta motifs of the various products traded within. The second-floor Main Hall was an astonishing 220 feet by 144 feet, with a huge latticework skylight 60 feet above the floor. As Nathan Silver sadly comments in his heartrending *Lost New York,* "The Produce Exchange, one of the best buildings in New York, was replaced after 1957 by one of the worst."

The United States Custom House is considered the finest example of the French Beaux Arts-style in the city. Although the government has moved the operations of the Customs Service to the World Trade Center, this magnificent building, designed by Cass Gilbert and completed in 1907, is a designated landmark, but its future is uncertain. Contrasting with the dark gray granite of the building are four monumental white limestone sculpture groups by Daniel Chester French. Left to right, they represent the continents of Asia, America, Europe, and Africa. Above the cornice are statues symbolizing the 12 great mercantile nations of history: Greece, Rome, Phoenicia, Genoa, Venice, Spain, Holland, Portugal, Denmark, Germany, England, and France. The heroic cartouche atop the upper balustrade is by sculptor Karl Bitter. Ranged around the richly adorned Custom House are 44 Corinthian columns.

The dramatic second-floor Rotunda has a splendid display of Reginald Marsh murals depicting early events on the site and various seafaring themes. Hopefully, some adaptive reuse will be found for one of our most magnificent public buildings.

The original fortification called Fort Amsterdam was constructed in 1623 with the arrival of the first settlers. Then a more substantial fort was built in 1626, going through eight name changes, until as Fort George, it was demolished in 1787. Government House, intended as the presidential residence, replaced the fort three years later, but with the removal of the nation's capital to Philadelphia, it became the Governor's Mansion. It later became a boarding house, then the Custom House, and after a fire, was razed in 1815. Subsequently, town houses lined the site, but by midcentury they were taken over as shipping offices and known as "Steamship Row," as the area became entirely devoted to commerce. (Detailed and colorful dioramas of the early Dutch fort and surrounding settlement are displayed at the Museum of the City of New York.)

Enter Battery Park at the main entrance, directly to the right of the Custom House.

Battery Park is named for the battery of cannon that, between 1683 and 1688, were mounted along what is now the sidewalk opposite the Custom House, extending to just below the present Battery Place. From then until 1807 the area was fortified with additional batteries of artillery pieces. Most of the Park is built on landfill, as the Island of Manhattan was periodically enlarged through the years.

Bowling
Green

BROADWAY

WHITEHALL ST.

GREENWICH ST.

'ASHINGTON ST.

Brooklyn
Battery
Tunnel

BATTERY PL.

STATE ST.

BRIDGE ST.

PEARL ST.

PETER MINUIT PLAZA

1

2

17

19

18

Parking

Eisenhower Mall

3

16

4

8

Pier A

5

15

7

13

11

14

9

10

12

6

ADMIRAL GEORGE DEWEY PROMENADE

Yawl "Petrel"

Upper New York
Bay

Statue of Liberty Ferry Embarking Point

To Staten Island Ferry

To Governors Island Ferry

THE BATTERY

1 — Netherland Memorial
2 — Fort George Memorial
3 — John Ericsson Statue
4 — Walloon Settlers Memorial
5 — Breakwater Memorial Flagpoles
6 — Emma Lazarus Tablet
7 — Castle Clinton National Monument
8 — Salvation Army Memorial
9 — Verrazano Statue
10 — Peter Caesar Alberti Tablet
11 — Wireless Operators Memorial
12 — East Coast War Memorial
13 — Coast Guard Memorial
14 — John W. Ambrose Memorial
15 — Marine Flagpole
16 — Pre-Revolutionary War Cannon
17 — First Jewish Immigrants Monument
18 — Watson House — Shrine
19 — Seamen's Church Institute

The tall flagpole and sculptured pedestal is the **Netherlands Memorial Monument,** inscribed in both English and 17th-century Dutch, giving a brief history of the settlement of the Colony of New Netherland.

Bear to the right at the first path to the Statue of John Ericcson.

John Ericcson was the Swedish-born mechanical engineer who designed and built the first ironclad warship, the *Monitor*—the famous "cheesebox on a raft," which, on March 9, 1862, at Hampton Roads, Virginia, engaged the Confederate frigate *Merrimac* (renamed *Virginia*) and altered the course of naval history. The *Monitor*'s deck stood only 18 inches out of the water, while its revolving turret carried two 11-inch guns. The statue was executed by Jonathan Scott Hartley in 1893.

Turn left to the entrance gate of Castle Clinton.

Castle Clinton National Monument. In 1807 it appeared that another war with England was imminent, and several fortifications were hastily erected to protect the unguarded harbor. Among them was Castle Williams on nearby Governors Island, and the West Battery (now Castle Clinton) on a small rocky islet connected to the tip of Manhattan by a 200-foot causeway. (The intervening land was not filled in until the mid-19th century.) Constructed from plans by John McComb, Jr., in a circular shape with red sandstone walls over eight feet thick, the Battery's 28 guns never fired a shot in anger. Renamed in 1815 in honor of DeWitt Clinton, former Mayor and later Governor, the fort remained in the hands of the military until 1821, when Commanding General Winfield Scott moved the garrison to Governors Island. Two years later Castle Clinton was ceded to the City of New York.

In June 1824 the city leased it as a place of public entertainment, and redecorated with a garden, shrubbery, a fountain, and a promenade above, it opened as **Castle Garden.** Among the variety of public events presented, including concerts, fireworks displays, and balloon ascensions, was Samuel F. B. Morse's demonstration in 1842 of his "wireless telegraph." Then, on September 11, 1850, P. T. Barnum, in the musical event of the century, presented Jenny Lind, the "Swedish Nightingale," in her American concert debut. At the close of the sellout performance at which more than 6,000 had paid the exorbitant fee of at least three dollars a seat, the audience broke into a "tempest of cheers."

In 1855 Castle Garden became the immigrant landing station, and for the next 34 years witnessed the arrival of over 8 million new Americans. With the closing of the Garden in 1890, the nearby Barge Office (now demolished) handled the growing tide of immigrants until the new immigration depot was opened two years later on Ellis Island.

The Garden was then remodeled by the architectural firm of McKim, Mead & White to serve as the **New York Aquarium,** opening on December 10, 1896, to a crowd of 30,000. In 1941 the Aquarium was closed, moving to

The Lusitania *arrived on her maiden voyage to New York on September 13, 1907. Crowds jammed the waterfront between the Aquarium (formerly Castle Garden) and Pier A, as the liner steamed up the Hudson, eight years before her ill-fated rendezvous with a U-boat off the English coast. (New-York Historical Society)*

new and spacious quarters at Coney Island, and the building slated for demolition to make way for access roads to the new Brooklyn-Battery Tunnel. However, a hue and cry from civic-minded citizens saved it, and in 1946 Congress authorized the establishment of Castle Clinton as a national monument. Under the administration of the National Park Service of the Department of the Interior, it has been carefully restored as a fort, and now provides a dramatic link with our past.

In the rear of Castle Clinton, facing the waterfront, is the **plaque to Emma Lazarus,** who in 1883 penned her immortal sonnet *The New Colossus* to help raise money for the pedestal and ultimate erection of the Statue of Liberty. Her oft-quoted lines, ". . . Give me your tired, your poor,/Your huddled masses yearning to breathe free . . ." are now emblazoned on the base of the statue she helped secure.

Follow the path around Castle Clinton leading to the Statue of Verrazano.

Giovanni da Verrazano was the first to sight these shores. Arriving in the small caravel *La Dauphine* in 1524, the Florentine merchant sailing for Francis I of France, claimed the new land for the king, naming it *Terre d'Angoulême*. The French, however, did not follow up the claim, and Verrazano himself fell victim to cannibals on a voyage to the Caribbean four years later. The statue is the work of Ettore Ximenes, and was completed in 1909.

An almost deserted view of Broadway, looking north from Cortlandt Street in the mid-1880s. Midday crowds often gathered in front of the tall Western Union Building to watch a ball descend the top of the pole precisely at noon. George B. Post's flamboyant Renaissance structure, built in 1873–75—and considered one of New York's first skyscrapers—was demolished when the City Investing Building was erected. After the Blizzard of 1888 the maze of telegraph wires was removed and buried beneath the street. (New-York Historical Society)

In the deep excavation for the World Trade Center, the two tubes of the PATH subway lines were exposed, and passers-by could hear the eerie roar of the trains in what at first glance seemed to be enormous sewer pipes. The eastbound tube is in the foreground, the westbound is just visible, passing to the right rear of the early framework of the WTC's North Tower. (Port Authority of New York & New Jersey)

The statue of stern-faced Abraham de Peyster, son of a leading Dutch burgher, and Mayor of New York from 1691 to 1695, will be returned to Bowling Green Park after subway renovations have been completed. Except for the Bowling Green Offices at left, not one building survives from the time this photo was taken about 1900. (Museum of the City of New York)

A lithograph of Wall Street looking east from Trinity Church in 1834. In the distance is the cupola of the Merchants' Exchange, destroyed the following year in the Great Fire of 1835. (The J. Clarence Davies Collection. Museum of the City of New York)

Looking west on Fulton Street across Broadway in 1892, horsecars have been replaced by electric trolleys, but dobbin still reigns. In the background are the Sixth and Ninth Avenue Els. The L-shaped building on the southwest corner is that of the Evening Mail. *(American Telephone & Telegraph Company)*

The former Equitable Building on Broadway, between Cedar and Pine Streets. The Second Empire-style structure, built in 1872, was destroyed in a spectacular fire which burned for three days in January 1912. A replacement, completed in 1916, caused objections due to its sheer bulk, leading to a drastic revision in the building code. (King's Views of New York, 1909. Author's Collection)

Firefighters work, vainly, to save the Equitable Building. The conflagration had begun in the basement Cafe Savarin and quickly engulfed the entire structure. (*Museum of the City of New York*)

Equitable founder Henry B. Hyde seems to be studying the destruction of the lobby. Only slightly damaged, the statue by J. Q. A. Ward now graces the lobby of the Company's new headquarters at 1285 Avenue of the Americas. (*Equitable Life Assurance Society of the United States*)

Metropolitan Telephone and Telegraph Company,
16, 18 & 20 COURTLANDT ST., NEW YORK.
One large STORE ROOM on ground floor, and rooms in suits or singly for
OFFICES to suit tenants
FOR RENT.
For Diagrams showing location and prices, apply to
THE METROPOLITAN TELEPHONE AND TELEGRAPH COMPANY,
144 GREENWICH STREET.

A mid-1880s advertisement for loft space in the headquarters of a predecessor of the New York Telephone Company (then located on the north side of Cortlandt Street between Broadway and Church Street). The Romanesque Revival-style building was one of several newly opened exchanges. (American Telephone & Telegraph Company)

Castle Garden in 1870 when it served as the State Emigrant Landing Depot. Millions of immigrants passed through its portals between 1855 and 1892, when a new center was opened on Ellis Island. (New-York Historical Society)

In this lithograph by Nathaniel Currier, "Swedish Nightingale" Jenny Lind makes her American debut on September 11, 1850, as P. T. Barnum inaugurates Castle Garden as the city's leading showplace. The structure has now been restored to its original appearance as Castle Clinton National Monument. (New-York Historical Society)

A Sunday promenade along the Battery in an 1830 engraving, depicting Castle Clinton to the right, and Castle Williams on Governors Island across the busy harbor to the left. (New-York Historical Society)

The City Hall area from atop the American Telephone & Telegraph Company Building, c. 1917. In front of the lofty Woolworth Tower (the tallest skyscraper in the world at the time) is the Second Empire-style "Mullett" Post Office which virtually obscures City Hall from view. To the left rear are the "Tweed" Court House and twin wings of the Emigrant Industrial Savings Bank. To the right, the massive Municipal Building faces the Beaux Arts-style Hall of Records and the diminutive Probate Court Building. Further to the right are the twin cupolas of the Park Row Building, just beyond the narrow St. Paul Building. (American Telephone & Telegraph Company)

The same year, Esteban Gómez, a Portuguese mariner sailing under the Spanish flag, entered the harbor and named the mouth of the river Río San Antonio. It was not until 1609 however, that Henry Hudson, in his *Half-Moon,* actually sailed up the river that bears his name and brought back to Holland extensive reports on this "Great River of the Mountains." Four years later Adriaen Block, a Dutch trader, landed at the tip of Manhattan Island with a small group of men. When their ship *Tiger* caught fire and burned to the water, they were forced to spend the winter. The following spring they built a new ship which they called the *Onrust* (Restless), and returned to Holland. One can only admire these stalwart men who with their bare hands were able to fashion a seaworthy vessel from the trees of the forest, and sail it thousands of miles safely across the rough Atlantic.

Nieuw Amsterdam as a permanent settlement was established in 1625, and one year later, Peter Minuit made his famous purchase from the Indians. In 1664 the Colony was captured by the English and named for the Duke of York. For a few months in 1673 the Dutch regained control, but lost it again to Britain.

Facing the waterfront, and looking to the right, one can see **Pier A,** the fire-boat station built in 1886. The 70-foot tower and clock were donated in 1918 by Daniel Reid, a founder of the United States Steel Corporation, as a memorial to the 116,000 servicemen who died while serving in World War I. The clock peals the time on ships' bells. Pier A is a designated New York City Landmark.

A short distance to the east (and a bit difficult to find) is the **Wireless Operators Memorial Monument,** dedicated to those radiomen who went down with their ship. A bronze plaque is added with each tragedy, and some are quite recent. Note the plaque for the wireless operator of the *Titanic,* which struck an iceberg on her maiden voyage to America, and sank on the night of April 14–15, 1912, with a loss of 1517 out of 2000 passengers.

Walk out on the **Admiral George Dewey Promenade,** at the water's edge. Considered the finest view in the city, the broad panorama includes (from left to right) Brooklyn Heights, Governors Island, distant Staten Island, The Statue of Liberty on Liberty Island, Ellis Island with its former immigration depot, and the New Jersey harbor front. And there is the constant parade of ships of all types, which bring the harbor to life. Turning around, the view of the lower Manhattan skyline (now somewhat obscured by modern, uninspired additions) is awesome. The finest view, of course, is from the Staten Island Ferry or from the Statue of Liberty excursion boat.

Facing the Promenade is the **East Coast War Memorial,** which honors every seaman, soldier, and airman lost in the American coastal waters of the North Atlantic during World War II. All the names are carved into the eight marble pylons. In the center is an immense sculpture of an American Eagle.

Follow the Promenade to the end, and walk north on the park side of State Street.

On the way, the landmark **Municipal Ferry Piers** can be seen to the right. These are the last remaining ferry terminals, which once served a number of routes. The huge green metal arched buildings were built in 1907–09 and served the ferries to Brooklyn. They were closed in 1938 and are now used only by the Governors Island Ferry, the Staten Island Ferry having its own new terminal alongside.

At approximately the site of the Governors Island Ferry slip was the point of embarcation in Dutch Colonial times for ships sailing to the mother country or to other distant points. The little wharf was soon called **Schreijers Hoek** (Weepers' Point), since the perils of a long sea voyage threatened the safe return of loved ones. The name was taken from the *Schreijerstoren* (Weepers' Tower) on the Amstel River in Amsterdam, where relatives bade a tearful farewell to those departing on distant journeys.

Just inside the Park fence is the **Oyster Pasty Mount Cannon,** a relic from English Colonial days which was uncovered during building excavations. The Oyster Pasty was a derisive name given to the battery mounted near a pile of oyster shells.

Cross Peter Minuit Plaza (Carefully!).

The flagpole in the mini-park is New York City's tribute to the first group of Jews to arrive at these shores in 1654—23 men, women, and children, refugees from the Inquisition in Brazil. Attempting to return to Holland, their ship was taken by a Spanish pirate who in turn was captured by a French privateer. Pledging their possessions to the French captain, they were brought to Nieuw Amsterdam, where Peter Stuyvesant gave them a less-than-cordial welcome, but permitted them to stay. The townspeople paid off the captain, allowing the refugees to discharge their debt and keep the clothes on their back. Practicing their religion privately, the small group of Sephardic Jews later was able to rent a room for services in a windmill, and ultimately built the first synagogue in America in 1730 on Mill Street (now South William Street), about one-half mile north.

Peter Minuit Plaza is named for one of the first Dutch governors, who purchased the Island of Manhattan in 1626 from the Canarsie Indians (who didn't really own it anyway), for an amount of trinkets valued at 60 guilders, or about $24.

At 7 State Street the former **James Watson House,** is now the **Shrine of the Blessed Elizabeth Ann Seton,** the first American-born saint. Mother Seton (1774–1821) was the founder of the American Sisters of Charity, the first order of nuns in the United States. She is also credited with the establishment of the American Catholic parochial school system. Mother Seton was elevated to sainthood in September 1975. The house is a lone survivor of a magnificent row of elegant Federal mansions that lined State Street. Note the freestanding, slender Ionic columns and the Georgian details. The building is completely original, and was built in the early 1800s, probably by John McComb, the architect of City Hall. What a splendid sight the long colonnade must have presented to approaching ships. The church of Our Lady of the Rosary, adjoining the shrine, occupies the site of a former residence of Mother Seton.

The Seamen's Church Institute (15 State Street), supported by Trinity Parish, provides lodging and services for seamen, including educational programs, a library, school, chapel, and cafeteria. The attractive modern building, with a nautical motif, replaces an earlier building, built in 1913 at 25 South Street, which occupied a conspicuous site overlooking the harbor. The Institute building is a veritable museum and is open to the public seven days a week (ground floor and second floor only). The cafeteria offers inexpensive meals, and visitors are welcome. After a look at the lobby with its nautical artifacts, visit the intimate chapel with its bright stained glass, capstan baptismal font, and ship models. Then, walk up the winding staircase to the second floor, noting the collection of bronze plaques from the former Institute building. Along the walls of the second floor corridor are prints and photographs of old ships; and mounted on pedestals are ship's bells salvaged from stranded vessels. The most tragic is the bell from the *Atlantic,* which sank in a gale off Fisher's Island in Long Island Sound, on Thanksgiving Day, 1846. The tale is recounted on a wall plaque. Nearby is the bell from the *Normandie.* (Tap them gently with a coin.) The Institute began in 1834 as a sort of houseboat seamen's mission, called the Floating Church of the Comforter, and was anchored at an East River pier at the foot of Pike Street. The site of the Institute was the birthplace of author Herman Melville, who in his youth served aboard a whaling ship.

End of tour. Walk up State Street to the Bowling Green station of the IRT Lexington Avenue subway. Take any northbound train two stops to Fulton Street for connections to other subways.

start

ANN ST.

FULTON ST.

DUTCH ST.

WILLIAM ST.

RYDERS AL.

GOLD ST.

FULTON ST.

CLIFF ST.

PEARL ST.

WATER ST.

BEEKMAN ST.

RONT ST.

JOHN ST.

PLATT ST.

LIBERTY ST.

NASSAU ST.

CEDAR ST.

FLETCHER ST.

Schermerhorn
Row

South Street Sea

PINE ST.

DE PEYSTER ST.

FRONT ST.

Federal
Hall

WALL ST.

SOUTH ST.

EXCHANGE PL.

HANOVER ST.

WATER ST.

GOUVERNEUR LA.

NEW ST.

BROAD ST.

HANOVER SQ.

OLD SLIP

SOUTH STREET VIADUCT (F.D.R. DRIVE)

East
River

BEAVER ST.

MILL
LA.

STONE ST.

S. WILLIAM ST.

OLD SLIP

MARKETFIELD ST.

CUYLERS AL.

STONE ST.

COENTIES AL.

COENTIES SLIP

WHITEHALL ST.

BRIDGE ST.

PEARL ST.

Downtown
Heliport

MANHATTAN'S FINANCIAL DISTRICT

2. Manhattan's Financial District

[IRT Broadway-Seventh Avenue line to Fulton Street station; IND A line to Broadway-Nassau Street station; BMT M, J to Fulton Street station; IRT Lexington Avenue line to Fulton Street station; Second-Third Avenue M-15 bus to Fulton Street]

The walking tour begins at the corner of Fulton and William streets.

William Street is known as **"Insurance Row,"** with its rows of tall buildings that house the offices of dozens of large insurance companies and brokerage firms. On the northwest corner is the massive Aetna Life & Casualty Company; on the northeast, the neo-Georgian style building of the Royal Globe Insurance Company; and on the southeast, in a similar style, the Fidelity & Deposit Company of Maryland. On the southwest corner is the site of the birthplace in 1783 of Washington Irving (No. 131 William Street), who, it will be remembered, wrote *Knickerbocker's History of New York,* among other works, and coined the expression, "The Almighty Dollar."

Turn right on Gold Street.

A few yards down Gold Street, on the right side, and almost hidden among its neighbors, is a surprising relic of the beginning of the mechanical age—the **Excelsior Power Company** building. Completed in 1888, it was one of the city's first power houses. The coal-loading docks and wagon-wheel deflectors are still in place, and one can almost hear the whine of the early dynamos. The architectural style is the typical dark red brick Romanesque Revival "Industrial" of the 1880s.

Walk up the little cobblestoned lane, called **Ryder's Alley,** which makes an abrupt left turn, returning to Fulton Street. The street is named for Robert Ryder, an English surveyor during the Colonial Period.

Looking east on Fulton Street toward the Fulton Ferry Terminal about 1900. The Fulton Fish Market building, to the left, is long since gone, but the gabled-roof block across the street, known as Schermerhorn Row, survives from the first decade of the 19th century, and is a designated landmark—the focus of the South Street Seaport Area. (South Street Seaport Museum)

The Southbridge Towers housing project was completed in 1972. The plans originally called for enormous high-rise apartment houses, but the city fathers felt that such height would overwhelm the adjacent South Street Seaport area. The result is a pleasant blending with surroundings with considerable "breathing space."

At the corner of Water and Fulton streets is New York's "fun skyscraper," known only by its official address, **127 John Street.** Walk around the building and see for yourself. According to the owners, it is designed "to create an atmosphere of pleasure, humor, and excitement for people." See for yourself, as you relax for a moment on the north-side sun deck; then enter through the main entrance's neon-lit "vacuum cleaner pipe" and step into either a red or blue elevator. Set your watch by the world's largest digital clock mounted on the east wall. Note, too, the iron "bicycle rack" sculpture; and from a distance, the gaily painted adornments up to the roof's water tank. The clock was built as an extension of the wall to hide an old building whose owner would not sell to complete the land parcel. This imaginative building, which houses the New York Cocoa Exchange, was designed by Emery Roth in 1972. The site was occupied in the mid-19th century by the famous United States Hotel.

Follow Fulton Street to the South Street Seaport Area.

The South Street Seaport is an early 19th-century waterfront area that somehow survived the encroachment of modernization. The area restoration project is under the aegis of the **South Street Seaport Museum,** at 16 Fulton Street (with offices at 203 Front Street, a Steamship Gallery at 205, a Model Shop at 207 Water Street, and an excellent Book Shop at 25 Fulton Street). The highlight of the Museum is the display of ships berthed at Piers 16, 17, and 18, just beyond South Street, near the site of the old Fulton Ferry, where visitors can visit the square rigger *Wavertree,* the lightship *Ambrose,* a wooden Gloucester schooner, a steel coasting schooner, a hospital ship, a St. Lawrence River steam tug, a steam waterboat, and a retired city ferryboat. An excellent walking-tour guidebook to the South Street Seaport is available in the Seaport's Book Shop.

The block of Fulton Street between Front and South streets (south side) is known as **Schermerhorn Row**—the only remaining group of Federal- and Greek Revival-style commercial buildings in the city. Dating from the years 1811–12, the group is a designated landmark. Stop in first at the **Seaport Museum** at 16 Fulton Street (and pick up a membership application when you leave).

South Street during the Great Age of Sail was the city's "street of ships." Extending to the southern tip of Manhattan Island was a vast forest of masts,

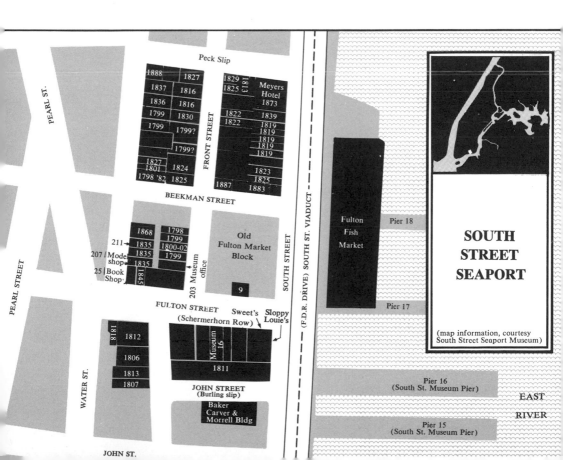

(map information, courtesy
South Street Seaport Museum)

as great sailing vessels from all over the world loaded and deposited their cargoes onto busy South Street. With the advent of steam, the commercial area shifted to the Hudson River, and South Street diminished in importance. Just north of Fulton Street is the Fulton Fish Market, where fleets of fishing boats unload their daily Atlantic catches for wholesale distribution throughout the city. Ultimately the Market will move out, and plans are underway to restore it to the appearance of the first public fish market of 1821. Other restoration work is in progress, and the area is envisioned as eventually an accurate working model of the early 19th-century nautical-commercial district.

Stop in, too, at Bowne and Company Stationers, **211 Water Street,** a re-creation of a 19th-century print shop typical of many that abounded in the area. This is another of the historic restoration projects that will eventually encompass a seven-block area. More than just a museum, Bowne and Company is a functioning commercial enterprise. In addition to more modern equipment, there are working hand presses with original typefaces and a display of early printing machinery, including one of the first typewriters. The

During the "Great Age of Sail" of the mid-to-late 19th century, South Street was lined with the tall masts of graceful sailing ships from all over the world. Here, near Burling Slip, are a four- and three-master, loading cargo for voyages to far-distant ports. (South Street Seaport Museum)

Looking north on New Street the morning after the Great Blizzard of 1888.
(Museum of the City of New York)

The block house and Water Poort *at the site of Wall Street and thè East River in 1674, as sketched for Valentine's Manual for 1862. (New-York Historical Society)*

Charming Hanover Square was not enhanced by the Second Avenue El roaring overhead along Pearl Street. At the time this photo was taken in the early 1880s India House was then the Cotton Exchange, and the lower level was rented to commercial tenants. (Museum of the City of New York)

At the turn of the century the Consolidated Stock Exchange operated briefly as a rival to the "Big Board," dealing mostly in mining stocks. The huge Greek Revival-style building stood at the southeast corner of Broad and Wall Streets. (King's Views of New York, 1909. *Author's Collection*)

Looking west on Wall Street, c. 1890, from South Street to Trinity Church, with the 2nd Avenue El passing overhead at Pearl Street. To the right of the church is the cupola of the Gillender Building, now the site of the Bankers Trust Company Building at the corner of Nassau Street. (*Museum of the City of New York*)

Young boys enjoying an illegal dip "in the raw" at the Fulton Fish Market pier at the foot of Beekman Street, c. 1892, apparently oblivious to the photographer, the man dragging the basket of fish, or the law banning swimming in the East River. Among the myriad sailing ships' masts in the background are the twin pilot houses of a Fulton Ferryboat. (New-York Historical Society)

The bow and figurehead of a square-rigger cast a long shadow across two curious onlookers at South Street near Maiden Lane in the late 1880s. (South Street Seaport Museum)

Greek Revival-style building dates from 1835–36, and a printer was its first tenant.

Spend some time exploring **Front Street, Beekman Street,** and **Peck Slip,** then take in the ships on the piers and the splendid views of the East River, including the beautiful Brooklyn Bridge.

The Brooklyn Bridge [*see* page 326], considered one of the most beautiful in the world, was designed by John A. Roebling in 1867 and took 16 years to complete. Injured in a fatal accident before the bridge was completed, he turned the job over to his son, Washington A. Roebling. It was the first bridge across the East River, and for many years was the longest suspension bridge in the world. Its pink granite towers with Gothic arches are a familiar sight against the dramatic New York skyline. Although the Bridge was opened in 1883, it was not until the completion of the Williamsburg Bridge 20 years later that the **Fulton Ferry** gave up its two-century-old river crossing service to Fulton Street, Brooklyn. The site also marks the location of General Washington's strategic withdrawal to Manhattan after the defeat of the Continental Army at the Battle of Long Island in August 1776.

At the entrance to the South Street Museum Piers is the **Titanic Memorial Lighthouse,** which formerly crowned the old Seamen's Church Institute Building at South Street and Coenties Slip before the building's demolition and relocation to its present site on State Street [*see* page 21]. Donated to the Museum, the lighthouse commemorates the sinking of the *Titanic.* Plans call for the relocation of the lighthouse to a mini-park to be built at Fulton and Water streets.

Return to Front Street, passing the old pitched-roof buildings of Schermerhorn Row. (Although it is not within the purview of this guidebook to recommend dining places, Sweet's, at 2 Fulton Street, is the oldest seafood restaurant in the city, and still retains its 19th-century atmosphere, including the sawdust on the floor; while around the corner on South Street, Sloppy Louie's is a more modest, but quite satisfactory dining establishment, also dispensing a variety of "denizens of the deep." Both are open weekdays only. It was in Sweet's during the mid-19th century that illegal slave traders, called "blackbirders," used to meet to make their nefarious deals.)

Turn left on Front Street.

The extension of John Street is still called **Burling Slip.** The "slips" (the others are Peck, Old, Catherine, Beekman, Pike, and Coenties) are reminders of the early days when these were still docking areas.

Look up Pine Street to the towering **Cities Service Building** one block west at Pearl Street. Until recently it had an annex at 60 Wall Street connected by a skywalk. The annex's demolition in 1975 left a gaping hole in the famous street wall of Wall Street. The skyscraper, built in 1932 from plans by Clinton & Russell, used to boast a Wall Street address; now it is merely called 70 Pine Street.

At Fletcher Street, turn right and continue south on Water Street.

No. 160 Water Street, completed in 1971, is more interesting for its side-walk geometrical designs than for its own architecture. Water Street was once the commercial hub of a thriving waterfront. The street was widened some years ago to provide a much needed traffic artery. In the process, however, many lovely old buildings were lost, and nothing now remains from the 19th century.

Maiden Lane, translated literally from the Dutch *Het Maagde Paatje,* was the site of a freshwater stream where young maidens in the 17th century did their laundry. Look up Maiden Lane to the impressive Florentine-style Federal Reserve Bank.

A refreshing change from the usual, uninspired "glass box" is **No. 88 Pine Street,** a breezy, light tower of white-painted metal and large windows. Designed by James I. Freed of I. M. Pei Associates, and completed in 1971, the building occupies a pleasant plaza, and with its see-through quality is ideally suited for a site close to the river. Look for the *QE* plaque on the south side of the mall.

On the southeast corner of Wall and Water streets was the **Merchants' Coffee House,** built in 1740. It was a popular gathering place for Revolutionary War plotters, and the area became known as Coffee House Slip.

The northwest corner was the site of the **Tontine Coffee House,** erected in 1792. It was here that the Stock Exchange had its beginnings, with transactions taking place on the street under a buttonwood (sycamore) tree and later within the Coffee House, the present site of No. 70 Wall Street. The building at the northwest corner (No. 82 Wall Street) commemorates the site in its name, Tontine House.

Turn right on Wall Street to Pearl Street.

Pearl Street was originally the shore of the East River in Dutch Colonial times and is named for the mother-of-pearl oyster shells that were scattered along the beach. **No. 100 Wall Street** on the north side, and **No. 111** on the south—the latter the downtown headquarters of the First National City Bank —were built on landfill added in 1801.

Wall Street is the site of the original protective wall, built by order of Governor Peter Stuyvesant in 1653, at the northern limits of the town of Nieuw Amsterdam. At the site of Wall and Pearl Streets, a blockhouse commanded the eastern end of the wall, and a large water gate was built between the blockhouse and the wall itself. It was called *'t Water Poort* to distinguish in from *'t Landt Poort* at Broadway. The Dutch referred to the path along the wall as *de Cingel* (the Rampart). The wall was a fortified palisade fence, not, as is commonly believed, to keep out hostile Indians, but to prevent an invasion by the English from the New England colonies. The fortification gradually deteriorated (helped by Colonists who "borrowed" planks for house repairs and firewood), and as the city grew northward, it was demolished around 1695. In 1709 the area became a slave market and later a grain market.

No. 74 Wall Street, at the northwest corner of Pearl Street, was built for the Seamen's Bank for Savings in 1926 from plans by Benjamin Wistar Morris, and is now occupied by a branch of the Williamsburgh Savings Bank. The handsome building has an attractive façade of multicolored seamed-face granite blocks, and upon completion was cited by the Downtown League as "the finest building of the year." The tall structure with its artistic setbacks cannot be categorized as belonging to any particular style, but the huge entrance arch is Romanesque in character, while the graceful upper buttresses are vaguely Gothic. Stretching a point, it might be called a very early example of Art Deco. Attractive are the low-relief blocks around the arch, representing nautical themes. The Seamen's Bank for Savings is the City's second oldest, chartered in 1829. Its original charter restricted banking activities to seamen only, in the belief that too many sailors were losing their hard-earned wages accumulated during long sea voyages, in waterfront saloons, as soon as their ships returned to port. When the building was dedicated, the directors decided to change the street address from 76 to 74 Wall Street, as some "old salts" who had been long-time depositors suggested that the combination of numbers totaling 13 "was a thing to make a good seaman wary."

A plaque on the building marks the site of the home of Edward Livingston, Secretary of State in 1831, who may hold the record in number of public offices held: Senator, Mayor, Congressman, and Minister to France.

Turn back (east) and take the first right into Beaver Street.

Beaver Street honors the little furry rodent on which so much of early commerce depended. Beaver pelts were shipped in such large quantities, and figured so vitally in the early colony's business life, that the animal was incorporated into the seal of New Amsterdam and later into the seal of the City of New York. The building at **82–92 Beaver Street** was formerly the New York Cocoa Exchange until its move to 127 John Street.

Return to the intersection of Pearl Street and turn right (south) on Pearl Street.

Note how **No. 140 Pearl Street** conforms to the curve in the street, preserving the unity of the "street wall." The name of the original owner is emblazoned in the pediment of this ornate cast-iron structure.

Hanover Square is an attractive oasis among the towering canyons of lower Manhattan. The intersection where Hanover, Pearl, Stone, and William streets meet Old Slip, it was originally a public common as far back as 1637, surrounded by elegant residences and situated very close to the river. At the site of nearby No. 119 Pearl Street, Captain (William) Kidd maintained a home. Captain Kidd was really not the pirate he was reputed to be. Although he was tried and hanged in England in 1699 for piracy, recent studies seem to indicate that he was an honorable sea captain who was the scapegoat of an unfair trial. The lower floor of India House is occupied by *Harry*'s, a restaurant popular with bankers and brokers. Hanover Square, named for the royal house of England, is one of the few public places whose name was not changed during the Revolution, perhaps because George I was not disliked as much as his descendant, two Georges later. As the district became commercial, Hanover Square was the first "Printing House Square" of the City [*see* City Hall, Old Newspaper Row, Five Points Nos. 2, 3, 4]. It was here that New York's first newspaper, the *New York Gazette,* was published by William Bradford in 1725. A plaque on No. 3 Hanover Square recognizes the event.

Dominating Hanover Square is the landmark **India House.** Built in 1837, two years after the Great Fire (see below), by Richard Carman as a commercial building, it was acquired in 1851 by the Hanover Bank. From 1870 to 1885 it was used by the New York Cotton Exchange, and later by W. R. Grace & Company (Grace Line). India House was organized as a private businessmen's club in 1914, and is dedicated to the furtherance of foreign trade. It contains a large collection of maritime artifacts and paintings in the charmingly reconstructed Marine Room. The brownstone exterior in Italianate style is reminiscent of a Tuscan villa. India House has been designated a New York City Landmark.

The parking lot across Pearl Street marks the site of the lovely Florentine style *palazzo* which once housed the corporate headquarters of W. R. Grace and Company. When the firm moved uptown in 1974 to their new "skirt-bottomed" skyscraper on 42nd Street [*see* 42nd Street, 10], they were unable to find a new tenant and had to demolish their lovely Hanover Square building, leaving an "open wound" in the street wall. A parking lot is apparently more lucrative than an office building.

Walk down Hanover Square to Water Street and turn left (north).

No. 77 Water Street, designed by Emery Roth in 1970, is another iconoclastic structure two years older than the same architect's 127 John Street Building. Although the superstructure is not particularly engaging, the handling of the ground floor with its surrounding "fantasies" is most pleasant. Walk through little Bennett Park, cross the mini-stream's bridges, examine the metal sculptures, including one made from compacted scrap steel (it might be your old automobile!), and visit Ye Olde Time Country Candy Store, with Virginia, the laughing soda dispenser, in the open lobby. It's all fun and a pleasant departure from the staid traditions of the Financial District.

Walk around the building to Old Slip, between the U.S. Assay Office and the Police Station.

The United States Assay Office, designed in 1930 by James A. Wetmore, is a solid five-story granite Italianate palace where the Government buys and sells silver and gold, assays them, and does its smelting (note the furnace chimney). Since the recent relaxation of the gold restrictions, the Assay Office has been somewhat busier.

Across Old Slip from the Assay Office, where sailing ships once docked, is the First Precinct Police Station, commonly called the **"Old Slip Station."** Also built in the style of an Italian *palazzo,* it is a trim, solid fortification with pleasing proportions, and was designed by Joseph Howland Hunt and Richard Howland Hunt in 1909.

Return to Hanover Square and turn left (south) just beyond India House into narrow Stone Street.

Stone Street's winding course parallels the old East River shoreline, and appears to be appropriately named. It was originally called *Brouwers Straet,* after Stephanus Van Cortlandt's brewery situated on the lane. Legend has it that his wife objected so strenuously to the dust raised by passing wagons on the unpaved street, that the good burgher was persuaded to have the street paved with cobblestones; and the practical-minded Dutch colonists then changed the street's name accordingly. Stone Street is said to be the Colony's first paved thoroughfare—the cobblestones were laid in 1657— and the paving stones today are erroneously thought by many to be original. These are Belgian blocks, laid in the 19th century.

Continue to Coenties Alley and turn left to Pearl Street.

At the northwest corner of Pearl Street and Coenties Alley once stood the **Stadt Huys,** the first City Hall. Built originally as the *Stadt Herberg,* or City Tavern, by Governor William Kieft in 1641, it was an imposing five-story stone structure—the tallest in town—overlooking the harbor. When Nieuw Amsterdam was granted its municipal charter 12 years later, New York's first hotel was converted into the *Stadt Huys,* and remained the seat of city government until 1790 when a new City Hall was built on Wall Street (on the site of the present Federal Hall). When the buildings which occupied the site of Nos. 71 and 73 Pearl Street were removed, the *Stadt Huys*'s foundations were discovered underneath. A team of archaeologists studied and mapped the foundations before the plot was resurfaced. The commercial building of the early 19th century which stood on the site of No. 71 was carefully dismantled, declared a landmark, and placed in storage pending reerection at the South Street Seaport. The old *Stadt Huys* served a number of functions, including a jail and debtors' prison, a courthouse, and a public warehouse. In front of the building, at the river's edge, stood the gallows, a pillory and stocks; and even a ducking stool, in which violators of the strict Dutch Reformed moral codes were tied and plunged repeatedly into the water.

Further north on Pearl Street, at the site of No. 81, William Bradford

The Stadt Huys, *the first New York City Hall, situated at the waterfront on Pearl Street and Coenties Slip, as seen in an 1869 print. (The J. Clarence Davies Collection, Museum of the City of New York)*

installed **New York's first printing press** in 1693. Note the commemorative plaque on the mid-19th century building.

Return to Coenties Alley and turn left into Coenties Slip.

Coenties Slip was one of the early city's largest wharfs, with a diagonally-shaped breakwater projecting far out into the East River [*see* Great Fire map]; however, the inlet has been completely filled in, even out beyond the end of the old pier. Coenties Slip is named for Conraet Ten Eyck who operated a tannery on nearby Broad Street. ("Coentje" is the Dutch diminutive for Conraet.) At this point the former Second Avenue El made a dizzying zigzag turn as it twisted sharply east from its southward path down Pearl Street, over Coenties Slip, then south again into Water Street—on the last lap of its tortuous route to South Ferry. Built in 1878, the El survived until 1942.

To the south of Coenties Slip is diminutive **Jeanette Park,** a paved multi-level plaza made entirely of similar brick to adjacent No. 4 New York Plaza. Terraced and equipped with an underground shopping mall, it is somewhat sterile in appearance, lacking much of the former park's shrubbery. The name is a memorial to the sailing ship *Jeanette* which met disaster on the George Washington De Long Expedition to the North Pole in 1881. The ill-starred venture was sponsored jointly by the U.S. Navy and James Gordon Bennett, publisher of the *New York Herald.* It was the *Herald,* in its tradition of sensationalism, which sent Stanley to Africa to find Livingstone. For years, Jeanette Park was a favorite port of call for unemployed seamen, and boasted a popular oyster bar in the middle of a shady mall.

To the left of Jeanette Park is enormous **55 Water Street**—a twin-build-

ing connected by an exterior escalator bank, and one of the latest additions
to the New York skyline. Take the escalator to the Plaza level and visit the
downtown branch of the Whitney Museum, then enjoy the river views from
the Plaza.

Across Water Street (opposite No. 4 New York Plaza) is an interesting
row of mid-19th century commercial buildings that survived only because the
street was widened on the east side. It was later decided to save the entire
block, which includes historic Fraunces Tavern, to re-create the atmosphere
of the mid-19th century commercial district. The group includes Federal,
Greek Revival, and Victorian buildings. It is also planned to convert the
parking lot on Pearl Street into a small park, to preserve the scale of the
environment.

**Continue south on Water Street and turn right at the next corner (Broad
Street).**

At the corner of Broad and Pearl Streets is one of our most cherished
landmarks, **Fraunces Tavern.** A handsome neo-Georgian building, it is a
splendid re-creation of the Etienne DeLancey house, built in 1719. Except
for some Dutch brick in the west wall, nothing remains of the original structure. Nonetheless, it is an excellent prototype of a formal English house of
the 18th century. DeLancey, a wealthy merchant with extensive land hold-

*The famous S-curve of the Second Avenue El, about 1879, at Coenties Slip. The
serpentine structure was scrapped in 1942 and melted into munitions for World
War II. (The New-York Historical Society)*

ings, was to lose all by choosing the wrong side in the American Revolution, and would suffer confiscation of his property. (Delancey Street on the Lower East Side is the only physical reminder of the family name.) In 1757 the building became a warehouse, and five years later was purchased by Samuel Fraunces who converted it into the *Queen's Head Tavern*. Fraunces, a West Indian of Black and French ancestry, operated the tavern successfully for a number of years and subsequently came into the employ of George Washington as his chief steward. What is now the New York State Chamber of Commerce was founded here in 1768, and just before the outbreak of the Revolutionary War, the Committees of Correspondence—soon to become the Continental Congress—held their first meetings at the Tavern. On November 24, 1783 Governor Clinton gave a gala dinner here to celebrate the British evacuation of the city, and that December 4th, Washington bade his famous farewell to his officers in the Long Room on the second floor. During the 19th century, the Tavern gradually deteriorated, suffered several fires, and fell victim to a number of unauthentic reconstructions. In 1904 the Sons of the Revolution of New York State purchased the building and spent three years restoring it to its present elegance. It is a National Historic Shrine and a New York City Landmark. Its Revolutionary War museum is open daily to the public (Monday through Friday, 10 A.M. to 4 P.M.). There is also a library and a charming ground-floor restaurant.

Take a moment for a brief lesson in Georgian-style architecture by crossing the street and admiring the details: the slate, hipped roof crowned by a balustrade, the tall chimneys, shed-roof dormers, a cornice set over a row of modillions, red brick walls with stone trim, and an ornate doorway flanked by classic columns and crowned by a pediment. The style was inspired by the north-Italian Renaissance as applied by the architect Palladio to many of the great Venetian and Lombardian villas.

On January 24, 1975, a bomb was exploded in the adjacent Anglers' Club, causing several deaths and many injuries. Allegedly placed by a Puerto Rican extremist group, the blast virtually destroyed the Club, but luckily caused only minor damage to Fraunces Tavern.

After walking north on Broad Street for about 100 yards, turn around and view the broad panorama of new "monoliths" that have sprung up along the downtown waterfront. From left to right (east to south): **55 Water Street;** Manufacturers Hanover's **No. 4 New York Plaza;** and behind it, **No. 2 New York Plaza;** Chase Manhattan's **No. 1 New York Plaza** with its recessed windows; **No. 1 State Street Plaza;** and **No. 1 Battery Park Plaza.** The erection of these behemoths has virtually obliterated the traditional Lower Manhattan skyline.

Continue north on Broad Street.

Across from Fraunces Tavern, at **No. 104,** is one of the many New York Telephone Company buildings, and on the triangular plot of land bounded by Pearl and Bridge streets, the austerely simple **New York Clearing House** (No. 100), which supervises the clearing of billions of dollars of member banks' checks daily.

Broad Street in Dutch Colonial days was a wide canal, called the *Heere Graft* (Great Canal) which extended from the East River as far as the present Exchange Place, with a small side canal up Beaver Street. (The broad dimensions of the old canal account for the disproportionately wide size of Broad Street today). By 1676, the canal became polluted and rather malodorous, and was filled in. The name of the resulting street, *Brede Straet,* survives to the present time. It is interesting to note that unlike other north-south streets, the numbers on Broad Street *decrease* in a northward direction.

No. 67 Broad Street, the **R.C.A. Global Communications Building,** also houses the **Commodities Exchange,** where "futures" are traded in silver, gold, hides, soybeans, pork bellies, wheat, etc. Note the splendid entranceway with its colorful mosaic ceiling. Visible on the roof are R.C.A.'s radio antennas.

Directly across the street, a narrow plaza leads to the rear of multicolored No. 2 Broadway.

A plaque at the entrance to tiny Marketfield Street marks the site of "the lost thoroughfare, Petticoat Lane." The diminutive street takes its name from the *Marcktveldt,* or Market Place, which once existed along the old canal. A market was held every Friday morning at the cattle bridge, one of several that crossed the *Heere Graft.*

Turn left on Beaver Street to New Street.

Nowhere else in the city can the expression **"The Canyons of New York"** be more dramatically visualized than from this point looking north on New Street.

No. 18 Beaver Street is an ornate survivor of the "Elegant '80s"—probably an elegant restaurant of yesteryear, better known then as a dining saloon.

At the southwest corner of Beaver and Broad Streets is the Renaissance Revival-style **American Bank Note Company Building.** Before the establishment of the government's Bureau of Engraving and Printing, many security printers such as the American Banknote Company printed our paper currency, bonds, and postage stamps. The Company still manufactures paper currency for many foreign countries and is the largest printer of securities in the world.

A number of interesting buildings can be seen on both sides of Broad Street: **Nos. 55, 50,** and **40** (the Journal of Commerce Building). During the Great Fire of 1835, when the *Journal of Commerce* was located on Garden Street (now Exchange Place), employees saved the building by dousing the flames with vinegar drained from storage vats in an adjoining yard. No. 25, **The Broad-Exchange Building,** when completed just after the turn of the century, was the largest office building in the world.

Exchange Place, named for a merchants' exchange located here during the Dutch Colonial period, is one of the city's narrowest streets. The surprising little hill leading to Broadway gives it the dubious distinction of being the steepest street in downtown Manhattan.

Across from the Broad-Exchange Building, on the northeast corner of Broad Street and Exchange Place, stood the **Old Ferry House** from which boats to Long Island shore points departed down the "Great Canal." Passengers were sometimes forced to spend the night here waiting for fair winds to make the trip. Looking up Exchange Place with its massed skyscrapers, it is hard to conceive that the area during the mid-17th century was a sheep pasture.

Approaching the end of Broad Street is one of the most famous panoramas of the financial center (left to right): **The New York Stock Exchange** (southwest corner), the **Bankers Trust Company** with its "ziggurat" atop the tower (northwest corner), **Federal Hall National Memorial** (northeast corner, directly ahead), the **Morgan Guaranty Trust Company** (southeast corner).

The New York Stock Exchange (8 Broad Street), synonymous with Wall Street, is the largest securities exchange in the world. The "big board" lists more than 3500 different stocks and bonds owned by about 30 million share- and bond-holders. Transactions are printed on a nationwide ticker network, and activity is centered on the trading floor, two-thirds the size of a football field, where member firms' telephoned orders to buy and sell are handled at 22 horseshoe-shaped trading posts on the main floor and in annexes. The often hectic scene, which seems almost incomprehensible to the casual visitor in the gallery, is explained on the daily tours given by the Exchange. The enormous classic building in a neo-Renaissance style was designed in 1903 by George B. Post, with a 22-story addition in 1923 by Trowbridge & Livingston. The sculpture in the pediment is by John Quincy Adams Ward and Paul W. Bartlett. The busy Stock Exchange is a far cry from the old Tontine Coffee House and buttonwood tree of 1792, when 24 brokers drew up the original trading agreement. A little reminder of those days is the recently-planted buttonwood tree in front of the Exchange.

Until the opening of the American Stock Exchange on nearby Trinity Place, some stock transactions were conducted along the sidewalks of Broad Street, with brokers or their representatives waving frenetic hand signals signifying "buy" and "sell" orders to correspondents in adjacent buildings. This very active "Curb Exchange" is now housed in the much more modern "Amex."

Federal Hall National Memorial, built in 1842 as the U.S. Custom House, is considered the Parthenon of public buildings in the city, and possibly its finest Greek Revival-style building. Its predecessor on the site was our second City Hall, which replaced the *Stadt Huys* in 1703. It was here that Peter Zenger, editor of the *New York Weekly Journal* was tried in 1735 for "seditious libels" against the royal government, and particularly against Governor William Cosby. His acquittal for printing the truth was the first major victory in the battle for a free press. Thirty years later, the Stamp Act Congress met to draft a Declaration of Rights and Grievances in which the colonists strongly protested the imposition by England of the Stamp Act. After this first public protest by a colony against "taxation without representation" and a subsequent boycott of the hated stamps, the British government repealed the tax. On July 18, 1776, the Declaration of Independence was read here. During the Revolutionary War, the occupying British forces used the City Hall as their headquarters. Upon cessation of hostilities, the new government met here and passed the Northwest Ordinance (explained on the building plaque to the left). In 1789 the building was renovated under supervision of Maj. Charles Pierre L'Enfant (who later designed the master plan of the City of Washington), and became the Capitol of the United States for just over a year. Congress met here for the first time on March 4, 1789, and, as its first official act, counted the electoral ballots for President George Washington's unanimous election. On April 30, Washington was inaugurated on the steps of the renamed **Federal Hall.** The statue of Washington, sculpted by J. Q. A. Ward in 1883, stands at about the same place where Washington took his oath of office. Congress also adopted the Bill of Rights here on September 25, 1789 and sent it out to the states for adoption.

Unfortunately, the building later fell into disuse and was sold in 1812 for scrap for the sum of $425. In 1862, after 20 years as the Custom House, the present building became a branch of the Independent Treasury System under President Van Buren. Of the six subtreasuries established, New York's was the most important and, as the Subtreasury Building, served until 1920. One of the old thick-walled vaults may be seen inside. Federal Hall is a National Memorial, and both exterior and interior are New York City Landmarks. Federal Hall was designed by Ithiel Town and Alexander Jackson Davis, under surveillance of John Frazee and Samuel Thomson, and is built of Westchester marble. The rather incongruously shaped interior rotunda (a circular space in a rectangular building) forms part of an extensive museum which should not be missed. [Federal Hall is open seven days a week, 8:30 A.M. to 4:30 P.M., enter on Pine Street.] It is one of six national monuments within the City of New York, and is administered by the National Park Service of the Department of the Interior.*

The Morgan Guaranty Trust Company Building, across from Federal Hall, was formerly the offices of J. P. Morgan & Company, America's most powerful private bank. The austere building, completed in 1914 from plans by Trowbridge & Livingston, was the assumed target of an anarchist's bomb. At about noon on September 16, 1920, a horse-drawn wagon parked in front of the bank exploded, killing 33 passers-by (and the horse), and injuring scores of others. The devastating blast occurred during the post-World War I period of anti-radical hysteria, and was said by some to be an act of violence

---

* **Castle Clinton,** in Battery Park; the **Statue of Liberty,** on Liberty Island; **General Grant National Memorial,** in Riverside Park at West 122nd Street; **Theodore Roosevelt Birthplace National Historic Site,** 28 East 20th Street; **Hamilton Grange National Memorial,** Convent Avenue between 141st and 142nd Streets.

In 1826 this charming Greek Revival structure was built by the government as the New York Branch of the Bank of the United States. Later, it became the Assay Office, and upon demolition in 1915 its dignified façade was carefully dismantled and re-erected on the American Wing of the Metropolitan Museum of Art. A subsequent Assay Office occupied the site briefly, and the building was acquired by the Seamen's Bank for Savings. (The Seamen's Bank for Savings)

against "one of the strongest bastions of capitalism." Another theory is that the wagon belonged to an explosives manufacturing company, and had been traveling on a prohibited street when the dynamite accidentally ignited. Numerous scars from the explosion are plainly visible on the bank's façade—and for some reason, the bank has never made an effort to patch them up.

Continue east on Wall Street.

No. 30 Wall Street, now the **Seamen's Bank for Savings,** has an interesting architectural history. Its predecessor on the site, a lovely Greek Revival-style building designed by Martin E. Thompson, was built in 1826 as the New York branch of the Bank of the United States. After 10 years the building was turned over to private banking interests, and in 1853 it was acquired by the Federal Government for the Assay Office. In 1915, the structure—by now the oldest federal edifice in the city—was demolished, but its charming Tuckahoe marble façade was carefully dismantled and stored away, to be reerected in 1924 on the American Wing of the Metropolitan Museum of Art, where it can be seen today. A new Assay Office was constructed on the 30 Wall Street site from plans by York & Sawyer, supervised by James A. Wetmore, and was completed in 1919, "designed to last a thousand years." However, it remained only until the most recent Assay Office was constructed at Old Slip, where Wetmore's experience was again called on for the design.

In 1955 the handsome building was purchased by the Seamen's Bank for Savings which found the five underground floors of bullion vaults in excellent condition, and preserved them for the Bank's archives. The old U.S. Assay Office Building was considered one of the best examples of Renaissance-style architecture. Because of its quality and beauty and the architectural harmony with adjoining Federal Hall, it was decided to preserve this historic landmark and retain the limestone façade of the old Assay Office, erecting the new 12-story building around it on the old foundations. Architects Halsey, McCormack & Helmer incorporated the limestone addition most successfully, proving that a good building need not be demolished when more space is required. In the lobby, to the right of the main banking rooms, are the original marble cornerstones of the 1826 and 1919 buildings. The Seamen's Bank for Savings maintains a collection of ship models, marine paintings, scrimshaw, antique coin banks, and sailing cards in a sixth floor museum, and portions of the collection are part of the decor in all offices of the Bank.

Across the street, at No. 37, is the **Cotton Exchange,** which recently moved from an earlier location at 60 Beaver Street. The Classic Eclectic-style building was designed by Francis H. Kimball in 1907 for the Trust Company of America, and at the time of its completion, was the tallest on Wall Street.

Across from the Cotton Exchange, is lofty **40 Wall Street,** built in 1929 for the Bank of the Manhattan Company. Designed by architects H. Craig Severance and Yasuo Matsui, it was planned as the tallest building in the world. At the same time, Severance's former partner, William Van Alen, was completing the Chrysler Building uptown—also touted as the world's tallest. The developing rivalry led Severance to add two feet to his 40 Wall Tower when it was announced that the Chrysler Building had reached its maximum height of 925 feet. To everyone's surprise (and Severance's chagrin), Van Alen's workmen secretly assembled a towering stainless-steel spire *inside* the building, and raised the Chrysler Building to a record height of 1046 feet— the uncontested winner. Within nine months, however, Severance enjoyed the last laugh, as the newly completed Empire State Building rose almost 40 feet higher! The Bank of the Manhattan Company (since merged with the Chase National Bank to become the sprawling Chase Manhattan Bank), began its career as the city's first water supply company, a quasi-public utility known as **The Manhattan Company.** Founded by Aaron Burr in 1799, and chartered by the State Legislature, the company was the target of severe criticism from Alexander Hamilton, for the terms of the charter permitted it to engage in rather disparate financial pursuits, including banking. Hamilton saw this as an opportunity for Burr to gain banking privileges for his political party. This was one of the first confrontations between the two men that ultimately led to their tragic duel in 1804. The Manhattan Company did provide water to the growing city by means of pine-wood pipes bringing water from a reservoir on Chambers Street; however, banking became its primary interest. When the Croton Water System was opened in 1842, The Bank of the Manhattan Company continued as a financial institution exclusively; and its assets still remain "liquid."

The imposing Classic façade of the **First National City Bank Building** at No. 55 (the southeast corner of William Street), is a dominant landmark on Wall Street. The original ground floor was built in 1836–42, from plans by Isaiah Rogers, as the Merchants Exchange. An earlier Merchants Exchange was destroyed in the Great Fire of 1835. From 1862 to 1907 it served as the Custom House after moving from its former Federal Hall site. When the present Custom House at Bowling Green was opened, the vacant building was remodeled for the National City Bank by the firm of McKim, Mead & White [Stanford White was murdered the year before; *see* Madison Square, 11], and a second tier was added, doubling the size of the building. Note that the lower colonnade is Ionic, the upper, Corinthian. In designating the building a landmark, the New York City Landmarks Preservation Commission called it "a remarkable example of how a notable building can be sympathetically extended." The successor, the First National City Bank, chartered in 1812, and an outgrowth of the First Bank of the United States, still occupies the impressive structure.

Turn right into William Street, to the corner of Exchange Place.

Named for William Beekman, who came from Holland with Peter Stuyvesant (not for King William of England, as is commonly believed), **William Street** forms another of the deep, winding canyons that give the neighborhood so much atmosphere. Beekman's descendants settled farther uptown in the area now known as Beekman Place [*see* East River Panoramas, 5].

The 20 Exchange Place Building (also known as No. 22 William Street and No. 65 Beaver Street) is a striking 57-story limestone Art Deco shaft on an irregularly shaped base, designed by Cross & Cross, and completed in 1931. Formerly the City Bank Farmers Trust Company and later the First National City Trust Company, it is now one of the major buildings of the First National City Bank. The history of coinage is vividly displayed on plaques above the ground-floor windows (even our old Buffalo Nickel is there!). A "Bridge of Sighs" connects with the No. 55 Wall Street "Citibank" building. Although the street pattern is helter-skelter, the tower of the tall building conforms to the north-south city grid.

The west side of William Street, between Exchange Place and Beaver Street, is still in the late 19th century. **The Lords Court Building** (27 William Street and 40 Exchange Place) is a functional Classic Eclectic structure of c. 1895 with the usual ornamentation found on the first skyscrapers built with structural-steel skeletons. The tiny adjacent building, **No. 23,** somehow survived—no doubt because of its small, irregular plot—and was likely an early residence. Note the ornate hooded lintels over the windows and the classic cornice supported by four console brackets—a real anachronism among its lofty neighbors. **No. 15,** built in 1894 and formerly the Corn Exchange Bank, is similar in dimensions to the Lords Court Building, but has a far more ornate façade. The repeating horizontal courses and "columns" of recessed windows serve to break up the feeling of verticality for aesthetic as well as psychological reasons (people were still wary of high buildings before the turn of the century).

Delmonico's Restaurant (now Oscar's Delmonico's, at 56 Beaver Street) was founded in 1827 by Peter and John Delmonico, recent immigrants from Italy. In 1836 they built Beaver Street House for their establishment, which remained until the present building, designed by James Lord, replaced it in 1890. Another branch of the restaurant was operated on Madison Square, and later at Fifth Avenue and 44th Street. The restaurant was always fashionable, and in Moses King's 1893 *Handbook of New York City,* it is described as "a familiar name among the epicures of two continents for nearly three-quarters of a century . . . where it will cost you from $3 upward for a good dinner" (a high price in those days, and a tradition apparently maintained by the successors).

Across William Street (now called South William Street) is the investment banking house of **Lehman Brothers.** The building was erected in 1907 in a Renaissance Revival style from plans by Francis H. Kimball and Julian C. Levi, for the banking firm of J. & W. Seligman & Company (who are still in business at 65 Broadway). The cupola set above an indented corner can be seen only from a distance.

Continue down South William Street to Mill Lane.

South William Street was originally called Mill Street, and near this site in 1626, the Dutch West India Company had erected a large mill. Not only did it grind flour, but its large upper room served as a house of worship for the first settlers until their Reformed Church was completed within Fort Amsterdam (on the site of the present Custom House). The room later served the first Jewish immigrants who arrived in 1653 but were not permitted to hold services until several years later. Two millstones from the old mill are preserved in the Spanish & Portuguese Synagogue at 8 West 70th Street [*see* West of Central Park, 1]. It was here, too, that on August 29, 1664, the Dutch formally signed the document of surrender of Nieuw Amsterdam to the English.

The view down Mill Lane to Stone Street (visited earlier in the tour) is in sharp contrast to the surrounding tall buildings, and with a little squinting it is not difficult to imagine oneself back in the early 19th century.

Farther down South William Street, at No. 26, is the site of the first synagogue in America, built in 1730; but spare yourself the walk, it is no longer there, and the garage at the address is not worth seeing. Even the commemorative plaque has disappeared.

Return to Beaver Street and turn right to Hanover Street (not Hanover Square).

Note again the coin motifs on the 65 Beaver Street entrance of the 20 Exchange Place Building, this time biblical coins. The corner of the building at the juncture of Beaver and Hanover Streets is the **site of the Great Fire of 1835** (*see* map).

At nine o'clock in the evening on December 17, fire broke out in the store of Comstock & Adams at 25 Merchant Street (the street has since been demapped). The temperature had dropped to a near record −17° and a howling gale was blowing. The fire, caused by a gas-pipe explosion, spread rapidly to adjoining buildings and within minutes the blaze raged out of control, fed by stores of dry goods and chemicals and driven by the wind. Fire companies fought desperately but ineffectively to stem the conflagration, hampered by frozen hydrants and hoses that became clogged almost instantly with ice. As the fire advanced in both east and west directions, whole blocks

THE
**GREAT FIRE
OF 1835**
December 17-18

Shaded area indicates extent of total destruction.

The Fire began at X.

East
River

The Merchants' Exchange, ablaze during the Great Fire of 1835, the worst conflagration in the city's history. A valiant attempt was made to rescue the statue of Alexander Hamilton (seen in this lithograph brightly lit by the flames) but the cupola, tilting dangerously, collapsed through the roof and shattered the sculpture. (New-York Historical Society)

seemed to erupt spontaneously into flames. By the early morning hours the blaze had engulfed almost every block to the East River from Wall Street to Coenties Slip, and west nearly to Broad Street. Help was summoned from as far away as Philadelphia, and pump wagons were hastily put aboard freight cars of the newly built railroad and transported to New York. It is said that the flame-reddened sky was visible as far away as Camden, New Jersey, and New Haven, Connecticut. By noon the following day, the fire had consumed all of Hanover Square, including the merchandise that had been saved from threatened buildings and stacked for protection in the Square. Adding to the horror were mobs of looters who converged on the area and overwhelmed the small police force in their mad scramble to steal what had not been burned. A supply of gunpowder was obtained from the Navy Yard in Brooklyn and rowed across the East River to blast a firebreak and hopefully to contain the still roaring inferno. Fortunately, the masonry walls of the line of buildings along Wall Street helped contain the flames, although the magnificent Merchants Exchange, one of the city's commercial and architectural showplaces was itself completely destroyed. By late December 18, the fire burned itself out, leaving an area of 17 blocks—about 20 acres—

The corner of Broad and Wall streets in 1882. In the center, the former New York Stock Exchange Building dominates Broad Street, and to the left are the banking offices of Drexel, Morgan & Company (now the site of the Morgan Guaranty Trust Co.). (The J. Clarence Davies Collection, Museum of the City of New York)

a smoldering field of ashes, with the incredible loss of 674 buildings from the very heart of the financial district! The disaster was compounded by the total destruction of many fire insurance companies, which left their insureds with no chance of compensation. The 1835 fire was the worst in our young nation's history and completely obliterated every remaining Dutch Colonial building in the city. That is why there is not a single structure left in Manhattan from the 17th century. As if this were not enough, another fire ten years later destroyed 345 buildings in the same general area.

Turn left on Hanover Street to Wall Street.

The building to the right, **No. 63 Wall Street,** is also decorated with coin plaques—drachmas of Ancient Greece on large plaques above the fourth-floor entablature.

Turn left on Wall Street to the northeast corner of William Street.

The view to Trinity Church down Wall Street is one of the best known scenes of New York. [Trinity Church is described in the tour of Lower Broadway and the Battery, *see* page 10.]

Wall Street in 1864, seen from the Subtreasury Building. In the rear is the Merchants' Exchange, rebuilt after the Great Fire of 1835, now sporting another story as the First National City Bank—and the only building in the view still standing. (Museum of the City of New York)

A classic view of Wall Street, Trinity Church and the Subtreasury Building (now Federal Hall), as seen in a magic lantern slide photo taken about 1875. (The Picture Decorator, Inc., N.Y.C.)

The oldest commercial bank in the country is the **Bank of New York,** founded by Alexander Hamilton in 1784. Several plaques describe its history, including the story of its predecessor on the site, the United States Branch Bank. The original cornerstone of the Bank of New York has been reset several times for each new building in its history. A low-relief bronze plaque above the subway entrance, commemorating the famous Wall, includes an early map, and was placed in 1909 during the Hudson-Fulton Celebration. The building, long a landmark in the lower Manhattan skyline, was designed in 1927 by Benjamin Wistar Morris. It is a graceful structure with a Georgian-style cupola and lantern, best seen at a distance.

Turn right (north) on William Street to Pine Street.

To the left soars the 800-foot aluminum and glass **Chase Manhattan Bank,** set on one of the largest plazas in the city. When completed in 1960 it was the trendsetter for the series of "plazas" to follow, conforming to the revised zoning regulations requiring more street-level space. The plaza is elevated at the William Street end due to the topography. Take a few minutes and climb the stairs to the plaza level. The sunken central courtyard with its fountain is paved with granite blocks in an unusual undulating form. It was originally planned to have fish and even dolphins in the fountain, but the idea was quickly abandoned, primarily because of the dangers of pollution (by air and people). Sculptor Isamu Noguchi is responsible for the innovative design, and Skidmore, Owings & Merrill for the towering box-like shaft. Stand beneath the edge of the lofty building and listen as the wind plays delicate tunes on the vertical metal strips. Dominating the plaza is Jean Dubuffet's enormous free-form white and black sculpture, *Group of Four Trees,* subject of considerable comment since its installation in 1972. A weekday visit to the building's concourse reveals an atomic clock, run by gamma rays from its cesium power supply; and to the left of the lobby a charming Japanese garden. The 60th-floor restaurant provides a spectacular view of the Financial District and its surrounding waterways. There are guided tours of the building (telephone for schedule), which include many antiques and works of art in the executive offices, as well as paintings from president David Rockefeller's private collection. The building also houses the world's largest bank vault, five levels below ground. The vaults are reputed to hold over $40 billion in securities, and just a few scant millions in cash. The Bank is the successor to the Bank of the Manhattan Company and the Chase National Bank. The latter was named for Salmon P. Chase, Secretary of the Treasury in Lincoln's administration, and founder of our national currency system and the Federal banking system. (There was no government-issued paper money prior to 1861.) Chase Manhattan occupies the first 35 of the 60 stories above ground.

Continue north on William Street to Liberty Street.

The Federal Reserve Bank Building, occupying the entire block between

Liberty Street and Maiden Lane, is *the* great bank for banks—one of 12 of our Federal Reserve System. A Florentine *palazzo* that would have warmed the heart of Lorenzo de' Medici, it is actually based on the design of the Strozzi Palace of the Italian Renaissance. Completed in 1924 from plans by York & Sawyer, The Federal Reserve Bank is a dramatic and imposing structure with its massive walls of rusticated Ohio sandstone and Indiana limestone, fortresslike machicolations, and extensive wrought-iron ornamentation. The lovely triple lanterns and the window grilles in the great arched windows were executed by Samuel Yellin. An enormous subterranean vault five stories below street level and protected by 90-ton doors contains gold bullion stored for many foreign governments; when trade balances are settled, gold is moved from one nation's room to another, rarely leaving the building. The tremendous volume of check handling and coin operations can be seen on visitors' tours, which begin in the impressive entrance lobby on Liberty Street. All paper currency issued by the Government through the New York branch of the Federal Reserve Bank bears the letter *B* on the face of each note. Bank notes issued by the Federal Reserve Bank in Boston have an *A*, Philadelphia, *C*, etc., through San Francisco, *L*. The Federal Reserve System, our nation's central banking establishment, was organized in 1913. All national banks must belong to a regional branch and keep a specific cash reserve on deposit. It is said that the vaults here house more gold than Fort Knox. The Federal Reserve Bank is a designated New York City Landmark.

The Home Insurance Company Building occupies a neat little plaza between Maiden Lane and John Street. Designed by the Office of Alfred Easton Poor, the building was completed in 1966. Enter on a weekday and zip up to the 15th floor for a visit to the **Harold V. Smith Firefighting Museum,** maintained by the Home Insurance Company. On display is the world's finest and most extensive collection of firefighting memorabilia. A splendid goose-neck fire pumper of 1838, named *Hope* (which was designed three years too late for use in the Great Fire) competes with one that saw service in the Great Fire of London of 1666. The American *Hope* was considered elegant enough to participate in President Grover Cleveland's inaugural parade. The Museum also boasts a large collection of fire marks—decorative plaques that early fire-insurance companies and volunteer brigades required homeowners to display prominently on their house fronts—or the fire would not be extinguished and compensation would not be paid. There is also a fine collection of Currier & Ives prints on "The Life of a Fireman," and many working models of old-time fire-fighting apparatus. The *pièce de résistance,* however, is the detailed re-creation of the firehouse of Eagle Engine Company No. 13, which in 1790 was located on Maiden Lane near Gold Street. A plaque in the triangular plaza marks the site of Thomas Jefferson's residence while he lived in New York City serving as the nation's first Secretary of State. New York was the seat of the Federal Government when Jefferson took office on March 21, 1790.

No. 100 William Street, on the northeast corner of Platt Street, is the city's

Intersection of William Street and Maiden Lane, looking west, c. 1760. The site is now occupied by The Home Insurance Company Building. In this E. P. Chrystie drawing, a beer barrel is being lowered from the third floor of Rutgers' Brew House. During the British occupation of New York it was a storehouse. (The Home Insurance Company)

first building to take advantage of the special 1970 zoning regulations that encourage builders to create a covered pedestrian space as an alternative to the open plaza—outdoor space that was often uninspired and of minimal utilitarian design and, of course, subject to the vagaries of the weather. This 21-story building, in a dark-textured façade, is reminiscent of the CBS Building uptown, and was completed in 1972 from plans by Davis, Brody & Associates with Emery Roth & Sons. Under provisions of the new law, the architects have designed an impressive 80-foot *galleria,* cutting diagonally through the ground floor of the building, providing an attractive arcade between William and John streets. The arcade is lined with shops, lit in part by angular windows and light troughs. The building received the Award for Excellence in Design for 1973 from the New York Society of Architects. A central escalator leads to the office of Chubb & Sons, one of the city's largest insurance brokerage houses. Walk through the stainless-steel, black-glass, and slate *galleria* (open weekdays only).

Continue to the corner of John Street.

About a hundred yards to the east, at the present corner of John and Gold streets, was a small hillock, covered with bright yellow flowers, which the Dutch had called *De Gouwenberg,* or Golden Hill. On January 18, 1770, it was the site of the first bloodshed between the colonists and the British Army.

Tempers had been running high since the imposition of the hated tax on tea, and particularly over the event of the previous night when soldiers knocked down a Liberty Pole and deposited the remnants in front of a tavern that was the meeting place of the Sons of Liberty. That afternoon several thousand citizens massed in "The Fields" near Broadway to vow punishment to any soldiers caught armed in the streets. The British reacted with taunts and ridicule, and after a series of provocative acts on both sides, a running brawl broke out between the mob and 20 British soldiers. Both groups then retired to nearby Golden Hill where they were met by a detachment of regulars who opened fire on the civilians, killing one and wounding several. The encounter, known as the **Battle of Golden Hill,** occurred several weeks before the Boston Massacre and five months before the first major hostilities at Bunker Hill.

Turn left on John Street.

   The John Street United Methodist Church, built in 1841, is the third on the site. Its position is now accentuated by the rising tower of the new annex of the Federal Reserve Bank, the plans for which were specifically drawn to shelter and highlight this old landmark. At this writing, while construction progresses on the 40-story building, lofted 13 stories above ground level, it is hoped that the little church will not be so overwhelmed as to be reduced to a mere curiosity. The first Methodist church in America was built on this site in 1768, and traces its roots to John Wesley, the founder of Methodism. Under the leadership of Philip Embury and Barbara Heck, the congregation, which had been meeting in a rigging loft on Horse and Cart Street (now William Street), established the meeting house. Since that time the building has been rebuilt twice, in 1818 and 1841, and was restored in 1965. Spend a moment and enjoy the intimate quality of the interior. Built in late Georgian style, the church is somewhat austere, yet cozy and inviting. Many of the original artifacts from the 1768 chapel still remain, including candelabra, John Wesley's great clock, foot warmers, and Embury's hand-carved pulpit. Climb the narrow staircase to the gallery for a good perspective of the interior. The Church has been designated an official New York City Landmark.

Broadway
Chambers

(A. T.
Stewart's
"Marble
Palace")
(Later
Sun Bldg.)
clock ● **15**

16

ELK ST.

Hall of Records
19

CENTRE ST.

Municipal Bldg.
1

20
Police Plaza

CHAMBERS ST.

Tweed Court House
17

IRT ■
2

WARREN ST.

Home
Life Bldg. **14**

18 City Hall

Nathan
Hale ●

Horace ●
Greeley

APPROACHES
TO Park Row U

BROOKLYN BRIDGE

MURRAY ST.

City Hall Park
13

3 Pace Univ.

(Frankfort St.)

Benjamin
Franklin

4

BROADWAY

PARK PL.

(Mall St.)
Site of
"Mullett"
Post Office

SPRUCE ST.

**Newspaper Row
(c. 1895):**

Staats-Zeitung

World

Woolworth
Bldg. **12**

5 Potter
Bldg.

Am.
Tract Soc.
Bldg.

Daily Recorder

Sun

BARCLAY ST.

BEEKMAN ST.

Tribune

Evening Telegram

Transportation Bldg.

N.Y.
County
Lawyers
Bldg. **11**

Evening
Post Bldg.

6

7 Park
Row
Bldg.

THEATER ALLEY

NASSAU ST.

PARK ROW

Evening Journal →

American →

Times

Press

VESEY ST.

Daily News

ANN ST.

Globe &
Commercial Advertiser

St. Paul's
Chapel **9**

Herald

Evening Post

Mail & Express

FULTON ST.

10

8

**CITY HALL
AREA**

3. City Hall, "Newspaper Row", Foley Square, and "Five Points"

[IRT Lexington Avenue Line to Brooklyn Bridge station; BMT Nassau Street Line to Chambers Street station; M-102 Bus to City Hall]

The tour begins at Centre and Chambers streets.

1. Classic in style and original in design, the imposing **Municipal Building** is our greatest civic skyscraper and the focus of the new Civic Center plan. In scale it is complementary to nearby City Hall as well as to the modern counterparts mushrooming about it. Built in 1914 from plans by McKim, Mead & White, it now houses only a fraction of the city offices which oversee the functioning of the metropolis. Particularly attractive is the row of freestanding columns, the extensive sculpture work, and the lofty colonnaded tower topped by Adolph A. Weinman's statue of *Civic Fame,* recently given a new coating of gold leaf. Pause for a moment to examine the sculpture: on the north arch, *Progress;* on the north panel, *Civic Duty;* on the central arch, *Guidance* and *Executive Power;* on the south panel, *Civic Pride;* and on the south arch, *Prudence.* Between the windows on the second floor are symbols of the various city departments. Note the collection of plaques, among which is the "triple-X" emblem of the city of Amsterdam, Holland. A lavish subway entrance is incorporated into the south section, under a vaulted ceiling. Chambers Street, which originally passed through the building, is now closed to vehicular traffic, and forms a part of a new pedestrian mall into Police Plaza. (We will return later after a loop around City Hall Park.)

Return to Centre Street and cross to City Hall Park.

2. Go down the IRT subway stairs directly across the street from the Municipal Building. At the foot of the staircase, mounted on the right-hand wall, are three enormous bronze plaques honoring those responsible for the construction of **"The First Municipal Rapid Transit Railroad of the City of New York."** The subway, a brainchild of financier August Belmont, took four years (and three mayors) to build (1900–04). The first station, City Hall, is no longer in service, but local IRT trains still rumble past it on a loop underneath the Park. The original line followed the present Lexington Avenue route to Grand Central, swung west under 42nd Street to Times Square, then north on Broadway to 145th Street.

Return to the street level and continue south about 50 feet.

3. Across Park Row (Centre Street joins it at this point), where modern Pace University is situated, was the beginning of the so-called **"Newspaper Row"** from the 1840s till after the turn of the century. In the year 1893, for example, there were 19 daily newspapers printed in the City of New York plus a score of foreign-language papers. In the year 1975, there were only three, yet the population of the city has grown from a million-and-a-half in 1893 to almost five times that number!

Where the Municipal Building's south section is now, was the site of the building of the *New-Yorker Staats-Zeitung,* the largest German-language newspaper in the country (and still publishing). To the right of the intertwining ramps of the Brooklyn Bridge stood the 26-story gold-domed *New York World,* the tallest building in the world when completed in 1890. Designed by George B. Post, the "World Tower" was a dominant feature of the lower-Manhattan skyline. Purchased by Joseph Pulitzer seven years earlier, the newspaper became one of the most literate and influential in the city.

Immediately to its right, across demapped Frankfort Street, stood the **Sun Building.** The *Sun* really "shone" after its acquisition by Charles Anderson Dana, becoming the city's first penny newspaper, with a broad popular appeal. The paper lived out its remaining years in a building which will be discussed shortly.

Adjacent to the *Sun* was the exuberant clock-towered **Tribune Building,** designed by famed architect Richard Morris Hunt. The *Tribune* was founded by Horace ("Go west, young man") Greeley in 1841, and soon was acknowledged as New York's most important newspaper. When Greeley departed from the *Tribune* to help found the Republican party, he left the management to Whitelaw Reid, himself an active political leader (Minister to France and unsuccessful candidate for Vice-President in 1892). Reid was one of a line of distinguished journalists who began their careers on the *"Trib";* others were

*City Hall Park and its panorama of newspaper office buildings around 1905.
Left to right, the domed* World, *the diminutive* Sun, *Richard Morris Hunt's*
Tribune Tower. *The* Times *had just moved uptown from the large building at
the right. Between City Hall and the* World *is the iron shed serving Brooklyn
Bridge trains and the Third Avenue El. Note the kiosk entrance to the IRT City
Hall Station in the lower left. Although the loop still runs underground, the
station was abandoned in the 1940s, and no more such elaborate cast-iron kiosks
remain.* (New-York Historical Society)

Carl Schurz, William Dean Howells, Charles A. Dana, Henry James, Bayard
Taylor, and Margaret Fuller, to name but a few. When the Tribune Tower
was demolished, the city lost a great architectural treasure.

Make a short detour into the Park in the direction of City Hall to the
Statue of Horace Greeley, done in 1890 by John Quincy Adams Ward, one of
the best known sculptors of the time. Below is a plaque honoring the donor
of the Pulitzer Prize and his *New York World.*

4. A bit farther we see little **Printing House Square** with Ernest Plassman's statue of Benjamin Franklin. Behind Franklin, at the corner of Spruce
Street, is the former **American Tract Society Building.** Designed in 1896 by

R. H. Robertson, it is a massive Romanesque Revival-style edifice that no longer houses any religious publishing concern, and is known merely by its address, No. 150 Nassau Street.

A block east of Printing House Square, on William Street, were William Randolph Hearst's *New York American* (an outgrowth of the earlier *Morning Journal*) and the *New York Evening Journal*. His *Journal* represented the archetype of "yellow journalism," for its rabble rousing and drum beating were held in great part responsible for our entry into the Spanish-American War.

To the right, at the corner of Park Row (No. 41), is the former **New York Times Building,** now an integral part of the Pace campus. Designed in 1889 by George B. Post, and later remodeled by Robert Maynicke (1895), it housed The *Times* until its move to Longacre Square (now Times Square) in 1904.

5. Abutting the former New York Times Building is the dazzlingly ornate **Potter Building** (38 Park Row) constructed in 1883. It has two "firsts" to its name, as the earliest surviving edifice built with a structural steel framework, and the first to sport an ornamental terra-cotta façade, in both cast and pressed forms. The fireproof quality of terra cotta was appropriately chosen, as the predecessor on the site, the old New York World Building, was de-

The Park Theater c. 1820 on Park Row, facing City Hall. One of the nation's first legitimate theaters, it was built at the time of the American Revolution. (Consolidated Edison Company of New York)

stroyed a year before in one of the city's most spectacular blazes. For a time, The *Press* was published in the Potter Building.

To the right rear, at 5 Beekman Street, are the twin pyramidal towers of the curious **Temple Court Building.**

6. "Newspaper Row" continued with a line of 5-story brick buildings that housed a number of popular dailies. The *New York Daily News,* at 26 Park Row, was a relatively small, evening paper at the turn of the century, and pro-Democratic at that. Adjoining was the *Morning Advertiser,* and two doors farther, The *Mail and Express.* Cyrus Field purchased the *Evening Mail* and the *Evening Express* in 1880 and 1882 respectively, and made them a financially successful enterprise. He subsequently built an interesting, rococo, T-shaped building near the corner of Fulton Street. The *Recorder* was at No. 21 and nearby, the *Evening Telegram.* Near Ann Street was the *Globe and Commercial Advertiser,* at the time the oldest newspaper in New York, dating from 1797.

7. When completed in 1899, the **Park Row Building,** at No. 15, was one of the tallest in the world. Its twin cupolas added interest and variety to the growing skyline. The skyscraper was designed by R. H. Robertson, and the four caryatids (including the 16 figures on the cupola) are attributed to J. Massey Rhind. The Park Row Building was also the birthplace of the Associated Press.

At the southeast corner of Park Row and Ann Street, on the site of P. T. Barnum's Museum, stood the white marble French Second Empire **Herald Building.** Founded in 1835 by James Gordon Bennett, it soon gained popularity for its frequent "scoops," as well as for printing news of the financial world. Although a penny newspaper, it made Bennett a fortune. His son, James Gordon Bennett, Jr., startled the "Fourth Estate" by moving the *Herald* uptown in 1894 to a magnificent McKim, Mead & White *palazzo* on what is now Herald Square. Although the Herald Building is now gone from the uptown Square, the Bennett Clock still rings the hours while figures with hammers strike an enormous bell. The building on "Newspaper Row" was later replaced by a 25-story, rather nondescript skyscraper, the St. Paul Building, which in turn was razed for the present Western Electric Building.

8. Occupying the same relative position one block south was the **Evening Post Building.** Founded in 1801 by Alexander Hamilton, the *Evening Post* was possibly the most conservative of all New York dailies. Under the leadership of editor William Cullen Bryant, the paper spoke out for free trade. Bryant, by the way, staunchly opposed allowing women to enter the journalism field. Later, under Carl Schurz, the paper adopted a more liberal attitude, both politically and toward women. In 1906 it moved to new quarters on Vesey Street (which will be seen shortly).

9. The oldest church in Manhattan (and the oldest building as well) is magnificent **St. Paul's Chapel.** Turning its back on Broadway, it faces a peaceful churchyard, oblivious to the noise and clamor of the crowded thoroughfare. St. Paul's, a branch of Trinity Church downtown, was completed in

1766, the tower and steeple in 1796. Architect Thomas McBean undoubtedly was influenced by London's St. Martin's-in-the-Fields when he designed this majestic landmark. It is built of locally quarried Manhattan schist, and the tower (by James Crommelin Lawrence) is of brownstone. The church is an almost perfect example of Georgian style, reflecting the elegant tradition of the Colonial period. Much of the interior decoration of this National Historic Landmark was done by Pierre L'Enfant, the French-born architect who later became a Major of Engineers in the Continental Army, and laid out the City of Washington, D.C. One can still see the pew where Washington regularly worshiped. Among the list of distinguished worshippers were Prince William (later King William IV), Lords Cornwallis and Howe, Maj. John André, the Marquis de Lafayette, and Presidents Grover Cleveland and Benjamin Harrison. (Further details on St. Paul's can be found on page 3.)

The quiet churchyard is well worth a visit. Note the numerous 18th-century headstones with names of well known families of early New York.

To the right of the churchyard on Vesey Street, are two interesting landmark buildings. At No. 20 is the **Garrison Building,** formerly the home of the *Evening Post,* from 1907 to 1926. This is a rare example of Art Nouveau architecture. The bronze-finished cast-iron spandrels are decorated with the colophons of well known 16th- and 17th-century printers, and the statues on the ninth floor represent "The Four Periods of Publicity," by Gutzon Borglum and Estelle Rumbold Kohn. The building, designed by Robert D. Kohn, was completed in 1906.

To its right, at No. 14, is the **New York County Lawyers Association Building**—"the Home of Law." Constructed in 1930 of Vermont marble and limestone, it was designed by Cass Gilbert in a neo-Federal style. Its auditorium is a reproduction of Independence Hall in Philadelphia. Vesey Street is named for William Vesey, first rector of Trinity Church.

10. Looking to the left from the churchyard across Fulton Street, is the multicolumned **American Telephone & Telegraph Building,** built in 1917 from plans by Welles Bosworth. Its crowning gilt statue, *The Genius of the Telegraph* (sometimes called *The Spirit of Communication*), by Evelyn Beatrice Longman, adds bright and artistic punctuation to the New York City skyline. A weekday visit to the spacious lobby reveals an interesting and educational display, including sculptor Chester Beach's marble and bronze statue, *Service to the Nation.* Interestingly, the American "Tel & Tel" Building, with its eight tiers of colonnades, has more columns than the Parthenon— or any other building, for that matter.

11. Turn north on Broadway to No. 225. The **Transportation Building,** designed by York & Sawyer in 1915, occupies the site of one of New York's most celebrated hostelries, the Astor House, which catered to affluent visitors from 1836 to 1913. Note the wall plaque with its scenic low-relief view of the Astor House in its heyday.

12. Possibly the most beautiful commercial building in the world is the dramatic, Gothic Revival-style **Woolworth Building.** When dedicated in 1913,

The Federal Building at the intersection of Broadway and Park Row became the city's main post office in 1875. An elaborate Second Empire pile designed by government architect A. B. Mullett, it obstructed the view of City Hall until its demolition just before World War II. (Museum of the City of New York)

the Rev. S. Parkes Cadman, a famous New York clergyman, in a burst of enthusiastic rhetoric, referred to it as a "Cathedral of Commerce"—and the sobriquet still stands. Many believe it to be architect Cass Gilbert's greatest triumph. Rising 729 feet (plus 1 inch!), the Woolworth Tower eclipsed the Metropolitan Life Tower to become the tallest building in the world for 17 years. The opening ceremony was climaxed when President Wilson pressed a button in Washington, illuminating 80,000 bulbs on the 60-story structure. Two years later, at the Panama-Pacific Exposition, it received a gold medal as the "most beautiful building in all the world erected to commerce." The observation deck on the 55th floor, which unfortunately is no longer open to the public, provided a breathtaking view, as visitors were whisked to the top at dizzying speed in the newest in high-speed electric elevators.

Frank Woolworth, the founder of the ubiquitous five-and-ten-cent-store chain, paid the $15,500,000 cost of the building in cash! The exterior has all the typical Gothic elements—look for the gargoyles, flying buttresses, arches, trefoils, etc. The style is followed in the interior as well. The lobby presents one of the most striking interior spaces in the city, with its vaulted, mosaic ceiling, which sparkles in a jewel-like effect; the delicate bronzework; the walls of veined marble; an imposing grand staircase; lacy, wrought-iron cornices covered with gold leaf; polished terrazzo floors; and the amusing little sculptured caricatures of Mr. Woolworth, Cass Gilbert (holding a model of his pet project), Louis Horowitz, the builder, and others involved with the construction of the "Cathedral." The 25th-floor office of Frank Woolworth, who died in 1919, is preserved as a private museum. (Ask the guard for a free descriptive leaflet.)

13. Cross Broadway to **City Hall Park.** Called the Common in the 18th century, it was then at the northern edge of the city, a triangular plot formed by the confluence of the Bloomingdale Road (now Broadway) and the Boston Post Road (now Park Row and farther north, the Bowery). On the Common, a prison was constructed, and nearby, a Poor House, as well as a Powder House and Barracks as part of the city's defenses. Just to the north was the Negroes' Burial Ground, and a short distance to the west, King's College (now Columbia University). As the city expanded northward, it became a popular public gathering place, and figured in a series of anti-British incidents for a ten-year period prior to the Revolution, in which patriots forcefully displayed their displeasure with the Crown by harassing the military post and erecting a series of Liberty Poles. After the Revolution, the city entered an era of prosperity and growth that required the construction of a new City Hall. In 1811 the present seat of town government was completed in what was the new City Hall Park. The Park was enlarged to its present size in the late 1930s with the razing of the old Post Office and Court House Building that occupied most of the southern corner of the triangle. The so-called "Mullett" (after the architect) Post Office was a massive granite pile of "wedding cake" built in 1878 in the French Second Empire style; its demolition provided light and space and a sweeping view of (and from) City Hall.

A bit farther north, beyond the private street leading to City Hall, is the famous **statue of Nathan Hale,** by sculptor Frederick MacMonnies, erected in the Park in 1893. On the lawn beyond, the flagpole commemorates the erection of the five **Liberty Poles.** Those poles were anathema to the British, not only for their symbolism, but also because they were cut from the prohibited white pine, a tree reserved exclusively for the masts of His Majesty's navy. The name Sons of Liberty was first applied to those who demonstrated against the hated Stamp Act by freedom-sympathizer Lt. Col. Sir Isaac Barré, a Member of Parliament, who is remembered with a plaque on the far side of the lawn (beside City Hall) and also in the names of Barre, Vermont, and Wilkes-Barre, Pennsylvania.

Located under Broadway, between Murray and Warren streets, was the City's first subway. In a short-lived experiment using compressed air for propulsion, Alfred Ely Beach constructed a 312-foot-long tube that was opened to the public in 1870. The subway was built in secret to prevent interference from corrupt "Boss" Tweed who had his own plans for mass transit. The passengers rode in a luxurious car, built to fit snugly against the tube's wall, and the "train" was propelled by air from a huge fan blowing through the tunnel. An elaborate waiting room was fully carpeted and furnished with

The recently completed American Telephone & Telegraph Company Building dwarfs St. Paul's Chapel at Fulton Street and Broadway, c. 1919. Nestled in the L-shaped structure is the Victorian-style Evening Mail Building which was later demolished when AT&T extended its building to Fulton Street. To the extreme left is the St. Paul Building, now the site of the Western Electric Building. (The American Telephone & Telegraph Company)

The oldest German daily in the United States, the Staats Zeitung, *began publishing in this Victorian pile on Park Row and Centre Streets in the 1870s. Statues of Gutenberg and Franklin by Ernst Plassman adorn the third floor. The site is now occupied by the Municipal Building. (Museum of the City of New York)*

The buildings at Centre and Chambers Streets represent a variety of styles. Note the pedestrian crossings, slightly elevated so rain would run off and vehicles would slow down, and also much easier on the feet than cobblestones. (Museum of the City of New York)

The Rhinelander Building at Duane and Rose Streets, demolished in 1971. The marble entrance columns as well as the barred "Old Sugar House" window are now preserved on Police Plaza. (New York City Landmarks Preservation Commission)

Mulberry Street with its infamous "bend" between Park and Bayard Streets in the early 1880s was, and remains, heavily Italian. Mulberry Bend Park (later Columbus Park) replaced the buildings on the left side of the street. (New-York Historical Society)

One of the few surviving photos (left) of the Beach Pneumatic Subway shows the approach to the Warren Street station in 1870. Below, the remains of the subway car found in an 1899 excavation. (New-York Historical Society)

paintings, a fountain, and even a grand piano. After his failure to secure adequate financial backing to extend the line, Beach abandoned the pneumatic underground railway. In 1912, workmen excavating for the BMT subway, came upon the old tube with its single car and lavish station.

14. No. 255 is the elegant former headquarters of the **Home Life Insurance Company.** Designed in Eclectic style by Napoleon LeBrun, its pyramided "temple" atop the building is best seen from a distance.

At the northwest corner of Chambers Street, No. 277, the **Broadway Chambers,** designed by Cass Gilbert, is a good example of "tripartite" skyscraper construction, where the building façade is divided into three basic sections, similar to the components of a Classic column.

15. Continue north to Chambers Street, where on the northeast corner is the former **A. T. Stewart "Marble Palace"** [*see* Ladies' Mile, 1]. Designed by John B. Snook and Joseph Trench, with marble cutting by Ottavino Gori, it was completed in 1846, and promptly became a trendsetter in American architecture. As the first commercial Italianate building, its *palazzo* style was copied widely; and with this extravagant edifice, the tradition of the large retail emporium was firmly established. After Stewart moved his flourishing dry-goods business uptown in 1862, he retained the building as a warehouse. His later successor added two additional floors, and in 1884 converted the now 7-story building for commercial use. In 1917, the *Sun* moved in from across the Park, publishing here until its demise in 1952. The attractive clock on the corner of the building, bearing the motto "The Sun it Shines for All,"

New York's first subway was the Beach Pneumatic Tube, built in 1869–70. It ran one block on Broadway between Park Place and Murray Street. In this rendering of the proposed car, the giant steam-operated fan which supplied the power through air pressure cannot be seen. (New-York Historical Society)

Faced with demolition as part of the projected Civic Center, the Criminal Courts Building on Chambers Street behind City Hall is a monument to civic corruption. Between 8 and 12 million dollars of taxpayers' money went into "Boss" Tweed's pocket. Supporters of this Italianate "villa" feel strongly that it should be preserved for aesthetic and historical reasons. (Photo by author)

has been preserved through the efforts of a local committee of businessmen and city employees who raised the funds to restore it, and it has become a kind of unofficial landmark. The *Sun*'s thermometer on the opposite corner, however, remains adamantly at 40°. In 1966, New York City acquired the Sun Building, and now its future is uncertain. Hopefully our City Fathers will recognize its historic and artistic value, and will find a role for it in the developing Civic Center plans.

16. To the east at 51 Chambers Street is the twin-sectioned **Emigrant Industrial Savings Bank Building.** No longer the bank's home office, its impressive double towers, topped by spread eagles and globes, and built in 1908, must have inspired confidence in the strength and security of the bank. Slated for possible demolition along with the Sun Building, it is now used by the City for office space.

17. The Italianate "villa" back-to-back with City Hall is the famous (or infamous) Criminal Courts Building. Known familiarly as the **Tweed Courthouse,** it stands as a monument to graft and corruption. Completed in 1872, it took nine years to construct, and the city's treasury found itself between $8 million and $12.5 million poorer. Approximately three-quarters of that amount was diverted into the pockets of "Boss" William Marcy Tweed and his Ring. Nonetheless, the city did inherit an attractive architectural addition. Its future, however, is now threatened, as the Mayor's Civic Center Task Force reports that the much needed renovation would be "substantially more costly" than building a new City Hall Annex. But considerable opposition has arisen from within the administration and from the public at large, and plans to destroy the historic Tweed Courthouse will doubtless meet with determined resistance. Visit the interior with its imposing central well, then walk around this Palladian country manor house to the *pièce de résistance* of the tour, City Hall.

18. The greatest architectural treasure in the city is palatial **City Hall,** built in 1811. The competition for its design was won by Frenchman Joseph F. Mangin, and Scotsman John McComb, Jr., who combined their talents to produce a French Renaissance–Georgian-style building of consummate beauty. McComb remained the guiding hand throughout the period of construction, but Mangin seems to have slipped into obscurity.

City Hall has always been the nerve center and civic hub of the metropolis, and has been the site of many public celebrations. Noteworthy were the receptions given in honor of Lafayette, the opening of the Erie Canal, the state visits of a parade of royalty, the welcoming of Lindbergh in 1927, and, in more recent times, of the hometown winners of the baseball World Series.

City Hall, 1826, from a colored aquatint by W. G. Hall. Mangin and McComb's French Renaissance and Georgian style building, completed in 1811, is considered one of New York's architectural treasures. (The J. Clarence Davies Collection, Museum of the City of New York)

The rotunda of City Hall was also the laying-in-state site of a number of famous citizens: Maj. Gen. William J. Worth [*see* Madison Square, 18], Horace Greeley, John Howard Payne, President U. S. Grant, and Mayors Gaynor and Mitchell. Nothing, however, could equal the homage paid to Abraham Lincoln after his assassination, when his remains lay in the rotunda on April 24 and 25, 1865. In the following funeral procession, 60,000 New Yorkers joined in the mournful parade up Broadway.

The structure has undergone many renovations and repairs throughout its history. The first addition was an illuminated public clock—the first in the city—installed in the cupola in 1831. In the same year an ugly fire tower was erected on the roof, remaining for 34 years until the volunteer fire department was replaced with a paid staff. In 1858 City Hall suffered extensive damage in a roaring blaze resulting from a fireworks display on the roof during the Atlantic Cable Celebration. Following the fire, City Hall began to deteriorate, neglected through the years by many corrupt City administrations. Someone referred to those days as the "tobacco juice period," as the building became more and more decrepit and dismal. It was even suggested that City Hall be demolished in favor of a new, "more modern" municipal building.

In 1895 the Board of Aldermen declared that ". . . the present appearance and condition of the City Hall is an offence to the sight of the community and a menace to the health of those whose business necessitates their presence in the building." A minor renovation followed. During the next 20 years, additional restoration was conducted with outside philanthropic assistance. In 1917, fire struck again, this time from a workman's charcoal burner in the cupola. Major reconstruction was begun under the direction of Grosvenor Atterbury, who restored the copper dome to its original appearance. Little was done, however, to save the decaying exterior until 1954, when the Board of Estimate voted the necessary funds for a complete restoration of the building. The eroded Massachusetts marble façade was carefully cut away and replaced with Alabama veined limestone, the base with Missouri red granite. The north façade, which was originally faced with brownstone ("Who would see it, since nobody of importance in those days lived north of City Hall"), was also refaced with limestone.

The interior, too, was completely restored to what was believed to be its original elegance. Although City Hall is closed to the public, the beautiful interior *may* be visited when the Board of Estimate or City Council are in session. Among the most attractive features are the Hanging Staircase, the colonnaded rotunda, the Office of the President of the City Council, the City Council Chamber, the Board of Estimate Chamber, the Mayor's Reception Room, the Committee of the Whole Room (for Board of Estimate executive sessions), and the Governor's Room (now a museum) with its Trumbull portrait of Washington.

Return to Park Row, past the Horace Greeley statue, to the corner of Chambers Street.

19. Directly across Chambers Street is the city's second most splendid Beaux Arts-style building (after the old Custom House at Bowling Green), the **Hall of Records,** and one-time Surrogate's Court. The sculpture groups at the entrance represent "New York in its Infancy" and "New York in Revolutionary Times," by Philip Martiny. The eight cornice figures are: David Pietersen de Vries, Caleb Heathcote, DeWitt Clinton, Abram S. Hewitt, Philip Hone, Peter Stuyvesant, Cadwallader D. Colden, and James Duane, all by the same sculptor. In the attic are ten allegorical figures by Henry Kirke Bush-Brown. The building dates from 1901 and was designed by architects John R. Thomas, and Horgan and Slattery. On a weekday, visit the colonnaded rotunda.

20. Return to the Municipal Building across the street, and walk through the pedestrian mall that was formerly Chambers Street into **Police Plaza.** As the first major accomplishment in the Civic Center plan, this three-acre public plaza (the largest in the city), and its adjoining modern structures, is a tribute to the Office of Lower Manhattan Development, as well as to the architectural firm of Gruzen and Partners.

Before walking into the Plaza itself, turn right to the small **"prison window" monument** of the Rhinelander Sugar House, which commemorates the dismal Revolutionary War prison that held hundreds of American patriots. When the original Sugar House was demolished in 1892, a window from the prison was preserved and built into the Rhinelander Building, which occupied the site until it, too, was razed in 1968, to make way for the new Police Headquarters Building. The window was rescued again and mounted here in the Plaza.

In the center of the Plaza is the arresting **steel sculpture** by Bernard Rosenthal, consisting of five enormous steel discs which will ultimately weather to a russet hue.

To the right are rows of newly planted honey-locust trees in front of the entrance to a five-tier **Municipal Parking Garage,** hidden beneath the Plaza. Just beyond is an 8-foot waterfall surmounted by fountains.

Looking ahead, the dominant feature of Police Plaza is the red-brick-and-concrete **Police Headquarters Building.** Designed by Gruzen & Partners in 1972, this $58 million center for "New York's Finest" is a restrained and tasteful addition to the city skyscape. Enter (ask permission at the desk), and enjoy the broad lobby, especially the vista of the Municipal Building and the panorama of City Hall Park skyscrapers seen through the plate glass entrance windows.

Leaving Police Headquarters, turn left and walk down the staircase to the Madison Street entrance, and the "Grecian Ruin." This **group of five Ionic marble columns** is a nostalgic artifact of the old Rhinelander Building, which stood on the site from 1892. To the east is the new **Murry Bergtraum High School for Business Careers,** named for a late president of the Board of Education; and behind it, a recently completed New York Telephone Company skyscraper.

Rhinelander's "Old Sugar House," at the corner of Rose and Duane streets, was erected in 1763 and during the Revolutionary War served as a prison during the British occupation of New York. It was demolished in 1892 to make way for an office building which kept the Rhinelander name. The building preserved a barred window of the "Old Sugar House" in its façade, and when it was razed in 1971 the window was removed and mounted on a special base adjacent to the Municipal Building, along with a commemorative plaque. (New-York Historical Society)

Return to the Plaza.

To the right is the spanking new **Federal Court House Annex** and the 12-story **Federal Metropolitan Correctional Center.** Also by Gruzen & Partners, the lines of its gray, split-faced concrete façade blend well with neighboring buildings. Note that the support columns are of the same height as those of adjoining St. Andrew's Church and the Municipal Building. A special type of tinted shatterproof glass with built-in alarm system has been installed in the prison section, replacing the traditional gloomy look of barred windows.

St. Andrew's Church was consecrated in 1939, replacing an earlier church, named Carroll Hall, built in 1842. Just before the Civil War when the City Hall area became the center of the printing and newspaper industry, the church received special dispensation to say a "Printer's Mass" at 2:30 A.M. for the night shift of newsmen and printers. It later became the first parish church to offer a noon mass for the growing number of businessmen in the area. The Latin phrase in the frieze means "Blessed are those who walk in the law of the Lord." The Plaza at this point, where Duane Street once penetrated, is now called St. Andrew's Plaza.

Walk through to Centre Street and Foley Square.

A STROLL AROUND FOLEY SQUARE

Follow the route of the broken line on the Foley Square Area map, beginning (and ending) at St. Andrew's Plaza:

U.S. Customs Court (1966). Our newest customs house in an attractive "glass box." Walk around it, exploring the broad, open passageways and ceramic tile murals. It has become somewhat of a local recreation spot on hot summer days, offering acres of shade for residents of nearby tenements.

U.S. Federal Building, 26 Federal Plaza (1967). Called the "checkerboard" by those who do not appreciate the massive, overpowering sensation caused by the grossly out-of-scale building and the odd treatment of the windows.

Department of Health of the City of New York Building (1933). A functional 1930s-modern-cum-Classical building. Note the names of great men of medicine emblazoned around the frieze.

Old New York Life Insurance Company Building, 346 Broadway (1870;

The original "Tombs" prison in an 1873 view. Built across Centre Street from the present "Tombs" site, this was the main city jail from 1838 to 1892. Compared to a pharaoh's tomb because of its columns, sun god motifs, and trapezoidal windows, this and the Croton Reservoir at Forty-Second Street were two examples of Egyptian style architecture in the city. (Museum of the City of New York)

remodeled on the Broadway side by McKim, Mead & White). Architect Griffith Thomas created a very imposing, but appropriately sober headquarters for the Company. Note the two clock towers, minus their cupolas, on this Renaissance Revival-style early skyscraper. The tower facing Broadway once sported a huge iron globe surmounted by an eagle. The Company moved its headquarters to Madison Square in 1928, and the building is now temporarily used for government offices. Cast-iron ornamentation on the Broadway side shows the New York Life Insurance monogram.

Family Court and Office of Probation (1973). The newest addition to Foley Square, its upper section, set askew from the street grid, is a bold departure from the usual modern "box."

Municipal and Civil Court Building (1960). This undistinguished building houses the Small Claims Court and the spillover from the Criminal Courts' calendar, as well as the courts of civil claims.

Engine Company 31 (1895, architect Napoleon LeBrun). This French Renaissance "château," no longer in use as a fire house, is a designated landmark, and a delightful gem of a building—a pleasant surprise in this neigh-

FOLEY SQUARE AREA

Dominating the lower Manhattan skyline at the turn of the century was the 26-story gold-domed "World Tower," the tallest building in the world when it was completed in 1890. Designed by George B. Post for Joseph Pulitzer's Evening World, it was demolished in the early 1950s to make way for new approaches to the Brooklyn Bridge. (*New-York Historical Society*)

The most notorious section of the city in the mid-19th century was the festering slum and den of criminals called Five Points. In this 1859 print from Valentine's Manual we see the crossing of three of the five streets: Baxter, Park, and Worth streets. (*Museum of the City of New York*)

borhood of towering monoliths. LeBrun was responsible for the design of a number of city fire houses as well as the Metropolitan Life Tower.

New York City Criminal Courts Building and former Manhattan Detention Center for Men (1939). The dramatic ziggurat-like towers represent the height of the 1930s "moderne" or Art Deco style. Known familiarly as the **"Tombs"** when it was the Men's House of Detention, it was built opposite the site of the original "Tombs" prison (so called because of its Egyptian-style architecture) which stood across Centre Street. The Men's House of Detention was moved in 1974 to Riker's Island, ending the building's 33-year history as a prison.

In the area encompassed by Franklin, Worth, Centre, and Lafayette streets was a small pond known as the **Collect.** A source of fresh water during colonial days, it became polluted as the city grew around it, and was ultimately filled in at the beginning of the 19th century. John Fitch tested his prototype of a steamboat on the Collect in 1796. Aboard was Robert Fulton who received all the accolades for the invention some years later.

Columbus Park, formerly Mulberry Bend Park, was created just before the turn of the century after the razing of many of the Five Points slums. Its name was changed in 1911.

State of New York Building (1928). Built on a wedge-shaped plot, this

The Old Brewery at Five Points was the City's most infamous slum. Known locally as the "Den of Thieves," it is shown in this pen and ink sketch, just before its purchase and demolition by the Ladies' Home Missionary Society for the construction of the Five Points Mission. (Museum of the City of New York)

functional building is known by all as the location of the automobile License Bureau.

Five Points [*see* special map] was probably the worst festering slum in the history of this country. So named because of the intersection of three streets, it began as a district of cheap amusement at the beginning of the 19th century, but by 1840 it had become a foul, crime-ridden "rabbit warren" of the most depraved elements of the city. Centered about an old brewery, whose surrounding lane was known as Murderers' Alley, it housed over a thousand men, women, and children in filth, squalor, and crime. More than a murder a day occurred in the former brewery and its surrounding slums; the area was so dangerous that even the police shunned it. It was the hangout of such notorious gangs as the "Plug Uglies," "Shirt Tails," and "Dead Rabbits." By mid-century the brewery was finally demolished and many of the ramshackle Five Points houses were razed. With the construction of the Foley Square courthouse complex, not a trace remains of that infamous district.

New York County Court House (1912). A designated landmark, this hexagon-shaped building has an enormous Corinthian portico. Architect Guy Lowell won the competition for the unique design of a building to occupy the irregularly shaped plot.

U.S. Court House (1936). Designed by Cass Gilbert and Cass Gilbert, Jr., its gold pyramid above a colonnaded "temple" is a familiar site on the city skyline. The neo-Classic-style building is a designated New York City Landmark. A pedestrian walkway has been created between the Court House and its brand-new Annex. Note the two connecting bridges in the rear. The old powerhouse was preserved, and can be seen nestled in the new addition.

GREENWICH
VILLAGE

(Shaded Area Indicates
Historic District)

4. Greenwich Village

[*IND A, B, D, E, F, or K lines to West 4th Street-Washington Square station*]

Greenwich Village, a town within a city, has a unique character and personality of its own. Designated a Historic District of New York City, the Village dates back to an old Algonquin Indian settlement called Sapokanickan. When the Dutch arrived in 1626 they named it Bossen Bouwerie (Farm in the Woods), and developed it as a large tobacco plantation. After the British captured Nieuw Amsterdam in 1664, the plantation was purchased by naval squadron commander Sir Peter Warren, who then renamed it Greenwich. Gradually the settlement was transformed into a small town, and by the early 19th century, "Village" was added to the name. A series of epidemics in the lower city in the early 1800s, and a disastrous fire in 1835 that virtually destroyed the southern tip of Manhattan Island, drove thousands of city dwellers northward to the town of Greenwich, seeking the "healthful climate and quiet" of this distant suburb.

You may note that the streets of the Village do not conform to the orderly grid pattern of most of Manhattan, since the town of Greenwich had already been established with its own layout of streets before the city expanded northward. As the Village grew, its crazy-quilt pattern of streets spread from the banks of the Hudson River to what is now Broadway. Many of the winding streets were originally cow paths, or followed meandering brooks. One of these waterways, Minetta Brook, still causes problems far beneath today's busy streets, especially when foundations are dug for new buildings. The visitor may be flabbergasted to discover that West 4th Street, for example, runs west only briefly, then abruptly swings north to intersect West 10th, West 11th, and West 12th streets!

In the 19th century the Village began to attract writers and artists, and

Engraving of the Jefferson Market Police Court on Sixth Avenue looking north from 9th Street, showing the first train of the Gilbert Elevated Railroad (later, the Sixth Avenue El) on April 29, 1878. (Museum of the City of New York)

boasted such residents as O. Henry, Mark Twain, Edgar Allan Poe, Henry James, Stephen Crane, Winslow Homer, John La Farge, and Augustus St. Gaudens. Rents were low and the atmosphere was very attractive. After the turn of the century, Greenwich Village began to earn its reputation as the cradle of Bohemia in America. The rents are much higher now, and many of the *literati* have departed, but the Village still retains much of its charm in its narrow, winding streets, the houses of many architectural styles, the variety of curious shops, and an assortment of colorful Village "types." There are many boutiques, exotic food stores, coffee shops, fine restaurants serving food from many nations, art schools, and drama workshops, as well as the world's largest private university.

1. The tour begins at the corner of **Avenue of the Americas and West 8th Street,** facing Village Square, the hub of the Village. Most Villagers refer to Avenue of the Americas by its former (and more logical) name, Sixth Avenue. The sidewalk along the Avenue just south of 8th Street is a gathering place during warm weather for exponents of a wide variety of political and religious views. On weekends particularly, throngs gather to listen—and often to heckle the speechmakers. Stroll along bustling, brassy 8th Street. It has become the main shopping thoroughfare of the Village in recent years. Turn right at the first corner (Macdougal Street), and walk the short distance to the gates of Macdougal Alley.

2. **Macdougal Alley,** with its picturesque and individually redesigned carriage houses, is a private dead-end street, of which there are several in the

Village. (Tiptoe in!) The little houses were built as stables in the 1850s for the wealthy residents of 8th Street (then called Clinton Place) and Washington Square. Some residents claim that the two gas lamps are the last remaining in the city maintained free by the Consolidated Edison Company, but " 'taint so!" At No. 1, now a restaurant, poet Edwin Arlington Robinson wrote his famous *Tristram,* winning himself his third Pulitzer Prize. Facing the Alley across Macdougal Street is the massive brick façade of the Tenth Church of Christ Scientist, remodeled in 1967. Turn left on leaving the Alley and walk to the corner of Washington Square.

3. Washington Square was originally a marshland teeming with wildlife, and a favorite hunting ground of the colonists. In 1797 it became a municipal Potter's Field. Recent excavations during the park's renovation revealed skeletons of some of the 10,000 early New Yorkers buried here. Equally grim was the field's popularity as a dueling ground and its use as a site of public executions. Directly across from you is the famous (or infamous) Hanging Elm, said to be the oldest tree in the city. It is one of 27 varieties in the park. The public hangings drew large crowds in a festive mood from the downtown districts. In 1824, on his triumphal return to America, the Marquis de Lafayette was the honored guest at the hanging of 20 highwaymen. Two years later, the park was officially designated as the Washington Military Parade Grounds, and at its dedication, two oxen, 200 hams, and a quarter-mile of barreled beer were consumed in the largest public picnic ever held here. In 1831, the grounds became the unofficial campus of the newly established University of the City of New York—now New York University, the largest private university in the country.

As you turn left and walk along Washington Square North, note the group of imposing town houses, Nos. 26–21. These elegant homes were built in the 1830s for the social elite, as were the houses farther down the street across Fifth Avenue. Known as "The Row," they represent the finest group of Greek Revival-style houses in America. Henry James's novel *Washington Square,* written in 1881, had its setting at No. 18—his grandmother's house. Unfortunately, the building was demolished along with neighboring houses in 1950 to make way for the huge apartment house at the corner. The five-story annex in a pseudo-Georgian style is a sad replacement, but represents a compromise, as the builders of the huge apartment house originally intended to erect it directly on the Square. Ask the doorman at the Fifth Avenue entrance to let you see the evidence of Minetta Brook, which bubbles under a glass dome in the lobby (when the pipes aren't clogged).

4. The Washington Arch, designed by famed architect Stanford White, is one of the world's finest triumphal arches. Built of marble in 1889, it commemorates the centenary of George Washington's inauguration as first President. This arch replaces an earlier model constructed of wood three years before, which spanned Fifth Avenue near the corner. The civilian statue of Washington was sculpted by Alexander Stirling Calder, the military statue, by Hermon Atkins MacNeil. The carved relief work on the Arch was done by

Frederick William MacMonnies, whose statue of Nathan Hale can be seen in City Hall Park. At Christmastime, a tall fir tree is placed in front of the Arch, illuminated with hundreds of colored bulbs. Neighbors gather to sing carols, often to the accompaniment of a Salvation Army band, or even guitars. At night, the floodlighting on the Arch can be seen from as far north as 42nd Street.

There is an interior staircase in the right section leading to the top, which figured in an unseemly escapade back in 1916, known as John Sloan's Revolution. Sloan, considered the father of the "Ashcan School" of painting, forced open the door to the stairs and led a group of slightly tipsy art students and fellow bohemians to the top of the Arch on a cold winter's night. They built a fire in a large beanpot, spread out food, and lit an array of colorful Japanese lanterns—all to the consternation and indignation of the very staid and proper residents of "The Row." The boisterous group read poems, fired cap pistols, and noisily declared the independence of the state of "New Bohemia." The arrival of a detachment of unsympathetic constabulary brought a quick end to the abortive "rebellion."

On weekends and during the warmer weather, the fountain and mall areas are a mecca for guitar players, longhairs, frisbee "pros," speechmakers, and exhibitionists of all kinds, as well as a gathering place for crowds of sightseers who come to watch them "do their thing." In June and September, the adja-

Fifth Avenue just north of Washington Square in 1869, showing the temporary wooden arch built for the centennial of Washington's inauguration. A horse-drawn omnibus waits for passengers as a street vendor dispenses goodies to well-dressed youngsters on this once fashionable avenue. (New-York Historical Society)

Stereograph view of the Washington Arch, taken as it neared completion in 1892. Many consider this monument one of architect Stanford White's outstanding achievements. (New-York Historical Society)

Celebrating the completion of the Washington Arch, community and civic leaders gather for their picture. William Rhinelander Stewart, one of the driving forces behind the building of the Arch, with ceremonial mallet and top hat, poses thoughtfully while architect Stanford White, at extreme right, seems distracted. In the rear is NYU's neo-Gothic building. (New-York Historical Society)

Nos. 4, 6, and 8 Fifth Avenue, corner of 8th Street—stately town houses designed by Henry J. Hardenbergh (the Plaza Hotel and the Dakota). The photo was taken in 1936 by Berenice Abbott for the Federal Art Project "Changing New York." All three buildings were razed in the early 1950s for an enormous apartment house. (Museum of the City of New York)

cent streets are host to the semiannual Greenwich Village Outdoor Art Show, where professional and amateur painters have the opportunity to "show and sell."

Cross Fifth Avenue and walk down Washington Square North to the lions in front of No. 6.

5. This magnificent row of **Greek Revival houses,** like their counterparts which you saw before, were built around 1831 for wealthy New York merchants. In later years, "The Row" was the residence of writers John Dos Passos and Edith Wharton, and artists Rockwell Kent and Edward Hopper. Although the houses are similar (except for No. 3), each has its own minor architectural differences. The stately entranceways, graced by marble columns and carved wooden colonnettes, are evidence of the graceful style of living of the original owners. Observe the brickwork—an alternating long and short brick in each row. This arrangement is called Flemish Bond, and was used on the more expensive early houses. Nos. 7–13 are mere façade, as all were gutted in 1939 to make way for an apartment house, magically hidden behind.

Sacrificed was the elaborate cornice, which still remains on the houses to the right, to make way for a fifth floor. How different, and how much more aesthetic a treatment than the architectural vandalism committed on the previous block! The cast-iron fence, in a remarkable state of preservation, helps unify the row of houses. Note the acanthus-leaf adornments, called anthemions, the intervening obelisks, the fret design along the base, and the lyres at intervals. These are all Greek motifs so popular during the Greek Revival period. As for the bronze lions in front of No. 6, they were cast in 1883 by sculptor S. Kitson.

Return to Fifth Avenue, turn right, passing the arcaded entranceway to the apartment house masked by the Greek Revival façade on the Square, and the little fake Greek Revival house of red brick, and enter Washington Mews.

6. Charming **Washington Mews,** like Macdougal Alley, was formerly a row of stables—in fact it was called Stable Alley until the 20th century. These converted carriage houses are vaguely reminiscent of London's Chelsea District, and were the residences of such celebrities as Gertrude Vanderbilt Whitney (founder of the Whitney Museum), diplomat and writer Walter Lippmann, and former Official City Greeter Grover Whalen. Walk through the cobblestoned mews to University Place. The last house on the right is

Stalled in the snow, on University Place and 9th Street, the morning after the Great Blizzard of 1888, the horse car's "motive power" is nowhere to be seen, in spite of the rush hour crowd aboard. In the rear is the Hotel Martin, an elegant French establishment with a famous basement restaurant. (Museum of the City of New York)

the French House of New York University, remodeled in an authentic rural French architectural style. Turn right and continue to the northeast corner of Washington Square.

7. Diagonally across the street (southeast corner) is the **Main Building of New York University.** Built in 1894, it replaced a handsome Gothic Revival structure completed in 1837, six years after the founding of the University. This largest private university in the country was founded by Albert Gallatin, Secretary of the Treasury under Thomas Jefferson, and boasted many creative teachers. Among them was a member of the art faculty, who in his spare time changed the course of history by inventing the telegraph— Samuel F. B. Morse. Professor John W. Draper made the first successful outdoor photographic portrait on the roof of his house adjoining the University building. Walt Whitman conducted classes in poetry, and Winslow Homer painted in a top-floor studio. Less academic perhaps was science professor Samuel Colt's invention of the "six-shooter." In later years, Thomas Wolfe gave courses in fiction writing.

The construction of the original building led to one of the first labor riots in the country. It seems that some of the founding fathers thought they could

The great neo-Gothic building of New York University completed in 1837, facing Washington Square. It was in this building that Samuel F. B. Morse perfected the electric telegraph, John W. Draper made the first successful outdoor photographic portrait, Walt Whitman conducted classes in poetry, Winslow Homer painted in a top floor studio, and science professor Samuel Colt invented the six-shooter. NYU demolished it in 1894 to build its present Main Building. (New-York Historical Society)

save money by using inmates from the nearby State Prison. This aroused the anger of guild laborers who demonstrated so forcefully that the local National Guard unit had to be summoned to quell the violence. The University gave in and peace was restored, and the incident became known as the Stone Cutters' Guild Riot.

Note the plaques honoring Manhattan's first schoolteachers, the founding of the American Chemical Society, Draper's photographic experiments, and Morse's telegraph; then walk south along the Main Building to Washington Place. Turn east to the northwest corner of Washington Place and Greene Street, noting the plaque indicating the birthplace of novelist Henry James.

8. This is the architecturally undistinguished Brown Building of N.Y.U. Built in 1900 for commercial use and known then as the Asch Building, it was advertised as a fireproof structure. Nevertheless, on March 25, 1911, fire *did* break out in piles of discarded cloth in the ninth-floor workroom of the **Triangle Shirtwaist Company.** Efforts to extinguish the blaze were unsuccessful, and within minutes the eighth, ninth, and tenth floors became a roaring inferno. Although the building was equipped with fire exits, the terrified workers discovered to their horror that the ninth floor exit doors had been locked by supervisors. A single fire escape was wholly inadequate for the crush of panic-stricken employees from the three floors, and the firemen's hastily stretched nets proved useless in breaking the fall from the upper floors of the dozens of workers who leaped—often hand-in-hand, and with hair and clothing ablaze—to their death on the pavement below. In less than an hour it was over. One hundred forty-six young people, most of them recent immigrants living on the Lower East Side, had perished—and the city was in a state of shock! As a result of the tragedy, improved fire-safety regulations were quickly adopted by the City Council, and the newly organized International Ladies' Garment Workers Union succeeded in having labor laws enacted to improve working conditions for the tens of thousands still working in similar sweatshops.

Return to Washington Square and enter the Park. Walk past the imposing statue of Garibaldi, the Italian patriot who made Staten Island his home for a number of years. Sculpted by Giovanni Turini in 1888, it is said that Garibaldi will always draw his sword to protect a damsel in distress. Spend a few minutes walking around the mall and fountain area, and observe the variety of people (most of the more colorful types enjoy being looked at, anyway). You may be drawn into a folk-music session, a frisbee tossing match, a political discussion, or a volleyball game.

Turn left and leave the Park at Washington Square South, opposite the tall tower of the Judson Memorial Church.

9. Named for the first American Baptist missionary, Adinoram D. Judson, the **Judson Church and Tower** are fine examples of the Italian Renaissance style. Designed by Stanford White, and built in 1892 by his architectural firm of McKim, Mead & White, the buildings are a designated New York City Landmark. If the church is open, look inside at the splendid stained-glass

Firemen pouring tons of water into the Asch Building at the corner of Washington Place and Greene Street on March 25, 1911, as the Triangle Shirtwaist Company burns in one of the worst disasters in the City's history. One hundred forty-six young garment workers lost their lives in this tragic fire which engulfed the upper three stories of the structure. The building still exists as the Brown Building of New York University. (Brown Brothers)

Burned out sewing machines are the only recognizable artifact in the charred debris of the 9th floor, the morning after the dread Triangle Fire. (Brown Brothers)

work of John LaFarge. The tower now serves as a dormitory wing of the adjacent Judson Residence Hall of N.Y.U. Looking east (left) across Thompson Street is the Generoso Pope Catholic Center with modern stained-glass windows, and farther east is the N.Y.U. Loeb Student Center. The Student Center occupies the site of Mrs. Marie Blanchard's Boarding House, demolished in 1948. Known as the "House of Genius," some of its famous boarders were Metropolitan Opera singer Adelina Patti; writers Theodore Dreiser, who penned his *American Tragedy* in a tiny garret room in 1915; Stephen Crane, who wrote *The Red Badge of Courage* in a neighboring room; O. Henry; Frank Norris; Gillett Burgess; Willa Cather; Eugene O'Neill; and Maxwell Bodenheim. Mrs. Blanchard outlived most of her celebrated tenants and died just after her 81st birthday in 1937.

Walk west, past the Georgian-style Vanderbilt Hall (N.Y.U.'s Law School) to Macdougal Street. On the Law School's site formerly stood the studio of painters William Glackens and Ernest Lawson, two of "The Eight" who rebelled against the sugary style of the National Academy of Art and staged their own show at the 69th Regiment Armory in 1913. The "Armory Show" is considered the birthplace of Modern American Art. Other artists who lived here were John Sloan, Maurice Prendergast, and Everett Shinn.

10. Macdougal Street and its adjacent blocks south of Washington Square are considered the "real Village" by the mobs of young people who throng here evenings and weekends. The scene is beginning to shift to 8th Street, but there's still plenty of "action" here. Before walking down Macdougal Street, you might want to visit the most authentic coffee house in the Village, the Peacock, at 149 West 4th Street (the continuation of Washington Square South). John Barrymore, "The Great Profile," lived at No. 132; and, at a former café at No. 148, Al Jolson and Grace Moore were discovered, while Norma Shearer worked as a hat-check girl. At No. 150, formerly "The Mad Hatter," Hendrik Willem van Loon wrote his *Story of Mankind*.

As you stroll down Macdougal Street, note the Provincetown Playhouse,

A Fifth Avenue bus parked in Washington Square in 1936. These popular "double deckers" disappeared after World War II, and there is now some movement to bring them back. In the rear is the Washington Arch and No. 1 Fifth Avenue. (Photograph by Berenice Abbott for Federal Art Project "Changing New York," Museum of the City of New York)

Eugene O'Neill's theater. Nos. 127 and 131 (best seen from across the street) are little Federal houses that were built for Aaron Burr in 1829 and are among the oldest in the city. Notice the typical dormer windows in the peaked roof, and the pineapples on the cast-iron newel posts—traditional signs of hospitality. Around the corner at 106 West 3rd Street, Aaron Burr's ghost is reputedly still haunting the Café Bizarre. At 130 Macdougal Street, Louisa May Alcott wrote her classic *Little Women.* Take an evening side trip one block farther to Bleecker Street and turn left. Try some of the exotic foods from around the world at the "hand held" food shops that line the street: souvlaki, tacos, sweet and hot sausage, empanadas, knishes, shish kebab, and Turkish coffee (but not all at one time!).

11. Turn down **Minetta Lane.** No. 1, at the corner of Macdougal Street is the birthplace of the *Reader's Digest.* Founded in 1922, its first edition had a press run of only 5000 copies. At narrow **Minetta Street** turn left. During the Prohibition Era, these narrow alleys were lined with speakeasies. Later these night spots became legitimate cabarets offering drink and amateur theatrical productions. Now, with stricter City licensing, few genuine cabarets remain, and the small theater groups have moved into their own "Off-Off" Broadway playhouses. Both streets follow the winding path of old Minetta Brook; and it is said that on a very quiet night, the gurgling waters can be heard below ground. However, there are very few quiet nights in this neighborhood. You will emerge at Sixth Avenue—rather, Avenue of the Americas, on Father Demo Square. Cross the avenue (carefully!), turn half right, and you will be at the corner of Bleecker and Carmine streets.

12. The Roman Catholic **Church of Our Lady of Pompeii** is the parish church of the large Italian community in this part of the Village. Mother Francis Xavier Cabrini, the first American saint, often prayed here. Walk along Bleecker Street for several blocks and savor the aroma of the many Italian food specialty shops. Then walk back and turn west on Leroy Street, and notice the variety of architectural styles, ranging from Federal-style houses to "Old Law" tenements. Cross Seventh Avenue.

13. As you round the bend on Leroy Street, the atmosphere suddenly changes. You are now on **St. Luke's Place,** with its charming row of Italianate brownstone town houses of the 1850s. The gingko trees, which line both sides of the street, are particularly resistant to air pollution. The twin lanterns on the stairway of No. 6 mark the former residence of Mayor James J. Walker —the popular "Jimmy" Walker of Prohibition Days. Rampant corruption in municipal government forced his resignation, but he remained a beloved and colorful figure till his death in 1946. Until Gracie Mansion was made the official residence of all New York City mayors, a pair of lanterns customarily adorned the entrance to "his honor's" home. Turn right at Hudson Street one block to Morton Street.

14. Had you stood on this spot 300 years ago, you would have been on the bank of the Hudson River. The land to the west was filled in gradually, until today the river is three blocks away. Looking down Morton Street, the

S.S. *John W. Brown, I* and *II,* Board of Education schoolships, are berthed at the Morton Street Pier. The ships, of World War II vintage, are quite seaworthy, but vital mechanical parts have been removed lest a group of adventurous students decide to make an unauthorized sea voyage. The Pier is open to the public and provides good river views and cool breezes.

To the northwest, on Washington Street, is the enormous red-brick **U.S. Federal Building.** Completed in 1899 as the Customs Appraisers' Warehouse, it took seven years to build, and its style is the fortresslike Romanesque Revival. It is a designated landmark and now houses records from the National Archives and serves as the Village Station of the U.S. Post Office. Continue north on Hudson Street two blocks to St. Luke's Chapel.

15. "St. Luke's-in-the-Fields," as it was called when the cornerstone was laid in 1821, stood at the river's edge and overlooked small farms, wandering streams, and shady country lanes. In those days most visitors came from the lower city by boat, as the trip by carriage was very arduous, and the canal that bisected most of Manhattan Island (site of present Canal Street), could be crossed only in two places. The first warden of St. Luke's was Clement Clarke Moore, who immortalized himself not with his dedicated church duties, but with the poem *'Twas the Night Before Christmas.* The church, a branch of the downtown Trinity Parish, has always been dedicated to education, and today boasts an excellent elementary school, visible behind the church. Explore the church and examine the fine Gothic-style high altar. The floor in front of the altar is paved with stones from the vaults in the church's crypt. Note the many names tied to the history of the Village. Ask the caretaker to let you wander through the lovely garden.

16. Adjoining the church are **Nos. 487–491 Hudson Street.** Observe how these restored Federal houses form a harmonious unit with the brick church. Built in 1825 they are the property of St. Luke's. Bret Harte, journalist, teacher, "gold rusher," and author of *Tales of Roaring Camp* and *The Outcasts of Poker Flat* lived at No. 487, and maintained a steady feud with his contemporary, Mark Twain, also a Villager.

Continue to Christopher Street, turn right, then right again into Bedford Street.

17. As you rounded the corner, you probably noticed the **Theater de Lys** on Christopher Street, one of the oldest off-Broadway playhouses. Kurt Weill's *Three Penny Opera* had its premier here and ran for nine years, with Weill's wife Lotte Lenya in a starring role. You now are entering the most charming section of the so-called West Village. Homeowners take special pride in restoring and preserving their attractive houses. There are more original Federal-style houses in this neighborhood than anywhere else in the city. Note the row of houses at Nos. 111–115 and 107–109. Stop just before the next corner, which is Grove Street, and stay on the right side of Bedford Street.

18. The wooden house on your left, **No. 100 Bedford Street,** was originally the workshop of sash maker William Hyde, who lived in the corner house. The sash maker's trade has now been assumed by the glazier and carpenter. In the early 19th century, window making was an important craft. The workshop is now a private residence. **No. 102,** which you just passed, is best seen from a distance. It is no accident that it resembles a fairy-tale house. Although the building dates from 1835, it was remodeled extensively in 1926 by Clifford Reed Daily and financed by Otto H. Kahn, who sought to convert the decaying house into "an inspiring home for creative artists." When the City's Building Department approved the radical plans, "Twin Peaks" was born.

At the corner, **No. 17 Grove Street,** which dates from the early 1820s, is the most complete wooden frame house in Greenwich Village. Turn right on Grove Street to No. 4.

19. The row of **Nos. 4–10** and **12–16** presents one of the most authentic groups of classic Federal-style houses in America. Enter **Grove Court** (unobtrusively!) and peek at this secluded, shady mews. Now converted into triplexes, the row of old houses was built as laborers' quarters in 1854, and Grove Court was known by the not-so-charming name of Mixed Ale Alley. Return to Bedford Street and turn right, stopping opposite No. 86.

20. Can you guess what **No. 86 Bedford Street** is (or was)? There are no visible signs of identification, but to Village *cognoscenti* it is Chumley's Restaurant. It was a notorious speakeasy during the Prohibition Days, and patrons had to identify themselves at the little glass window in the door before being admitted. It was also a favored hangout for writers, and faded dust jackets of long-forgotten titles line the walls inside. The restaurant's popularity is so widespread in the Village, that owner Lee Chumley never felt the need for a sign. During Prohibition, when the premises were raided by the police, patrons could beat a hasty retreat out a back exit in the rear of the restaurant, opposite the bar. This passageway, which leads through the courtyard of the adjacent building to Barrow Street, is still there. Turn right on Barrow Street to No. 70.

21. No. 70 Barrow Street, when built in the 1840s, was Empire Hose Company No. 1. In those days each neighborhood had its own volunteer fire brigade. Look carefully and you will see where the old carriageway was bricked in.

Across the street is a rather large double house with mansard roofs, **Nos. 39 and 41 Commerce Street.** Both halves were built in 1831 by a sea captain for his two unmarried daughters. The ladies for some reason lost to history were never on speaking terms—hence two separate houses with a common garden between. Walk ahead into Commerce Street, around the bend to the little theater.

22. A group of local playwrights seeking a stage for their own works converted an old brewery malt house into the **Cherry Lane Theater** (Commerce Street was then called Cherry Lane). Recent original premiers were Samuel Beckett's *Waiting for Godot* and *Endgame,* as well as plays by Ionesco and Edward Albee.

23. At the corner of Bedford Street is the **Isaacs-Hendricks House,** built in 1799. Like the two wooden houses seen earlier, it is typical of the architecture of old Greenwich, and is the oldest surviving house in the Village. Its entrance is in the rear, behind the fence. Around the corner at **No. 75½ Bedford Street** is the narrowest house in the city, measuring only 9½ feet wide! The first floor was formerly a carriage entrance, with living quarters above. A cobbler had his shop here, and later it was a candy factory. In the early 1920s, poet Edna St. Vincent Millay lived here. Like the Isaacs-Hendricks House, this diminutive structure had its entrance facing the rear. Spend a few moments looking at Nos. 70, 66, and 64, noting the historical plaques. Turn right on Commerce Street to No. 17.

24. Two years before killing Alexander Hamilton in that fateful duel in 1802, Aaron Burr lived briefly at **the site of No. 17.** Nos. 16–18 across the street are worthy of note, being virtually in original appearance. At **No. 11,** the plaque informs us that Washington Irving resided here when he penned his *Legend of Sleepy Hollow.* Continue to Seventh Avenue, turn left one block, and cross to Barrow Street.

25. At the corner of Barrow Street and Seventh Avenue is **Greenwich House.** Originally a settlement house, it has expanded its services to the community with recreational facilities, arts and crafts studios, concerts, antique

A row of pristine Federal town houses, Nos. 3 through 6 West 4th Street, facing Sheridan Square, was lost forever when an apartment was erected on the site in the early 1950s. The photo by Wurts Bros. was taken in 1915. A saddle and harness shop is barely visible at right. (Consolidated Edison Company of New York)

shows, and cultural programs for senior citizens. Proceed along Barrow Street. Nos. 17 and 15 were once stables. Note the horse heads on No. 15, indicating that it was a public livery stable.

26. At **Sheridan Square,** turn right briefly on West 4th Street to Numbers 175–185, charming houses dating from the 1830s. West 4th Street has many interesting little shops, and, except for the storefronts, most of the buildings remain unchanged. Return to Sheridan Square, bearing to the right, and make a sharp right turn into Grove Street, just before reaching Seventh Avenue.

27. Sheridan Square is shaped like a huge butterfly, with two distinct "wings." So many streets converge at this point that visitors often become confused (Villagers, too, for that matter). Because of heavy traffic at this intersection, the corner has been called "The Mousetrap." Pass through the second "wing" of the butterfly by walking along Grove Street, opposite the little park with the equestrian statue of General Philip Henry Sheridan. Actually, this half of Sheridan Square is called **Christopher Park,** but nobody ever calls it that. The Ellsworth Flagpole honors a 24-year-old colonel, the first of his rank to be killed in the Civil War. The Square figures in another aspect of the Civil War—the Draft Riots. In 1863, mobs of bloodthirsty rioters, in the worst civil insurrection in the city's history, gathered in the Square and attacked a number of freed slaves. They would certainly have hanged them from nearby lampposts, had not the residents of **No. 92 Grove Street** risked their lives to save them. The house has since been extensively remodeled, and is now called the Burges Chambers Studio. Its design won a prize from the American Institute of Architects.

28. Grove Street now becomes Waverly Place, and as you stand before the **Northern Dispensary,** you are at the corner of Waverly Place and Waverly Place! Since the street divides at this point to meet Grove Street and also to swing northward, it has given rise to the saying that the Dispensary "has two sides on one street, and one street on two sides." Built in 1831, and surprisingly unchanged in appearance, the Northern Dispensary still functions as a public clinic. According to its records, Edgar Allan Poe was treated here (free) for a head cold in 1837.

Continue in the same direction, and turn left into narrow Gay Street.

29. Gay Street was the center of a small Negro neighborhood in the latter half of the 19th century. In the 1920s the street was lined with speakeasies. **No. 14** was the site of Ruth McKenny's play *My Sister Eileen.* Later it was filmed here on location. Walk ahead to Christopher Street, and spend a few minutes window shopping in the curious shops to the left. Then turn right to Greenwich Avenue. Turn left to the corner of West 10th Street.

30. The vacant lot across the street is the **site of the former New York City Women's House of Detention.** The massive orange brick Art Deco structure was demolished in 1973–74 after considerable community pressure, and the inmates were moved to Riker's Island. Cross Greenwich Avenue to Sutter's and enjoy an ice-cream cone or some of their tempting pastry. Turn right on West 10th Street to the entrance gates of Patchin Place. Lighting the entrance is **one of the last remaining cast-iron "bishop's crook" lampposts** in the city.

31. The houses on quaint **Patchin Place** were built in the mid-19th century to house workers of the then-elegant Brevoort Hotel on Fifth Avenue. The narrow street later became the residence of such famous authors as poet-laureate John Masefield, Theodore Dreiser, e. e. cummings (at No. 4), as well as Harry Kemp (the "Hobo Poet"), and William Brinckley, who wrote *Don't Go Near the Water.* Enjoy the peaceful atmosphere of this unusual cul-de-sac, away from the noise and clamor of nearby thoroughfares. Turn left, walk to Avenue of the Americas (we'll get to the "castle" across the street shortly), and turn left again. Watch carefully, or you'll miss the iron gates marking the entrance to Milligan Place.

32. Milligan Place is named for the original landowner, Samuel Milligan, who settled here in 1799. His daughter married the surveyor of his property, Aaron Patchin. Perhaps part of the dowry was the small street named for him. Many native Villagers are unaware of this tiny, secluded mews. Walk ahead to West 11th Street, turn right and cross the avenue. Fifty feet down the street is a small cemetery.

33. The Second Cemetery of the Spanish & Portuguese Synagogue was one of three burial grounds of this first Jewish congregation in New York. The first cemetery, near Chatham Square, and the third, on West 20th Street, kept pace with the northward growth of the Jewish community from the 17th through the 19th centuries. The peculiar triangular shape of the cemetery resulted from the opening of West 11th Street through to Sixth Avenue in the mid-19th century, cutting off a substantial piece of the graveyard. Return to Avenue of the Americas, turn left, and stop at the "castle."

34. The Jefferson Market Library, the Village's most magnificent Victorian Gothic structure, was built in 1874–77 as a courthouse, with an adjoining jail, firehouse, and market. Designed by architects Frederick Clark Withers and Calvert Vaux, it was listed among the ten most beautiful buildings in America at the time. (Vaux, by the way, helped design Central Park.) Note the striking effect of the red brick and white stone, the Gothic motifs, stained-glass windows, and dramatic clock tower. The tower replaces an earlier wooden fire lookout, one of many throughout the city, long before the advent of the electric fire alarm system. In 1967 the building was saved from the wrecker's ball at the eleventh hour by a dedicated committee of neighborhood residents, who not only saved it, but convinced the City to restore it and make it a branch of the New York Public Library. The clock, known affectionately as "Old Jeff," was repaired and illumination for the dials installed. During the Christmas season the belfry is festooned with gaily colored lights. Read the plaques at the base of the tower and visit the Library. Take the elevator to the third floor and walk down the intriguing spiral staircase to the dungeonlike basement, which houses the reference room. As you leave the building, turn right to Village Square and West 8th Street where the tour began.

THE
LAFAYETTE
HISTORIC
GROUP
and
THE EAST
VILLAGE

5. The Lafayette Historic Group and the East Village

[*IRT Lexington Avenue line to Bleecker Street station; IND B, D, F lines to Broadway-Lafayette station; Broadway-City Hall or South Ferry bus to Houston Street; Fifth Avenue M-5 bus to Houston Street*]

With the end of the American Revolution, New York City, which had stagnated under years of British occupation, came alive again, regaining its position as an important port and commercial center. A burgeoning population began to push the city's frontiers northward, swallowing up the once-remote and peaceful farms of mid-Manhattan and crisscrossing them with a latticework of newly opened streets.

In 1811, the City Commissioners drew up their famous Plan, laying out a gridwork street pattern for the entire island, numbering all east-west streets and north-south avenues, commencing roughly at the point of departure of this tour. By the end of the 19th century the last farms disappeared from Manhattan, yielding to the ever increasing needs for *Lebensraum*.

By the 1830s this neighborhood became the "gold coast" of the city, boasting the most lavish residences—including that of the nation's wealthiest citizen, John Jacob Astor. Within 20 years the area gave way to commerce and public entertainment, and by the 1880s and 1890s it became a center for the printing trades. Light industry followed with factories, loft buildings, and warehouses.

Surprisingly, so many vestiges remain from each period of development that within the half-square-mile area can be found such diverse "artifacts" as opulent Greek Revival residences, Italian Renaissance cultural institutions, Romanesque Revival industrial structures, cast-iron commercial "palaces," plus a number of historic and architecturally unique buildings—most in an excellent state of preservation.

The tour begins at Houston and Lafayette streets. [For background information on Houston Street, *see* SoHo Cast-Iron District, page 149.]

1. On the southwest corner stands the **Puck Building** (295–309 Lafayette Street). Built in 1885, with an addition in 1892, it is a fine example of the monolithic Romanesque Revival style so popular in the last two decades of the 19th century. Architect Albert Wagner designed it for the publishers of the humor magazine *Puck,* whose Shakespearean character proclaimed "What Fools These Mortals Be!" across the magazine's cover. The publication lasted more than a "Midsummer's Night," entertaining New Yorkers for some 30 years, until it was absorbed by the now-defunct *New York Journal-American,* which kept only the old magazine's logo. Puck, however, lives on in two larger-than-life statues perched on third-floor ledges at the north corners of the building. Note the original elegant marble-columned entranceway, which opens on Lafayette Street. The present owner, the Superior Printing Ink Company, deserves credit for wisely choosing a handsome gilt-lettered sign appropriate to the genre of the building.

Walk west on Houston Street to Crosby Street. Turn north (right), and stop about three-quarters of the way to Bleecker Street.

2. The startlingly beautiful building directly ahead (65 Bleecker Street), almost hidden in the shadows of the dark, narrow streets is the **Bayard Building,** New York City's only Louis H. Sullivan treasure. The guiding spirit of the "Chicago School," Sullivan was the teacher (and employer) of Frank Lloyd Wright. Ignore the altered ground floor and study the radical façade, noting the vertical clarity and romantic detail leading up to an astonishing cornice with six supporting angels. It is said that Sullivan objected strenuously to the figures, but placed them there at the insistence of Silas Alden Condict, the original owner. When the building was completed in 1898, Condict was quoted as asking, "Who would expect an aesthetic experience on Bleecker Street?" The building is a designated New York City Landmark.

To the right, on the southeast corner, are the decaying remains of a once-proud Federal-style residence, with dormers in the front and rear of the typical peaked roof.

The last horse car in the City of New York on the Bleecker Street and Broadway line, making its farewell trip on Bleecker Street, between Crosby Street and Broadway, July 26, 1917. Horse car service began in 1832. For some reason, New York held on tenaciously to its "horse power" long after most other cities had electrified their lines. (Museum of the City of New York)

Turn east (right) to Lafayette Street, then left past Shinbone Alley, turning left into Bond Street.

3. In the 1830s Bond Street was one of the city's most fashionable. Lined with Greek Revival-style houses, it was a secluded, peaceful street whose most celebrated resident, Albert Gallatin, lived (appropriately) at No. 1. As Secretary of the Treasury under Thomas Jefferson, he helped reshape the financial structure of the country, and in later years was a founder of the nearby University of the City of New York, later N.Y.U. A few badly misshapen Federal-style houses survive on the north side of the street. Curiously, Shinbone Alley makes a right turn in the middle of the block, and emerges as Jones Alley for a brief block-and-a-quarter.

On the site of Gallatin's residence is one of the best preserved cast-iron "palaces" in the city. Built in French Second Empire style, it was designed by Stephen D. Hatch in 1871 for the D. D. Appleton (publishing) Company. The style is typified by the enormous mansard roof with pavilions; however, the "Palladian" façade is strictly out of the Renaissance. The main portico, still intact, with graceful broken pediment, shelters the company's emblem— the torch of learning—on both sides of the keystoned fanlight. The old firm is still in business at another address as Appleton-Century-Crofts.

Broadway, looking north from the old Broadway Central Hotel toward Great Jones Street, c. 1895. Elegantly clad ladies and gentlemen walk by hansom cabs waiting at the curb, while horse drawn traffic and Broadway cable cars clatter by. (Consolidated Edison Company of New York)

The adjacent building on the east side also has a cast-iron façade, but is just not in the same league.

Return to Lafayette Street again, and continue east on Bond Street.

4. No. 26 Bond Street is an unusually large Greek Revival-style house, and was probably the residence of a very affluent family.

5. At the northwest corner of the Bowery, the former Bond Street Savings Bank is pure wedding cake in cast iron. Built in 1874 from plans by Henry Engelbert, it is another attractive example of the French Second Empire style. With the influx of many German immigrants into the neighborhood, it later became the German Exchange Bank; and with its subsequent failure in the early 20th century, it ended its banking career as a deteriorating loft building. But in 1963, with the growing popularity of off-Broadway theater, it gained a new lease on life as a playhouse. The newborn **Bouwerie Lane Theater** won additional recognition when it was designated an official New York City Landmark. Note the lovely façade with its rows of paired Corinthian and Ionic columns flanking the windows, the ornate modillions under the cornices of the roof and surmounting pediment, and the stately entranceway guarded by paneled cast-iron newel posts.

Continue north one block.

Originally **"Bouwerie"** in Dutch, the street's name hearkens back to the days of Peter Stuyvesant, when he had it built as a road from the lower city past the "bouweries," or farms, to his own estate a half-mile north. Although the Bowery is now synonymous with the unfortunate flotsam of society who inhabit much of this now-dismal thoroughfare, it was for a time a lively center of entertainment. Music halls, theaters, and beer gardens were numerous in the late 19th century, and the street is recalled in the humorous lyrics of the Gay '90s song "The Bowery—I'll Never Go There Anymore!"

The building on the southeast corner of Bowery and East 3rd Street (do not bother to cross the street!) is the **Men's Shelter,** administered by the City's Social Services Administration. It offers a free bed and meals to the indigent. Careful scrutiny of the near wall reveals an old sign indicating that this was once the Bowery Branch of the Y.M.C.A.

Turn left (west) on Great Jones Street.

There never was anyone named "Great Jones"! It seems that when the street was first opened, some official "street-name-giver" in City Hall decided to call it Jones Street, overlooking the fact that neighboring Greenwich Village already had a Jones Street. When the fact was brought to his attention, this

The Broadway Central Hotel, built in 1871, in Second Empire style by Henry Engelbert, replaced an earlier hotel called the LaFarge House. A year after it opened, it witnessed the sensational shooting of Jim Fisk. The enormous hotel deteriorated badly in its last years and gave up the ghost in a spectacular cave-in of its north wing in 1973. (New York City Landmarks Preservation Commission)

unimaginative civil servant then changed it to Great Jones Street. Why it wasn't just given the former name of 3rd Street (Amity Street) is anyone's guess. In any case, local residents claim that the name is appropriate since it is much wider than the Jones Street in the Village.

6. Midway down the block, at No. 44, is the home of **Engine Company 33 and Hook & Ladder 9.** Formerly the headquarters of the New York City Fire Department, it is a splendid example of the French Beaux Arts style—almost too grandiose for a fire house. Designed by Ernest Flagg and W. B. Chambers in 1898, it is now a designated landmark. Flagg, incidentally, is responsible for the design of many of the city's fire houses built at the turn of the century.

Across the street, at **Nos. 31 and 33,** are two run-down commercial buildings. A glance at the pediment reveals that they were once a pair of livery stables. Serving a similar purpose as today's public garage and rent-a-car establishment, Bienecke's boarded horses and also rented various types of rigs to those who couldn't afford to maintain their own private stable.

7. Reaching the corner of Lafayette Street, look through the parking lot on the northeast corner, and seek out the apse of an old neo-Gothic church protruding from the rear of a nondescript commercial building. About a hundred years ago it was St. Bartholomew's Protestant Episcopal Church. With the industrialization of the neighborhood, the congregation departed, and the building was sold. Don't look for the front of the church on the East 4th Street side . . . it isn't there any more.

8. No. 376–380 Lafayette Street (on the northwest corner) is a solid and imposing Romanesque Revival-style loft building. A designated landmark built in 1888, it is by Henry J. Hardenbergh, who gave us, among others, the Plaza Hotel, the Dakota Apartments, and the Consolidated Edison Building.

Turn right (north) on Lafayette Street, then right into East 4th Street.

9. The Old Merchant's House, at 29 East 4th Street, is probably the only surviving Greek Revival-style house in the city—intact within as well as outside. Built in 1831–32 by Joseph Brewster from plans attributed to famed architect Minard Lafever, it was purchased in 1835 by Seabury Tredwell, a wealthy merchant. It remained in the Tredwell family until the last surviving member, Gertrude Tredwell, died in 1933. To save the house and its original furnishings from the auctioneer's block, the property was then purchased by George Chapman, a distant relative, whose sole interest was to maintain it as a unique example of a New York City family's house and style of living. Among the furnishings are the original furniture, mirrors, carpets, draperies, chinaware, and a collection of dresses, shawls, and bonnets. The interior architectural elements also preserved are the mantelpieces, wainscoting, moldings, columns, banisters, and the kitchen. There is even a secret passageway that leads under the house from an upstairs closet. Chapman organized the Historic Landmark Society to maintain the Old Merchant's House as a public

Lafayette Place (now Lafayette Street) was an elegant, tree-lined cul-de-sac around 1870. Not visible on the left of the street are the imposing façades of Colonnade Row, the houses of the wealthiest citizens in town. Note the raised pedestrian crosswalks and Greek-Revival-style fence. The view is north from Great Jones Street. (New-York Historical Society)

museum. The house subsequently received official New York City Landmark designation.

Time and neglect, however, began to take their toll. To protect and preserve the landmark, which had suffered from the effects of weather and vandalism, a major renovation was undertaken in 1973–74 under the supervision of New York University architect Joseph Roberto; and now the Old Merchant's House, completely restored with all its furnishings, is open for all to enjoy.

10. At 37 East 4th Street, a few doors east, is the **Samuel Tredwell Skidmore House.** Built in 1844–45 for a cousin of Seabury Tredwell, it is a late Greek Revival-style house, and much less imposing than its richer cousin. At one time the entire block was lined with similar houses.

Return to Lafayette Street.

11. On the northeast corner, at No. 393–399 Lafayette Street, stands the massive **De Vinne Press Building.** One of the great printing "giants" of the late 19th and early 20th centuries, De Vinne was the founder of the Grolier Club and the publisher of such popular magazines as *Scribner*'s, *Century,* and *St. Nicholas.* The De Vinne Press was famous for its innovative typefaces and high-quality books. The architects, Babb, Cook, & Willard, designed this "Romanesque Utilitarian" structure in 1885, in a style reminiscent of the aqueducts of Ancient Rome. Notice how thick the masonry bearing walls are. The name of the establishment is still visible on the upper façade. The De Vinne Building is a designated landmark.

12. No. 409–411 Lafayette Street demonstrates how different building mediums can be employed together successfully (in this case, cast iron and brick) to produce a functional and aesthetic effect. Viewed from a distance, the ornate two-story-high cast-iron columns of the **Durst Building** are an imposing base for this former men's clothing store and factory. The "squared" style of the larger columns adds a feeling of strength, while lightness results from the beaded bands on all the columns, the ornate design on the spandrel panels above the ground floor, and the round-arch windows on the second floor; while slender iron columns divide the paired windows above. Designed by Alfred Zucker in 1891, it is the newest building on the block.

13. The superb Corinthian colonnade across the street (Nos. 428, 430, 432, and 434) is all that remains of one of the most magnificent rows of Greek Revival town houses in America. On the site of John Jacob Astor's Vauxhall Gardens Amusement Park, and completed in 1838 by developer Seth Geer from plans by Alexander Jackson Davis, **Colonnade Row** is an architectural treasure and an outstanding example of early urban design. Originally named LaGrange Terrace, after the Marquis de Lafayette's country estate in France, the group consisted of nine mansions on what was then Lafayette Place. (Lafayette Street was not opened till much later; Lafayette Place was a shady, cobblestoned cul-de-sac extending only to where Great Jones Street is now.)

Colonnade Row, on the west side of Lafayette Street, was a group of nine marble town houses built in 1838, which became the most fashionable addresses in the city. Today, only four of these survive. A nineteenth-century-style restaurant now occupies the ground floor of the right-hand building where the Churchman, *a religious publication, once had offices. (Museum of the City of New York)*

Constructed of Westchester marble and set back behind a 30-foot court-yard, the impressive row was protected from the "masses" by an iron fence. The nine houses were reduced to four when the John Wanamaker Department Store callously destroyed them early in this century to make way for a garage for their delivery trucks. (The John Wanamaker name appears on the ugly building to the left.) When he built the row, Geer was criticized for speculating "so far out in the country," but his plan was vindicated when possession was taken by such notables as John Jacob Astor, Cornelius Vanderbilt, Warren Delano (Franklin Delano Roosevelt's grandfather), and other wealthy cit-izens. Washington Irving stayed here for a time, as did two distinguished visitors from England, William Makepeace Thackeray and Charles Dickens. In 1844, then-President John Tyler secretly married the daughter of resident David Gardner. John Jacob Astor died in 1848 at the age of 85, leaving a fortune of $20 million. An interesting reminder of John Jacob Astor's lucra-tive fur business can be seen in the colorful ceramic panels depicting beavers, imbedded in the tile walls of the IRT Astor Place subway station, one block north.

The houses, now subdivided into apartments and commercial properties, are in a rather depressing state. The original stoops have been removed, outrageous disfigurements have sprung up on the roof, and many of the ornate details are either damaged or missing (observe what is left of the lovely row of anthemions on the cornice). In addition, a patina of a hundred years of neglect covers the entire façade. Some attempt at preservation and restoration is being undertaken by a few of the owners, which hopefully may eventually return this landmark to a modicum of its former elegance.

14. Facing the beautiful Row is the former Astor Library, now the **New York Shakespeare Festival Building.** Begun in 1849 as Astor's bequest to the City of New York, the Library was built in three stages (south wing, by Alexander Saeltzer, completed in 1853; center wing, by Griffith Thomas, in 1859; and north wing, by Thomas Stent, in 1881). It was the City's first major library accessible to the public, and was combined in 1912 with the Tilden Foundation and the Lenox Library to form the nucleus of the New York Public Library.

From 1921 to 1965 the building was the headquarters of the HIAS—the Hebrew Immigrant Aid & Sheltering Society—which since 1884 has been a worldwide migration agency responsible for the rescue of almost four mil-lion refugees and their settlement in lands of freedom. When the HIAS moved uptown to larger quarters, the survival of this lovely Italian Renais-sance *palazzo* was seriously threatened. Virtually at the eleventh hour it was saved through the efforts of impresario Joseph Papp and a group of concerned citizens who ultimately convinced a skeptical City Council to recommend municipal purchase of the building as a permanent home for the New York Shakespeare Festival.

Renovation began in 1967 under the supervision of architect Giorgio Cavaglieri (who restored the Jefferson Market Courthouse; *see* Greenwich

Village, 34), and was completed several years later. The Festival Building is an ideal example of adaptive reuse, proving that one can deal with old spaces and make them work. Contrary to the custom of gutting the interior and merely preserving the façade, Cavaglieri saved the elaborate interior, converting the two-tier skylit atrium of the former main reading room into the 300-seat Anspacher Theater. Two other large spaces were likewise made into theaters. The entrance and lobby remains a classic Corinthian colonnade. (Walk in, look around . . . and purchase a subscription to a performance series!)

15. No. 436–440 is a large cast-iron commercial building in virtually pristine condition. Although no architectural beauty, it is typical of this type of construction [*see* SoHo Cast-Iron District walking tour]. It was designed by Edward Kendall in 1870 for Alfred Benjamin & Company, which manufactured men's clothing. Note their initials on the six escutcheons mounted on the pilasters. Interesting are the ram's horn volutes on the capitals, and the full ram's horn on the shields.

Adjacent **No. 442–450,** occupying the corner lot, is maintained in almost original appearance by appreciative owners. Built in 1875 from plans by Griffith Thomas, it was for many years the headquarters of book publisher J. J. Little & Company (now, Little, Brown & Co.), and is another example of the pleasing wedding of cast iron and masonry.

16. The **District 65 Building,** formerly Clinton Hall, and before that the Mercantile Library Building, has little to recommend it architecturally; however, it occupies the site of the old Astor Place Opera House, and "thereby hangs a tale. . . ."

A black page in New York City history was written on the evening of May 10, 1849, when a rampaging mob of thousands stormed the theater in one of the city's bloodiest outbursts of violence. **The Astor Place Riot,** as the event came to be called, stemmed from a bitter rivalry and on-going feud between English tragedian William Macready and America's greatest actor, Edwin Forrest. Against a background of anti-British sentiment and a general antipathy toward foreigners as well as home-grown aristocrats, feelings had been running high for a number of weeks—spurred in great measure by rumor mongers, know-nothings, and a sensationalist press.

That evening, when the curtain rose on the English actor's performance of *Macbeth,* a large and noisy crowd gathered in Astor Place, spilling over into the adjoining streets from Broadway to the Bowery. During the play, Macready was pelted with a steady stream of rotten eggs, copper pennies, and an assortment of vegetables. In the third scene a group of gangsters, led by small-time politician Isaiah Rynders, interrupted Macready's performance with screams and epithets, while a group of supporters of the English actor hurled back abuse with equal vigor. When the play was able to resume, the continuing commotion drowned out the stage. By the time the third act had begun, the mob outside started to assault the theater with bricks and stones. The police, although forewarned, were hopelessly outnumbered, and could do nothing to quell the screaming, cursing multitude that was now advancing on the theater's entrance. Estimates numbered the raging crowd at between 10,000 and 20,000.

In the meantime, the militia had been summoned from the nearby Tompkins Market Armory, but was restrained from action by nervous Mayor Caleb Woodhull, who feared the political consequences of any drastic action. Woodhull himself quietly fled the scene, leaving decisions to the unit's commanding officer. Finally, the order was given to fire, and after a warning volley over the heads of the rioters, the militiamen reluctantly fired volley after volley at point-blank range, killing 31 persons and leaving 150 wounded, putting an end to the worst theater riot in history.

17. At the time of the Riot, Astor Place extended to where the "black cube" now rests, at the juncture with 8th Street (then called Clinton Place). Little St. Ann's Church occupied the site until Lafayette Street was pushed through to meet Fourth Avenue. The present occupant of the traffic island is sculptor Bernard Rosenthal's stabile, **Alamo,** erected in 1967. Another recent work, an enormous five-disk steel sculpture, adorns Police Plaza, near the Municipal Building downtown.

18. Against the backdrop of a wide-open sky, the stunning **Cooper Union**

Watercolor drawing of the Astor Place Riot of May 10, 1849, as militia from the nearby Tompkins Market Armory were firing into the crowd. A rampaging mob of between 10,000 and 20,000 stormed the Astor Place Opera House as the culmination of bitter feelings against English actor William Macready. When order was finally restored 31 lay dead and 150 were injured. (Museum of the City of New York)

Foundation Building stands as a most pleasing sight. Completed in 1859, this gift to the people by industrialist-engineer-philanthropist Peter Cooper played a significant role in the development of the city. The "Union" was established as the first free, private, nonsectarian, coeducational college. Dedicated to the fields of science and art, it occupies a special place of respect among American colleges and universities.

Peter Cooper (1791–1883), a self-educated "Renaissance Man," was responsible for the first successful American railway locomotive (the "Tom Thumb"); he worked with Cyrus W. Field in the laying of the Atlantic Cable, and, with Samuel F. B. Morse, developed the telegraph. Cooper also battled

Around the corner from Clinton Hall and the former Astor Place Opera House was Aberle's Theater, previously St. Ann's Roman Catholic Church. The theater opened in 1879, changed its name to the Germania in 1894, and was demolished in 1903. (The J. Clarence Davies Collection, Museum of the City of New York)

The Astor Place Opera House at the intersection of Astor and Clinton places (later 8th Street) was rebuilt after the riot of 1849 and later became Clinton Hall and the Mercantile Library. In this photo taken c. 1868, the building also houses auction rooms and the Sixpenny Savings Bank. The present building on the site, the District 65 Center, was also called Clinton Hall. (New-York Historical Society)

corrupt politicians and helped to improve the city's public-school system. With the profits from his ironworks and a glue factory, he built Cooper Union. In 1876 he ran unsuccessfully for President on the Greenback ticket, although his son Edward was elected Mayor of the City, as was his son-in-law, Abram S. Hewitt.

The building, designed in a kind of "Italian Renaissance cum Industrial" architectural style, is a unique achievement in itself, being the first to be constructed with wrought-iron beams as its framework. The exterior is of brownstone and rough-hewn sandstone, with cast-iron columns, pilasters, and arches. It was originally a five-story building, but the "factory-roof" art studios were subsequently superimposed. The street level was built with rows of small shops to provide a steady source of revenue for the institution. On the south end of the roof, the cylindrical protuberance houses the shaft of the original circular elevator. Cooper anticipated a lift system and installed the shaft even before a practical elevator was available. The novel construction of the building, employing steel railroad rails produced in his Trenton foundry, demanded that the supported sections of the "Union" coincide in measurement with the standard length of these rails. The rails spanned the brick bearing walls and supported the brick floor arches. In a recent renovation, architecture students were fortunate in obtaining a first-hand view of the original rail placement, as the central section of the interior was literally jacked up several floors while the old masonry walls were replaced by more modern steel and reinforced concrete.

The showpiece of the interior is the Great Hall, a magnificent auditorium, crisscrossed by arcades of supporting columns topped by granite arches. It was in the Great Hall that the Institution's inaugural lecture was given by Mark Twain. A year later Abraham Lincoln delivered his momentous "Might makes Right" speech, establishing a Cooper Union lecture tradition followed by every President up to Woodrow Wilson.

The reconstruction, adhering essentially to the original plans of architect Frederick A. Peterson, was carried out by Cooper Union graduate architects under the direction of Architecture Department Head, John Hejduk. Cooper Union is both a New York City Landmark and a National Historic Landmark (note the plaques on the north end).

Walk south along the Cooper Union Building to the small park on Cooper Square.

An engraving of Cooper Union, with the Tompkins Market (right) and Bible House (left), enlivened by prancing horses and richly clad citizens as seen in Valentine's Manual of 1861, looking north from Fourth Avenue and 6th Street. (Museum of the City of New York)

19. The **statue of Peter Cooper** was executed in 1897 by one of the country's foremost sculptors, Augustus Saint-Gaudens. Among his best known works are the equestrian statue of General Sherman near the Plaza Hotel, the statue of David G. Farragut in Madison Square Park, the marble altar relief in the nearby Church of the Ascension, as well as the design of one of our former 20-dollar gold pieces. The base and canopy of the monument are by Stanford White.

Notice the attractive, and very visible, Cooper Union clock with its seven-foot frosted glass face. Once driven by an enormous weight and pendulum, it is now powered by a tiny electric motor.

The Bowery, which becomes Third Avenue at this point, was once darkened by the **3rd Avenue El,** which rumbled by, from 1879 to shortly after World War II, on its way from South Ferry and Chatham Square to several points in the Bronx. Old-timers still look back with relish at the speedy, open-air ride provided by the old El. Although the Bowery and Third Avenue were never thoroughfares of scenic beauty, the exciting cityscape panoramas provided by these overhead trains cannot be duplicated by the much slower-moving ground-level buses.

20. The **Abram S. Hewitt Memorial Hall** of Cooper Union (Clinton & Russell, 1905), named for Peter Cooper's partner and son-in-law, occupies the site of the Tompkins Market Armory. Before it burned down, the old barnlike structure was a public market on the ground floor and an armory above. It was from here that the 27th Regiment of the New York National Guard was summoned to quell the Stone Cutters' Riot at the Washington Parade Ground [now Washington Square; *see* Greenwich Village, 7]; some years later, the Astor Place Riot; and in 1863, the Draft Riots (although in the latter disturbance, the militia had to be hastily called back from the just ended Battle of Gettysburg). The unit later became the 7th Regiment and is now based in the landmark Seventh Regiment Armory, at Park Avenue and 67th Street.

Cross the Bowery to the northeast corner of East 7th Street.

The area east of the Bowery, roughly between East 4th and East 13th streets, and extending almost to the East River, is the **"East Village,"** formerly considered part of the Lower East Side.

From the early 19th century, successive waves of immigrants occupied the crowded tenements, leaving their individual ethnic stamp on the neighborhood. First came the Irish, followed by Germans, Jews, Poles, Ukrainians, and after World War II, the Spanish-speaking, mainly from Puerto Rico. In the 1950s and '60s the low rents attracted artists, writers, "beatniks," "hippies," and many who just liked the ethnic mix.

In the several-square-block area just east of the Bowery, centered on East 7th Street, there remains an active, tight-knit **Ukrainian enclave.**

21. The former Metropolitan Savings Bank, now the **First Ukrainian**

Assembly of God, is an ornate pile of marble, very similar in style to the cast-iron buildings for which it served as a model. Attributed to architect Carl Pfeiffer, and built in 1868, its stately French Second Empire façade must have presented a convincing appearance of strength to its depositors. (The old name is still barely visible above the first floor.) This designated landmark was one of the city's first fireproof buildings.

22. At 11 East 7th Street is **Surma's Ukrainian Shop**—a fascinating emporium offering Ukrainian books, music, and records, colorful "peasant" clothing, painted (real) eggs, jewelry, and owner-cultivated honey.

23. McSorley's Old Ale House (No. 15) antedates the Ukrainian influx by many years, and claims to be the oldest saloon in the city (1854). Formerly a man's domain, it now permits women to share the authentic old-time atmosphere. In the dimly lit tavern, dozens of aging photographs and yellowing newspaper clippings hang on the grimy sheet-tin walls.

24. St. George's Ukrainian Catholic Church was oroiginally the Seventh Street Methodist Church. It was "converted" with copper-clad onion domes in the Slavic manner, and is now the religious and cultural center of most of the Ukrainian community.

Continue to Second Avenue.

At the height of the Jewish immigration, Second Avenue from Houston Street to 14th Street was known as the **Yiddish Rialto.** Little now remains of the once lively Yiddish theater except for an occasional on-Broadway presentation. The old playhouses that lined Second Avenue were either demolished or stand vacant. The lone survivor is the Eden (formerly the Phoenix) at East 12th Street, which still functions occasionally with an avant-garde production.

Turn left (north) to just beyond St. Mark's Place.

A few doors north of St. Mark's Place are two interesting buildings: the **Stuyvesant Polyclinic** and the **Ottendorfer Branch of the New York Public Library.** Both are contemporaries and reflect the architectural tastes of the late 1880s. Local wags have commented that the institutions were appropriately placed side by side, the former to care for the community's physical wants, the latter for their intellectual needs.

Continue west on St. Mark's Place.

25. St. Mark's Place is the "main drag" of the East Village, and to an extent, the center of New York City's "counterculture." It is difficult to conceive that this was a most fashionable residential block in the early 19th century, with rows of elegant Federal and Greek Revival-style town houses. Vestiges still survive here and there along the block, covered by coats of garish paint and hidden by all manner of "improvements."

No. 20, a designated landmark, was once the **Daniel LeRoy House** (1832). The last holdout of the row of town houses on the south side of the street, it shows many Federal and early Greek Revival features.

The Dom, at No. 23, was once a large Polish social center. In more recent times it has been a sometime discotheque, and for several years the home of the Electric Circus, one of the first rock 'n' roll establishments.

No. 12 was built for the German American Shooting Society in 1885. Like the Dom, it was also a social club. (The beer drinking was done here, the shooting elsewhere.)

No. 7 is another survivor of the early town-house row.

A plaque on the next-to-last building on the south side claims that James Fenimore Cooper once lived in a house on the site.

26. Diagonally across St. Mark's Place, between 8th and 9th streets, is the modern **Cooper Union Engineering Building** (1961, Voorhees, Smith, Smith, and Haines). It occupies the site of the old "Bible House," headquarters of the American Bible Society from 1852 to 1956, when it moved uptown to the Lincoln Center area—probably the last publishing house to move from the district.

27. With the large number of local institutions dedicated to books and book production (Astor Library, Mercantile Library, Cooper Union, Scribner's, Bible House, the many publishing houses, as well as nearby New York University) it was no surprise that Fourth Avenue north to 14th Street became the second-hand book center of the city. The five blocks that comprise **"Booksellers' Row"** boasted no fewer than two dozen book dealers. Sidewalk stands in front of the shops were always piled high with cheap books of every description, but the *cognoscenti* would seek out the real "finds" on the dusty shelves of the dark, labyrinthine interiors. Only a scant few of the booksellers remain: Pageant Book Company, No. 59; Biblo & Tannen, No. 63; Fourth Avenue Bookstore, No. 138; and Strand, at 828 Broadway. As in the past, browsers are always welcome.

28. On the west side of Fourth Avenue, between 10th and 11th streets, is the charming Gothic Revival-style **Grace Church School.** Enriching the appearance of the street, it was built in harmony with the landmark Grace Church, around the corner on Broadway. [For a description of Grace Church, *see* Ladies' Mile, 2.] The building was built in sections, beginning in 1888, by the architectural firm of Renwick, Aspinwall & Russell.

Continue north to 14th Street. End of tour.

LOWER
EAST
SIDE

STANTON ST.

RIVINGTON ST.

Park

DELANCEY ST.

WILLIAMSBURG
BRIDGE

BOWERY

CHRYSTIE ST.

Delancey Roosevelt

FORSYTH ST.

ELDRIDGE ST.

BROOME ST.

ALLEN ST.

ORCHARD ST.

LUDLOW ST.

ESSEX ST.

NORFOLK ST.

SUFFOLK ST.

CLINTON ST.

GRAND ST.

Sara

HESTER ST.

Seward
Park

start

CANAL ST.

DIVISION ST.

JEFFERSON ST.

EAST BROADWAY

RUTGERS ST.

HENRY ST.

MANHATTAN BRIDGE

PIKE ST.

6. The Lower East Side

[*IND F line to East Broadway station, walk one block east on East Broadway.*]

The first tides of mass immigration to this country began sweeping across our shores just before the mid-19th century, with millions of refugees, mostly from Europe, seeking a haven from famines, wars, economic and political repression, and religious persecution. In successive waves they came—Irish, English, Germans, Swedes, Jews, Italians, Slavs—from Northern Europe to the Eastern Mediterranean, enduring the hardships of a long steerage voyage in crowded, foul ships. Mostly poor and strange to our ways, they would frequently gather together in the larger cities, creating with their fellow countrymen sprawling ghettos that were to become a kind of staging area in the gradual process of assimilation into the new culture.

Among the largest of the immigrant groups were the Jews from Eastern Europe, who after 1870 began arriving in ever increasing numbers, fleeing the widespread pogroms and economic restrictions that had become commonplace throughout Poland, Hungary, Bohemia, Russia, and the Balkans. Settling largely in Manhattan's Lower East Side—a four-square-mile triangle bounded roughly by 14th Street on the north, the Bowery on the west, and the East River on the east—they moved into the squalid, hastily constructed tenements that filled every block in the area. As new arrivals continuously swelled the teeming ghetto, it became the most densely populated district in the world. By 1894, the population reached an astonishing 986 people per acre—one-and-a-half times that of Bombay, India! The immigrant Jews, seeking to maintain their Old World ties, also tended to band together by country of origin, thus creating within the Lower East Side enclaves of Russians, Poles, Rumanians, Lithuanians, Hungarians, and Levantines. In common, however, they shared their religious beliefs and rituals, their miserable living conditions, and their hopes for a better life. Many of the immigrants were drawn to the needle trades, and eked out a meager existence working in the unregulated sweatshops, or laboring in their tiny, crowded cold-water flats in what soon became a cottage garment industry centered about the family sewing machine. Others were employed in the numerous small retail shops and factories that proliferated on the street floors of the tenements, while many chose "private enterprise" as pushcart vendors, hawking an endless variety of wares from these peripatetic two-wheeled establishments that lined the main thoroughfares of the Lower East Side.

In spite of their grinding poverty, the struggle for survival, and the drudgery of daily life, Jewish institutions flourished. More than 500 synagogues and *talmud torahs* (religious schools) were constructed; a Yiddish theater was founded; Hebrew and Yiddish book publishers flourished; and more than a dozen Yiddish newspapers appeared on the newsstands. Rapid naturalization was the immediate goal of all immigrants, and evening classes in English and Americanization at the neighborhood public schools were always jammed to overflowing. Every newcomer dreamed of the day when, no longer a greenhorn, he could climb the economic ladder, become a "real American," and make a better life for himself and his children.

With the passage in the 1920s of restrictive laws, the great flood of immigration was finally halted, and the growth of the ghetto stemmed. As families moved to better neighborhoods in the city, the "old neighborhood" began to decline, and the Jewish ghetto is now largely gone. The depressing tenements are being replaced with high-rise apartments; the small family-run shops are giving way to supermarkets and large retail stores; the hundreds of synagogues—many of them awesome architectural masterpieces—are reduced to a scant, crumbling handful; and the *lingua franca,* once exclusively Yiddish, is yielding to a babel of Spanish, Chinese, and Hindi.

The walking tour of the Lower East Side is largely an imaginative glimpse of the past through a number of the vestiges and surviving artifacts of that era of Jewish immigration—a sort of last look at the remnants of the old neighborhood, which in a few short years will be no more. In *Portal to America: The Lower East Side, 1870–1925,* editor Allon Schoener describes the neighborhood as recalling ". . . a wonderfully rich and fruitful period of American history in which millions of Jews came to the United States through a small portal and spread across the entire country making their contributions to the total fabric of American Life."

Begin the Lower East Side tour at the corner of East Broadway and Jefferson Street (on the park side), one block east of the IND East Broadway subway station.

    1. The Educational Alliance, known as the Hebrew Institute when the building was erected in 1891, was organized by a group of "uptown Jews" as an educational, cultural, intellectual, and social service center for the residents of the Lower East Side. It provided training in Americanization for the newly arrived immigrants, and is credited with helping speed up the immigrants' process of assimilation with its day and evening classes in English and citizenship. It housed a free library at a time when no public libraries existed in the city, and its classes were later used as models for the New York City Board of Education's citizenship program for the foreign-born. Classes for children were also offered in Jewish religion and history, and the Alliance conducted free High Holy Day services for those too poor to be members of a synagogue congregation.

Through the years the Alliance has expanded its educational work, offering free courses in a wide spectrum of disciplines: art, music, philosophy, drama, science, and vocational skills. Although its original constituency is largely gone, it holds classes in English and citizenship for new Spanish- and Chinese-speaking immigrants. It is also very active in community social service projects, especially senior citizen activities.

The Lower East Side's population is now approximately 45 percent Puerto Rican (and other Spanish-speaking groups), 15 percent Chinese, 10 percent Black, 5 percent others (Indian, Ukrainian, Polish, Albanian, and Italian), and only 25 percent Jewish. The original East Broadway building of the Alliance was modernized in 1970–71 and renamed the David Sarnoff Building, and a new annex added on the Jefferson Street side.

2. To the left (in the park) is the **Seward Park Branch of the New York Public Library.** Built in 1910, it was one of the first branches of the newly established free municipal library system. The Public Library was founded by Andrew Carnegie, who was instrumental in merging the Astor, Tilden, and Lenox Libraries—the three largest private collections in the City.

So great was this free library's popularity with the immigrants when it opened, that it was not uncommon to see long lines of adults and youngsters patiently awaiting their turn to enter the crowded building. Until recently this branch had the largest Yiddish collection in the city.

3. Across the street, at 175 East Broadway, towers the ten-story **Jewish Daily Forward Building.** The building is no longer occupied by the *Forward,* as the newspaper has moved its offices uptown, where it continues to publish the only surviving Yiddish daily in the world. Founded in 1897 by Abraham Cahan, the *Forward* became the most influential newspaper in the Jewish community, and was read with a dedication second only to that given to the religious books. As an ardent campaigner for the improvement of the Human Condition, Abe Cahan and the *Forward* supported the labor movement, fought dishonest politicans, and led in the battle to eliminate the sweatshops, at the same time helping the immigrants adapt to the New World and encouraging them to be informed, loyal citizens. The *Forward* always lent a sympathetic ear to the problems of its readers, and still conducts a daily column called the *Bintel Brief* (Bundle of Letters), in which problems of readers are printed and answered by the editor. The paper has always provided a forum for the greatest Yiddish writers (Isaac Bashevis Singer is still a contributor). The *Forward* also maintains a small staff of foreign correspondents who provide material not available from the usual wire services. Its present circulation is only a third of the 1924 peak of 200,000, but there is still sufficient interest in Yiddish to keep it alive and well.

The building, which not only housed the *Forward,* but an active Yiddish theater and the offices of many Jewish labor organizations, is now in the hands of a Chinese syndicate, which is converting it to use by the fast-growing Chinese community of the Lower East Side.

4. Triangular **Nathan Straus Square** is named for the Jewish philanthropist who in 1919 sponsored a program of free sterilized-milk stations for children throughout the country. Nathan Straus, a partner in the R. H. Macy enterprise, was active for many years in charitable causes.

The circular marble column was erected in tribute to the servicemen of the Lower East Side who gave their lives in both World Wars.

5. The **Garden Cafeteria,** at the corner of Rutgers Street and East Broadway, is very much a Lower East Side landmark, albeit unofficial. For years, the "Garden" has been a favored meeting place of writers, actors, and other local "intelligentsia," as well as for a colorful assortment of East Side characters. It offers such typical Jewish gastronomical delights as blintzes, borscht, chicken soup (of course!), herring, carp, pirogen, kashe varnishkes, and a tempting variety of vegetarian steaks and roasts, as well as sinfully luscious desserts. The establishment is a cafeteria in front and a restaurant in the rear. The waiters in the restaurant section add a special touch with their zealous dedication to stuffing patrons "just like mother did," frowning in undisguised disapproval if a recommended specialty is rejected or if food is left afterward on the plate. Don't miss the mural on the wall of the cafeteria depicting the former artisans' market of Hester Park (now Seward Park). In former times, if one needed a plumber, carpenter, or electrician, he went to the artisans' market, bargained for the man's services, and brought him to the apartment for the job.

6. Seward Park, carved out of a former slum district, provides a pleasant retreat for the inhabitants of the surrounding crowded and shadeless streets. A small but busy "thieves market" near the Essex Street entrance should be avoided.

7. St. Teresa's Roman Catholic Church, at the corner of Rutgers and Henry streets, was founded in 1863 to serve the growing Irish immigrant community that at the time occupied much of the Lower East Side. Built in 1841 as the First Presbyterian Church of New York, it was purchased through the efforts of then-Archbishop Corrigan, and now serves new immigrant groups. It is possibly the only trilingual Catholic Church in the city, offering masses in English, Spanish, and Chinese. (Only one other Catholic church offers services in Chinese, the Church of the Transfiguration, on Mott Street in Chinatown.)

Hester Street was the main shopping thoroughfare of the Lower East Side, with pushcarts, shops, and stalls lining both sides of the street. This view, looking east from Essex Street to Norfolk Street, was taken in 1899, at the height of Jewish immigration. (Museum of the City of New York)

Rutgers Street is named for the Henry Rutgers family whose farm occupied much of the land from this point to the East River during the Colonial period. Their property bordered the Etienne DeLancey farm, and the boundary line is now appropriately called Division Street.

8. The nameless square (or triangle) formed by the confluence of Canal and Division streets is particularly colorful during the Jewish festival of Succoth, or Feast of Tabernacles, which according to the lunar calendar can fall anywhere from late September to mid-October. The sidewalks are lined with vendors, many in Hasidic garb, selling the myrtle leaves, palm fronds, and citrons imported from the Holy Land. These are bought by religious Jews to decorate their *Succah,* or outdoor lattice hut, where meals are taken during the holiday in celebration of the harvest.

9. Walk one block west on Canal Street, noting the number of Hebrew and Yiddish bookstores as well as some new East Indian retail establishments. A faint aroma of curry emanates from several Indian restaurants on the south side of Division Street.

Turn right on Ludlow Street. On the right is the massive structure of the now-defunct **Canal Theater.** When you return to Canal Street, see if you can discover the somewhat altered, but still ornate former entrance to this former silent film movie house. It is now occupied by a discount electrical appliance store, and the dark recesses of the theater are used as a warehouse.

Across Ludlow Street is the equally defunct **Independent Kletzker Brotherly Aid Society** building, whose name and founding date (1892) may be read in the pediment. It was customary for newly arrived immigrant groups to maintain association with those from the same *shtetl,* or small town. If the group were large or wealthy enough, they would build a synagogue and a *talmud torah,* purchase a cemetery lot, and sometimes establish a benevolent or mutual-aid society for their members. This is the only such surviving building in the neighborhood, and was constructed for an immigrant group from the Polish village of Kletsk. Now owned by a funeral parlor, the building is divided into apartments.

Return to Canal Street and continue west to Orchard Street.

10. Orchard Street for the seven blocks north of Canal Street has been the principal commercial thoroughfare for many years. For those living outside the neighborhood, Orchard Street is synonymous with the Lower East Side. Hectic, bustling, and noisy, it is the closest thing to a "native market." Before the pushcarts were ruled off the streets by city ordinance, it was even busier. Here on Sundays come thousands of bargain hunters from all over the New York Metropolitan Area, taking advantage of the discounts—real and fanciful—offered by the endless row of small retail shops. It is said that the Lower East Side is the only complete mercantile district in the city, where virtually everything can be purchased, and at a lower price than anywhere else. Orchard Street is primarily a clothing center, each block having its own specialization. (A stroll along Orchard street comes later in the tour.)

11. On the southwest corner of Canal and Orchard streets looms the tallest structure on the Lower East Side—**Jarmulovsky's Bank** building. Only a few old-timers remember that active financial institution, founded in 1873 (the building dates from about 1895), which served as the local Baron Rothschild for more than 40 years, ultimately bringing grief to thousands of unlucky depositors when it collapsed during World War I. Federal banking regulations were quite lax in those days, and private banks flourished throughout the country. Sender Jarmulovsky was a shrewd financier whose success was climaxed in the construction of this imposing building at the height of the immigration period. However, the Panic of 1907 and Yarmulovsky's subsequent passing, left the bank in shaky condition. A few years later it closed its doors, insolvent, owing its creditors millions and ruining thousands of trusting immigrants.

In addition to the grand entrance to the old bank with its low-relief sculpture and clock, some evidence of the former institution can be seen inside, on the walls of the luncheonette that now occupies the former main banking floor.

12. Allen Street, one block west, was once a dark and dingy thoroughfare, echoing with the rattle of the former Second Avenue Elevated, and boasting one of the largest red-light districts in town. With the El gone and the street widened (note the absence of building fronts on the east side), it is a main north-south artery of the city, and now has a rather extensive antiques center. Dealing mostly in old (and not-so-old) brass and copper, these shops offer hours of interesting browsing, and good buys can occasionally be had in old candelabra, chandeliers, lamps, and fixtures. But don't try to outsmart the dealers—they've been in business for a long time.

At Eldridge Street turn south (left).

13. The Old Law tenement at **Number 19** is purported to be the birthplace of actor Eddie Cantor. Old Law tenements prevail throughout most of the Lower East Side. Prior to the passage of the "Old Law" in 1879, there was little regulation of the construction of multiple dwellings. Houses were often built of wood, without fire escapes, toilets, or water supply; and there was no provision for the ventilation of interior rooms, as only the front and rear rooms had windows. The 1879 law corrected many of these evils, and included among its requirements that an airshaft be built between adjacent tenement houses to provide (some) light and air for inside rooms, that hallways and stairways be wider and constructed of fireproof materials, that water be piped into each apartment, and that there be a toilet for each two apartments. Thus backyard privies and curbside water pumps became a thing of the past, and the tenements became a bit safer, and possibly a trifle more comfortable. Another prohibition was the construction of the so-called "backyard houses"—multiple dwellings that were built behind other houses, without direct access to the street. The addition of the airshaft to the tenement changed the overhead shape of the building from a simple rectangle to that of an exercise dumbbell—and the name "dumbbell tenement" is still applied to those built under the Old Law. In 1901, the "New Law" was passed, further modifying the building code, including a provision that houses higher than five stories must be equipped with an elevator. Seven-story walk-ups were not uncommon in the old days!

Compare this row of Old Law tenements with the building at **Number 18,** built c. 1870. Notice the narrow hallways, sheet-tin walls and ceilings, and the wooden floors and staircases. Fire escapes were added as mandated by the 1879 Law, otherwise this nonfireproof building would be a frightening fire trap. Scores of pre-Old Law tenements still exist throughout the Lower East Side.

14. The adjacent synagogue, **Congregation Khal Adath Jeshurun and Anshe Lubz,** was once the largest Jewish house of worship in the district. Built in 1886 from plans by the renowned architectural firm of Herter Brothers, it is built mainly in Moorish Revival style with some Gothic elements. Except for missing finials on the cornice, the façade is in an excellent state of preservation. The stained-glass windows, however, have suffered from vandalism and neglect. The interior is exceptional, with a hand-carved ark of Italian walnut, sculptured wooden balcony, enormous brass Victorian chandeliers and candelabra, high-quality stained glass, brightly painted wall murals, and a lofty, barrel-vaulted ceiling. Since the building has fallen into disuse, the effects of weather and lack of upkeep have taken a dreadful toll. A leaking roof and smashed windows have allowed years of rain and snow to wreak havoc, with the result that the stairways and balcony are threatened with imminent collapse. As the Jewish population of the neighborhood declined through the years, the congregation dwindled to the point where fewer than 20 active members remain to support this great temple. The magnificent sanctuary was abandoned in the mid-1930s, and services are held in the basement whenever a *minyan,* or quorum of ten adult males, can be assembled.

The future of this synagogue—surely one of the most beautiful anywhere —is very uncertain. To visit the sanctuary, come on a Saturday morning, and if services are being held, ask the volunteer sexton to show it to you . . . and "you don't have to be Jewish." Occasional tours of the building are conducted by the Jewish Museum of New York (telephone 860-1875). A small donation would be received with gratitude.

Continue south on Eldridge Street, turning left on Division Street to Allen Street.

15. The **Manhattan Bridge** overhead was begun in 1905 and completed four years later. It is the last built of a trio of downtown bridges connecting Manhattan with Brooklyn. (The first, the Brooklyn Bridge, was begun in 1883, and was referred to in Yiddish as the *Alte Brick,* or Old Bridge. The Williamsburg Bridge, opened in 1903, was the *Naiye Brick,* or New Bridge.) A three-cent fare was charged on the creaky trolley that shuttled back and forth when the Manhattan Bridge was opened. In addition to four lanes of motor-vehicle traffic, it also carries several subway lines.

At the corner of Allen Street (which changes its name to Pike Street as it curves toward the East River) is the **former power house of the Second Avenue El.** Note the old metal letters on the wall of the original Manhattan Elevated Railway building, as well as the row of holes for the former power cables. Since the El made a sharp curve at this point to swing into Division Street, the corner of the power house was flattened. It is now a Chinese-owned warehouse. Allen Street was widened in 1930. Look closely and you will notice that there are no building fronts on the east side, except for a few small houses built later.

Diagonally across the street at 15 Pike Street is another threatened synagogue, the **Congregation Sons of Israel Kalwarie,** built in 1903. This Classic Revival-style building also suffers from a dwindling congregation, and can no longer afford to employ a rabbi. The interior is very impressive and well worth a visit (on Friday evenings or Saturday mornings).

Continue north on Allen Street, past Canal Street and a few antique shops, to Hester Street.

The Police Court on Essex Street at the corner of Broome was replaced by Seward Park High School. In this view, taken in 1892, the high wall visible in the background was the Ludlow Street Jail, where corrupt "Boss" Tweed had died 14 years before. (New-York Historical Society)

The opening of the Manhattan Bridge in 1909 improved transportation to Brooklyn, and to an extent encouraged further emigration from the Lower East Side. The Manhattan Bridge Three Cents Trolley provided a cheap trip across the East River. (Long Island Historical Society)

(Left) This photograph of a poor Jew with his chalah preparing for the sabbath in a coal cellar, is touching evidence of the struggle for human dignity under conditions of abject poverty. The sign at left indicates that the man may be a shoemaker by trade. (Photograph by Jacob A. Riis. The Jacob A. Riis Collection. Museum of the City of New York)

(Left, below) The squalor of tenement life is dramatically apparent in this picture by an unknown photographer, taken, according to the wall calendar, some time in June 1916. The rear room, without window or ventilation, indicates that this is a pre-Old Law tenement, built before 1879. (Community Service Society of New York)

(Below) Sociologist-photographer Jacob Riis visited the old Essex Market School and recorded this crowded little classroom with its coal stoves and gas illumination. The closely-shaven-headed youngsters seem rather well-behaved, doubtless after strong admonition by the usually very strict teachers. (The Jacob A. Riis Collection. Museum of the City of New York)

(*Photograph by Jacob A. Riis. The Jacob Riis Collection. Museum of the City of New York*)

(*Museum of the City of New York*)

For youngsters growing up in the crowded, unsanitary Lower East Side tenements, the daily life of grinding poverty left little time to enjoy the pleasures of childhood. They were expected to work in the sweatshops and shoulder their share of the family's struggle for survival.

(*Community Service Society of New York*)

(*Photograph by Jessie Tarbox Beals, Community Service Society of New York*)

Sweatshops took many forms. Here a family of Bohemian cigar-makers work busily at their trade. (Photograph by Jacob A. Riis. The Jacob A. Riis Collection. Museum of the City of New York)

Tightly parked rows of pushcarts virtually block access to the sidewalk in this Lower East Side street scene taken in the 1890s. Youngsters generally sought the freedom of the streets to escape the overcrowded condition of their squalid tenement homes. (Community Service Society)

A group of three women buying eggs just before the Sabbath on Hester Street, 1895. (Photograph by Alice Austen. Staten Island Historical Society)

Photographer Jessie Tarbox Beals posed this Italian immigrant family in the kitchen of their East Side flat. Few apartments consisted of more than a kitchen, small in-between room, and a parlor, or "front room." Communal toilets in the Old Law tenements were located in the halls, adjacent to the cold water faucet. Note the tiny bedroom whose only window opens into the kitchen. The gas stove was considered a "modern improvement," and the kerosene lamp on the stove was the room's only source of illumination. (Museum of the City of New York)

The intersection of Delancey and Clinton Streets at the entrance to the Williamsburg Bridge was the busiest on the Lower East Side when this photo was taken in 1919. Motor vehicles and horse-drawn wagons shared the bridge with trolleys and the BMT subway. Then, many more pedestrians than now used the wide bridge walkway, saving themselves the two-cent carfare. The ornate square buildings in the foreground were entrance kiosks to the underground bridge trolley station. Most of the Old Law tenements along the north side of Delancey Street are still lived in. (*The Edward B. Watson Collection*)

A smoky elevated train has just passed the Chatham Square junction of the 2nd and 3rd Avenue Els in the mid-1880s. The station was later rebuilt with an upper level to eliminate the dangerous rail crossovers. The train is headed for South Ferry, while the tracks on the left lead to City Hall. Below the elevated structure are Park Row (*left*), East Broadway (*right*), and the Bowery (*rear*). The 2nd Avenue line swings around the left side of Congress Hall up Division Street. (*Museum of the City of New York*)

16. By the 1880s **Hester Street** had become the busiest market in the Lower East Side. With both sides of the street lined with pushcarts and the wares of all the shops piled high on the sidewalks, the crowded street took on the atmosphere of an Oriental bazaar. Especially on Thursday evenings, the congestion and clamor reached its weekly peak, as housewives shopped for the sabbath. Anything could be bought on Hester Street—dry goods, food, housewares, books, jewelry, furniture—and haggling was always the rule. On hot summer days the lack of refrigeration was very much in evidence, as fish peddlers pressed to sell out before nature took its course. Everywhere was the smell of decay as the gutters and sidewalks accumulated "mountain ranges" of fruit peels, paper, fish scales, nutshells, rotting vegetables, and rubbish of all sorts. The horses that pulled the many peddlers' wagons added their contribution, too.

Continue to Orchard Street and turn left.

17. Note the partially abandoned **seven-story walk-up** on the left side of Orchard Street, a short distance from the corner. One can only speculate on the number of unfortunate souls whose hearts were surely overtaxed by the wearying daily ascents to the upper floors. Jewish stars in terra cotta appear on the façades of a number of tenements—no doubt a ruse by the builders to attract religious, but naïve tenants.

18. At the southwest corner of Orchard and Grand streets is the **former Ridley's Department Store.** Its imposing rounded corner and rusting ornate cast-iron façade are all that remains of one of the most fashionable stores in the city during the Gay '90s. Together with competitor Lord & Taylor's, four blocks west on Grand Street, they presented an almost incongruous element of elegance in a neighborhood that could ill afford their wares.

Ridley's gave up the ghost in 1901, and a year later, Lord & Taylor's moved all of its retail operations to its main store at Broadway and 20th Street [*see* Ladies' Mile, 27]. A bizarre epilogue to the Ridley story is contained in a newspaper clipping from the defunct *New York World-Telegram,* pasted conspicuously in the window of the present store. One day in 1964, the owner received a letter in one of Ridley's self-addressed envelopes, in which the sender requested a mail-order catalog—63 years after the establishment's demise! The article also recounts the mystery of the unsolved murders of one of the Ridley brothers as well as his bookkeeper in the subcellar of their former establishment.

Turn west (left) on Grand Street.

19. Across the street at the corner of Allen Street, the Romanesque Revival building now occupied by a bank and a furniture store was formerly a very popular **sports arena** when it opened in the mid-1880s. Indoor sports at that time were mainly confined to boxing.

20. Look across Allen Street, about 100 yards to the left of Grand Street.

The Yiddish Theater was an important aspect of Lower East Side cultural life. The Grand Theater which stood on the southwest corner of Grand and Chrystie streets until the blocks between Chrystie and Forsyth streets were leveled for the construction of Sara Delano Roosevelt Park, boasted many famous actors. In this 1908 photo, Jacob Adler stars in the Yiddish version of King Lear. (*Museum of the City of New York*)

The tall building now housing a public garage was **formerly the wagon house and stables of Ridley's Department Store.** A closer look will reveal the old bumpers designed to prevent the wagon wheels from striking the wall, and many of the Romanesque Revival details so popular with architects in the mid-1880s.

21. Continue west on **Grand Street,** which for many years was one of the city's major east-west thoroughfares. Its double horsecar line connected the New Jersey ferries on Manhattan's West Side with the East River ferries to Long Island. On the north side of Grand Street, between Allen, Eldridge, and Forsyth streets are four diminutive **Federal-style houses** of the 1820s. No longer residences, these old houses with peaked roofs and twin dormers somehow managed to survive.

22. At the corner of Eldridge Street, look left at No. 87, formerly a synagogue, and now serving the small Black community as the **Lincoln African Methodist Episcopal Church.** The Jewish symbols in the façade still remain.

23. On the other side of Grand Street, at 107 Eldridge Street (now a fabric store), is the **former Eldridge Street Police Station.** The building is in surprisingly good condition, and except for first-floor modifications, looks very much as it did when built as the local station house in the late 1870s.

24. Seven blocks of tenements were demolished in the late 1930s between Forsyth and Chrystie streets to make the way for **Sara Delano Roosevelt Park,** named for the mother of F.D.R. The Lord & Taylor department store stood at the southwest corner of Grand and Chrystie streets.

25. One block farther west on Grand Street, at the Bowery, is **"Bank**

The Third Avenue El looking north from the Grand Street station in 1895. Before the els were electrified, the little steam locomotives created problems for those below, spewing hot cinders and oil, and littering the streets with ashes. In this photo, made from a magic lantern slide, the buildings seen on the left of the street are still standing today, from the Bowery Savings Bank (extreme left), the early nineteenth-century houses with dormers, the long defunct Germania Bank (tall white structure), to distant Cooper Union. (The Picture Decorator, Inc., N.Y.C.)

Corner." The landmark **Bowery Savings Bank,** occupying the L-shaped plot on the northwest corner, was built in 1894 by the famed architectural firm of McKim, Mead & White, and represented the newly popular Classical Revival style. On the same corner, surrounded on two sides by the Bowery's "temple of savings" is the former **Butchers' & Drovers' Bank** (note their old insignia in wrought iron), now a branch of the First National City Bank. Across the street on the southwest corner, in a building now used by the Manufacturer's Hanover Trust Company, was another victim of the Depression, the **Chatham & Phenix Bank.** Disgruntled depositors sometimes referred to it as the "Cheat 'em & Fix 'em" Bank.

26. Turn north on the Bowery, observing the number of Federal-style houses remaining, particularly **Nos. 133, 134, 136,** and **140.** For years this block has been the "interior lighting center" of the city. Formerly specializing in gas lighting equipment, the dozen or so brilliantly lit stores now offer just about every type of electric lighting fixture known.

27. Turn right into **Delancey Street.** Once a rather fashionable retail center, it is now shabby and forlorn, serving mainly as an approach route to the Williamsburg Bridge, a half mile to the east. In its heyday, the city fathers renamed it Schiff Parkway in honor of philanthropist Jacob Schiff; but the name didn't stick, and so it again honors Etienne DeLancey, the original 18th-century landowner. DeLancey chose the wrong side in the American Revolution, and at the conclusion of the war, his property was confiscated and he left for England. Delancey Street is the sole public reminder of his name.

28. On the southeast corner of Forsyth Street is the **former Forsyth Street Synagogue,** Congregation Anshe Ileya, now occupied by a Dominican Seventh-Day Adventist Church. The old synagogue was once one of the wealthiest and most exclusive *shuls* on the Lower East Side. The designers of the building shrewdly planned for future financial security by having a row of stores built into the Delancey Street side.

29. Take a short detour north on Allen Street to the **Municipal Bathhouse.** Built in 1905, it is the only remaining free public bathhouse in a city that had 15 such facilities at the beginning of the century. There are 54 men's showers and 34 women's showers in the white brick and limestone building. Few residents of this or any poor neighborhood had the luxury of bathing facilities in their dismal apartments, so the city built a series of public baths in the more densely populated districts. To this day, occupants of most of the tenements do not have adequate bathrooms. Some have a bathtub in the kitchen, but must still share a common toilet in the hall. Central heating and landlord-supplied hot water are still the exception.

30. The tall building with templelike columns at the southeast corner of Delancey and Allen streets is the home of the **Hebrew Publishing Company.** Founded before the turn of the century to cater to the immigrants' thirst for Yiddish and Hebrew reading material, it is the world's largest publisher of prayer books, language texts, and literary works in both languages. Stand directly in front of the building, near the curb, and examine the wide con-

Looking west on Hester Street at the turn of the century. The excavation at left is for Seward Park, which was to become a welcome oasis in the maze of crowded, depressing tenements. In the background, a horse car passes on Essex Street while in the distance, the Second Avenue El structure can be seen on Allen Street. (New-York Historical Society)

crete panel above the first floor. With a little squinting one can discern the old sign, "Bank of the United States." This was the Lower East Side branch of a largely Jewish-owned bank. Doing business with branches throughout the city, it prospered for many years. It is said that part of its success was due to immigrants' belief that because of its name, the Bank of the United States was actually a government institution, hence safe beyond a doubt. Its failure in 1932 is rumored to have been caused by the collusion of several big city banks that refused to grant it short-term credit. It was customary for banks to help each other when one was momentarily short of working capital, but in this case it was felt that anti-Semitism was the reason. Depositors ultimately received most of their money, but the bank's collapse was a sensation for a number of years.

31. Across the street, the crumbling **Delancey Theater** is the last of the former silent-film playhouses. Note the aging advertisements on the walls of the building behind the theater, some dating from the turn of the century.

32. Turning north on **Orchard Street,** the atmosphere suddenly changes. Formerly identical in character to the blocks to the south, it has in recent years become a Latin American neighborhood. The sights, sounds, and smells are reminiscent of a typical "south of the border" public market. There is a gaiety and liveliness absent until now, with Latin rhythms blaring from record shops, storekeepers aggressively peddling their merchandise on the sidewalk, and the aroma of an assortment of savory, exotic delicacies being cooked in nearby restaurants. So busy is this street that vehicular traffic is banned on Sundays. Walk through to Rivington Street and turn right.

33. The First Roumanian Congregation in America, *Shaari Shamoyim,* was organized in 1885. Only the name is Rumanian now, as the synagogue serves a new generation of East Siders. One of the few remaining large houses of worship, it still maintains a Hebrew School and is very active in community affairs. The building, in Romanesque Revival style, was built as the Allen Street Methodist Church in 1888, four years before its purchase by the Hebrew congregation. The sanctuary is very spacious, with a particularly beautiful pulpit set against an array of brightly colored stained-glass windows.

Busy Grand Street was the major east-west thoroughfare of the Lower East Side as its crosstown streetcars connected with both New Jersey and Long Island ferries. Here a crowd is attracted by the derailment of a streetcar at the intersection of Eldridge Street. Behind the disabled streetcar is the Grand Theater, and in the distance, the Third Avenue El, at the Bowery. (Community Service Society of New York)

Rivington Street is named for James Rivington, a well-known printer and newspaper publisher during the late 18th century. Thought to have been a Tory during the American Revolution, recent historical discoveries show that he was a very successful spy for General Washington, and is credited with breaking the British naval code.

34. At the corner of Essex Street is another gastronomical landmark, the **Economy Food Shop.** The counters, both inside and on the sidewalk, are stacked high with such goodies as dried fruit, nuts, gelatin candies, and halvah.

A few doors north is **Bernstein-on-Essex Street,** a Jewish delicatessen and also a genuine kosher Chinese restaurant! Peek inside at the Chinese waiters wearing *yarmulkes.*

Farther down Rivington Street are two other food landmarks: **Shapiro's Wine Company,** at the corner of Norfolk Street; and **Streit's Matzoth Company,** one block farther at Suffolk Street. The winery and matzoth bakery are the only ones left in Manhattan.

Along the east side of Essex Street, extending for several blocks, is the **Essex Street Market,** built by the city just before pushcarts were banned from the streets.

35. Turn south on Essex Street to **Delancey Street.** This busy intersection, with its approach to the Williamsburg Bridge, was once even busier! When the bridge was opened in 1903, Delancey Street became a major artery, not only for the horse-drawn vehicles and early motorcar traffic, but for horsecars and the new electric trolleys as well. A few years later, the newly built Brooklyn & Manhattan Transit extended its subway line over the bridge, and beneath the intersection a new station was constructed for the train and bridge trolleys. The bridge trolleys have long since disappeared. Their elaborate subway entrance kiosks have been demolished, and the large underground station lies dark and abandoned.

The **Loew's Delancey** was one of the grandiose movie palaces of the 1920s, its façade still showing traces of the then-popular Moorish Revival style. Adjacent is **Ratner's,** a well known Jewish restaurant. Many famous dining places were located here, but only Ratner's survives.

Continue to Broome Street.

36. The building on the northwest corner (with the "Bell Yarn" sign) was formerly the **Eastern Dispensary,** one of four large privately endowed clinics that provided free medical care for the needy. Only the Northern Dispensary remains [*see* Greenwich Village, 28].

Seward Park High School occupies the entire block between Ludlow, Essex, Broome and Grand streets. The school was built on the site of the Essex Market Court House and Ludlow Street Jail, which stood on the western half of the block. Infamous politician William Marcy "Boss" Tweed died there in 1878 [*see* City Hall, 17]. On the eastern half of the block was the Essex Market Court House.

Virtually every tenement had its share of "sweatshops," operating in crowded apartments from dawn to late night, six days a week. In this view taken around 1905 in a Ludlow Street tenement, renowned photographer Jacob Riis captured the activity and working conditions of a group of cloth cutters. (The Jacob A. Riis Collection, Museum of the City of New York)

37. Walk east on Broome Street to Norfolk Street, and turn right to the **Beth Hamedrash Hagodol Synagogue,** a designated New York City Landmark. This Gothic Revival building was built in 1852 as the Norfolk Street Baptist Church and was sold to this congregation in 1885. Priding itself on having been the largest Russian synagogue in the country for many years, its membership is now quite small. Open on the sabbath, the sanctuary is magnificent and should be visited. Most attractive are the ornate ark and pulpit, the center *bimah* (reader's platform) with etched glass lamps, cantilevered balconies, Gothic vaulted ceiling, and colorful wall paintings. When the converted gas fixtures are illuminated at twilight, the atmosphere is awesome!

At Grand Street turn right to Essex Street. Delicious bagels, bialys and other exotic breadstuffs can be purchased at the bakery across the street, adjacent to the theater.

38. In the two blocks between Grand and Canal streets are a variety of small retail establishments catering to the Orthodox Jewish community. Working in ground-floor tenement shops, much as they did almost a hundred years ago, are the *yarmulke* (skull-cap) makers, torah scribes, *talith* (prayer-shawl) manufacturers, *tefillin* (prayer-phylacteries) repairers, and vendors of religious articles and books. There are also *glat* (strictly) kosher groceries and restaurants. The proprietors, many belonging to the Hasidic sect and wearing their traditional garb, will often stop business operations, close their doors, and with the shop filled with patrons, pause to conduct afternoon prayers. Miller's Kosher Cheese Agency, at 13 Essex Street, is known throughout the city, and before the Passover Holiday, long lines of customers are a usual sight.

Adjoining Miller's at No. 13½, is the small workshop of Rabbi Moses

The synagogue was the center of spiritual and cultural life of most Jewish immigrants in the Lower East Side. At times, the need for new houses of worship could not keep up with the influx of new worshippers. Typically, a new congregation would purchase and recondition an old church. The Sineerer Shul, which stood at Madison and Montgomery Streets until destroyed by fire in 1972, was formerly the Madison Street Presbyterian Church. (New York City Landmarks Preservation Commission)

Eisenbach, a *sofer,* or torah scribe. The venerable rabbi can be seen repairing torah scrolls or phylacteries, or even writing delicately on a piece of parchment with the traditional quill pen made from a turkey feather.

A few steps around the corner on Hester Street is Guss' Pickle Works (follow your nose!), where dozens of varieties of tasty pickles are dispensed from large casks on the sidewalk. At the corner of Ludlow Street are two more food shops to tempt the palate of those wishing to explore further the world of Jewish appetizers.

This corner had another function during the sweatshop era. It was here that the garment industry contractors would gather every morning to hire their daily contract laborers. The noise and commotion was so great that the intersection and its surroundings earned the name **Khazzer Mark,** or Pig Market.

Return to Essex Street, and continue to Canal Street, where the walking tour began.

Two additional short tours can be made to other Lower East Side points of interest. Supplementary Tour "A" is a visit to the old Chatham Square Cemetery and a few other landmarks. Tour "B" visits the Henry Street Settlement, the remaining great synagogues, and some additional points of interest.

SUPPLEMENTARY TOUR "A"
TO THE HISTORIC CHATHAM SQUARE CEMETERY

Follow East Broadway about a half-mile west to Chatham Square. Some old-timers still recall the lumbering battery-operated "Green Cars," which rolled along East Broadway at an exasperating eight miles per hour, and which in the winter trailed smoke from a pot-belly stove mounted on the side of the car. In the distance is a striking panorama of new and old New York, with the Municipal and Telephone buildings set against the twin towers of the World Trade Center; while almost hidden below is the dark spire of St. Paul's Chapel.

At Chatham Square, with its Chinese-American War Memorial, turn left into St. James Place. Just beyond Oliver Street is the **Chatham Square Cemetery,** called officially the First Shearith Israel Cemetery. Built in 1682, this National Historic and New York City Landmark is the burial ground of the first Jewish congregation in the United States which arrived in 1654 (*see* page 20). It also has the distinction of being the oldest surviving man-made artifact on Manhattan Island! An earlier cemetery was consecrated in 1656 farther downtown, but no trace of it exists today, and its exact location is uncertain.

The historic burial ground is still maintained by the descendants of the original Sephardic congregation, *Shearith Israel,* the Spanish & Portuguese Synagogue, at 8 West 70th Street. The cemetery contains the graves of many of the early founders, including Gershon Mendes Seixas (1745–1816), the first American-born Jewish minister. Seixas served as a trustee of Columbia College and represented the Jewish community at Washington's inauguration. His brother Benjamin, also buried here, was a lieutenant in the New York militia and a founder of the New York Stock Exchange. The graves of 18 Jewish soldiers who fought for our independence have been marked by the Daughters of the American Revolution. The tombstone of Benjamin Bueno de Mezquita (1683) is the city's oldest. The site also played a role in the defense of the city during the early days of the Revolutionary War, when General Charles Lee mounted two batteries of cannon in the burial ground in an attempt to thwart the British invasion. The cemetery was closed in 1831, and two subsequent burial grounds were opened [see Greenwich Village, 33; and Ladies' Mile, 16].

Return to Oliver Street, and turn right to the **Mariner's Temple.** Now a Chinese Baptist Church, this brownstone Greek Revival-style church was designed in 1842 by architect Minard Lefever, and is a designated New York City Landmark. The attractive building replaces three earlier churches that were destroyed by fires, the most recent of which was called the Oliver Street Baptist Church. Note the enormous ship's bell to the right of the portico, hearkening back to the days when this was primarily a seamen's house of worship.

Turn left at Henry Street. This block was known as **"Doctors' Row"** in the 1840s. Don't miss "Dr. Naughton's Office" carved into the wall of No. 46.

St. Christopher's Chapel (No. 48), now the Chinese Church of Our Saviour, was once an elegant Federal-style residence.

At the corner of Market Street is the landmark **Sea and Land Church.** Another "mariners' temple," it was built in 1817 of local Manhattan schist in Georgian style for the First Dutch Reformed Church, but with some elements that anticipated the later Gothic Revival period. In 1869 it became the Sea and Land Church, but now is the First Chinese Presbyterian Church.

At **51 Market Street** is the former William Clark House. A New York City Landmark, it is a late Federal-style house of rather large proportions, retaining much of the original architectural detail.

Follow Henry Street, past Mechanics Alley (nothing remains to explain its name), under the Manhattan Bridge to Pike Street; turn left one block to East Broadway, then right to where the tour began.

SUPPLEMENTARY TOUR "B"
TO OTHER LOWER EAST SIDE LANDMARKS

Turn east on East Broadway (the opposite direction of Chatham Square), past the Educational Alliance building. In the block between Jefferson and Clinton streets are over a dozen small synagogues incorporated into the row of apartment houses that line the street. Some belong to small ultra-Orthodox groups; and it was in such a house of worship that the Young Israel movement was founded in 1910. The organization was established for Orthodox young people as a bulwark against the growing liberalization of the religion as exemplified by Reform Judaism, and is still very strong to this day. Many of these storefront synagogues, or *shtiebls,* however, belong to Hasidic groups, of which there are two major communities, the Lubavitcher and the Satmar sects. The *hasidim* are a very special ultra-Orthodox group (*hasid* means "pious one") who dress distinctively and stay apart from other Jewish groups, mingling with the outside world only when necessary. Modern hasidism was founded in 18th-century Poland by Israel ben Eliezer, called *Baal Shem Tov* ("Master of the Good Name") by his followers. The movement began as a reaction to the overly academic attitudes of Jewish religious leaders at the time. The essence of the Hasidic spirit is in their intense concentration while performing religious acts and their unbounded joy in devotion—believing that to be truly religious, one must enjoy his relationship with God. The Hasidim frequently sing, sway, and dance during prayers. Although considered extremists by fellow Jews who do not accept their fundamentalist philosophies, dress, and attitudes toward worldliness and women, the Hasidic move-

A cigarette factory sweatshop, c. 1910. The worker in shirtsleeves at the extreme left is the author's grandfather. (Photograph, courtesy Samuel Wolfe)

ment has nevertheless been growing in popularity since the arrival in this country of so many Hasidim after World War II. The Lubavitchers came mostly from Poland, while the Satmar Hasidim are Hungarians who fled their country after the 1956 Russian invasion.

While there are variations, the traditional Hasidic attire is adapted from the costume of the Polish nobleman of the 18th century, with a long black coat (*kapote*) and a broad-brimmed beaver or sable hat. Hasidim wear the traditional side locks and do not shave their beards. Married women shave their heads and wear a wig, and never expose bare arms or legs.

At Clinton Street, turn right one block to Henry Street. The trio of houses, Nos. 263, 265, and 267, is the **Henry Street Settlement.** Built in 1827 as residences when the neighborhood was just beginning to lose its rural character, these Federal-style houses are a designated New York City Landmark as well as a National Historic Landmark. In 1893 the Settlement was organized through the efforts of social reformer Lillian Wald with the financial backing of Jacob H. Schiff. It was the pioneer social agency on the Lower East Side, and a model for later neighborhood settlement houses throughout the country. It is still carrying on its original purpose of helping to improve living conditions and providing a health and social center for the neighborhood. Among its cultural activities is a highly successful drama and creative arts program.

Return to East Broadway, turn right to the intersection of Grand Street.

The Classic Revival building at the intersection of East Broadway and Grand Street, formerly a school, is now a **ritualarium,** or *mikveh.* Among Orthodox Jews it is customary for the bride-to-be to take a ritual bath prior to the wedding ceremony, and for all women to go to the *mikveh* at least once a month. In former times, many synagogues had their own ritual bath chamber, although there were many nonaffiliated mikvehs such as this.

Turn west on Grand Street to Willett Street, then right (Marinus Willett was a patriot in the Revolutionary War and mayor of New York City in 1807–08). Standing alone in the middle of the block is the **Bialystoker Synagogue.** Built in 1826 in Federal style, its fieldstone construction gives it a simple but rugged appearance. Originally the Willett Street Methodist Episcopal Church, it was sold in 1905 to an immigrant Jewish congregation from Bialystok, Poland which had arrived in the late 1870s. Still serving an active constituency mostly from the adjacent Sidney Hillman Houses, the synagogue is well maintained and has an impressive interior. A three-story-high carved wooden ark dominates the simple sanctuary. Colorful ceiling and wall paintings represent the signs of the zodiac and views of the Holy Land, while sparkling rays of blue and red stream down from a huge, arched stained-glass window. Contrary to the custom of facing east, the Bialystoker Synagogue must, because of its original design, face west.

Returning to Grand Street and continuing west, we pass the spanking new

Playhouse of the Henry Street Settlement, and walking down Pitt Street toward the Williamsburg Bridge we see the modern **Police Station and Fire House,** completed in 1974. The new 7th Precinct building replaces the former Clinton Street station house, which for over 70 years stood at the southeast corner of Delancey and Clinton streets, near the bridge exit.

Walk under the bridge, turn left on Delancey Street to Attorney Street, then right to the small synagogue in the middle of the block.

This diminutive Greek Revival building was erected about 1845 as the First Protestant Methodist Church. Some years later it was acquired by a Negro congregation, which renamed it the Emanuel African Methodist Episcopal Church. The adjacent house, which now stands abandoned, served as the former church's rectory. With the influx of Jewish immigrants in the 1880s the church was sold and converted to a synagogue. **Congregation Beth Haknesseth Mogen Avraham** ("Synagogue of the Shield of Abraham") is little changed, however. Only a *bimah* (reader's platform) was added in the sanctuary, and the stained-glass windows modified with Stars of David; the tall windows and brightly painted walls give the interior a cheerful and cozy atmosphere. The downstairs *beth medresh* ("house of study"), reached by a narrow wooden staircase, is used for weekly services. On sabbath eve, when the handful of elderly worshippers draped in their prayer shawls gather together in the small, dimly lit room, the somber scene is reminiscent of a Rembrandt canvas. The building, never really modernized, is probably the only synagogue still to have outside plumbing.

At Rivington Street, turn left one block to Clinton Street.

At the beginning of the century, **Clinton Street** was the center for religious-goods merchants. Store after store offered such articles as prayer books, prayer shawls, *yarmulkes, mezzuzahs,* phylacteries, torahs, candelabra, and ceremonial wine goblets. The street is now almost entirely Spanish-speaking and has become an important commercial thoroughfare. Turn right one-and-one-half blocks to the **Chasam Sopher Synagogue.** Built in 1853 for the German congregation Rodeph Shalom, it is the second oldest surviving synagogue in New York. Its design, rather unique for a synagogue, is of the Round-Arch Romanesque Revival style. In 1886, Rodeph Shalom moved uptown and sold the building to a Hungarian immigrant congregation which renamed the *shul* in honor of a 19th-century religious leader. The exterior has suffered many alterations through the years, losing an ornate iron balustrade and the street-level doors that gave access to the women's galleries. The sanctuary, however, is virtually unchanged—spacious, bright, and unpretentious, its quiet atmosphere a relief from the tumult of busy Clinton Street. The design of the hand-carved ark is a model of the synagogue's front façade, with most of the architectural details faithfully reproduced in miniature. The future of Chasam Sopher is uncertain. The small group of devoted members can no longer support a rabbi and must rely on a volunteer "reader."

At the corner of Stanton Street, turn right, walk two blocks to Norfolk Street and turn right again.

Halfway down the block, almost hidden by its taller neighbors, is **Congregation Anshe Slonim.** Little evidence remains of the former glory of this, the oldest synagogue in New York, and one of the oldest in the country! The smashed windows and doors, peeling stucco, broken fence, and overall state of deterioration are a melancholy end for such a historic building. Designed by architect Alexander Saeltzer in 1849 for the first Reform Congregation in America, Anshe Chesed, it was for a time the largest synagogue in the city. Gone now are the polygonal pyramids that once graced the twin towers of this Gothic Revival-style building, as well as the elaborate windows, traceries, and other medieval details of the façade. It is said that the architect was influenced by Germany's Cologne Cathedral, which had just celebrated its 600th anniversary the year before. In any case, the decade of the 1840s was the period of the Gothic Revival. Saeltzer's reputation as an architect was assured two years later when he designed the famous Astor Library on Lafayette Street, later the Hebrew Immigrant Aid Society building, now the New York City Shakespeare Festival Theater [see Lafayette Historic Group and East Village, 14]. As with neighboring Rodeph Shalom, the German Anshe Chesed congregation also moved uptown, and the building eventually passed to another Hungarian immigrant group. Changing names several times as different organizations took over the building, it ultimately became Anshe Slonim in 1922, taking its name from a tiny village in Poland. Most of the membership has long since departed, and the neighborhood, now in transition, is slated for urban renewal. What lies ahead for this venerable institution is anyone's guess. Lack of maintenance and the inability to cope with constant vandalism have taken a terrible toll. Its future is bleak, if not hopeless.

Return to Stanton Street, turn right one block to Essex Street. The IND subway station at Delancey Street is two blocks south.

SOHO CAST-IRON DISTRICT

Buildings with Complete Cast-Iron Façades

(Shaded Area Indicates Historic District)

7. SoHo Cast-Iron District

[*BMT Broadway line or IRT Lexington Avenue line to Canal Street station; Broadway M-1 bus to Canal Street*]

Cast iron as a building material had its origins in England in the mid-18th century. It was discovered that pig iron could easily be heated to the melting point by the use of coke, later coal, thus freeing it of impurities while maintaining the proper carbon content needed for strength. The molten mass could then be cast into sand molds of the desired size and shape. In 1779 a cast-iron bridge was completed over the River Severn, and in the last decade of the century a number of iron-framed buildings, mostly textile mills, demonstrated the feasibility of this type of construction. Subsequently, the use of cast iron to support large glass greenhouses became very popular, and in 1851 the world was treated to the awesome spectacle of architect Joseph Paxton's London Crystal Palace Exhibition Building. Two years later New York City was witness to another Crystal Palace Exhibition, which was built on the present site of Bryant Park on 42nd Street. The style lent itself successfully to the construction of the dome of the U. S. Capitol, completed in 1865, and to numerous railway train sheds around the world. Many of those expansive iron and glass stations are still in use today.

Cast iron, however, achieved its greatest popularity here in the United States during the period 1860–90, when more commercial buildings with iron fronts were built in New York City than anywhere else in the world! A surprising number of these structures still stand, and can be found within the one-half-square-mile area shown on the map.

Recognizing the importance of cast-iron architecture to the growth and development of the city, as well as its aesthetic and historic importance, the New York City Landmarks Preservation Commission in 1973 designated this 26-block area as the SoHo Cast-Iron Historic District—the first such commercial district to be so named. "SoHo" is an acronym for the area *So*uth of *Ho*uston Street. Although still a commercial neighborhood, it has become in recent years a popular center for artists and sculptors who find the high-ceilinged loft buildings ideal for studios and workshops. The influx of these artists has given the area a new dimension, demonstrating that with imaginative zoning, industry and art can coexist successfully.

Until the end of the 18th century the area was largely rural, difficult to reach by road from the lower city because of extensive marshland. With the filling in of the Collect Pond, the draining of Lispenard's Meadow, and the subsequent paving of Broadway to Astor Place in 1809, the character of the area soon changed to middle-class residential. By 1825 it had grown to be the most populous ward in the city, with a large freed-slave population. Large, fashionable retail emporiums established themselves along Broadway with such familiar names as Arnold Constable, Lord & Taylor, and Tiffany's; while elegant hotels were erected alongside. For years to come, such hotels as the St. Nicholas, the Metropolitan, and the Prescott House were synonymous with extravagance and luxury. An array of theaters and music halls soon followed, and by 1850, the Bowery was displaced by Broadway as the entertainment center of the city. It also became one of the biggest red-light districts in town.

But the glitter and gaiety lasted only ten years. Keeping pace with the northward growth of the city, the entertainment district moved up to 14th Street, and what was left of the former residential section gradually disappeared. In its place came large textile and other mercantile establishments, which commissioned the construction of new buildings, selecting for the most part the new cast-iron front designs. For the next 30 years some of the largest and most prestigious textile firms in the country were housed side-by-side in those cast-iron "palaces" whose surviving Renaissance façades are reminiscent of Venice's Grand Canal. By the early 20th century, the industrial pattern changed again, as the district became New York's millinery manufacturing center. And with the felt hatmakers came the fur and feather processers to add the essential details to milady's headgear. Until recently the area was devoted exclusively to diverse light manufacturing and to warehousing; but with the rapidly growing colony of artists, it is acquiring a new and charming atmosphere not seen in any of the city's other commercial districts. Many claim that SoHo has now replaced Greenwich Village as the center of artistic creativity.

CHARACTERISTICS OF CAST-IRON CONSTRUCTION. In a masonry building, the weight (load) is borne by the exterior and interior walls, which must be built correspondingly thicker as the height increases. On the other hand, in pure iron construction, the load is borne by a skeleton of vertical and horizontal rolled-iron beams, with the exterior brick walls attached to the framework, serving only as a "skin." The cast-iron parts making up the façade are then attached to the street wall. Cast iron, in effect, anticipated

The aesthetics of cast-iron architecture are shown to advantage in the Dittenhoffer Warehouse, 427–429 Broadway, erected in 1870. (Photo by author)

the principle of modern skyscraper construction, where similar "curtain walls" surround a structural steel framework.

Cast iron was employed not only functionally, but decoratively as well. Each iron foundry employed its own architect who designed the building details. At first architects imitated the style of stone buildings, copying in cast iron the ornate French and Italian Renaissance motifs which were so fashionable in the mid-19th century. Some went so far as to add sand to the beige-colored paint to give the finished product the look of rough stone. It is interesting to note that after cast iron achieved widespread popularity, many builders copied the Palladian cast-iron fronts in masonry! It is therefore difficult at times to visually determine whether a façade is of iron or stone . . . unless, of course, one has a magnet handy.

Later architects developed their own particular style, which will be examined on the tour. Most of the iron-front buildings erected from the 1850s through the mid-1870s were essentially Renaissance in style, followed by the influence of the French Second Empire. The French neo-Grec style, characterized by incised floral and geometric designs, using slender columns and mostly Ionic capitals, became popular in the 1880s. By the '90s, cast iron was falling out of fashion, and only an occasional example can be found. Structural steel was developed, and skyscraper architecture followed.

Representation of the first cast-iron building erected in 1848–49 at the corner of Centre and Duane Streets by James Bogardus for his Eccentric Grinding Mill. (Museum of the City of New York)

There were many advantages to the novel cast-iron medium. In 1835 New York suffered a disastrous fire that literally burned off most of the southern tip of Manhattan. Again in 1845 another conflagration, this one consuming 300 buildings! Less combustible building materials were sought (masonry was expensive), and cast iron seemed to offer the solution. It could only be melted in a blast furnace. It was also lightning-proof—the iron framework acting as a "Faraday's Cage," conducting the electricity safely to the ground. Cast iron was lighter and cheaper than stone, and much cheaper to erect. It could be mass-produced from standardized molds—the iron parts being interchangeable and easily replaced from the foundry's catalog. Cast iron, once painted, was weatherproof and required little maintenance. The building's appearance could be "renewed" with a different color paint. Iron's coefficient of expansion and contraction was similar to that of the brickwork to which it was attached, obviating the danger of separation under extremes of weather. In addition, an iron framework had greater structural integrity than other building materials, and could withstand stresses that would collapse wood or stone structures. A particular advantage was the space gained by the elimination of massive bearing walls. With a cast-iron façade, large windows were now possible for the first time, affording light and ventilation hitherto impossible. Finally, the simplicity of erection was such that an iron front could be raised almost overnight, with no more tools than a wrench, much like a child's Erector Set, since all parts were fastened together with nuts and bolts.

There were, however, some disadvantages. Although the builders described cast-iron structures as fireproof, in many cases they were not. Flooring, beams, joists, and staircases were frequently made of wood; and while a fire would not damage the cast-iron front, it would gut the interior. Cast iron, although highly compressible, was brittle, lacking the tensile strength of modern steel. The iron panels, which could withstand the heat of a building fire, would often crack under the shock of cold water from the firemen's hoses.

The success of cast iron as a structural and architectural medium is credited to two contemporary engineers, Daniel D. Badger and James Bogardus, whose foundries mass-produced the first complete iron-front buildings. Bogardus, who invented the I-beam, built the longest surviving cast-iron building in New York, the famous Edgar Laing Store, which stood on the corner of Washington and Murray streets from 1848 to 1971, about a mile from the Historic District. The store was carefully dismantled when the neighborhood was urban-renewed, to be reerected later on the new campus of the Borough of Manhattan Community College. Measured drawings were made by students in a Restoration and Preservation of Historic Architecture Program of Columbia University, and the pieces were inventoried, all under supervision of the Landmarks Commission. Unfortunately the remains fell

The former Edgar Laing Store, until recently the oldest surviving cast-iron building in New York. Built in 1848 at the corner of Murray and Washington streets, it was dismantled in 1971 for future re-erection. Thieves subsequently made off with most of the iron sections. (Photo by author)

victim to thieves, and most of the parts were stolen—sold as scrap iron! Hopefully, molds will be made from the drawings so that replacement parts can be recast, and the landmark Bogardus building erected again. Bogardus's original warehouse still stands at 85 Leonard Street, a few blocks south of Canal Street.

Badger and his Architectural Iron Works left us with possibly the finest example of commercial cast-iron architecture in America, the Venetian Renaissance-style Haughwout Building, to be seen later on the tour. Completed in 1857, it is the city's oldest surviving iron-front building.

Within a few years at least three dozen iron foundries were busily producing façades and decorations for the hundreds of new buildings going up in the area. The names of these iron works can be seen embossed in the base blocks of many of these structures: *Aetna, Architectural, Atlantic, Cornell, Excelsior, Jackson,* etc. With the lone exception of the Cornell Iron Works, which now casts other iron products, all the original building foundries are now gone. The advent of the "iron age" also brought immortality to architects such as Isaac F. Duckworth, Henry Fernbach, Robert Mook, Jarvis Morgan Slade, Jonathan B. Snook, Griffith Thomas, and Samuel Warner.

The walking tour map indicates *every* building with a complete cast-iron front; however, there are at least as many masonry buildings whose ground floors are full cast iron. Some stone buildings have only cast-iron ornamentation, such as columns, cornices or simply designs. Notice the iron loading docks, light platforms, and sidewalk vault covers. Watch also for old Bishop's Crook lampposts, built of cast iron and once prevalent throughout the city.

Note: A glossary of architectural terms appears on page 159.

BROADWAY TO GREENE STREET (along Canal Street)

The tour begins at Canal Street and Broadway. Named for the drainage ditch that was built in the late 18th century to connect the old Collect Pond with the Hudson River, Canal Street was paved in 1820, and has grown to become one of the city's busiest crosstown thoroughfares.

Walk west on Canal Street to **No. 307–311**. Built in 1856–65 for the Arnold Constable "Marble House" [*see* Ladies' Mile, 29] this stone building is in a good state of preservation. It has an Italianate marble façade on Canal Street, and brick on the Mercer and Howard Street sides. Note the second-story round-arched windows with decorative keystones, flanked by pilasters with Corinthian capitals. The windows on the third through fifth floors are topped by segmental arches. Above the fifth-floor windows, paired volutes rise toward the center, forming a modified pediment. The building is capped by a simple cast-iron cornice. Walk around this old department-store building and compare the three façades; then continue west on Canal Street to Greene Street and turn right (north).

The Arnold Constable Store, called the "Marble House," was erected in 1856 when the firm moved to Canal and-Mercer Streets, to open one of the city's most elegant dry goods emporiums. Constructed of brick and stone, the Italianate building survives today in a surprisingly good state of preservation. (The Edward W. C. Arnold Collection, lent by the Metropolitan Museum of Art. Museum of the City of New York)

CANAL STREET TO WEST HOUSTON STREET (along Greene Street)

Greene Street, named after Revolutionary War hero General Nathanael Greene, was opened just after the turn of the 19th century. It is still cobblestoned (they are actually called Belgian blocks), and boasts the largest aggregation of cast-iron buildings in the world! The view up the street is virtually unchanged in a hundred years. On a Sunday, when few automobiles are to be seen, only the modern lampposts and the buildings' fire escapes give any hint that we are not walking up the street in the year 1876.

The row of ten buildings on the east side of the street, from No. 8 through No. 32–34, is the longest continuous row of such iron-front buildings anywhere. **No. 8** dates from 1883, and **Nos. 10–14** from 1869—all four designed by architect Jonathan B. Snook. **Nos. 16** and **18,** built in 1882, and **No. 20–26,** built in 1880, were designed by Samuel Warner. In front of No. 10–12 is the original iron stoop and light platform, which was converted into a loading platform. Note the glass circle lights on the risers. These glass disks also permitted sunlight to illuminate the basement. The system was invented by Thaddeus Hyatt in 1845 for installation in sidewalk vaults, and is still to be seen throughout the city. Note the founder's mark, S. B. Althause & Co., on the vault covers.

Warner also designed **No. 15–17,** across the street, in 1894. A rather late cast-iron building, its "flattened" façade shows the simpler style that supplanted the earlier ornate Renaissance motifs. There is a Cornell Iron Works trademark at the base. Adjacent **No. 19–21** is by Henry Fernbach, and was built as a warehouse in 1872.

No. 23–25, designed in a French Renaissance style by Isaac F. Duckworth (1873), is particularly impressive with its triangular pediment with delicate finials set over two central bays, its iron moldings, partially fluted columns, and stylized Corinthian capitals topped by a symmetrical cornice line. There are rosette designs in the frieze panel and two flanking vertical rows of quoins that extend from the base of the building to the cornice.

The block, however, is dominated by **No. 28–30** on the east side of the street, designed in 1873 by Duckworth (who had a strong predilection for the French Second Empire style) for Picaut, Simon & Capel Company. Note the immense mansard roof with central pavilion, dormers, half-round attached columns, bell-shaped capitals, keystoned and segmented arches over wide windows, and projecting central bays which give a dramatic third-dimensional effect—to say nothing of the effect of the bright blue coat of paint! Notice, too, the light disks in the iron vault covers surrounded by six metal studs. The risers have circle lights with hexagonal frames. What was formerly the stoop now serves as a loading platform. Except for the removal of the acanthus leaves from the columns' capitals, this imposing building is in as pristine condition as the day it was built!

No. 32, with a small bonnet cornice, is another Duckworth building (1873). Its neighbor, **No. 34,** by Charles Wright, and built the same year, continues the cornice line.

No. 31, across the street (George W. DaCunha, 1876), is interesting because of its neo-Grec details. Note the three square-topped windows on each floor, the freestanding Corinthian columns, flanking pilasters with neo-Grec designs on the terminal blocks at each floor's cornice level, and the repeating rosettes and concave brackets on the entablature. The building, unfortunately, is in a sad state of decay and its future is uncertain. There is another identical building by the same architect at 74 Grand Street (to be viewed soon).

Turn east briefly on Grand Street.

Nos. 91 and **93** (Jonathan B. Snook, 1869), are quite unusual in that their façades are not copied from the Renaissance or French Second Empire styles but cast in the appearance of ashlars (large masonry panels). At first glance one would take these for stone buildings. A dead giveaway is the "J. L. Jackson & Bro. Iron Works" label at the base.

Return to the corner of Grand and Greene streets.

No. 83–87 Grand Street (on the southwest corner) is a rather large

The remains of the once opulent St. Nicholas Hotel, this pair of stone buildings at
521 and 523 Broadway. Completed in 1854, the hotel was second in luxury only
to the Astor House downtown. (Photo by author)

Looking north on Greene Street near Broome Street in the heart of the Soho Cast-Iron District where an almost unbroken panorama of cast-iron buildings presents itself. (Photo by author)

James Bogardus's only surviving iron-front building, his former warehouse at 85 Leonard Street, erected in 1862. (Photo by David Bishop)

The old New York Life Insurance Company building at 346 Broadway at Leonard Street, built in 1870 from plans by Griffith Thomas, still stands but is hardly recognizable from this early engraving. A turn-of-the-century addition by McKim, Mead & White added nine floors, a clock tower, and winged globe (now removed). The company moved to Madison Square in 1928. (New York Life Insurance Company)

An 1870s steel engraving showing the lavish interior of the New York Life Insurance Company building at 346 Broadway. (New York Life Insurance Company)

The Greene Street side of this neo-Grec style cast-iron building at 112–114 Prince Street is painted, simulating rows of windows—a pleasant solution to a blank brick wall. (Photo by author)

An 1865 advertising poster for Daniel D. Badger's Architectural Iron Works, located between 13th and 14th streets, Avenues B and C. (Museum of the City of New York)

structure in a modified neo-Grec style, designed in 1872 by William Hume. The date appears conspicuously over the central bays. The iron for this former silk warehouse was cast by the firm of Lindsay, Graff & Megquier (see label on base).

Across the street, **No. 80–88** Grand Street (B. W. Warner, 1873) was built for a large importing and commission merchant. **No. 78,** alongside was designed in 1882 by Robert Mook.

No. 72 and **74** (1885), as well as **No. 68–70** (1887) on the northwest corner of Wooster Street, are by George DaCunha who favored the neo-Grec style. In the latter building, a high cornice is set on paired concave brackets above three wide pilasters.

No. 71–73, on the southeast corner (Mortimer C. Merritt, 1879, corner section 1888), demonstrates how a cast-iron front permits the use of large plate-glass windows. Set between fluted Corinthian columns on paneled bases, the ground floor presents a light and expansive appearance. Each floor has its own cornice, partitioned by ornamental blocks. The bays are framed by smooth pilasters topped by stylized neo-Grec capitals with incised floral designs. The relief panels above the fourth floor serve as a transition to the splendid upper cornice with its paired elongated brackets above each column and similarly elongated modillions. Merritt was the architect of the great Hugh O'Neill Department Store, which still stands on Avenue of the Americas between 20th and 21st streets [*see* Ladies' Mile, 15].

Return to Greene Street and turn left (north).

No. 37–43 (Richard Berger, 1884) is undistinguished and has lost its cornice.

No. 45 (J. Morgan Slade, 1882) is another typical neo-Grec-style ironfront building. The pilasters and columns are topped by Ionic capitals. Note the egg-and-dart molding above the windows, the deep columnar base blocks and connecting panels, and the architrave above the ground floor in the form of a scrolled grillwork strip. The economy of cast-iron construction can be seen in the similarity of sections on each floor—all cast from the same mold.

Although **No. 49** is a stone building, its street number is a lovely cast iron plaque set into a fluted iron column. Look for D. D. Badger's "Architectural Iron Works" label on the plinth.

Across the street, **Nos. 42–44** and **46–50** are both masonry buildings that have attractive ornamental ironwork details. The former has an iron store front with fluted columns and pilasters. Its neighbor to the north is far more ornate. Observe the twin iron pilasters on the ground floor with bolted-on scrollwork and medallions, and the small stone pediment on the second floor. With all the surviving details on the lower façade, one can only speculate on the appearance of the now-missing cornice.

Turn left (west) on Broome Street.

Named for the lieutenant governor of New York State in 1806, Broome Street is somewhat wider than its parallel neighbors, as it was a major east-west artery in former times. It is still heavily traveled as an alternate route to the west side.

One of the best preserved cast-iron "palaces" in the city is the imposing Gunther Building, on the southwest corner, **No. 469–475** Broome Street. A Griffith Thomas masterpiece, it was built by the Aetna Iron Works in 1871–72 as a warehouse for William H. Gunther, a leading furrier. (The building that housed his old showroom still stands on the west side of Broadway just south of 23rd Street, near Madison Square.) Among its outstanding features are the impressive curved corner with unusual curved windowpanes flanked by columns of quoins, the bold cornice at each floor level, the rows of flat-arched windows, and a simple but firm roof cornice supported by heavy brackets over symmetrical rows of pilasters. The protruding pedestal blocks on both sides of the "Gunther Building" plaque once supported life-size statues (draped in furs?). A balustrade, similar to the one on the second floor, once graced the roof cornice. A significant architectural feature—handed down by the Ancient Greeks—is the foreshortening of each successive story. By progressively diminishing the height of each floor, an illusion of greater height is achieved. The Aetna Iron Works was located in former times at 104 Goerck Street, near the corner of Grand Street, on the Lower East Side. Goerck Street has long since disappeared, demapped for a large housing project.

The adjacent building to the west, **No. 477–479,** was erected in 1872–73 by the Excelsior Iron Works from plans by Elisha Sniffen. A very classical building in the French manner, it was built for the Cheney Brothers Silk Mills. While the neighboring Gunther Building has a uniform treatment of the windows, this building shows great variety. Some bays are flanked by engaged columns with Corinthian capitals, others are capped by keystones, and still others are decorated with balustrades. Twin pediments surmount a bracketed cornice, giving the structure an appearance of great width. No. 477 has a four-step iron entrance stoop while 479 has five steps. Note the circle lights surrounded by six raised metal studs, and the name of the iron works.

Across the street, **No. 470** is a typical Griffith Thomas building in stone, completed in 1867. The ground-floor columns and the entablature, however, are of cast iron.

No. 472–474 was built by Thomas two years later, and was probably one of his last stone buildings, for from late 1869 on, he devoted himself exclusively to cast iron.

No. 476–478 is still another Griffith Thomas building (1872), now representing his cast-iron period. L-shaped, it wraps itself around No. 480 to become No. 62 Wooster Street, around the corner. Typical Thomas touches are a cornice line at each floor, flattened window arches, flanking three-quarter round Corinthian columns in the center section with connecting balustrades, and flat pilasters at the sides of the façade.

No. 480 was designed by Richard Berger in 1884.

Return to the corner and continue east on Broome Street.

Situated in one of the finest cast-iron blocks in the district, **No. 465–467** Broome Street is another product of the Aetna Iron Works and was designed by Isaac F. Duckworth in 1872. The beauty of the building is severely diminished by the ground floor "modernization."

The stone building at the northwest corner of Broome and Greene streets, **No. 464–468,** designed in 1860 (architect unknown), was built for Aaron Arnold of the Arnold Constable emporium. Nine bays wide on Broome Street, it is divided into three sections of three windows each. The two-story high columns flanking the windows are in the "sperm candle" style, for they resemble candles made from whale's sperm oil. (More buildings, in both iron and stone, employing the "sperm candle" feature will be seen later on Broadway.) The graceful, fluted iron columns on the ground floor were cast by the nearby Nichol & Billerwell Foundry on West Houston Street. The building is extremely handsome, and was a prototype for many later cast-iron copies.

No. 461 (1871) is another Griffith Thomas "iron-fronter."

Still in "Griffith Thomas Territory," **No. 457–459** (1871) is somewhat simpler than the adjacent corner building. Quoined pilasters are set at each end of this six-story, six-bay edifice. The windows are separated by modified Doric columns with egg-and-dart and floral motif moldings above. Note the balustrade at the bases of the second-story windows. Above the cornice is a rather large pediment.

No. 453–455 (Griffith Thomas again, 1872–73) was built for the Welcome G. Hitchcock silk and veilings store. Two of Hitchcock's early partners were Aaron Arnold and James Constable. Five stories of foreshortened Corinthian columns, wide flat-arched windows, a cornice line at each floor, and quoined pilasters flanking the end bays give a bold look to this well preserved cast-iron building. Lightness and charm result from the delicate Corinthian capitals, the second-story balustrade, the floral motifs, and the intricate modillions and brackets under the ground-floor and roof cornices. Above the fifth floor is a classic attic that once sported finial-tipped cast-iron urns.

At the southwest corner of Broome and Mercer streets is the stem of a 19th-century cast-iron lamppost. When returning to Greene Street look for another on the southeast corner. Many of the city's older fire alarm boxes are also made of cast iron.

No. 448, on the north side of Broome Street, just beyond Mercer Street, is an outstanding cast-iron creation. Designed in 1871 by the firm of Vaux & Withers, it has a style of ornamentation not seen elsewhere in the city. Capped by delicately ornate friezes and outlined by pellet moldings, the windows with their flanking triple groups of colonnettes are the most unusual feature of the building. The fifth-floor windows are subdivided into round-arched

The "Queen" and "King" of Greene Street cast-iron architecture; (left) No. 28–30, in Second Empire style; (right) No. 72–76 in Renaissance style, both designed by Isaac F. Duckworth in 1873. (Left, photo by author; right, New York City Landmarks Preservation Commission)

groups of two, separated by colonnettes. The intervening spandrels repeat the floral motifs. Observe the striking entablature with its rosettes set in panels in a concave architrave and the upper frieze; while "sprouting" from the fifth-floor colonnettes are elaborate brackets. One cannot but condemn the first-floor alterations. Calvert Vaux and Frederick Clark Withers designed the landmark Jefferson Market Courthouse (now Library) in Greenwich Village [*see* Greenwich Village, 34]. Vaux also teamed up with Frederick Law Olmsted to give us Central Park and Prospect Park.

Returning to Greene Street, note **No. 458,** a three-bay stone building between Mercer and Greene streets. Built in 1867 by David and John Jardine, who shortly thereafter were "converted" to the cast-iron medium, the structure has interesting molded drop-lintels over the windows whose keystones incorporate an incised fleur-de-lis. The ground floor stone entablature, and its row of columns beneath, divides the building into two distinct sections. The decorative main entablature is of cast-iron capped by a raised, curved pediment. It appears that this former store and warehouse is a kind of structural parasite as it has no side bearing walls of its own, and relies on its two stalwart neighbors for support. D. and J. Jardine ten years later designed the palatial B. Altman Store that still occupies the northwest corner of Avenue of the Americas and West 18th Street [*see* Ladies' Mile, 10].

Turn right (north) on Greene Street.

The block from Broome to Spring Street has no fewer than 13 full iron-front buildings, representing the height of cast-iron architectural development.

No. 58–60 (1871) is one of nine buildings in the block designed by architect Henry Fernbach.

No. 62–64, erected one year later, is also by Fernbach. Observe how the first-floor columns are fluted on the lower section and topped by Ionic capitals. Each floor has its own entablature with Tuscan columns separating the four central bays. The ornamental double brackets in the roof entablature are a very dominant feature. The restrained curved pediment above the cornice shows the date of construction.

In front of No. 62–64 is one of the few remaining **"bishop's crook" lampposts.** The lamppost weighs 835 pounds, almost twice that of today's modern aluminum tubular posts. The base shows the ornate fluting, acanthus-leaf motif, rosettes, and egg-and-dart elements. In the "crook" above is the traditional curlicue known as a *feuille rinceau,* French for curling leaf. The next time you pass an older fire-alarm box, note the cast-iron flambeau above and the palmetto-leaf design on the shaft.

No. 66 (Jonathan B. Snook, 1873) was built as a store for the Lorillard (tobacco) Company. **No. 68,** identical in appearance, is also by Snook, and was built later in the same year.

Across the street, **No. 65 and 67** (1872) are another look-alike pair, although the former is by Jonathan B. Snook, and the latter by Henry Fernbach. It appears that both buildings were ordered from the same catalog.

Looking to the east side again, we are confronted by the most regal cast-iron building in the block, **No. 72–76,** known as the "King of Greene Street." Considered to be the finest example of French Renaissance style in the district, this masterpiece was designed by Isaac F. Duckworth and completed in 1873 for the Gardner Colby Company, whose initials can be seen on the pilasters. From its pedimented portico to its pedimented cornice, this stately "commercial palace" must have been considered the last word in cast-iron elegance. This ten-bay structure gives an imposing third-dimensional effect with its ranks of free-standing Corinthian columns—each group supporting its own cornice, with projecting centrally paired bays, as well as side bays that are set off on rusticated piers separated by Ionic pilasters. The broken pediments over the entrance and on the roof with their ornate iron urns further accent the central projection. In the roof pediment are decorative birdlike ornaments topped by a fleur-de-lis motif.

No. 69–71 on the west side (Henry Fernbach, 1876) is identical to **No. 73,** its next-door neighbor. Both were erected at the same time, designed by the same architect, are from the same Cornell Iron Works foundry . . . and were built for the same owner! **No. 75** is another member of the family, with only minor differences in the façade. **No. 77** is a "younger brother," completed in 1878 as the office for the Jennings Lace Works, the firm that introduced Chantilly, Point d'Alençon, and Breton lace to this country. And **No. 81** is the fifth member of the Fernbach family, built in 1877.

No. 80–82, on the east side, was built as a store and warehouse (Griffith Thomas, 1872).

No. 84–86 (122–124 Spring Street) is a Henry Fernbach building in stone (1883), with brickwork trimmed with cast-iron ornamentation. It has an interesting, restrained façade with such features as wide stone window lintels and sills, segmentally arched lintels with keystones on the sixth floor, with alternating soldier courses of brick under each window.

(For a glimpse of two surviving Federal-style residences that somehow remained relatively undisturbed since they were built in 1819, turn left [west] on Spring Street to Nos. 156 and 146. Both still retain their peaked roofs, dormer windows, and original doorways.)

Turn east on Spring Street.

On the north side of the street are a trio of late-1870s iron buildings. **No. 119** (1878) is by Robert Mook, **Nos. 115–117** and **113** (1878) are by Henry Fernbach. Typical of the Fernbach touch are the separate cornices on each floor ending in a heavy terminal block supported by double brackets, windows flanked by columns with egg-and-dart molding, plus paneled pilasters delineating the buildings.

At the northwest corner of Mercer Street stands the **oldest•house in the neighborhood, No. 107,** built *before* 1808! Its brickwork has been covered by stucco, but it shows its splayed lintels and keystones over the windows.

Across Mercer Street, on the northeast corner, is lovely **No. 101** (Nicholas Whyte, 1870). See how the expanses of plate glass, framed by slender columns, give it a light and airy look. Unusual decorative motifs appear in the clustered corner columns, which rest on piers with a unique rectangular design. Bizarre motifs also appear in the corners of the upper windows, while the ground-floor columns have ball-shaped capitals. The whole is an outstanding example of the success of cast iron as a functional and decorative medium. The building is now occupied by a sculptor.

Adjacent **No. 99** (D. and J. Jardine, 1871), a brick structure with an iron storefront, was built as a hotel. It has several architectural features worthy of note: all the windows have cast-iron drop-lintels with a spiral molding and foliate design; above the storefront windows, two panels of stained glass still survive; and the roof displays an intricate iron cornice.

Return to Greene Street and turn right (north).

On the west side, **Nos. 93–95, 97,** and **99** are all neo-Grec-style buildings designed in 1881 by Henry Fernbach. At the base of the second-story windows is a row of vertically incised panels with a neo-Grec motif that, from a distance, simulates a balcony.

Across the street, **No. 96** is by Henry Fernbach (1879), while **Nos. 98** and **100** are by Charles Mettam (1880). The latter two are identical although built for different clients. The pair are flanked by two designed by Fernbach. Both Mettam and Fernbach were contemporaries, and quite similar in taste, but Mettam's work is lighter and somewhat more imaginative.

No. 103–105 (Fernbach again, 1879), occupying a double lot, was formerly one-third larger. **No. 101,** originally an iron-front building, was rebuilt in 1957 after a fire. The three central bays are framed by Corinthian columns, and each floor has a simple molded cornice. In spite of its present asymmetry it is a pleasing Fenrbach building.

No. 112 across the street (1883) is another in the Fernbach line, but its neighbor, **No. 114–120** is a superlative example of his work. Occupying four lots, it is six stories high and ten bays wide. It was built in 1881 as a branch of the Brooklyn-based Frederick Loeser Department Store (which went out of business shortly after World War II). This is an appropriately elaborate building with a typical Fernbach cornice and entablature. The ground-floor piers are quite ornate, as is the treatment of the broad square windows, which are separated by fluted Ionic columns. Note the different arrangement of the top floor, with segmentally arched lintels separated by columns with egg-and-dart motifs. Imitation fanlights appear between the cornice brackets. Dominating the cornice are stylized acanthus-leaf antefixes located above the pilasters in the middle and at the ends.

(For refreshment, there are a number of restaurants on Prince Street, running the gamut from prosaic diners to organic food establishments.)

Turn right (east) on Prince Street.

No. 102–104 (Henry Fernbach, 1881) was also built for Frederick Loeser & Company, and was connected to No. 114–120 Greene Street in the rear. **Nos. 100** and **96–98** were also designed by Fernbach and completed in 1882.

Now turn west on Prince Street to No. 112–114.

By now you must have noticed the spectacular *trompe l'oeil* painting covering the entire east wall of the building. The details are so accurate, and the visual effect so realistic, that passers-by often fail to realize that an entire wall of windows has been painted, complete with all the traditional cast-iron details, where none exists. The painstaking work even includes a window air conditioner and a cat! The painting was done by artist Richard Haas with the assistance of City Walls, Inc. Much of the building is occupied by the SoHo Center for Visual Artists. This is a rather late cast-iron building in neo-Grec style (Richard Berger, 1889), and the only full cast-iron building on the south side of the block. Among its graceful elements are the banded pilasters at each end of the building, fluted colonnettes with neo-Grec capitals flanking the windows, lintels with acanthus-leaf designs, an entablature dividing each story,

Iron foundries took pride in their prefabricated cast-iron buildings, and frequently mounted a distinctive builder's plaque at the base. (Photos by author)

and each cornice surrounded by incised terminal blocks and elaborate brackets. Above, the raised pediment encloses a fanlight motif.

The corner building, **No. 109–111** Prince Street, is discussed later as No. 119 Greene Street. **Nos. 113–115, 117–119,** and **121** share a common façade. The three were designed by Cleverdon & Putzel for the Frank Seitz Warehouse in 1890. The whole is replete with French Renaissance designs in its frieze motifs, medallions and leaf ornaments. Note how the design changes at each successive story. Only No. 113–115 retains its original entablature; nonetheless, the unity of the group is striking.

Return to Greene Street and turn left (north).

No. 119 Greene Street (Jarvis Morgan Slade, 1882) is beautifully adapted to its corner site. The diagonal bay was once the grand entrance. Slade used French Renaissance motifs very effectively. Note how the projecting cornices separate each floor, and how all architectural features are simply realized. The main cornice is plain, as are the pilasters and window groupings. A circular design appears in the paneled frieze in the entablature.

No. 121–123 (Henry Fernbach, 1882) is doubtless the most ornate structure in the block. With its fluted pilasters with acanthus-leaf design, its columns with ornamented capitals, an elaborate "Fernbachesque" cornice topping the whole, we have a wedding of the architect's skill with the founder's technique.

No. 125 and 127 are twins. The former was one of Fernbach's last works, completed in 1883. The latter is credited, however, to William Baker, and was not completed till the following year. Possibly Baker was an associate of Fernbach, carrying out the design after his death. Again we have the typical Fernbach style: pilaster moldings with egg-and-dart; fluting; acanthus-leaf and pellet details separating the two buildings; and the cornice above also ornamented with egg-and-dart, as is the upper frieze with rosettes.

Across the street, No. 130 (Richard Berger, 1888) is an almost perfect example of the neo-Grec style. The designs on the pilasters and pier capitals are clear and precise. The colonnettes are delicate and topped by huge Ionic capitals with egg-and-dart motifs. They are attached to the building wall by means of a screenlike element, pierced with a stylized flower-and-leaf design. Each story is separated by a simple cornice, and even the upper cornice is simply detailed, supported by curved brackets above the colonnettes and pilasters with a row of dentils under its molding. The slender colonnettes emphasize the verticality of the building and demonstrate the decorative possibilities of cast-iron.

No. 132–134, 136, and 140–142 share a common façade. All are by Alfred Zucker (1885).

No. 142–144 (1871) is another by Henry Fernbach.

No. 146 is a stone building, but still retains its cast-iron vault covers. Note the "S. B. Althause & Co." foundry name on the edge of the covers, and the "Galls & Mark" trademark on the edge of the light platform. The light platform has the typical circle lights surrounded by six metal studs.

Back across the street, Nos. 133–135 and 137 are others by Henry Fernbach (1882).

No. 143, a brick, stone, and iron building, was designed by the architectural firm of DeLemos & Cordes in 1887. Nine years later they drew the plans for the famous Siegel-Cooper Department Store, the world's largest store at the time. Their professional skill can still be admired on the northeast corner of Avenue of the Americas and West 18th Street [see Ladies' Mile, 11].

GREENE STREET TO BROADWAY

Turn right and walk two blocks to Broadway.

No one can ascertain the origin of Houston Street's name. It is either named after early settler Nicholas Bayard's son-in-law, or is an adaptation of the Dutch *huis* and *tuin* (house and garden). The latter seems more likely, since its pronunciation is almost the same (which confounds out-of-towners who can only think of the Texas hero). In any case, it is "HOUSE-ton." The buildings along the south side of the street were razed in 1963 when the thoroughfare was widened.

The enormous building at the northeast corner of Broadway is McKim, Mead & White's **Cable Building.** Designed in 1894 by Stanford White, it was the headquarters of the Broadway Cable Traction Company, whose initials in wrought iron can be seen over the entrance. Above the entrance (611–621 Broadway) are two relief sculptures, and topping the main cornice is a row of antefixes in the typical Greek anthemion design.

Across the street, **No. 620** (John B. Snook, 1858) may be the second-oldest cast-iron building in New York. A gem of the Italian Renaissance *palazzo* style, this delightful former gaslight-fixture factory building has somehow survived intact, except for some ground-floor modifications. The façade, in imitation of rusticated blocks, gives a third-dimensional effect behind the rows of paired, free-standing Corinthian columns. Each pair of fluted columns supports its own entablature and is joined to its neighbor by ornate semicircular arches rich in design. The structure is a tribute to Daniel D. Badger's Architectural Iron Works. A larger version of this delightful structure is the Cary Building, located at 105 Chambers Street, downtown.

A quick glance over your shoulder is all that **No. 623** Broadway requires. It is almost hidden by its larger neighbors, perhaps justly, as little remains of it that is worthy of mention.

No. 622–626 (1882) occupies the site of the former Laura Keene's Varieties Theater, a popular entertainment spot from 1856 to 1881, when it was destroyed by fire. Having suffered the ravages of "modernization," little remains except for the five floors of columns, and a rather attractive upper story. Curved-arch windows with keystones and an intricate cornice give some idea of its original ornamentation. Oddly, the building is unevenly divided into two sections of two and six bays, possibly because it was first planned as two separate entities.

No. 628–630 (1882) was designed by Philadelphia architect Henry Schwarzmann, the supervising architect of the 1876 Centennial Exposition. Built for Henry Newman's New York Mercantile Exchange, it has a rather flat, but pleasing façade, with bamboolike colonnettes and extensive floral designs. The firm name emblazoned across the front adds to the overall effect.

The decorative cornice is made of galvanized iron, and the wrought-iron cresting has disappeared.

Return to Houston Street and continue south on Broadway.

HOUSTON STREET TO CANAL STREET (along Broadway)

Broadway, in the four long blocks south to Canal Street, offers as diverse an array of commercial architecture as can be found anywhere. Virtually every style is represented, in both cast iron and masonry, dating from the period of the late 1850s to the early 20th century. Although the tour is concerned primarily with cast-iron architecture, one should not overlook the great variety of brick and stone buildings—some of which were the forerunners in style of the early cast-iron edifices, as well as those later steel-framework behemoths whose over-ornateness often approaches decadence. As if searching for an architectural style of their own, the enormous commercial loft buildings of the 1890s through the 1900s cling tenaciously to all the old classic motifs, draping themselves in reckless abandon with a profusion of carved stone and terra-cotta adornments, apparently unwilling to face the stylistic demands imposed by the new "skyscraper" heights permitted by structural steel.

With the widening of Houston Street, **No. 600–602** Broadway is now the corner building. Built in 1882 from plans by Samuel Warner, it is another example of the *palazzo* style.

Across the street, **No. 597,** a marble building (John Kellum, 1867), looks so much like a typical early cast-iron building that one is tempted to test it with a magnet. **No. 593** and **591** are also an interesting pair. The former is an attractive Classical-style building dating from 1860, and still shares part of the original cornice line with its neighbor. No. 591, extensively altered about 1900, still has a great deal of charm. The iron doorways and ground-floor window seem to be original. The window treatment, light and cheerful, is varied, particularly in the projecting bay. The sixth-floor entablature has an attractive decorated frieze.

No. 569–575, a brick and stone building (Thomas Stent, 1881), has a cast-iron storefront by the Heuvelman Iron Works (see label at the base).

No. 568–578 (the corner building across the street) is a typical 12-story stone, terra-cotta and brick structure of the mid-1890s, not unlike many in this four-block length of Broadway. It was designed by noted architect George B. Post, who produced buildings of much greater interest: the New York Stock Exchange, City College north campus, the Long Island Historical Society, and the Williamsburgh Savings Bank.

(Look east on Prince Street to the diminutive red-brick Federal style house at the southeast corner of Crosby Street, a remnant of the former residential district of the early 19th century.) On the northeast corner of Broadway, in the mid-19th century, stood the famous Metropolitan Hotel, one of the City's largest at the time.

One of the outstanding architectural achievements of the early 20th century is **No. 561–563,** occupying an L-shaped plot on the southwest corner of Prince Street. Known as the "Little Singer Building," it was designed in 1903 by architect Ernest Flagg as an office and loft building for the Singer (sewing machine) Manufacturing Company. Flagg was also responsible for their famous tower—once the tallest skyscraper in the world—which was located at the corner of Broadway and Liberty Street, until its unfortunate demolition in 1967. One of the most avant-garde uses of iron, the "Little Singer" presents an innovative 12-story façade of cast iron, decorative terracotta panels, and broad expanses of plate glass. Delicate balconies and balustrades with wrought-iron traceries, supported by fragile cast-iron colonnettes, are surmounted by a graceful, lacy arch; while, above, curved wrought-iron brackets support the 11th-story cornice. The Prince Street side has a narrower, but similar façade.

No. 560–566 (Thomas Stent, 1883), a six-story brick and stone building, occupies the entire Prince Street side to Crosby Street. Heavy brick piers flank both the end and center bays; and at the first, second, fourth, and sixth floors, the piers are decorated with floral capitals. Foliated iron pilasters separate the windows, which have curved lintels, and the entablature between each floor has its own foliated frieze.

On the west side of Broadway, **No. 549–555,** in gray granite with cast-iron colonnettes and spandrels, is the massive Rouss Building. Designed in 1889 by Alfred Zucker for Charles Rouss, it stands as a symbol of success of the self-made millionaire who arrived penniless in New York from Maryland shortly after the Civil War. Making his fortune as a wholesale merchant, Rouss attributed his success not only to hard work, but to the opportunities afforded him by Broadway, and in gratitude, he took "Broadway" as his middle name, emblazoning it for all to see in the scrolled pediment above. When an identical section was built in 1900, the roof was altered and the triangular mansardlike attic dormers added. The windows of the façade are divided into groups of three by heavy, quoined pilasters, each window grouping having a pair of intervening, slender colonnettes. Cast-iron spandrels separate each pair of stories. Although the much altered ground floor spoils the unity of the building, it is, nonetheless, a bold and impressive structure.

Nos. 554 and **552,** across the street, are among the oldest on Broadway (Jonathan B. Snook, 1855). Both are of stone and have two-story iron fronts, joined together later in 1897. Note the wide central window on the second floor, the four large console brackets that support the second-floor cornice, the rounded window lintels with incised keystones, and the elaborate upper cornice with its modillions and decorated brackets.

No. 550, alongside, completed in 1854, was formerly the Tiffany & Company store. However, little can be seen of the original façade as it was refaced with cast iron in 1901, probably one of the last such fronts to be erected.

In front of No. 542 is another "bishop's crook" lamppost.

On the west side of Broadway, much altered **No. 545** (1885) is by Samuel A. Warner.

Nos. 537–541 are a pleasing trio in cast iron (Charles Mettam, 1868). If one ignores the remodeled ground floor, the beauty can be seen in the harmonious treatment of the eight-bay façade set off by three-quarter round columns with Corinthianesque capitals and the flat arches with rope moldings. In the spandrels are rosettes above each column. The roof line, however, dominates the building. Above a paneled frieze are three pediments—two curved, and one triangular—supported by scrolled brackets and modillions. Ornate urns further highlight the intricate cornice.

Back across the street, **No. 542–544,** built of marble in 1864, has undergone several modifications; nevertheless the arrangement of the upper floors is quite eye-catching. The bays are separated by Corinthian columns, but on the very top floor they are separated by caryatidlike figures. The cornice, topped by two urns above the outer figures, is supported by large scrolled brackets.

No. 540 (D. & J. Jardine, 1867), built of marble, was once a store and warehouse. It has a most unusual two-dimensional effect created by the flatness of the pilasters, "capitals," window arches, lintels, and keystones—all with carved fleur-de-lis designs. Above the cornice, set in a small semicircular pediment, is the date of construction. Again, one can only speculate on how the motif was handled on the original ground floor.

The northwest corner of Broadway and Spring Street is the site of the luxurious Prescott House, built in 1852.

No. 521–523 is all that remains of the once opulent St. Nicholas Hotel. Completed in 1854, it was one of the most elegant hotels in the city, competing in luxury only with the Astor House on lower Broadway. There is some controversy over who the architect was. Whether it was Griffith Thomas or Jonathan B. Snook, no one knows for sure. The 1000-bed establishment occupied 11 lots from 507 through 527 Broadway, extending to the corner of Prince Street, opposite the Prescott House, which was built two years earlier. During the Civil War, the St. Nicholas was taken over by the War Department as a headquarters, becoming one of the nerve centers of the Union Army. The life of the hotel, however, was relatively short. With the uptown move of the entertainment district, the plush hotels soon followed, and by the mid-1870s it closed its doors. This remaining section of the old hotel is faced with stone, showing only a trace of its former appearance. No. 521 still retains its ornamented moldings, and above each window there is a cornice ledge beneath which some carved designwork is evident. The old cast-iron Corinthian storefront has long since been removed, but the original stone entablature over both halves of the building is still in place. Virtually nothing remains of No. 523's original façade.

No. 513–519, designed by Samuel A. Warner in 1884 (on the site of part of the old St. Nicholas Hotel) is a 13-bay-wide commercial building in the then-popular Queen Anne style. It incorporates newly adopted terra-cotta elements into the building's multicolor façade. Heavy brick pilasters adorned with terra-cotta plaques and topped with ornate capitals divide the bays into three groups between the first, second, and fifth floors. The windows in the outer bays are separated by delicate cast-iron Ionic pilasters, while the center bay sections have iron columns with very ornate capitals. Scrolled brackets supporting the iron cornice alternate with terra-cotta plaques in the frieze. A half-story mansard roof is offset by three pediments—the center one enclosing an elaborate design. The dark red brick throughout is also typical of the Queen Anne style and became very popular in the contemporary Romanesque Revival style of the 1880s.

A "bishop's crook" lamppost stands in front of No. 515.

Nos. 503–505, 507–509, and 511 were all designed in cast iron by Jonathan B. Snook in 1878 to form a harmonious grouping, after the demise of the St. Nicholas Hotel. So many alterations have taken place that only the ornate entablature is really worthy of note. A row of vertical pseudo-brackets stretch across the broad concave frieze below the narrow cornice, with larger brackets topped by neo-Grec terminal blocks above the pilasters supporting the cornice. Note how the capitals have been stripped of their acanthus leaves, with only rusting bolt holes remaining. (Rusted bolts often caused cast-iron ornaments to break off and fall to the street, presenting a serious hazard to passers-by.)

Across the street, No. 502–504, designed by Kellum & Son in 1860, presents a striking façade with its "sperm candle" style. Named after the shape of old whale oil candles, the motif is credited to Daniel D. Badger, whose Architectural Iron Works constructed the original storefront, and who used the design in full cast iron on a building erected in 1861 at 55–57 White Street (two blocks below Canal Street). The smooth white marble columns separate each window grouping into two-story units, forming a giant "double arcade." Under the cornice is a row of "inverse crenelation," and rising above the molded end brackets are small urns. Architecture buffs have long been arguing whether the "sperm candle" style originated in stone or cast iron.

Cross to the southwest corner of Broadway and Broome Street for the best view of the most beautiful commercial cast-iron building in the country, the **Haughwout Building,** at **No. 488–492** Broadway. Referred to as the "Parthenon of Cast Iron Architecture in America," this impressive building was one of the first designated New York City Landmarks. Architectural writer Ada Louise Huxtable said of it: "The Haughwout Store's iron elegance contained all the seeds of the future; its metal façade was to lead in turn to the metal frame; the elevator, combined with the metal frame, was to produce the skyscraper; and its repetitive Palladian rhythms were to become the basis of today's aesthetic of pre-fabricated, mass-produced structural units." In 1856 Eder V. Haughwout engaged architect John P. Gaynor to design an appropriate store and showroom for his china and glassware business. The result a year later was this superb Venetian Renaissance *palazzo*. The finely detailed iron façade was cast by Daniel D. Badger's Architectural Iron Works, and later appeared in his illustrated iron works catalog [*see* Related Bibliography]. Haughwout's chinaware was so highly esteemed that it was used in the White House and was displayed at New York's Crystal Palace Exhibition. He also commissioned Elisha Graves Otis to install a steam-driven passenger elevator—the first of its kind anywhere—which years later was to make skyscrapers feasible, at the same time launching the industrial empire of the Otis Company. The basic design motif, repeated on each level, is a keystoned round-arch set on fluted Corinthian columns, flanked by taller columns supporting a full entablature, with an underlying balustrade in each bay. A delicate cornice rises above several bands of elaborate friezework; and in the center bay of the second floor hangs a large iron clock, now minus its hands. The building is in virtually pristine condition (although a coat of paint would help); the ground floor, so often altered, is completely intact; even the present owners' sign is "authentic." Because of its architec-

Considered to be the "Parthenon of Cast-Iron Architecture" is the landmark Haughwout Building at Broadway and Broome Street. This superb Venetian palazzo was cast by Daniel D. Badger's Architectural Iron Works in 1856, and was equipped with the first commercial steam elevator by Elisha Graves Otis. It is probably the oldest extant cast-iron building in the city, and certainly the best-preserved. (Photo by author)

tural and historic significance, the Haughwout Building has been listed in the National Register of Historic Places.

On the west side of Broadway, **No. 483–485** is a five-story cast-iron building, very simply styled in the classic manner. Designed by Robert Mook in 1869, its cornice line with urns above the pilasters gives it a curious appearance, while the capitals of the columns have a "fake" Doric look, given by the egg-and-dart moldings.

The adjoining **No. 477–479** (H. W. Smith & Sons, 1869), contrasts strongly with its neighbor. A center molded pilaster divides the bays into two distinct groupings. The bays themselves are separated by columns with hexagonal bases and stylized Corinthian capitals. The windows have rounded lintels, and abstract geometric detail decorates the spandrels. Simple cornices separate the upper stories. Note the fine leaf-pattern design on the brackets of the upper cornice.

The Roosevelt Building across Broadway, at **No. 478–482,** is the only surviving Richard Morris Hunt commercial building in New York. The Paris-trained architect also designed the Metropolitan Museum of Art, the base of the Statue of Liberty, the bronze doors of Trinity Church, and the late lamented New York Tribune Building, which dominated Park Row, downtown. This unusual building, owned by Roosevelt Hospital, was built as a store for income-producing purposes in 1873. The visual impact of this original statement in cast iron is often lost on the thousands of riders and pedestrians who pass it daily, as few New Yorkers are in the custom of looking any higher at buildings than ground-floor level. Built to utilize the advantages of iron architecture to the utmost, it resembles no masonry predecessor nor any other cast-iron building either. The enormous front is divided into three main sections by four fluted pilasters at the tall ground floor level and continued by bold Ionic columns for the next three levels. Slender colonnettes separate the triple windows, disappearing behind a curved screenlike tracery arch set over each group. The top floor, which repeats the three-window pattern, is shaded by a broad projecting cornice, now minus much of its former decoration. On each incised pilaster is mounted a large circular escutcheon with the street address in bold numerals. A single section of the building extends back to Crosby Street (No. 40), where its one-third-smaller front is graced with a proportionately scaled version of the Broadway façade.

Nos. 466–468 and **462–464** at the northeast corner of Grand Street combine to form a striking pair. Built from plans by John Correja in 1879, the pair was leased by the large textile importing firm of Mills & Gibb, specializing in linens and laces. An earlier tenant on the site was the Brooks Brothers Store, which during the Civil War established its reputation by supplying uniforms for the Union Army. An interesting variation on the decorative theme is the sawtooth motif that embellishes the window lintels, and the rows of incised banding on the second- and fourth-story entablatures. On the third, fifth, and sixth floors, the pilasters have unique scallop-and-bandwork capitals, with a medallion motif halfway up the shaft. The cornice

Now a vacant lot on the northwest corner of Broadway and Grand Street, the Lord & Taylor store occupied the site from 1860 until fire destroyed it a hundred years later. The firm sold the building shortly after the turn of the century when the retail district moved uptown to "Ladies' Mile." (The Edward W. C. Arnold Collection, lent by the Metropolitan Museum of Art. Museum of the City of New York)

is rather heavy and is supported by brackets, while a row of modillions lines the architrave.

The parking lot across the street is the site of an early Lord & Taylor Department Store (1860–1872). The original Griffith Thomas designed building recently suffered a disastrous fire and had to be demolished. During the Draft Riots of 1863, Lord & Taylor armed its employees for protection against the raging mobs that surged down Broadway (the rioters were dispersed by Union Army artillery about a mile north, at what is now 3rd Street). In 1865, when President Lincoln's funeral cortege moved up Broadway, early photographs depict the store draped in mourning, with merchandise removed from the windows and replaced by seats for the viewing of the procession.

Midway down the east side of the block are **Nos. 452, 450, 446–448,** and **444**—an interesting quartet in cast iron. The two outer buildings (Nos. 452 and 444) are identical (by Schweitzer & Gruwe); while the inner pair (Nos. 450 and 446–448) share a common façade (Jonathan B. Snook). All were completed in the same year, 1877. The flanking outer buildings immediately bring to mind Hunt's Roosevelt Building (at 478–482 Broadway), with their pierced stylized arches and wide spandrel panels, together with the slim colonnettes separating the windows. Crowning the front is a bold projecting cornice decorated with anthemions alternating with raised circular motifs, with neo-Grec console brackets at the ends. Look for the foundry label, which unexpectedly gives the names of the architects along with the Long Island Iron Works. The inner group of buildings is distinguished by quoined pilasters at each end, Corinthian columns defining the window bays and ground floor openings; while above, the entablature is flanked by large console brackets topped by neo-Grec terminal blocks, a common cornice stretches above a paneled frieze, and additional concave brackets with their own incised terminal blocks alternate with the frieze panels. The cast-iron fronts were supplied by the J. B. & J. W. Cornell Iron Works (see label).

Across the street, **No. 447** (architect unknown, 1860) has an iron storefront listed in D. D. Badger's Architectural Iron Works catalog of 1865.

No. 443–445 (Griffith Thomas, 1860) gives a very aesthetic appearance. Rows of pleasing round-arch windows are topped by individual projecting cornice slabs supported by brackets. A projecting balustrade runs along the second floor, with decorative urns at each end. Ornate scrolled brackets support the main cornice, above which a pediment adds the final touch.

Except for No. 441, built in 1876, the entire west side of the block dates from the 1860s.

"The Bank in the Park" at the northwest corner of Howard Street (Eggers & Higgins, 1967) offers a pleasant oasis of restful greenery. In spite of its "pseudo-Williamsburg" style, the effect of the diminutive European-American Bank building and its landscaped plot is quite successful.

Howard Street is named for Harry Howard, a volunteer "fire laddie" of the early 19th century. It was called Hester Street until 1825, which, incidentally, is still the street's name after it makes a small zigzag at Centre Street on its way toward the Lower East Side.

Turn left (east) on Howard Street for a brief glance at **No. 27** and **29.** The former, a modified neo-Grec style building, was designed by Samuel Warner in 1888. No. 29, 20 years its senior, is by the firm of Renwick & Sands. One must look beyond the added fire escape and the dingy atmosphere abetted by the narrow and dark street, to enjoy the profusion of decorative elements. The rolling iron shutter in the center window was a novelty introduced in the "iron age." Amazingly, both buildings' ground floors remain completely intact.

A "bishop's crook" lamppost stands on the northeast corner of Crosby Street.

Return to Broadway and continue west on Howard Street.

No. 48, a stone building with a cast-iron storefront, was built in 1860 as an annex to the Arnold Constable "Marble House" across the street. The façade with its rows of round-arched windows, pilasters, heavy entablature, and elaborate cornice is a typical example of the masonry prototypes of early cast-iron buildings.

No. 50–52 was built in 1860 as a store for a gun dealer. Also a stone building with a cast-iron storefront, it is more imposing than No. 48. The ground level has lovely fluted Corinthian columns, above which are rows of French-style segmental-arch windows in a kind of "recessed" style that creates a flat, two-dimensional effect. The overall restrained appearance ends at the cornice, which is disproportionately ostentatious. During the Civil War, the building became the New York State Soldiers' Depot, a rest home and hospital for troops on leave.

Return to Broadway and turn right (south).

On the southwest corner of Howard Street and Broadway is the exquisite Dittenhoffer Warehouse, **No. 427–429,** built (as advertised in the ornate triangular pediment) in 1870. The success of foreshortening is clearly demonstrated in a feeling of much greater height than would be expected from a five-story building. Architect Thomas Jackson used both Venetian and French motifs to highlight this palatial edifice. Particularly noteworthy is the beautifully ornate façade, as exemplified by the spandrels between the window arches, the decorated column shafts, the Corinthian capitals, the keystoned arches over the windows, and the frieze below the bracket-supported cornice, which repeats the florid details of the spandrels. Except for one remaining show window on the Howard Street side, most of the ground floor has been altered beyond recognition. The foundry label carries the trademark of the Excelsior Iron Works. The corner was the site of the City Hotel from 1852 to 1869.

Adjacent **No. 425,** erected in 1869, is one of architect Griffith Thomas' first full iron-front buildings (Aetna Iron Works). How different from its neighbor are the square-headed windows with curved corners, the unadorned entablatures, the almost bare columns, and the curved broken pediments. It was built for the LeBoutillier brothers who later moved their store uptown, opening one of the most fashionable women's wear emporiums during the gaslit era. [*See* Ladies' Mile, 20].

The tour ends here.

A short walk through the neighborhood from Canal Street to Chambers Street, using Broadway as an axis, reveals a number of additional cast-iron buildings of more than casual interest. A few are listed below. *Except where indicated, all cast-iron buildings are located in the one block west of Broadway.* [*See* street map.]

CANAL STREET: **No. 268** (one block east) and **No. 351–353** (two blocks east).

LISPENARD STREET: **Nos. 48–40.** See also cast-iron decoration on **No. 39–41** (Clark Building).

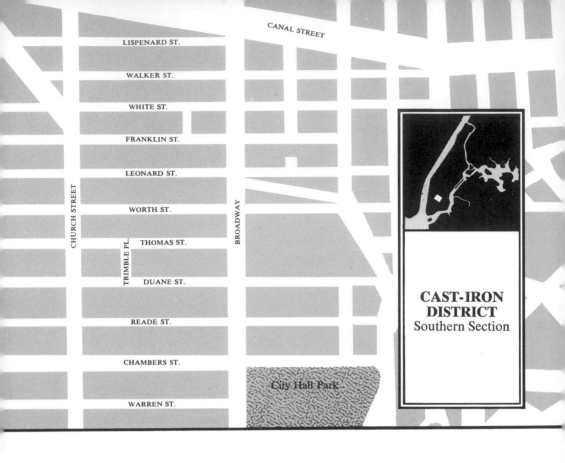

CAST-IRON
DISTRICT
Southern Section

WALKER STREET:	Nos. 57, 49–43, 42.
BROADWAY:	No. 385 (Grosvenor Building).
WHITE STREET:	Nos. 57–55, 60, 41, 37–35 (and the avant-garde Civic Center Synagogue. Not cast iron, but astonishing!).
FRANKLIN STREET:	Nos. 83–85, 86–88 (both east of Broadway).
BROADWAY:	No. 361 (James S. White Building).
LEONARD STREET:	No. 85 (Bogardus's former warehouse).
BROADWAY:	No. 346 (east side). Not cast iron, this was the former New York Life Insurance Company Building.
BROADWAY:	No. 319 (corner of Thomas Street). No. 287 (corner of Reade Street).
READE STREET:	No. 96–100. Walk one block farther to Church Street to admire the Cary Building at No. 89–91. No. 93. Walk south to Chambers Street.
CHAMBERS STREET:	No. 105–107 (the rear façade of the Cary Building). No. 120 (just a bit farther west). The building has an identical façade in the rear at 50 Warren Street.

If you are still interested in cast iron . . .

There is a small but active organization, Friends of Cast-Iron Architecture, which conducts walking tours, sponsors lectures, and fights determinedly for the preservation and restoration of our cast-iron buildings. It is primarily to this group of dedicated cast-iron buffs that credit is due for the designation by the Landmarks Commission of the SoHo Cast-Iron Historic District. (For more information, write to the Friends at 44 West 9th Street, New York, N.Y. 10011.)

GLOSSARY OF TECHNICAL TERMS USED IN THE SOHO CAST-IRON DISTRICT WALKING TOUR

ANTEFIX, an ornament projecting above a roof cornice, frequently incorporating an anthemion motif

ANTHEMION, a conventionalized leaf motif based on a honeysuckle or palmette form, originating in Greek ornamental forms

ARCHITRAVE [*see* ENTABLATURE]

BALUSTRADE, a row of baluster columns topped by a railing, forming a parapet, usually set on a cornice or in front of a window

BAY, the general term for the window section

BEARING WALL, a wall upon which the structural load of a building rests

BRACKET, a projecting L- or S-shaped support used frequently below a cornice, balcony, or projecting sill

    CONSOLE BRACKET, an elongated ornamental bracket, frequently in the form of an S-curve

CARYATID, a decorative column in the form of a female figure

CLASSICAL ORDERS. In discussing the buildings dating from the second half of the 19th century within the Historic District, references to the classical orders must be interpreted loosely. The architects of these buildings took great liberties in adapting Greek and Roman forms to commercial buildings. Reference to a specific order refers only to the capital (the design element at the top of the column shaft).

    TUSCAN CAPITAL, a very simple, unadorned capital, resembling the Doric, but frequently of heavier proportions

    DORIC CAPITAL, a relatively simple capital with a flat topmost member

    IONIC CAPITAL, a capital with spiral volutes beneath its topmost member

    CORINTHIAN CAPITAL, a capital embellished with carved acanthus leaves

    CORINTHIANESQUE CAPITAL, a capital incorporating stylized leaf forms

    COMPOSITE CAPITAL, a capital combining volutes and acanthus leaves (a composite of the Ionic and Corinthian orders)

CONSOLE BRACKET [*see* BRACKET]

CORNICE [*see* ENTABLATURE]

CORNICE SLAB, a cornicelike projection placed above a window

CURTAIN WALL, an exterior wall, separate from the structural framework, that supports only its own weight

DROP LINTEL [*see* LINTEL]

EGG-AND-DART MOLDING, a classical molding consisting of alternating egg-and-dart-shaped forms

ENTABLATURE, the group of horizontal members directly above column capitals. It consists of:

ARCHITRAVE, the lowest member, resting upon the column capitals. An architrave is also occasionally extended to enframe the sides of a door or window opening that is topped by an entablature.

FRIEZE, the middle member of an entablature, which in 19th-century architectural styles is frequently embellished by panels or medallions, and interrupted by large cornice brackets; 19th-century adaptations of classical orders often combine a frieze and cornice without an architrave

CORNICE, the horizontally projecting topmost member of an entablature. It is frequently found by itself as the crowning motif of a façade.

FANLIGHT, a semicircular window placed over a door, with bars radiating from its center like spokes of a fan

FINIAL, an ornamental form at the top of a pediment, spire, pinnacle, etc.

FRIEZE [*see* ENTABLATURE]

IRON VAULT COVERS, a number of iron plates with lights (*see below*) that lie over the vaults, and are on the same level as the sidewalk

KEYSTONE, the central voussoir (block) of an arch

LIGHT, generally, a pane of glass, but in this district it refers to pieces of hardened glass of various shapes, sizes, and colors that are inserted in iron plates

LIGHT-PLATFORM, a flat, raised area in front of the façade of a building that is made up of a number of iron plates with lights, and which stands on the vault

LINTEL, a horizontal member placed over a window or door to support the superstructure

MODILLION, a small ornamental bracket used in a closely spaced, regular series below a projecting cornice

PALAZZO, an Italian "palace," usually associated with those from the Renaissance. When referring to 19th-century architectural styles, however, a *palazzo* can be any large, impressive building whose style was derived from the Italian Renaissance.

PEDIMENT, a low, usually triangular gable constructed in a classical style that is often filled by sculpture and usually framed by a cornice. It is used decoratively to crown central bays, porticoes, and important windows of a façade, and is sometimes segmental in shape or broken away in the center.

PIER, in masonry architecture, an upright supporting member carrying a structural load. When interpreted in cast iron, an exterior pier is, in most instances, merely a solid part of the curtain wall placed between the windows and/or on either side of a façade.

PILASTER, a shallow, flat engaged (attached) column, normally serving only a decorative function

QUOIN, in masonry architecture, large stones used to reinforce a corner or salient angle of a building. When interpreted in cast iron, rusticated quoins were used decoratively to emphasize the flanking piers.

RISER, the vertical member between the treads of a stair

RUSTICATION, in masonry architecture, an emphasis of individual (usually large) stones by recessing their connecting parts

SEGMENTAL ARCH, an arch in which the curvature is a segment of a circle, but less than a semicircle

SOLDIER COURSE, a course (row) of bricks set on their ends

SPANDREL, the space between the outer curve of an arch and its rectangular enframement, or between two adjacent arches and a horizontal member above them

SPANDREL PANEL, in skeleton-frame construction, the wall panel between the head of one window and the sill of a window directly above it

TERMINAL BLOCK, a decorative block placed at the extreme ends of a cornice between floor levels, thus interrupting the quoin lines or flanking piers of a façade

TREAD, the horizontal surface of a step

VAULT, a cellar room used for storage, often extending under the sidewalk

VOLUTE, a spiral or scroll-like form, as with the Ionic capital

VOUSSOIR, a wedge-shaped stone forming part of a masonry arch

LADIES'
MILE
and
FASHION
ROW

c. 1900

Fint &
Horner

James McCutcheon

Western Union
Bldg.

23RD ST.

(19) (20) (21) (22) (23)

Riker's

Ehrich
Bros.

Stern
Bros.

Flatiron Building

(18)

Site of
Best & Co.
and
Bonwit Teller

22ND ST.

Adams
Dry
Goods

Site of
James
McCreery

Sohmer
& Co.

(24)

BROADWAY

(17)

Scribner's

21ST ST.

(16)

3rd
Spanish
& Port.
Cemetery

Hugh O'Neill

Church of
the Holy
Communion

156
Fifth Ave.

(25)

903
5th Ave.

20TH ST.

(15)

(26)

(14)

Lord &
Taylor's

(27)

Simpson-
Crawford

Cammeyer's

150 5th Ave.
Methodist
Book Concern

Gorham
Mfg. Co.

(28)

19TH ST.

(13)

(29)

(12)

Arnold Constable

(30)

W. & J.
Sloane

B. Altman

(11)

Siegel-Cooper

(10)

18TH ST.

17TH ST.

UNION SQUARE N.

SIXTH AVE.

FIFTH AVE.

UNION SQUARE WEST

Union
Square

PARK AVE. SOUTH

16TH ST.

15TH ST.

Dead Men's
Curve

14TH ST.

(9) (8)

(7)

(6)

Macy's

Hearn's

Bau-
mann
& Co.

Rogers
Peet

(Site of Wallack's Theater)

13TH ST.

(5)

UNIVERSITY PLACE

12TH ST.

(4)

James
McCreery

BROADWAY

4TH AVENUE

11TH ST.

Hotel
St. Denis

(3)

Grace
Church

10TH ST.

(2)

Site of A. T.
Stewart
Cast-Iron
Palace

WANAMAKER PL.

9TH ST.

John
Wanamaker

(1)

8TH ST.

start

8. Ladies' Mile and Fashion Row

[*BMT RR Broadway line to 8th Street station; IRT Lexington Avenue line No. 6 train to Astor Place station, walk west one block on 8th Street*]

The department store as we know it today had its genesis in the small wholesale and retail dry-goods shops that began to proliferate along the busier thoroughfares of lower Manhattan during the 1820s. With the upsurge of immigration in the following decades, and the rapid growth of commerce and industry, many keen merchants seized the opportunity to expand and diversify, making fortunes by catering to the changing tastes and increased demands of the burgeoning city. By the 1870s and 1880s, the main shopping center of the city had moved uptown, following the northward growth of the city, to an area between 8th and 23rd streets, along Broadway, and also on Fifth and Sixth avenues. With women shoppers always in the majority, it did not take long before this bustling row of large retail stores was known as Ladies' Mile.

Today not one of those fine old establishments can be found on the Mile. The stores either relocated farther uptown to keep abreast with the inexorable northward tide, or, unable to update their merchandising techniques, closed their doors forever. Astonishingly, most of the buildings that housed those elegant department stores still remain intact, although now occupied by other tenants.

Our itinerary takes us on a "shopping tour" of those glamorous "ghosts" of a bygone era, and, using a little imagination, we can return to the bustling streets of those gaslit days. Listen carefully for the rhythmic clip-clop from the profusion of horse-drawn vehicles and the clatter of their iron-clad wheels on the cobblestoned street, the persistent bell clanging of horsecars caught in the tangled traffic—their impatient conductors exchanging abuse with draymen and carriage drivers—and the shrill cries of "Extra! Extra!" from little boys hawking their penny papers at the street corners. When we reach Sixth Avenue, our walk will take us under the gloomy structure of the old El, whose wooden trains roar by overhead in an endless, ear-splitting clatter, their smoky locomotives spewing hot cinders and oil on the unwary below. Standing stiffly at the entrance portals to the fancy "magazines" that line the Avenue, liveried doormen await the arrival of the "carriage trade," and as a coach draws up, rush forward to escort the affluent patrons to the door. And clustered about the elaborate show windows, we glimpse elegantly clad women in trailing dresses, billowy hats, and frilly parasols, pressing to catch the latest fashions in furbelows, veils, shirtwaists, millinery, and high-button shoes.

1. The tour begins at 8th Street and Broadway, the southerly end of Ladies' Mile. The huge building at the northeast corner was formerly the **Wanamaker Department Store,** now known simply as 770 Broadway. Construction of this 16-story giant began in 1902 and took five years to complete. Designed by Daniel H. Burnham, architect of the Flatiron Building [*see* Madison Square, 24], the structure was planned as a modern extension to the older "Cast-Iron Palace" that occupied the block directly north. John Wanamaker came to New York in 1896 to open a branch of his Philadelphia store, and purchased the old cast-iron building from the successors of the faltering A. T. Stewart Company. Alexander Turney Stewart, who had been considered a merchandising genius, in 1846 opened New York City's first large department store, at Broadway and Chambers Street. Called "The Marble Dry-Goods Palace," the building still stands today [*see* City Hall, 15]. In 1862 he leased a portion of the old Randall Farm in Greenwich Village, and while maintaining his Marble Dry-Goods Palace as a warehouse, built the first large store in what was to become Ladies' Mile. His new emporium, employing the novel architectural medium of cast iron, occupied the entire block from 9th to 10th streets. Each of the six stories was supported by iron beams, the roof area enclosed by an enormous glass dome over a central court. Rows of cast-iron columns lined the façade, permitting sunlight to stream in through the wide intervening Palladian windows. A grand staircase and six steam-driven elevators provided easy access to all shopping floors. The exterior, painted a mottled white, and sparkling like an architectural gem of the Italian Renaissance, was an immediate success.

When Stewart died in 1876, he was the second richest man in America, although his wealth had come mostly from real estate investments. His fashionable emporium, so successful during his lifetime, was now under the management of a former business associate, and the store was renamed Hilton, Hughes & Company. Later it was taken over by a firm called Dennings, and the once-great Stewart store began to founder. It would have gone under altogether were it not for an eleventh-hour reprieve from John Wanamaker who purchased it in 1896. The establishment was completely reorganized, a new building erected alongside (connected to the "Cast-Iron Palace" by a double-decker "Bridge of Progress" and three subterranean passageways, as well as having a direct entrance from the newly built IRT

The great Palladian cast-iron palace which had been the A. T. Stewart Store on Broadway at 9th Street was under the operation of Hilton, Hughes & Co. when this photo was made in 1889. In the distance is Grace Church, the Gothic-style landmark which still stands at Broadway's bend at 10th Street. (New-York Historical Society)

subway station at Astor Place). Business began to boom again, and for nearly half a century the name Wanamaker's was synonymous with the ultimate in department store merchandising.

By 1952, the center of retail trade had moved far away and patronage fell off rapidly. Although the southbound end of the Fifth Avenue Bus line was still called the Wanamaker Terminal, few customers were to be seen getting off. The older store building was vacated and all operations shifted to the newer facility next door. Time was running out for the once-popular Wanamaker Store. Two years later the end came, and all retail business was transferred to a small downtown shop and to their suburban stores. In a rather dramatic exit, the old cast-iron building which occupied the entire block between 9th and 10th streets, fell victim on July 15, 1956 to one of New York's most spectacular conflagrations, blazing out of control for two days in a fiery farewell to the Stewart-Wanamaker enterprise. In a somewhat unglamorous tribute to the old merchant prince, the apartment building that now occupies the site of the "Cast-Iron Palace" is named Stewart House.

2. Grace Church, at the northeast corner of Broadway and 10th Street, is an outstanding example of the Gothic Revival style. This lovely church, built on land formerly owned by Peter Stuyvesant, was designed in 1843 by James Renwick, Jr., when only 23 years of age. Renwick was also the architect of St. Patrick's Cathedral and the Smithsonian Institution, but many consider Grace Church to be his crowning work. Renwick himself was a parishioner and later vestryman. Particularly beautiful are the 46 medieval stained-glass windows and the intimate Chantry. The garden beside the Chantry is the site of the former Fleischmann's Vienna Model Bakery, a popular

Fleischmann's Vienna Model Bakery, at the northeast corner of Broadway and 10th Street, photographed in 1898 by Percy C. Byron. Conveniently located between Grace Church and the former A. T. Stewart Store, it was a European style café which produced its own baked goods and was one of the most popular places of refreshment along Ladies' Mile. (The Byron Collection. Museum of the City of New York)

continental café in the days of Ladies' Mile. Bought by Grace Church and named Huntington Close, after a former rector, the plot adds much charm to the setting. The steeple is illuminated at night and can be seen for miles down Broadway. Among the scores of architecturally notable structures of the city built before 1930, the Municipal Art Society places Grace Church in its first category of seven buildings "of national importance to be preserved at all costs." The church and rectory are designated New York City Landmarks.

The view of Grace Church is a debt to early settler Henry Brevoort, whose family owned the lands where Grace Church now stands. He was so intent on preserving a much loved apple orchard that stood in the way of Broadway's northern march, that he succeeded in forcing the city fathers to divert the street to the west.

3. On the southwest corner of 11th Street and Broadway stands a rather nondescript 19th-century building, whose extensively altered façade masks its former identity. **The Hotel St. Denis,** built in 1848 and renovated in 1875, was one of the more fashionable hostelries in the city. *King's Handbook of New York,* 1893 edition, praises the attractiveness of this 250-room hotel and adds, "The equipments of the house, as to steam heating, electric lighting, ventilating, and hydraulic elevators, are supplemented by a perfect corps of polite and well-disciplined attendants." In its heyday, it hosted Presidents Lincoln, Grant, and Arthur, as well as Sarah Bernhardt, P. T. Barnum, and Col. William "Buffalo Bill" Cody. Probably the most significant date in the hotel's history was May 11, 1877, when Alexander Graham Bell gave a preview demonstration of his telephone to a spellbound audience of prominent guests in the second-floor parlor room. The wire was strung from the hotel across the Brooklyn Bridge. The St. Denis closed in 1917, and shortly thereafter was converted to commercial use. At that time all the adornments were stripped from the façade. Enter at the 11th Street door, walk almost to

The St. Denis Hotel and Taylor's Saloon at the southwest corner of Broadway and 11th Street, c. 1875. It was in the corner parlor room on the second floor that Alexander Graham Bell demonstrated his "speaking telephone" to a group of prominent New York citizens May 11, 1867. The hotel closed in 1917, but the building, much altered, still stands. (Museum of the City of New York)

the bank of elevators, turn right and admire the original cast-iron staircase, as well as a few stained-glass windows.

4. Across 11th Street is the Palladian cast-iron establishment of the former **James McCreery & Co. Store.** Arriving in this country as a 20-year-old immigrant from Ireland in 1845, McCreery started in business opening a small shop selling Irish lace. Gradually expanding to larger quarters, and following the uptown tide, he commissioned architect John Kellum to build this large dry-goods store in 1868. He was reputed to be a kindly, tolerant man, whose flowing white beard and long shock of hair, together with a thick Irish burr, made him a very striking figure. He always showed great concern for the welfare of his employees in an era when social conscience in business was relatively unknown. McCreery, self-educated, became a patron of the arts and dedicated much of his later fortune to philanthropic and artistic causes, including helping to found the Metropolitan Museum of Art.

In 1895 he moved to an even larger building at the northern end of Ladies' Mile, at Sixth Avenue and 23rd Street. The present building miraculously survived years of occupancy by a variety of users, but a few years ago suffered a disastrous fire, which all but sealed its fate. Demolition seemed the only alternative until a developer, sensing the value of such a rare example of cast-iron elegance, converted it into an apartment house. The interior was gutted, but the beautiful façade was restored to its original appearance. Except for the ugly two-story addition on the roof, it looks much the same today as when it was first built. Since the interior vertical iron beams had to be retained, a curious result is that many tenants have an ornate Corinthian supporting column adorning the middle of their living room! This creditable restoration is an excellent example of adaptive (and profitable) reuse.

5. The building with the smooth mansard roof at the northeast corner of Broadway and 13th Street marks the location of the famous partnership of Charles B. Peet and Marvin N. Rogers. Although both gentlemen died before the firm moved into this building, **Rogers Peet Company** had been in business manufacturing men's clothing and army uniforms since 1874 at two previous lower Broadway addresses. A relative latecomer (1902) to Ladies' Mile, the company was the last to leave (1970), moving its executive offices to one of its Fifth Avenue stores uptown.

From 1861 to 1881, the site was occupied by famed Wallack's Theater. John Lester Wallack, who managed the playhouse, was also a leading actor, performing in many of the old comedies and contemporary English dramas which were so popular in the late 19th century. When Wallack's moved to the new Rialto district on 30th Street, the house was renamed the Star Theater (1893) and continued to offer dramatic productions until its razing for the Rogers Peet building.

6. Turn west on 14th Street and pause briefly at **Union Square.** Called "Union Place" in the Commissioners' Plan of 1811, its present attractive layout was not achieved until 1831, a credit to Samuel B. Ruggles who planned nearby Gramercy Park [*see* Gramercy Park, 9]. The name "Union" derives

The equestrian statue of Washington, by Henry Kirke Brown and John Quincy Adams Ward, executed in 1856 and considered one of the finest in America, is seen here at the intersection of Fourth Avenue (now Park Avenue South) and 14th Street. With the advent of the motor age, it was moved into adjacent Union Square. (Museum of the City of New York)

not from Civil War days, nor from any association with the labor unions whose activities were later identified with the Square, but merely from the fact that this was the "place of union" of the Bowery Road with the northern extension of Broadway. Until the early 1860s it had been a beautiful residential district; then business took over the area. The statuary in the Park is particularly worth seeing (return another time, however, for a closer view of the greatest equestrian statue in America and for other great works of sculpture). Gone from the west side of the Square are the well known establishments of Tiffany & Company and Brentano's, as well as the array of piano manufacturers that lined the north side of 14th Street on both sides of Union Square, from Irving Place to beyond Sixth Avenue.

For the Broadway horsecars and omnibuses, making the detour around Union Square presented no problem; but when the later cable cars were installed, a major traffic hazard was created. The forward progress of the Broadway Cable Traction Company's cars was controlled by continuous sections of underground cable laid in a slot between the rails. To negotiate the sharp curve, the operator of the car, called the grip-man, had to get up speed, release his hold on the 14th Street cable section, stamp furiously on his warning bell as the car swung wildly around the bend, then catch the next underground cable section on Broadway. This repeated act of derring-do always attracted crowds of onlookers, and resulted in numerous accidents—some fatal. The spot soon earned the grim appellation, **"Dead Man's Curve."**

7. Continue west on 14th Street, passing the former **Baumann Brothers & Co.** store, at 22 East 14th Street, a large cast-iron edifice whose "modernized" ground floor belies its Classic-style upper façade. Baumann Brothers was a furniture dealer in the Gay '90s and for a time in the 20th century.

8. Midway between Fifth and Sixth avenues, on the south side of 14th

Street (Nos. 34–40), a small vestige remains of what was once a prosperous and dynamic enterprise, **James A. Hearn & Son.** Arriving on 14th Street in 1879 after a brief association downtown with his uncle Aaron Arnold (later of Arnold, Constable & Company), James A. Hearn built up a large dry-goods business, and soon became an aggressive rival of R. H. Macy, then at the corner of Sixth Avenue. The two merchants often indulged in cutthroat competition, to their mutual detriment and the customers' delight. It is said that Japanese silk, a favorite with the ladies of the day, was offered by Macy at 41¢ per yard, whereupon Hearn immediately dropped the price by a few cents; and Macy followed suit. Again and again the price was slashed, until at the next day's closing, the fabric was being "sold" at 11 yards for 1¢!

Son George, who inherited the business on his father's death in 1886, followed the same merchandising path. He, like neighbor James McCreery, was very philanthropic and also became a benefactor of the Metropolitan Museum of Art.

The original building, with an immense cast-iron façade, was many times the size of the present relic. An apartment house to its left now occupies much of the old site, but still remains "tied" to Hearn's by a series of exposed reinforcing girders. For three-quarters of a century Hearn's remained a family "bargain" store. Older New Yorkers still recall the annual mini-riot at the Washington's Birthday Sale, when thousands of bargain-hungry shoppers pushed their way into the store, smashing plate-glass windows and doors, in

The perils of Dead Man's Curve at Broadway and 14th Street are depicted in this woodcut from Harper's Weekly *of March 27, 1897. (New-York Historical Society)*

A rare old photograph of Lord & Taylor's dry goods store at 47–49 Catherine Street on the Lower East Side, just before the move to Grand and Chrystie streets. At this address Samuel Lord founded the oldest retail store in New York in 1826, taking on partner George Washington Taylor in 1838. Judging from the "selling off" signs, the picture by an unknown photographer was probably taken in 1853. (The Consolidated Edison Company of New York)

The business office of the Siegel-Cooper Department Store in a photograph taken c. 1899 by Byron. (The Byron Collection. Museum of the City of New York)

The sales staff of Siegel-Cooper's sheet music counter poses for photographer Percy C. Byron with the latest tunes of 1889. (The Byron Collection. Museum of the City of New York)

An 1861 lithograph of Wallack's Theater, at the northeast corner of Broadway and 13th Street. The site is now occupied by the former Rogers Peet Building. (*Museum of the City of New York*)

The Eden Musée, an amusement hall and wax museum, stood in the middle of the north side of 23rd Street, between Fifth and Sixth Avenues. It was so popular in the gaslight era that all street cars made a special stop at the door. The Eden Musée was opened in 1884 and survived until 1916. Robert J. Horner's Furniture Store is at left. (*The J. Clarence Davies Collection. Museum of the City of New York*)

Simpson Crawford Company occupied the west side of Sixth Avenue from 18th to 19th streets and opened a new building in 1900. In this 1905 view of their unusually large show window, photographer Percy C. Byron captured the latest fashions of the day. The building is still there, although the company closed in 1915. (The Byron Collection. Museum of the City of New York)

Demolition is already in progress on the old James W. McCreery Store on the southeast corner of Sixth Avenue and 23rd Street. Erected in 1884, it replaced the Edwin Booth Theater. The company moved uptown in 1907, and in 1975 its old building was razed. (Photo by author)

Fourteenth Street decked out in patriotic bunting for the presidential election of 1892. The north side of the street, just west of Union Square, displays the signs for at least six different piano manufacturers as this was the music center of the city in the Gay Nineties. Steinway Hall and the Academy of Music were just a few blocks east. (New-York Historical Society)

their stampede to purchase a television set or major appliance for one cent! The store closed in 1955, although it did operate a liquor store for a brief period. Its name is still preserved in a store in the Bronx at East 149th Street and Third Avenue, now run by a department store chain.

9. At 56 West 14th Street, look up above the first floor, and with a little squinting, the faded name of the original occupant, emblazoned on a wide stone panel, can be vaguely distinguished: **MACY'S.** This narrow, Beaux Arts-style building is all that remains of a cluster of buildings that marked the early days of what is now the world's largest department store.

After a brief career as a whaler, Rowland Hussey Macy tried and failed three times to establish himself in the dry-goods business. His fourth attempt in 1858 with a small shop around the corner on Sixth Avenue, "buying and selling for cash," met with more success; and within a few years he acquired several adjacent buildings, connecting them with passageways, and offering a wide selection of merchandise. The store prospered, and by 1877 when Macy died, it had grown to a row of 11 buildings, with an annual sales volume of well over a million dollars. The store's well known emblem, a large red star,

The opening of the Metropolitan Elevated Railroad, later the Sixth Avenue El, gave impetus to the commercial growth of the thoroughfare. Here, along Fashion Row looking north of 18th Street in 1899, flags wave from (left to right) Simpson, Crawford, & Simpson, Hugh O'Neill (with the cupolas) and Cammeyer's, across the street. All have gone out of business, but the buildings remain. (New-York Historical Society)

was adopted by Macy from his arm tattoo, a reminder of his whaling days. The whale motif is also used to promote big sales.

After several changes in management, direction of the store was assumed by brothers Isador and Nathan Straus who earlier had obtained from Macy a concession to operate a china and glassware department. Under their leadership, business boomed, and R. H. Macy & Company became the city's largest department store. Its more than 500 red-and-black delivery wagons could be seen all over town. Using novel sales and advertising techniques, manufacturing many products under its own name, and offering a wide selection of merchandise sold at highly competitive prices, Macy's set the trend for the future retail industry. Its stock ranged in variety from five-cent ice-cream sodas, straw hats, fabrics of all kinds, furniture, men's and women's clothing, to the newly popular bicycle. Bicycles, by the way, were demonstrated by professional riders on a specially designed track where customers could give their own new "wheels" a trial spin. Another innovation, soon copied by other stores, was the annual Christmas toy display—an event that attracted thousands of visitors.

By the turn of the century it became evident that newer and larger quarters were essential. Fourteenth Street's popularity as a shopping center had begun to wane, and in 1901 a site was chosen for a new buidling. Purchasing Oscar Hammerstein's Manhattan Opera House, located on the north side of 34th Street west of Sixth Avenue, Macy's demolished the theater and erected the first of its present buildings, opening its doors three years later.

Turn right on Sixth Avenue (Avenue of the Americas) to the northwest corner of 15th Street, and look back at the old Macy's Store. On the west wall of the building one can still discern part of a 100-year-old advertisement, proudly proclaiming in letters several stories high, "Macy's—World's Largest Store."

Proceed north to the northeast corner of 6th Avenue and 18th Street.

The old Sixth Avenue El, which cast its dark shadows from 1878 to 1940, is now just a memory. Its demolition, however, opened a vista not possible in the gaslit era. Lining both sides of the street in a five-block silent array from 18th to 23rd streets, stand "The Ghosts of Sixth Avenue." Huge, overbearing, and pretentious edifices—in stone, brick, or iron—they evoke the spirit of another day.

10. Across the street (northwest corner of 18th Street), the dark gray, shabby-looking cast-iron building was once **B. Altman & Company**—"The Palace of Trade." From 1877 till 1906, Altman's was the trend-setter of women's fashions, specializing in the finest silks, satins, and velvets. Ceramics and sculpture, too, graced the show windows and shelves, for Benjamin Altman was not only a keen entrepreneur, but a lover of objets d'art. A collector himself, he presented his accumulation of art works, worth over $15 million, to the Metropolitan Museum of Art shortly before his death in 1913.

As the age of the sewing machine had just arrived, women flocked to his block-long emporium in quest of the high quality dress goods that made Altman's famous. Benjamin Altman, a solitary man who remained a bachelor all his life, devoted himself exclusively to his enterprise. He took particular pride in appearances. His home delivery wagons, seen in the more affluent precincts of the city, were rubber-tired, painted a shiny maroon, decorated with brass carriage lamps, and pulled by a matched team of horses driven by a pair of nattily uniformed men. Altman was a considerate employer who shortened the generally accepted 64-hour work week and installed restrooms and a subsidized cafeteria for his workers. In 1906 the store moved uptown to Fifth Avenue and 34th Street, and is still there today—continuing Ben Altman's tradition of selling only quality merchandise and maintaining good employee relationships. Across 6th Avenue stood one of Altman's biggest competitors, Siegel-Cooper & Company.

11. New York was never the same after Henry Siegel arrived from Chicago! Fresh from successful participation in the 1893 Columbian Exposition, he joined with partner Frank H. Cooper to found a profitable department store in the windy city, and now sought to build the greatest one of them all in New York City—which he did in five short months! Six stories high and capped by a tall tower, the block-wide store extended almost to Fifth Avenue. Designed by architects DeLemos & Cordes in a grandiose style reminiscent of the Exposition, the new store was unprecedented in proportions. With great fanfare and a record-breaking crowd of 150,000, **Siegel-**

When the great Siegel-Cooper Company opened its doors in 1896, it seemed that all New York flocked to the event. In this Byron photo, overflow crowds jam Sixth Avenue between 19th and 18th Streets, as el trains bring even more sightseers. (The Byron Collection. Museum of the City of New York)

Cooper & Company opened its doors on Saturday evening, September 12, 1896.

Its motto "The Big Store—A City in Itself" was no exaggeration. Henry Siegel soon earned the reputation as "the father of merchants," for he was shrewd, innovative, and bold. Never before had such a variety of merchandise been seen under one roof. The central feature of the main floor, however, was the Fountain. A circular marble terrace surrounded an enormous white marble and brass statue of *The Republic,* a replica of Daniel Chester French's towering sculpture at the Chicago Fair. Jets of water, illuminated by myriad colored lights, played around the granite pedestal; and from the open "well hole" in the second floor, protected by a mahogany balustrade, customers looked down in awe. The Fountain was not only the prime attraction, but the major rendezvous place for shoppers, businessmen, lovers, and tourists. For Gothamites, "Meet Me at the Fountain" became an institution for years to come. To this day, old-timers will quote the slogan without hesitation when asked if they remember Siegel-Cooper.

Siegel showed great understanding of human nature when he introduced the "free sample," especially in his novel food department. After a round of

The latest styles are worn by mother and children entering the Siegel-Cooper store. Elaborate bronze columns and lanterns flank the Sixth Avenue entrance. (Photograph by Byron. The Byron Collection. Museum of the City of New York)

Siegel-Cooper advertisement in Pearson's Magazine *for September 1908 advertises the latest styles at prices which today seem unbelievable. Note the shirtwaists for only $1.00. (Author's collection)*

taste-tempting goodies, people *did* buy. He also began the very effective demonstrator system, illustrating the possibilities of such disparate items as kitchen gadgets, wing collars, and sheet music. Among other revolutionary ideas, he installed an air-cooling system, which really brought in the masses on stifling summer days; he hired women in many of the sales departments; and he advertised widely in the daily newspapers and on billboards all over town.

But by the first decade of the 20th century the inevitable uptown exodus of the shopping trade had begun again. Henry Siegel, however, had resolute faith in his magnificent palace of retailing. Surely the Fountain would always remain the favorite meeting spot in town. Alas, time proved otherwise, for the crowds were now meeting at Macy's and Altman's, and the great empire was beginning to crumble. A reorganization with the backing of financier Joseph B. Greenhut failed to pump new life into the faltering enterprise, and by World War I, Siegel-Cooper was no more.

The best view of the Big Store is from across Sixth Avenue. Note the intricately designed terra-cotta plaques with the firm's monogram, the huge bronze columns set in dramatic archways, and the overall effect of grandeur.

On the north side of West 17th Street, between Seventh and Eighth avenues, Siegel-Cooper's enormous wagon house and stable can still be seen. It, too, is heavily ornamented with distinctive terra-cotta S-C emblems and the company name in large letters on the parapet. During World War I, the store served for a time as a military hospital. Incidentally, the famous statue that graced the Fountain now rests in Forest Lawn Memorial Park ("The Happy Cemetery"), in Glendale, California.

12. The large, somewhat restrained granite and limestone building occupying the whole block on the west side of Sixth Avenue between 19th and 20th streets reflects the type of establishment it was; for **Simpson Crawford & Simpson** catered exclusively to the "carriage trade." Partners Thomas and James Simpson and William Crawford opened their first retail store on the site in 1879, aiming for the patronage of the conservative moneyed classes, and dealing mostly in high-priced merchandise. A new building, designed by architects William H. Hume & Son, was opened in 1900—the first on the avenue with the newfangled Otis Escalators. It still shows evidence of the very large show windows, and even a trace of the mosaic floor (at the entrance). Price tags on merchandise and in advertisements were considered superfluous, as their elite clientele would never think of asking anyway. This led to Henry Siegel's sarcastic remark that this was indeed a "priceless" store. Tailor-made dresses were a specialty of the house, with men tailors working overtime to make up the orders for delivery in 24 hours! After James Simpson died, the name was shortened to Simpson Crawford Company, and in the ensuing reorganization, Henry Siegel became president. After the demise in 1914 of the great Siegel-Cooper Store across the street, Simpson Crawford limped on for another year, then expired.

13. The red-brick and limestone Italianate building occupying most of the block across the avenue was built in 1893 for the largest shoe "department" store in town, **Cammeyer's.** The stately, well maintained *palazzo* remains as a tribute to the imagination and industriousness of Alfred J. Cammeyer and later partner Louis M. Hart. Together they raised the standard of the retail shoe business from the early custom of stringing up pairs of shoes on storefront poles, to a distinguished and reputable enterprise on a scale comparable to their department-store neighbors. The store prided itself in its "standard of merit" slogan, which became synonymous with quality footwear. When the uptown exodus put an end to Ladies' Mile, Cammeyer's, still in the forefront of retail merchandising, moved to 34th Street in 1917, and four years later, opened an elegant branch on Fifth Avenue. The pitfalls of specialization, however, ultimately doomed the firm, which disappeared after the Depression.

14. The Church of the Holy Communion, on the northeast corner of 20th Street, dates from 1846, when the busy shopping center was a quiet and somewhat remote residential district. Architect Richard Upjohn, who designed this landmark church, was one of the best known advocates of the popular Gothic Revival style of the 1840s; his *chef d'oeuvre,* however, is Trinity Church on lower Broadway.

15. When the **Hugh O'Neill Store** opened in 1876, it must have been a dazzling site to its first visitors. With flamboyant round towers topped by huge bulbous domes, an imposing pediment rising high above five stories of Corinthian columns and pilasters, and a building almost unrivaled in size, O'Neill's began a tradition that was to cause amazement and surprise to patrons and competitors alike for years to come. Hugh O'Neill was no ordinary merchant, but an aggressive, extravagant, and colorful salesman. Hardly a week went by without a dramatic sale accompanied by much hoopla and publicity, for his appeal was not to the staid, conservative clientele of his neighbors, but to the working classes. With the advent of Elias Howe's great invention, the motto of O'Neill became "Put a Sewing Machine in Every Home!" He offered the machines as loss-leaders and was thus able to move his tremendous stock of piece-goods at a healthy profit. His tactics of undercutting and and doing battle with his competitors earned him the name, "The Fighting Irishman of Sixth Avenue." Although a bit crusty and brusque, he was a deeply religious man who commanded the love and respect of his employees. He always insisted that they observe their religious holidays, no matter what their faith, and would give them time off with full pay; nor was he ever above discussing their personal problems with them. A special source of pride to Hugh O'Neill was his shiny fleet of delivery wagons; he frequently would be seen making an early morning inspection round, like a general reviewing his troops, as the teams lined up for the day's deliveries. After he died, there was no one to carry on in the same spirit. To save the store, a merger was arranged with its neighbor to the north, the Adams Dry-Goods Company, resulting in a most unlikely partnership that was destined to last only for a few years. Adams had a different retailing style and an even more dissimilar clientele, so the O'Neill-Adams alliance disintegrated and collapsed completely in 1915.

16. Around the corner on 21st Street, seemingly hidden and protected by the L-shape of the Hugh O'Neill Store, is the diminutive **Third Cemetery of the Spanish & Portuguese Synagogue.** This shady burial plot is the northernmost of three early cemeteries of this first Jewish congregation in America, and was in use between 1829 and 1851. [*See* Lower East Side *Supplementary Tour A;* Greenwich Village, 33.]

17. The ornate Beaux-Arts **Adams Dry-Goods Store** reflects the architectural style that came into vogue around the turn of the century. A relative latecomer to the avenue, A.D.G. tried to capture the fancy (and patronage) of the "carriage trade" through conservative merchandising and a high-priced inventory. One of its novel offerings was men's ready-to-wear and made-to-measure clothing. Its founder, Samuel Adams, started in business much earlier, but did not erect this building until 1900 (note the date, set near the cornice). Since most department stores were family enterprises, Adams had no one to carry on the name. His only daughter, Eileen, showed no inclination for the retail trade, and married the son of march-king John Philip Sousa. When he sold out to Hugh O'Neill, the newly formed O'Neill-Adams Company made a desperate attempt to create a new image. The two firms now were connected not only by a hyphen, but also by an underground tunnel beneath 21st Street; and considerable sums were spent in promoting the new venture—but all in vain. They apparently could not keep abreast of the new, more scientific merchandising techniques, and in 1915, joined the roster of "ghosts."

18. Ehrich Brothers, the last of the old-timers in the Sixth Avenue row, stands dark and dingy, straddling the southwest corner of 23rd Street. The small corner plot, occupied by a cream-colored cast-iron building that juts into the old department store, was always a thorn in the Ehrich Brothers' side—they were unable to acquire the property and had to build around it (much the same as the problem that later faced Macy's when they purchased the 34th Street and Sixth Avenue site in 1904). This corner buidling, recently restored almost to its original appearance after a destructive fire, shows what cast-iron structures looked like when new. It was formerly a branch of the **Riker's Drug Company,** later absorbed into the Liggett chain.

Ehrich Brothers (Julius S. and Samuel W.) was known as a "bargain store," perhaps even more so than Hugh O'Neill. The store was famous for its sales of manufacturers' closeouts and for its "omnibus advertising" (many categories of merchandise grouped into a single large advertisement). Saturdays were "Children's Days" at Ehrich's, when mothers could leave their young ones to enjoy specially provided entertainment and be free to shop at leisure. One of Ehrich Brothers' young trainees learned the retail trade quite well, and after the store ultimately closed, went into business for himself, establishing the name of Nathan Ohrbach as one of the city's successful retail merchants.

In 1911 Ehrich's ceased operations for much the same reason as its neighbors. The brothers tried their hand briefly in a "horseless carriage" dealership, but that, too, proved a failure. On the 23rd Street side, one can still see the faded name "Ehrich Brothers" on a rusty panel above the ground floor.

19. On the southeast corner of 23rd Street and Avenue of the Americas from 1869 to 1883 stood the **Edwin Booth Theater,** with Booth himself as manager and frequent star performer. When **James W. McCreery,** known as the "Dean of the Retail Trade," acquired the site, he demolished the theater and erected his second department store. In 1907 he joined his competitors in the great move uptown, building his newest emporium on 34th Street at Fifth Avenue. McCreery's went out of business unexpectedly in 1954 and the store was purchased by Ohrbach's. The 23rd Street structure survived until 1975 as a loft building. When McCreery opened the store in 1884 he installed a marble bust of Shakespeare into the façade—a memento from the Booth Theater, together with a bronze commemorative plaque honoring the theater. Both the bust and plaque were rescued when the building came down and were donated by the former owner to New York University Library. It is said that Booth, dressed as Shakespeare, posed for the sculpture.

20. Further east, where Nos. 62 and 60 are now, stood the twin buildings of **Best & Company,** which came to 23rd Street in 1881. Specializing in children's wear, it was known by its more popular name, "The Lilliputian Bazaar." The store departed in 1910, moving to Fifth Avenue and 35th Street (the impressive building still occupies the southwest corner); and later to 51st Street, where to the dismay of many New York shoppers, it closed its doors forever in 1970. The new Olympic Tower now stands on the site.

Adjacent, at the site of No. 58, was the famed partnership of **Paul J. Bonwit and Edmund D. Teller.** "Bonwit's" began at Sixth Avenue and 18th Street in 1895, selling fine-quality apparel for women. It opened its 23rd Street store three years later, then in 1911 followed the crowd uptown. In 1930 Bonwit Teller settled at Fifth Avenue and 56th Street, where it still sells fine apparel for women.

The third member of the departed triumvirate was fashionable **LeBoutillier Brothers** (pronounced by all, "Le-boo-ti-LEER"—even by founder Philip LeBoutillier, himself). Arriving in 1898, the store soon became a mecca for the latest in women's styles. By 1913, hard times struck again, and Philip LeBoutillier, the only brother left in the business, closed his shop and joined Best's, ultimately rising to the rank of president of the company.

Across 23rd Street, No. 61–65 is another venerable cast-iron front building, looking not much different from when it opened in 1877 as Robert J. Horner's Furniture Store. Designed by the noted architect of cast-iron buildings, John B. Snook, it later merged with the Flint Furniture Company to become the well known **Flint & Horner Furniture Company.** Occupying the building until 1912, the firm then joined the great uptown procession to 34th Street. Like Wanamaker's, Stern's, and most recently Arnold Constable, the company abandoned the city and continued operations in a suburban location, in this case, Manhasset. Cast iron was ideally suited to the retail trades, as the showrooms could be well illuminated by the large areas of window glass that an iron front permitted. Note the building's feeling of height created by the foreshortening of each successive story—an illusive device credited to the architects of Ancient Greece.

21. In the middle of the block is the gargantuan white cast-iron building of the former **Stern Brothers Department Store** (best viewed from the parking lot across the street). From humble beginnings when they arrived from Buffalo in 1867, the children of poor immigrants, Stern brothers Isaac, Louis, and Bernard, plus three sisters, opened a small dry-goods shop around the corner on 22nd Street. Business prospered, and in 1878 they erected this imposing seven-story edifice—200 feet wide, extending through to 22nd Street, engulfing their old one-room store. Until the opening of the Siegel-Cooper Store 18 years later, it was New York's largest. A far cry from the

Stern Brothers original store, in an 1878 print, shares the south side of 23rd Street with residences, a church, and the Edwin Booth Theater, as well as the recently completed Sixth Avenue El. (Museum of the City of New York)

West 23rd Street looking east from Sixth Avenue, c. 1900, shows the northern limit of Fashion Row. Right to left are the stores of Best & Company, Bonwit Teller, and the enormous white cast-iron front of Stern Brothers. The newly completed Flatiron Building appears in the distance. The Stern Brothers building still remains in a good state of preservation. (Museum of the City of New York)

little family shop was this luxury store, in front of which were posted blue-liveried doormen with top hats, giving the establishment a touch of class that it was to retain for years to come.

Although priding itself in its appeal to the carriage trade, Stern Brothers did not overlook the working classes, for their merchandise was priced for both extremes of the economic spectrum. Isaac, the guiding spirit of the firm, was frequently to be seen greeting customers by name; and it is said that on occasion he would make an urgent home delivery in his own carriage. A fourth brother, Benjamin, joined the partnership after Bernard's passing in 1884. A number of men working in the department stores of the gaslit era achieved later fame as merchandisers in their own right. One of them, a 13-year-old youngster starting as a stock boy, worked his way up in Stern's eventually opening a store on 34th Street in 1902 bearing his own name, Franklin Simon.

By 1913, seeing the handwriting on the wall, Stern Brothers built a new store on 42nd Street and Sixth Avenue and joined the "uptown club." To the regret of many, the store ceased operations in 1970, leaving only its suburban branches to carry on the name.

Note the company monogram and the ornate design motifs in the well preserved façade. It is apparent that the present owners of the building take pride in the historic and aesthetic value of this beautiful cast-iron front.

22. At 14 West 23rd Street is a small iron-front building, now rather woebegone in appearance, which was once **James McCutcheon & Company.** Known as "The Linen Store," it arrived in Ladies' Mile in 1886 after progressive moves uptown, having started 31 years before at Broadway and Astor Place. Dealing exclusively in fine linens, its tablecloths, napkins, doilies, sheets, pillowcases, and such were in great demand from the moneyed classes. In 1907 the store moved to more fashionable quarters on Fifth Avenue. Ultimately it merged with Plummer & Company, becoming Plummer-McCutcheon. More recently it was taken over by Hammacher Schlemmer on 57th Street, and now functions as one of its departments. The building, incidentally, was the birthplace in 1862 of novelist Edith Wharton. The building, then a brownstone, was converted in 1882 to a retail store by architect Henry J. Hardenbergh (the Dakota, Plaza Hotel, etc.). The cast-iron front was installed ten years later by another architect, George H. Billings, for the new occupant, James McCutcheon's Linen Store.

23. Just before reaching Fifth Avenue, pause briefly at the red-brick Queen Anne-style building that **The Western Union Company** built in 1883 as its uptown office. A terra-cotta plaque above the second floor bears the company name. Across the street is the unique Flatiron Building, erected in 1902 [*see* Madison Square, 24].

24. Turn south on Fifth Avenue to No. 170. The interesting cupola atop this narrow building built in 1897 could be seen from quite a distance, marking the location of the **Sohmer Piano Company.**

Across the avenue at No. 153, was **Charles Scribner's Sons** store. Look for the "S" on the fourth-floor balcony. Not only was the firm a well known book dealer (as it is today), but the publisher of one of the most popular periodicals of the time, *Scribner's Magazine.*

25. At **150 Fifth Avenue** (southwest corner of 20th Street) is a particularly handsome building in a mixture of Queen Anne and Italianate styles of architecture. Emblazoned at the top are the letters M.B.C., announcing the home office of one of the largest religious book publishers of the "Mauve Decade," the Methodist Book Concern, as well as the headquarters of the Methodist Church in New York. There were, in fact, so many publishers of religious books along the street that the district was known as "Pater Noster Row." Except for a dreadful modernization of the entrance, the building is in a very good state of preservation. By contrast, note the splendid original "grand entrance" to **No. 156,** on the northwest corner, built in a Romanesque Revival style. Both buildings date from the last decade of the 19th century.

Walk east to the northeast corner of Broadway and 20th Street.

26. The yellow brick and terra-cotta Italianate "palace" on the northwest corner, **No. 903 Broadway,** is a fine example of McKim, Mead & White's favored Renaissance Revival style adapted for commercial use, and built in 1887.

27. One of the most enduring partnerships in the retail trade was that of Messrs. **Lord and Taylor.** The spectacular structure on the southwest corner of 20th Street is a tribute to the courage and resourcefulness of these two English immigrants who together built one of the most respected fashion establishments in the trade. Opening a little shop on Catherine Street in 1826, Samuel Lord joined the growing number of dry-goods merchants; 12 years later he took on as a partner his wife's cousin, George Washington Taylor, and soon the firm of Lord & Taylor had the reputation for honest business practices and quality merchandise. A year after Taylor retired in 1852, the much expanded firm opened its first "department store" on the corner of Grand and Chrystie streets, a large gray stone building capped by an imposing glass dome, which was to remain a local landmark for almost 50 years. Grand Street at that time was one of the busiest shopping streets and also a primary east-west thoroughfare whose crosstown horsecars connected with the New Jersey and Long Island ferries.

Rapid development of business encouraged the firm to open another store farther west on Grand Street, at the corner of Broadway. This latter branch lasted only 12 years, as the shopping trend was on the march north again. It was during this period in the 1863 Draft Riots that some 100 employees ran to secure arms and ammunition from an uptown armory, barricaded the building, and successfully discouraged an attempt by the unruly mobs to sack the store.

In 1872 this extraordinary five-story iron-front building, designed by James Giles in what was described as Bohemian Renaissance style, was opened to the public. Equipped with a steam elevator and other "modern" conveniences, it was an instant success. Surviving the following year's Panic of 1873, Lord & Taylor continued to be one of the most fashionable women's stores on the newly developing Ladies' Mile. When the Grand and Chrystie streets store was finally closed in 1902, the present building was greatly enlarged. Much of the elaborate emporium, however, has disappeared. A parking lot on the 20th Street side now separates the main building from a segment that once extended to Fifth Avenue. Particularly attractive is the mansard roof on the corner pavilion, complete with dormers, and all in cast iron. Note the plaque on the Lord & Taylor building, placed by the New York Community Trust, in recognition of the building's historic and aesthetic merit.

The year 1914, when so many of these great establishments either failed or departed, saw Lord & Taylor move to its present location at Fifth Avenue and 38th Street.

28. The building at the northwest corner of 19th Street, whose irregular and picturesque roof is reminiscent of an English Victorian castle, was the sales office of the **Gorham Manufacturing Company.** The name survives today and is still synonymous with fine silver. The structure, designed by architect Edward H. Kendall in 1883, housed the company whose specialty was custom-designed silverware and a wide variety of ecclesiastical metalwork. The firm subsequently moved its operations uptown, erecting an appropriately impressive building on the southwest corner of Fifth Avenue and 37th Street.

29. A year after Lord & Taylor opened its magnificent store on 20th Street, its die-hard competitor **Arnold Constable** followed suit one block south. The saga of Arnold Constable, New York's oldest department store, began with Aaron Arnold, a young English immigrant, opening a small dry-goods shop on Pine Street in what is now the financial district. With business flourishing, he moved to progressively larger sites; and taking in two nephews, George and James Hearn—the partnership became Arnold, Hearn & Co. [*see* 8.] A recently hired friend of the Arnold family, James Mansell Constable—in typical Horatio Alger fashion—fell in love with the boss's daughter, married her, and was taken into the partnership. Apparently disgruntled by the sudden rise of Constable, the Hearn brothers left Arnold and went into business for themselves. After another change in location, the firm built a large establishment at the corner of Canal, Mercer, and Howard streets, with an impressive white marble façade which Arnold referred to as his "Marble House." It was here that he renamed his firm Arnold, Constable & Company, and made his reputation selling luxury merchandise, soon becoming the darling of the carriage trade—with a customer list reading like the social register. The building, stripped of its fancy trappings, still stands.

In 1869, Arnold retired, leaving the reins of the company in the hands of James Constable. The same year marked the move to the 19th Street site. In a series of land acquisitions, the store grew in size, until 1877 when it covered the whole block to Fifth Avenue. The five-story brick and limestone structure, topped by an enormous French Second Empire mansard roof, was a sensation. Devoting itself exclusively to the sale of fabrics, carpets, and upholstery materials, it remained a prestige store for years to come. The vast selection of its dry goods, ranging from children's wear to mourning apparel, led to the comment that "Arnold Constable provides elegant clothing, from cradleside to graveside." The *New York Daily Graphic,* in its January 8, 1877, edition, described the store as "a new Emporium of Trade—a dominant and ornamental addition to the street architecture of New York."

In 1914, that famous "uptown moving year," the company abandoned its pretentious building and moved to its final location at Fifth Avenue and 40th Street. It is interesting to note that from 1860 to 1975, the two fierce competitors, Arnold Constable and Lord & Taylor, had never been more than two blocks apart! With the demise of Arnold Constable after 150 years, its rival survives as the oldest retail store in the city.

30. "The house of **W. & J. Sloane** stands indisputably at the head of the carpet and rug industry of this country," wrote Moses King in his *Handbook of New York,* for 1893. Unlike the other department stores that had their origin in the dry-goods business, Sloane's dealt almost exclusively in rugs and floor coverings.

Arriving on a sailing ship in 1834, William Sloane, a young weaver from Scotland, found work in a Connecticut mill, learning American weaving techniques. Nine years later he established a small "Carpeting and Floor Cloth Shop" on lower Broadway, using the slogan "Dependable Merchandise at an Honest Figure." In 1852, brother John, the "J" of W. & J. Sloane, was taken into the business, but stayed with William for only nine years. At the closing of the 1876 Centennial Exposition in Philadelphia, William Sloane purchased a superb collection of Oriental rugs that had been a major display at the Fair, offering them to his growing list of wealthy clients. This marked the first time Oriental rugs were sold by a retail house. In the meantime, he had moved up Broadway twice, keeping abreast of the familiar northward push, and a few years later accomplished another "first," contracting with a weaving firm in India to become the only American rug store with its own Oriental source of supply.

William Sloane achieved fame of another sort a few years earlier, when the criminal jury of which he was foreman convicted "Boss" Tweed. While on the jury he learned that merchant-prince A. T. Stewart was about to foreclose a mortgage on the Alexander Smith Carpet Company in Yonkers, N.Y. Sloane raised the money, saved the Smith Company, and in return received an interest and became its exclusive agent for many years. On his death in 1879, the firm's direction was taken over by his eldest son, John II. It was under John Sloane that the company achieved its greatest growth, inaugurating in 1881 the large store across the street from Arnold Constable, and an equally spacious outlet in San Francisco. W. & J. Sloane achieved national fame with a contract to carpet some of the swankiest hotels in the city, including the newly opened Waldorf-Astoria on 34th Street; and the company won international fame with the commission to supply all the carpeting for the coronation of Czar Nicholas II. At the same time, the store expanded its operations into home decorating, selling antiques, and manufacturing "registered reproductions" of antique furniture.

As the gaslit era waned, Sloane's moved in 1912 to Fifth Avenue and 47th Street, where they remained until 1962. In a subsequent move down the avenue to 38th Street, they sold their building to E. J. Korvette and acquired the store formerly occupied by Franklin Simon.

Find the "S" monogram on a small cast-iron shield set high on the building, as well as the date of construction in terra-cotta Roman numerals.

EAST 23RD ST.

LEXINGTON AVENUE

⑥

EAST 22ND ST.

⑤ ④ ⑦

③ ⑧

GRAMERCY PARK N.

GRAMERCY PK. E.

GRAMERCY PK. W.

GRAMERCY PARK

⑨

EAST 21ST ST.

GRAMERCY PARK S.

start EAST 20TH ST.

① ②

BROADWAY

PARK AVENUE SOUTH

IRVING PLACE

EAST 19TH ST. ⑩

THIRD AVENUE

⑪ ⑫

EAST 18TH ST.

⑬

EAST 17TH ST.

⑭

EAST 16TH ST.

⑮

Union Square

EAST 15TH ST.

⑯

⑰

EAST 14TH ST.

⑱

GRAMERCY PARK

(Shaded Area
Indicates
Historic District)

9. Gramercy Park

[*IRT Lexington Avenue line to 23rd Street station; BMT Broadway line to 23rd Street station*]

In Dutch Colonial days the locality was known as *Crommessie Fly* (crooked stream), an area of woods and marshes situated just above the country estate of Governor Peter Stuyvesant. It later became the property of James Duane, mayor of New York City from 1784 to 1789, who named it Gramercy Seat. In 1831 land developer Samuel B. Ruggles purchased a substantial parcel from the Duane Farm, and laid out the residential lots and park. Ruggles also laid out lower Lexington Avenue, naming it after the Revolutionary Battle of Lexington, and Irving Place, which he named for his friend Washington Irving. In spite of the growth of the surroundings, and the encroachment of high-rise buildings, Gramercy Park has managed to remain one of the most charming residential districts of the city.

1. The tour begins at **28 East 20th Street,** just east of Broadway, at the birthplace of one of Gramercy Park's most illustrious residents, Theodore Roosevelt. This trim townhouse of the 1840s is a National Historic Site and a New York City Landmark. Built of brownstone and remodeled in Gothic Revival style, it was restored in 1923 and is maintained by the U.S. National Park Service in cooperation with the Theodore Roosevelt Association. The rooms have been restored to the period of "Teddie's" boyhood. The drawing room is furnished with crystal chandeliers, magnificent mirrors, and blue satin hangings, characteristic of the elegance of the day. The front bedroom in which he was born contains the original furniture and a portrait of his mother, Martha Bulloch Roosevelt. Next to it is the nursery and, beyond, the open porch that was used as a gymnasium. In addition to his widely known political accomplishments, Theodore Roosevelt was also an effective, reform-minded Police Commissioner of New York City. Proceed east to Park Avenue South, known formerly by its more prosaic name, Fourth Avenue.

2. At **250 Park Avenue South** is a large industrial building in a neo-Gothic style. Built at the turn of the century when decoration served a more important function of architecture than it does today, it is typical of many such commercial structures in the city.

3. Across the avenue, one block north, is the **Calvary Church.** Designed in 1846 by James Renwick, Jr., architect of Grace Church and St. Patrick's Cathedral, it is in the tradition of the Gothic Revival so popular in the 1840s. The stone towers, which replaced earlier wooden steeples, were removed in 1925.

4. At No. 281 is the **Church Missions' House.** Built in a lavish Romanesque Revival style in 1894 by R. W. Gibson and E. J. N. Stent, this imposing edifice houses the headquarters of the domestic and foreign missionary service of the Protestant Episcopal Church, which was founded in 1821.

5. Across the street, at the southwest corner of 22nd Street, in a much altered Classical style is the "temple" of **The New York Bank for Savings—** the "Beehive Bank." Chartered in Greenwich Village in 1819 as the Bleecker Street Savings Bank, this oldest savings institution in the city moved into its present home office in 1894.

6. The United Charities Building, at 105 East 22nd Street, was erected in 1891–93 from plans by R. H. Robertson and Rowe & Baker in a modified Romanesque Revival style, for the New York Association for Improving the Condition of the Poor, now the Community Service Society, ". . . to improve the condition of the working classes, and to elevate their physical state." It also houses, among other charitable institutions, the Children's Aid Society. Turn east on 22nd Street to Lexington Avenue.

7. The lavish Renaissance-style building on the southwest corner was built for the **Russell Sage Foundation** at the turn of the century. Sage, a financier and philanthropist, died in 1906, leaving an enormous fortune to charity. Among the legatees was Russell Sage College, in upstate Troy, N.Y. He was known to be strongly opinionated, and it is said that upon being approached by August Belmont to share in the financial backing of the newly begun subway, he turned to the president of the Rapid Transit Construction Company and commented scornfully that "New Yorkers would never go into a hole to ride it." In recent years the building was occupied by Catholic Charities, and in 1975 it was purchased by a developer who converted it into an apartment house—a most appropriate adaptive reuse.

Across 22nd Street is the **Mabel Dean Bacon Vocational High School,** formerly the Manhattan Trade School for Girls. It was built in 1917 from plans by C. B. J. Snyder whose Collegiate Gothic style for school buildings was very popular early in the century.

Walk south one block to 21st Street. The northeast corner is the **site of the Cyrus W. Field Residence.** Field, with help from Peter Cooper (who lived just a few doors north, at 6 Lexington Avenue) promoted the Atlantic Cable, which after some initial failures, was laid successfully in 1866. He was also responsible for the building of most of the elevated railroads in the city during the late 1870s, only to lose them a few years later to railroad tycoon Jay Gould.

The Hewitt Cooper House, built by Peter Cooper in 1848 at 9 Lexington Avenue was later occupied by his son-in-law Ambram S. Hewitt, Mayor of New York, 1887–88. The house was demolished in 1939. (Museum of the City of New York)

8. Gramercy Park, whose name probably derives from the original Dutch *Crommessie Fly* (crooked stream), is a tribute to Samuel B. Ruggles's foresight, and is an excellent example of urban planning. By taking the 42 lots that comprise the 1½ acre park, and deeding the parcel to the 60 surrounding lot owners, he established the only surviving private park in the city. (An earlier private plot, St. John's Park, owned by Trinity Parish, was destroyed by the takeover of adjacent land by the Hudson River Railroad, and ultimately obliterated by the entrance ramps to the Holland Tunnel.) The cast-iron fence was erected in 1832, with extensive planting undertaken thereafter. Although formerly restricted to adjacent property owners, this private park is now accessible to all who live close by and who pay the annual fee. The Park and surrounding lots, including the Calvary Church, and a stretch of property on 18th and 19th streets, were designated in 1966 by the Landmarks Preservation Commission as the **Gramercy Park Historic District.**

Turning west at the Gramercy Park Hotel, we pass **the site of Stanford White's residence** from 1901 until his untimely death in 1906. White is acknowledged not only as an exemplary architect, but as one who established the American tradition of art collecting. His private collection of paintings and sculpture is now distributed among several museums.

At what was **formerly No. 70** stood the home of diarist George Templeton Strong, the peripatetic chronicler of mid-19th century life and events, who acquired the property by marrying Ruggles's daughter. To the east of his house lived Robert "Bob" Ingersoll, orator and lawyer, who, because of his highly publicized lectures on religion, was dubbed "The Great Agnostic."

Rounding the corner, **Nos. 1 and 2 Gramercy Park West** date from 1849–50. Dr. Valentine Mott, probably the most renowned surgeon in the days just before the Civil War, lived in No. 1. He was responsible for the founding of the New York University Medical College and Bellevue Hospital.

Lovely **Nos. 3 and 4,** with their ornate cast-iron porches, were built in 1846 and are attributed to famed architect Alexander Jackson Davis. The pair of lanterns in front of No. 4 indicate that it was once a mayor's residence. James Harper, founder of the Harper & Row publishing house, was elected to the city's highest office in 1844 after a scurrilous anti-Irish, anti-"Popism" campaign.

Turning east at the corner, we see the large double brownstone mansion of the **National Arts Club** at **15 Gramercy Park South.** Built in 1845, the two single houses were remodeled and converted in 1874 by Calvert Vaux for

Charming Nos. 3 and 4 Gramercy Park West still remain, adding to the pleasant atmosphere of the neighborhood. This pair of houses, built in 1846, are attributed to architect Alexander Jackson Davis. Twin lanterns in front of No. 4 denote the residence of former Mayor James Harper. (Photograph by Berenice Abbott. Federal Art Project "Changing New York." Museum of the City of New York)

Samuel J. Tilden (Vaux, with Frederick Law Olmsted, designed Central and Prospect parks). Although the façade is not surviving well against air pollution and pigeons, it is nonetheless an engaging example of Ruskinian Gothic, inspired by the Medieval Revival style made famous by the 19th-century English author and artist John Ruskin. Tilden, an eminent lawyer and reformer, was governor of New York in 1875–76, but resigned the office to run as Democratic presidential contender against Rutherford B. Hayes. History records that he won the popular majority by a quarter of a million votes, but lost the election—defeated by a group of Southern Republican Electors. The National Arts Club purchased the landmark building in 1906.

The adjacent **Players' Club,** also a landmark, was built for a banker in 1845. It was later purchased by actor Edwin Booth who, in 1888, commissioned Stanford White to remodel it as a private club for the theatrical profession. Note the huge stone porch and elaborate ironwork, including the two graceful lanterns. Not all the great "Players" were actors, however. The membership included such notables as Walter Damrosch, Thomas Nast, Mark Twain, Booth Tarkington, and even General William Tecumseh Sherman. But they were all *men,* as the Players' Club was, and still is, "no-woman's-land."

"No-man's-land," on the other hand, is just next door at **No. 17,** the **Salvation Army's Parkside Evangeline Residence Hall.**

Before crossing Irving Place, look through the Park gates at the statue of Edwin Booth as Hamlet, sculpted by Edmond T. Quinn in 1916.

At **No. 19 Gramercy Park South** is the **Stuyvesant Fish House.** Built for a Horace Brooks in 1845, it was acquired in 1887 by Stuyvesant Fish, wealthy socialite and President of the Illinois Central Railroad. The line had so many of the "400" on its board of directors that it was called the "Society Railroad." His wife, Mary "Mamie" Fish, succeeded Mrs. William Astor as the head of New York society. It is said that Mamie Fish curtailed the traditional dinner hour from a several-hour affair to a mere 50 minutes; she was also responsible for a new informality among members of society, by encouraging the use of guests' first names. The Victorian mansard roof with ornate iron cresting is a later addition to this beautifully maintained house. Its prideful owner today is well known public relations counsel Benjamin Sonnenberg.

No. 21, next door, built in 1853–54, was the residence of John Bigelow, author and diplomat. Bigelow was co-owner with William Cullen Bryant of the *New York Evening Post* from 1848 to 1861, when he gave up his newspaper business to become minister to France during the Civil War. He is credited with depriving the Confederacy of recognition by the French Government, and with stopping the construction of rebel warships.

Ignoring several nondescript remodelings, we come to the former **Friends' Meeting House,** 144 East 20th Street. Built by King & Kellum in 1859, it is a fine example of the dignified Italianate style so popular in the 1850s. For a time the fate of the Meeting House was uncertain, as the Friends had merged their meetings with the Stuyvesant Square congregation, selling the house to the United Federation of Teachers. There was even talk of demolition and the erection of a high-rise apartment house, in spite of its designation as a New York City Landmark. But early in 1975, the Brotherhood Synagogue, which had been sharing quarters with the Village Presbyterian Church on West 13th Street, purchased the building from the U.F.T. for conversion to a synagogue. Only minor interior changes were made, and the lovely landmark's future is now assured.

The lot at the corner of 20th Street is occupied by "The Gramercy," a former "French flats," or luxury apartment house of the 1880s. Now a co-op, its sumptuous lobby still reflects the aura of the Elegant '80s. Its neighbor to the north, a neo-Gothic apartment house, is guarded by a pair of incongruous armored knights.

Return to Irving Place, walk one block south to 19th Street, and turn east.

9. The tree-lined and serene block between Irving Place and Third Avenue is known as the **"Block Beautiful."** Frederick Sterner was the prime mover in the rehabilitation of many of the old houses. Although none are particularly outstanding by themselves, they form a unity of "harmonious differences." Note the three "Gothic" conversions at **Nos. 127** (1854), **129** (1861), and **135** (1845). **No. 139** (1842–43), in a Tuscan style, earned Sterner his initial popularity. **No. 141** (1843), with its jockey hitching posts, belonged to the late sportscaster Ted Husing. **No. 132** (1910) was the residence of silent film ingenue Theda Bara, and of Mrs. Patrick Campbell, who in 1912 created the role of Eliza Doolittle in Shaw's *Pygmalion*. It was also the home of "muckraker" Ida M. Tarbell, who wrote the highly critical two-volume *History of the Standard Oil Company*. George Bellows, a founder of the Ashcan School of American painting, lived at **No. 140** (1852–53). The ceramic reliefs over the entrances of **Nos. 147–149** (1861) are the work of resident artist Robert Winthrop Chanler.

Return to Irving Place and continue south to 18th Street.

10. Pete's Tavern, at 66 Irving Place, dating from 1864 when it was called "Healy's," boasts to be the oldest saloon in New York City. The assertion, however, is strongly disputed by McSorley's Old Ale House, on East 7th Street, which opened 10 years earlier. Pete's also claims to have been a favorite haunt of O. Henry; but, knowing his proclivities, almost any saloon could have earned that distinction! Legend (and a few faded newspaper clippings) maintains that he wrote *The Gift of the Magi* in the second booth on the right (this is also disputed by a café across the street at No. 55 —in fact, they have a plaque on the building to "prove" it). Be that as it may, the Tavern has been a popular local landmark for many years. Two old carriage houses in the rear have been absorbed into the expanded establishment, and much of the flavor of the gaslit era remains.

11. Around the corner, **Nos. 135–143 East 18th Street** are a row of pre-

The Academy of Music, built in 1854 at the corner of Irving Place and 14th Street was New York's most popular and fashionable opera house until the advent of the Metropolitan Opera House in 1883. In 1910 it was razed to make way for Con Ed's new office building. Note the ad for Drake's Plantation Bitters painted on the curb. (The Consolidated Edison Company of New York)

Civil War houses (1855), each only two bays wide. When neighbors get together in a common effort to restore their properties, the result can be very gratifying. **Nos. 145–151** date from the same period (1853–54).

12. No. 55 Irving Place is the site of William Sidney Porter's (O. Henry's) residence. Now an apartment house, little remains of the original building or the old Blue Bell Tavern at the corner (another purported "favorite" of the author). A vestige of the former saloon does remain, however, in the wine cellar, whose brick arches can be seen in the redecorated lower level of the plant store.

13. The little red-brick Greek Revival house on the southwest corner of 17th Street, **No. 40 Irving Place,** claims (on its bronze plaque) to have been the residence of Washington Irving. The house was actually built (c. 1845) for his nephew, John T. Irving, but Washington Irving *was* a frequent visitor. (His home for a time was at 11 Commerce Street, in Greenwich Village). From 1894 to 1911 the house was occupied by two remarkable women, Elsie de Wolfe and Elizabeth Marbury. Miss de Wolfe was considered "the best-dressed woman in town," and later shocked the interior design profession by becoming the first "lady decorator." Her friend Miss Marbury was a noted literary agent. Their Sunday afternoon socials for the literary world were the talk of the town.

14. In front of Washington Irving High School, built in 1912, is an enormous bust of the school's namesake, executed by Friedrich Baer in 1885 and originally placed in Bryant Park. One wonders what the sculptor (or Irving, himself) would think if he could see the shade of paint that is supposed to protect the bust from the effects of pigeons, air pollution, and students' graffiti.

15. At the southwest corner of Irving Place and 15th Street is a mournful-looking pile. Now a warehouse for the former S. Klein Department Store, the woebegone appearance belies its history as the **Amberg Theater.** It opened in 1888 with the American premier of several Ibsen plays. Nearby 14th Street was still in its heyday as an entertainment district. When the theater district moved uptown, the Amberg became the Irving Place Theater, offering silent films and vaudeville. For a time the hall even echoed the lines of the best known actors of the Yiddish theater, but by the early 1930s it went back to films. It did achieve brief popularity again when Gypsy Rose Lee gave her burlesque performances, but the staid city fathers put a quick end to that

Tammany Hall, on the north side of 14th Street between Irving Place and Third Avenue in a c.1870 photograph. Chief Tamanend, above, presides over the Society which was founded in 1789 as an outgrowth of the Sons of Liberty. Tammany became a political power through the efforts of Aaron Burr. (New-York Historical Society)

lively theater art. Reverting once more to its movie-house status, it became a center for Russian film festivals, but after World War II it gave up the ghost.

16. Occupying the entire block to Third Avenue, between 15th and 14th streets, is **the headquarters of "Con Ed."** The main building was designed by Henry J. Hardenbergh (architect of the Plaza Hotel and the Dakota Apartments). Begun in 1911, the structure and its extensions developed in stages, and took 18 years to complete. The unique clock tower, a pleasing contribution to the cityscape, was planned by Warren & Wetmore (architects of Grand Central Station) and completed in 1926. The company's predecessor, the Manhattan Gas Light Company, was located near the corner of 14th Street from 1885 to 1910; and at the corner was the Academy of Music, a competitor of the Metropolitan Opera. Farther east in the block was Tammany Hall, and at the Third Avenue corner, the popular entertainment spot, Tony Pastor's Music Hall. The Academy of Music hosted such greats as Jenny Lind, Adelina Patti, Helena Modjeska, E. H. Sothern, Edwin Booth, and Julia Marlowe. When the Metropolitan Opera House opened at Broadway and West 39th Street in 1893, the Academy of Music soon declined, and for a number of years presented only vaudeville and silents. In 1926, it finally surrendered to the wrecker's ball, making way for the Consolidated Edison Company's main building extension. Across the street, the Academy of Music lives on, but in name only. Note the fading advertisement on the upper stories of the movie house, offering "the finest in photo plays for 25¢ and 50¢."

17. Nearby **Lüchow's,** at 110 East 14th Street, is a typical German restaurant of the Gay '90s. The building dates from 1840 when the neighborhood was still residential. With the arrival of the entertainment district in the 1870s and 1880s, the house found a new tenant with the opening of Lüchow's Restaurant in 1882. It soon became a gathering place for the big names in the musical world. Frequent habitués were Paderewski and Caruso. It was here, in 1914, that Victor Herbert founded the American Society of Composers, Authors & Publishers (ASCAP); and songwriter Gus Kahn penned "Yes, Sir, That's My Baby." Although Lüchow's name still survives, it is now run by a restaurant chain. Nonetheless, the décor remains authentic *Münchener Bierhalle,* the "oompah" bands still play, the waiters wear *lederhosen,* and the place is always jammed at the annual *Oktoberfest* and Christmas *Tannenbaum* celebrations. The interior is a designated New York City Landmark.

MADISON
SQUARE

E. 31ST ST.

W. 31ST ST.

W. 30TH ST.

W. 29TH ST.

E. 29TH ST.

BROADWAY

FIFTH AVE.

MADISON AVE.

W. 28TH ST.

E. 28TH ST.

start

W. 27TH ST.

E. 27TH ST.

W. 26TH ST.

E. 26TH ST.

Madison
Square
Park

W. 25TH ST.

E. 25TH ST.

W. 24TH ST.

E. 24TH ST.

W. 23RD ST.

E. 23RD ST.

10. Madison Square

[*BMT RR Broadway line to 28th Street station*]

Along Broadway from 23rd to 42nd streets, during the 1880s and 1890s, was the Rialto of New York—the celebrated Great White Way. Keeping pace with the northward drive of the city, the theater district, in a series of moves up Broadway, now reached to Longacre Square (called Times Square after 1904). Our uniquely American theater idiom, the musical comedy, was coming into its own, and the heyday of songwriting had begun. Along 28th Street, music publishers and tunesmiths by the score worked around the clock in a cacophony of musical sounds, to give birth to the appropriately named Tin Pan Alley. Facing nearby Madison Square arose Stanford White's monumental "Garden" to present a variety of entertainment on a scale hitherto unheard of by American audiences. Competing with the live entertainment of Broadway came the infant motion-picture industry, grinding out its silent films in hastily constructed studios in the West 20s.

Gone now are the legitimate theaters and music halls, the budding film industry, and the opulent hotels, restaurants, and cafés that lined Fifth Avenue and Broadway. Gone, too, is the din, glitter, and excitement that drew the throngs of nightly visitors. Even lavish Madison Square Garden bade farewell to its namesake site in 1925 and moved (twice) to other locations.

Broadway and adjacent Madison Square have quite a different flavor now. The 20th century witnessed the development of a bustling business district, bringing with it some of the most imposing commercial structures in the city. Shady Madison Square Park, however, still retains its quiet elegance—a refuge from the congestion and clamor of surrounding streets. And here and there, dwarfed by modern, multistoried neighbors, some architectural vestiges of the past still survive—mute reminders of that vibrant, exciting era of 80 years ago.

1. The tour begins at **West 28th Street and Broadway,** the former heart of "Tin Pan Alley." Walk north on the west side of Broadway, noting several examples of the skyscraper era of the 1890s; for example, Nos. 1170 and 1181 Broadway. At that time architects seemed to feel that tall buildings should not be just dull vertical shafts, so they bestowed them with considerable ornamentation, and frequently divided the façades into three distinct sections, similar to the divisions of a Classic column: the "base," usually the first three or four stories; the "shaft," the tall, relatively unadorned center section; and the "capital," the top group of stories, frequently very ornate, and topped with a projecting cornice. This "Tripartite" style of commercial building architecture remained popular until about 1910.

2. On the northeast corner of West 29th Street and Broadway is the "gray ghost" of the **Gilsey House.** Built of marble and cast iron in 1871, it is a splendid example of the French Second Empire style. It was the favorite hotel of Oscar Wilde during his American lecture tours, and was also a frequent haunt of James Buchanan "Diamond Jim" Brady, the financier and *bon vivant* of the Gay '90s, whose wild parties with nude girls on high-flying swings made lusty copy for the morning dailies. The Gilsey House was the first hotel in the city to boast a telephone. A block-and-a-half farther north, between 30th and 31st streets on the east side, its dark mansard roof almost hidden, is the former Grand Hotel. Built about the same time as the Gilsey House, it was considered one of the great hostelries of New York. Turn east on West 31st Street to the Hotel Clinton.

3. This rather seedy establishment is **the former home of Life Magazine.** Before its purchase by the Time-Life Corporation in 1936, it was a rather sophisticated humor weekly. Visible on the upper stone balcony is its name, as are groupings of L's on the ornate cast iron balconies, together with the inscriptions of "wit" and "humor." The future is uncertain for this Classical-style building, designed in 1894 by the noted architectural firm of Carrère & Hastings.

4. The Wolcott Hotel at 4–10 West 31st Street is a fine example of Classic Eclectic-style hotel architecture so popular at the turn of the century. Turn south on Fifth Avenue to the southwest corner of West 27th Street. (Incidentally, Fifth Avenue is the east-west dividing line of all numbered streets, from 8th Street north.)

5. The dark-red apartment house across the street (284 Fifth Avenue, entrance on West 30th Street) is the **Wilbraham Apartments.** Built in the mid-1880s, it was one of the first "French Flats," or residential apartments for the wealthy. Actress Lillian Russell occupied the top floor during the heyday of her career.

6. The building at 276 Fifth Avenue was formerly the **Holland House.** Built in 1892 and named for a similar hotel in the Kensington section of London, it was a gathering place for intellectuals and gourmets. Its staircase of Siena marble and bronze and its famous restaurant made it a showplace until its closing in 1920. In its 1903 edition, *King's Views of New York* called it "The peer of any hotel in America . . . where the most fastidious people are its 'instant guests.' "

7. At the northwest corner of 29th Street is the well known **Marble Collegiate Church,** where Dr. Norman Vincent Peale's Sunday sermons originate to reach a nationwide radio audience. Built in 1854 from plans by architect Samuel A. Warner, the church is a fine example of early Romanesque Revival style applied to what is essentially a Gothic Revival-style building, and is a designated New York City Landmark. The congregation dates back to the founding of the Dutch Reformed Church in America in 1628. Note the huge bronze bell on the lawn. Cast in Holland, it summoned the faithful while it hung in the old North Church downtown on William Street in the 18th and 19th centuries.

8. Turn east on 29th Street to the landmark Episcopal Church of the Transfiguration. Known as the **"Little Church around the Corner,"** it dates from 1848–1856, and is New York City's unique example of the Cottage Gothic style of the 14th century. It earned its nickname from an incident that occurred in 1870. When actor George Holland died and was refused burial rites at a nearby church, a friend, Joseph Jefferson, was informed that there was a *little church around the corner* that would perform the rites—and the name stuck. The church has been closely connected with the acting profession since that time. The lich-gate at the entrance recalls the custom of conducting a preliminary burial service outside the church (*lic* is the Anglo-Saxon word for "body"). The interior is unusually beautiful, with a quiet, intimate atmosphere. Look for the stained-glass window (in the south transept) of actor Edwin Booth as Hamlet, done by John LaFarge. The reredos of the *Last Supper,* as well as the lich-gate, were designed by architect Frederick Clark Withers. Note also the Chantry with its Brides' Altar, the carved wooden screens at the entrance to the nave, the Joseph Jefferson Memorial Window, the Mortuary Chapel with stained-glass copy of Raphael's *Transfiguration,* and the little chapel dedicated to actor José María Muñoz. The church takes pride in its history of helping the less fortunate. During the Draft Riots of 1863, it sheltered runaway slaves, and in the depressions of 1907 and the mid-1930s, it operated bread lines. It is still very active in community service, and also supports a small professional theater company, appropriately called "The Joseph Jefferson Players."

Return to Fifth Avenue.

9. At **250 Fifth Avenue,** now a First National City Bank branch, is a fine Italianate *palazzo,* built in 1907 by the architectural firm of McKim, Mead & White as a commercial building.

Turn east on 28th Street.

10. The Prince George, another Classic Eclectic-style hotel, has kept up appearances since its opening in 1902. At the time, its ballroom was considered among the most elegant in town. It was another partying place for fast friends "Diamond Jim" Brady and Lillian Russell, and the splendor of the old hall

The first Madison Square Garden building was originally the Union Depot of the New York & Harlem Railroad at 28th Street and Madison Avenue. It served for a time as P. T. Barnum's Hippodrome, then in 1879 it became the "Garden." It lasted only until 1890, when Stanford White's great masterpiece replaced it. (New York Life Insurance Company)

is still quite evident. To the right of the ballroom entrance, and dominating the entire lobby, is the spectacular Martinique Clock. Made in England in the early 17th century, with a cabinet of intricately carved mahogany, this enormous long-case clock is undoubtedly one of the largest in the world. Examine the collection of grandfather clocks scattered about the extensive main floor. Most of them date from more recent times. The tap room is a rather good imitation of an English country pub. Leave through the 27th Street entrance, and turn left to Madison Avenue.

11. The New York Life Insurance Company Building, designed by Cass Gilbert, and built in 1926–28, is a New York City Landmark. Although of no particular architectural style, the *AIA Guide to New York* refers to it as "Limestone Renaissance at the bottom, Birthday Cake at the top." The gilt pyramid that caps this mammoth structure is similar to the one Gilbert later designed for the top of the U.S. Court House on Foley Square. The lobby of the New York Life Building is particularly attractive. Its coffered ceiling, enormous hanging lamps, and ornate doors and paneling—all of bronze— make it one of the great interiors of the city. The "grand staircase" leading to the IRT subway station belies what is below. Compare this lavish lobby with Cass Gilbert's treatment of his Woolworth Building, built 13 years before.

This is the **site of the first two Madison Square Gardens.** Originally, the Union Depot of the New York & Harlem Railroad was built here after it had been moved uptown from its earlier location near City Hall. (The city fathers objected strenuously to the noise and air pollution of the old steam locomotives.) In 1871 the railroad terminal was shifted to the present site of Grand Central Station, and the Depot sold to P. T. Barnum, who converted it into his popular Hippodrome. Nine years later it became the first Madison Square Garden.

In 1890, Stanford White designed the second Madison Square Garden, an imposing Spanish Renaissance-style structure, which occupied the entire block. Its central tower, modeled after the *Giralda* in Seville, and topped by Augustus St. Gaudens's statue of Diana, was to be a dominant feature of the city skyline for 35 years. Complete with the largest amphitheater in the country, Garden Theater, Roof Garden, concert hall, café, and even an immense swimming pool, it was an immediate sensation. Among some of the events staged in the Garden were operatic concerts, prize fights (Jack Dempsey knocked out Bill Brennan), Wild West Shows, aquatic exhibitions, the first American automobile show, six-day walks, six-day bike races, and Barnum & Bailey's circus.

Planned at first to be the site for annual horse shows, Stanford White designed Madison Square Garden to include a theater, concert hall, roof-garden, and restaurant, graced with a dramatic tower—the second highest in the city—and surmounted by a gilt statue of Diana. (New York Life Insurance Company)

Architect White had an eye not only for beautiful buildings, but for beautiful women as well. His two homes nearby were the scenes of frequent and wild all-night parties. Rumor had it that White installed a high red-velvet swing on the top floor of his West 24th Street love nest, on which girl friends were offered all manner of inducements to oscillate "in the altogether." One of these steady "swingers" was young Evelyn Nesbit, a former *Floradora* show girl who later married eccentric millionaire Harry K. Thaw. On the evening of June 25, 1906, Stanford White entered the Roof Garden Theater and was observed by Thaw and his recent bride, who were dining at a nearby table. Evelyn whispered something about White to her husband that infuriated him; whereupon he leaped up from the table, stalked across the floor, drew a revolver, and fired three fatal shots at the architect. After nine years and three prolonged trials, Thaw was acquitted.

After its demolition in 1925, the Garden was rebuilt at West 50th Street and 8th Avenue, where it remained until 1968. Ironically, its present location at Eighth Avenue between 31st and 33rd streets is on the site of McKim,

The elegant Leonard Jerome Mansion built in 1859, later the Manhattan Club, graced the southeast corner of 26th Street and Madison Avenue. Daughter Jennie Jerome, later became Lady Randolph Churchill, mother of Sir Winston. The Landmark Law came too late to save the beautiful house, and in its place is the enormously out-of-scale Merchandise Mart Building. (New York Life Insurance Company)

"Dr. Parkhurst's Church" as the Madison Avenue Presbyterian Church was called, was built in 1853 when the neighborhood was entirely residential. On this peaceful site of the late 1880s—the corner of 23rd Street and Madison Avenue—now stands the Metropolitan Life Tower. (Metropolitan Life Insurance Company)

Madison Square has managed to escape most alterations made in the name of progress. The drinking fountains and pavilion are gone, but the trees remain, sporting the foliage of more than three-quarters of a century of growth since this 1901 photo by Byron. (The Byron Collection. Museum of the City of New York)

The young boy drinking from the common cup was a participant in a Madison Square clean-up campaign sponsored by the Metropolitan Life Insurance Company in 1913. (Metropolitan Life Insurance Company)

An early 1900s sightseeing bus in front of No. 1 Madison Avenue. (Metropolitan Life Insurance Company)

The triangular site of the Flatiron Building, the intersection of Broadway and Fifth Avenue at 23rd Street, as seen from the Fifth Avenue Hotel in 1884. Note the white Broadway omnibus at left. (*New-York Historical Society*)

The expression "Twenty-Three Skidoo!" is said to have come from the efforts by Officer Kane, stationed at Fifth Avenue and 23rd Street, to "shoo" away the young men who gathered at the breezy corner to catch a glimpse of a lady's ankle. (*Metropolitan Life Insurance Company*)

The Twenty-third Street crosstown car was one of the last to exchange horsepower for electric. In this undated photo, a two-horse team passes in front of 45 East 23rd Street on its way to the New Jersey ferries. (Metropolitan Life Insurance Company)

Prim young ladies serving tempting desserts in Maillard's elegant confectionery shop, on the ground floor of the posh Fifth Avenue Hotel. (Photograph by Byron. The Byron Collection. Museum of the City of New York)

Mead & White's greatest architectural achievement—Pennsylvania Station—which fell victim to the wrecker's ball and civic short-sightedness!

12. No. 50 Madison Avenue was built in 1896 by Renwick, Aspinwall & Owens for the American Society for the Prevention of Cruelty to Animals (ASPCA). This limestone structure is now occupied by various tenants, including the Child Study Association.

13. The glistening new **Merchandise Mart Building** (41 Madison Avenue), on the southeast corner of 26th Street, is a shocking example of utter disregard for scale. It would appear that the designers cared not at all about the height, shape, and style of adjacent buildings when they planned this one. By acquiring the air rights from the Court House to the south, they could legally raise this enormous "cracker box" to an eye-boggling height, thus overwhelming its neighbors, destroying a pleasing skyline, and casting a visual pall over the park below. To make the picture even more dismal, the former occupant of the site was the Leonard Jerome House (Jerome's daughter, Jennie, became Lady Randolph Churchill—Winston Churchill's mother). The attractive mansion, built in 1859, later became the Manhattan Club where, it is said, the Manhattan cocktail was invented. Demolition took place with indecent haste, just before the passage of the Landmarks Preservation Law, and New York suffered another irretrievable loss.

14. The Appellate Division, New York State Supreme Court resembles a stately Greek temple, and is a tribute to its architect, James Brown Lord. Built in 1896–1900, this magnificent building miraculously escaped the fate of its ex-neighbor, the Jerome House. Public clamor prevented the Court's consolidation into the Foley Square complex. Perhaps by surrendering its air rights to the "bully" next door, it was given a reprieve. An examination of the exterior sculpture is a must:

Madison Square side:

> Four caryatids: "The Four Seasons" (Thomas Shields Clarke)
> *Peace* (Karl Bitter) [*on balustrade*]
> *Moses* (William Couper) [*on balustrade*]

25th Street side:

> Entrance: *Force and Wisdom* (Frederick W. Ruckstuhl)
> Portico Windows: *Morning and Night, Noon and Evening* (Maximilian M. Schwartzott)
> Balustrade (right to left): *Mohammed* (Charles Albert Lopez) [removed at the request of the Moslem community of New York], *Zoroaster* (Edward C. Potter), *Alfred the Great* (Jonathan Scott Hartley), *Lycurgus* (George Edwin Bissell), *Justice* flanked by *Study and Power* (Daniel Chester French), *Solon* (Herbert Adams), *Louis IX* (John Donoghue), *Manu* (Augustus Lukeman), *Justinian* (Henry Kirke Bush-Brown), *Confucius* (Philip Martiny) [facing Madison Avenue].
> Pediment: *Triumph of the Law* (Charles H. Niehaus)

A visit to the interior is most rewarding (open weekdays only). The furniture was designed by the architectural and interior design firm of Herter Brothers, the cabinetry by George C. Flint Company, the sculpture of Charles O'Connor by James W. A. MacDonald, and the stained-glass windows by the Maitland Armstrong Company. Nothing was spared in making the Appellate Court House an aesthetic, architectural masterpiece.

15. The Metropolitan Life Insurance Company buildings complete the panorama of the west side of Madison Square. The original main building, at the corner of 23rd Street, was built in 1893. Its crowning glory, however, came in 1909 with the 700-foot tower addition, making it the tallest building in the world at the time, and the identifying symbol of the company—"the Light that Never Fails." Designed by architect Napoleon LeBrun, the tower is based on the *Campanile* of St. Mark's Square in Venice. Four years after its completion, its height record was surpassed by the 60-story Woolworth Building, downtown. In the mid-1950s, the original main building was demolished and the present 12-story structure erected in its place. The tower was given a "facelifting" as part of the overall modernization project, with most of the ornamentation stripped off the façade. Only the four 3-story-high clocks and the surmounting gilded lantern escaped this architectural butchery, leaving the tower gaunt and denuded.

An interesting event in the history of the 50-story tower occurred on election night 1908, one year before its completion. The *New York Herald* installed a giant searchlight among the still-exposed girders near the top of the spire to signal the election results far and wide. A northward-swinging beam would indicate a majority for the Republican presidential candidate William Howard Taft, and a southward beam for Democrat William Jennings Bryan. As the first returns showed a plurality for Taft, the beacon moved slowly up and down in a northward direction. By a little after 8 P.M., as the telegraphed vote count gave a clear majority to the Republican, the searchlight's rays were held steadily northward. Thus New Yorkers and suburbanites for miles around were the first to get the election results transmitted from the tall tower's beacon.

The **North Building,** occupying the block between 24th and 25th streets, was designed by Wald, Corbett, & Angilly, and built in three stages from 1932 to 1950. A striking example of the Art Deco style, the massive Alabama limestone exterior was planned to conform to the city's building regulations requiring extensive setbacks on tall buildings. Their "stepped" arrangement, along with the interesting angular upper walls and chamfered corners, can best be appreciated from across the Square. Arched loggias at the four corners provide entrance arcades that lead to central elevator halls, and the huge building is connected to the Home Office Building by a skywalk and a tunnel. The lobby walls are faced with handsome Italian cremo marble. Just before the outbreak of World War II the company stockpiled huge blocks of this marble for fear that a war might destroy the northern Italian quarries and prevent a uniform completion of the building's interior. The North Building holds the distinction of being the first commercial structure in New York City to have central air conditioning.

On the site of the adjacent Metropolitan Life Tower stood the brownstone Gothic Revival-style Madison Square Presbyterian Church, built in 1853. Its outspoken minister, the Reverend Charles H. Parkhurst, led a vociferous campaign in 1893–94 against citywide crime and police corruption. Accused by angry Tammany politicians of being self-serving, Dr. Parkhurst documented his charges by personally visiting the dens of iniquity that City Hall denied existed and proving complicity and brutality by the police. After these revelations from Parkhurst's pulpit, the State Legislature convened the Lexow Committee, whose subsequent investigation corroborated Dr. Parkhurst's accusations and led to the defeat of Tammany Mayor Hugh Grant, a major shakeup in the Police Department, and the appointment of Theodore Roosevelt to the Board of Commissioners. The Metropolitan Life Insurance Company acquired the church property for needed building expansion, and in exchange for the corner plot, agreed to build a new house of worship across the street for Dr. Parkhurst's congregation. Stanford White was commissioned to design the new church which was completed in 1906 in Italian Renaissance style. The bright, white granite New Madison Square Presbyterian Church was White's last public building and is considered by many authorities to be the most beautiful building he ever designed. In 1919, the ever expanding company purchased the property and

For a brief period in 1906 there were two *Madison Square Presbyterian Churches standing side-by-side. Needing additional land to erect its famous tower, the Metropolitan Life Insurance Company bought and razed the older Gothic Revival-style church and built another for Dr. Charles H. Parkhurst's congregation. The neo-classic "temple," Stanford White's last commission, survived only until 1919 when the Insurance Company again acquired the property to build its North Building. (Metropolitan Life Insurance Company)*

demolished the lovely church. (The parishioners had, for the most part, moved to more fashionable precincts uptown anyway, as the neighborhood by that time was almost exclusively commercial.) A "new" annex was erected to the Home Office, but it, too, was razed when the new North Building was designed.

16. Madison Square Park became the pleasant oasis it is now in 1870. At the time of the Revolution it was a swampy grassland traversed by a meandering stream, abounding with game. Later it became a paupers' burial ground. By the first decade of the 19th century, a military outpost was established as part of the defenses of the lower city at the junction of the Eastern Post Road and the Middle Road—now Broadway—near the present intersection of Fifth Avenue. In 1811, the famous New York City Commissioners' Report officially designated the street pattern of much of Manhattan Island, and a "Parade" was laid out between 23rd and 34th streets, and Third and Seventh avenues. A few years later it was greatly reduced in size and named in honor of the then fourth president, James Madison. In 1844 the Square was again reduced, to its present size. In its concept the plan was a forerunner of the one that subsequently gave us spacious Central Park.

Enter the Park at the Statue of Roscoe Conkling.

Elected as a Republican to the U.S. Senate in 1867, Conkling served the Empire State for 14 years. He resigned in 1881 after a dispute with President Garfield and retired to law practice. During the Great Blizzard of March 12, 1888, he was caught without transportation home from his downtown office, and set out on foot against the mounting drifts and sub-zero cold. He became lost in Madison Square, but was rescued and carried to his nearby home. The effects of the exposure, however, were fatal, and he died six weeks later. This bronze memorial statue, by sculptor John Quincy Adams Ward, was erected in 1893 through contributions by friends, and stands on the precise site where he was felled by the blizzard.

Hansom cabs line the west side of Madison Square, across from the fashionable Fifth Avenue Hotel, as two young ladies stroll toward the camera of Percy C. Byron, 1905. (The Byron Collection. Museum of the City of New York)

Three types of horse-drawn carriages wait outside Delmonico's, at Fifth Avenue and 26th Street, in 1888, then the most fashionable dining place in town. A number of years later, the restaurant moved up Fifth Avenue to 44th Street where it finally closed in 1923. The restaurant on the site of Delmonico's first establishment at Beaver and South William Streets still preserves the name. (New-York Historical Society)

Walking to the northwest corner of the Park under the broad elms and horse chestnuts, we come to the imposing **statue of Admiral David Glasgow Farragut.** In a dramatic posture as a rugged sailor facing the wind, Farragut is memorialized as the great naval hero of the Civil War. His victories at New Orleans and Mobile Bay finally closed all Gulf ports to the Confederacy. One can almost hear him shout that celebrated order, "Damn the torpedoes, full speed ahead!" Appropriately, he is represented in bronze by famed sculptor Augustus St. Gaudens, with Stanford White as the designer of the pedestal and bench.

A short distance to the west is the **statue of Chester A. Arthur,** 21st President, who assumed the office after the assassination of James Garfield in 1881. The monument, by George Bissell, was unveiled in 1898 and was a gift of Catherine Lorillard Wolfe, who lived in a brownstone on the site of the Metropolitan Life Tower.

17. Directly north of Madison Square, at the northeast corner of Fifth Avenue, is the attractive **Art & Gift Center Building.** Built of red brick and limestone in a Renaissance Revival style, this commercial building's excellent state of preservation is a tribute to the artistic sensibilities of its present owners. It was formerly called the Brunswick Building, after a posh hotel that once occupied the site. Notice the *palazzo*-like features, the elaborate iron balconies, and the ornate copper cornice.

18. Cross Fifth Avenue to the **General William J. Worth Monument.** Designed by James C. Batterson and erected in 1857, this monument marks the only burial site of a public figure under a Manhattan thoroughfare. Worth fought in the Seminole and Mexican wars, and the names of some of his famous battles are carved on the granite shaft. Although a downtown street is named for him, he is perhaps more of a hero in the state of Texas, where the city of Fort Worth honors his memory. Interesting is the cast-iron fence with repeating sword motifs, now in a sad state of disrepair. The mysterious marble-faced structure behind the monument is a City water-metering station. The Catskill Water Supply tunnel passes just below.

Along Fifth Avenue and adjacent Broadway stood many famous landmarks of the gaslit era. On the northeast corner of Fifth Avenue and 26th Street was Delmonico's, the most fashionable dining spot in town. On the southwest corner of Broadway and 26th Street stood the St. James Hotel, whose name is borne today by the Gothic Revival skyscraper on the site.

Looking north on Fifth Avenue at Madison Square Park. In 1876 the arm of the Statue of Liberty was brought from Philadelphia's Centennial Exposition to New York as a means of raising money for the base and the costs of assembling France's gift to America. The statue was finally erected ten years later. Behind the General Worth Monument is the Brunswick Hotel. The first spire on the left belongs to the Marble Collegiate Church. (New-York Historical Society)

Occupying the west side of Broadway between 24th and 25th streets was the Hoffman House, an elegant hostelry of the time, whose bar was also a noted art gallery. Remembered particularly is Adolphe Bouguereau's huge, somewhat risqué painting, *Nymphs and Satyrs,* which created quite a sensation in those Victorian days. The painting can be seen today, no longer causing a stir, at the Clark Art Institute, in Williamstown, Massachusetts.

19. Make a brief detour along West 25th Street to the **Serbian Orthodox Cathedral of St. Sava.** Designed in 1855 by noted church architect Richard Upjohn, it was built in Gothic Revival style for the Trinity Church's uptown Chapel, and is now a designated landmark. Alongside is the 1860 Parish House, in Victorian Gothic style, by J. W. Mould. The buildings were purchased by the Serbian Church in 1943.

Walk through the alleyway between the buildings and return to Broadway, turning south to the corner of 24th Street.

20. The building occupying the entire block to 25th Street, as well as its neighbor to the south, are linked together not only by a skywalk, but by the same street number: **200 Fifth Avenue.** This pair of commercial buildings is the Toy Center, home for most of the city's wholesale toy manufacturers and distributors.

A few yards down 24th Street stood the Madison Square Theater, famous at the turn of the century for its hydraulically operated double stage.

Across the street, at the edge of the Park, is the **Eternal Light Monument** currently under repair. Erected in 1924 from plans by Thomas Hastings (of the architectural firm of Carrère & Hastings) and Paul W. Bartlett, its star-topped light burns day and night to honor the fallen of World War I. At a point just to the left, the arm of the Statue of Liberty was displayed from 1876 to 1884 while funds were being raised to pay for the base. The arm and torch were first sent by France to the Philadelphia Centennial Exposition, then brought to Madison Square Park. The arm was later returned to France for completion of the statue which was finally erected in 1886.

21. The tall **sidewalk clock** in the next block is one of the last remaining on the streets of New York, a vestige of the days when wristwatches were unknown and pocket watches were for the affluent. They were usually placed in front of a commercial establishment as an advertising gimmick. This cast-iron street clock, which still runs perfectly, was built by the Hecla Iron Works in the 1880s with a movement by Seth Thomas—the oldest surviving American clockmaker.

22. The plaque on the massive Toy Center Building at the corner of 23rd Street describes some of the former tenants of the site. The **Fifth Avenue Hotel** was the most luxurious in the city when it was completed in 1859. Earlier in the 19th century, there was a post tavern used for changing horses, and later a road house, known as Corporal Thompson's Madison Cottage. The *New York Herald* of May 9, 1847, carried the following notice about the inn:

> MADISON COTTAGE—*This beautiful place of resort opposite Madison Square, corner of Twenty-Third Street and Broadway, is open for the season, and Palmer's omnibuses drive to the door. It is one of the most agreeable spots for an afternoon's lounge in the suburbs of our city. Go and see!*

In 1853, Franconi's Hippodrome replaced the Cottage, offering a variety of public entertainment in an open-air arena, which included chariot races and circus performances.

The elegant dining salon of the subsequent Fifth Avenue Hotel was a favorite gathering place for the financial and political bigwigs of the day. A nightly spectacle at the main entrance was the steady procession of flashy carriages with matched teams of horses, bringing such giants as "Jay" Gould, "Jim" Fisk, "Larry" Jerome, Commodore Vanderbilt, and "Boss" Tweed. The powerful politico "Tom" Platt—credited with Theodore Roosevelt's presidential victory in 1898—held court before a coterie of adulating yes-men near the bar, in his so-called "Amen Corner." O. Henry, in his *Voice of the City,* vividly described the life and spirit of the times. The Hotel was also

Madison Square c. 1916 is no longer dominated by the "Garden" but by the Metropolitan Life Insurance Company buildings rising on the east side. Horse-drawn vehicles are still plentiful, but the age of the motorcar has already begun. (Metropolitan Life Insurance Company)

frequented by Mark Twain, Edwin Booth, William Cullen Bryant, and Stanford White.

Cross Fifth Avenue to the Park.

   23. The Statue of William H. Seward, by Randolph Rogers, was unveiled in 1876. As U.S. Senator from New York before the Civil War, and later as Lincoln's Secretary of State, Seward so distinguished himself as a statesman that President Andrew Johnson retained him in his own cabinet. A wise choice indeed, as Seward foresaw the importance of Alaska and was responsible for its purchase. However, the statue was not well received. One critic proclaimed that "Mr. Seward was a man 'all head and no legs,' whereas the statue represents the statesman with unusual length and prominence,"—an observation that lends credence to the legend that the statue originally was not Seward, but *Abraham Lincoln Signing the Emancipation Proclamation!* (Note that one hand holds a scroll and the other a pen.) It is believed that Rogers, lacking the necessary funds to complete a Lincoln statue, switched heads at the last minute.

   24. Directly across 23rd Street, in the triangle formed by the confluence of Fifth Avenue and Broadway, stands the striking **Flatiron Building.** Newly arrived from Chicago and his successful participation in the planning of the Columbian Exposition of 1893, Daniel H. Burnham designed this innovative and daring commercial structure in the Italian Resaissance style. With a steel framework and rusticated limestone walls, this "Italian palace" in the shape of a flatiron startled even blasé New Yorkers when it was completed in 1902. Visitors at first shunned the rooftop observation deck, predicting that strong winds would soon topple "Burnham's Folly." With fears allayed by the passage of time, the panoramic view attracted crowds of sightseers. On a clear day, the New Jersey palisades and Coney Island's beaches were easily visible. Although originally designated the Fuller Building, popular insistence on calling it by what it resembled forced the owners to yield and make the building's nickname official. It is now a designated landmark. Note the ornate, yet restrained façade, whose undulating walls and sharp corners, topped by a classic cornice, result in a dramatic perspective. The protuberance on the ground floor extending toward 23rd Street was added a few years later, and was dubbed "the cowcatcher."

   The busy intersection in front of the Flatiron Building has always been a particularly windy spot, and in the era when skirts trailed on the ground, it was a favorite vantage point for girl watchers hoping for a glimpse of a trim ankle. It is said that nearby traffic policemen would turn from their task of untangling the confusion of horsecars, omnibuses, wagons, and carriages, to shoo away these young voyeurs—hence the expression, **"Twenty-Three Skiddoo!"**

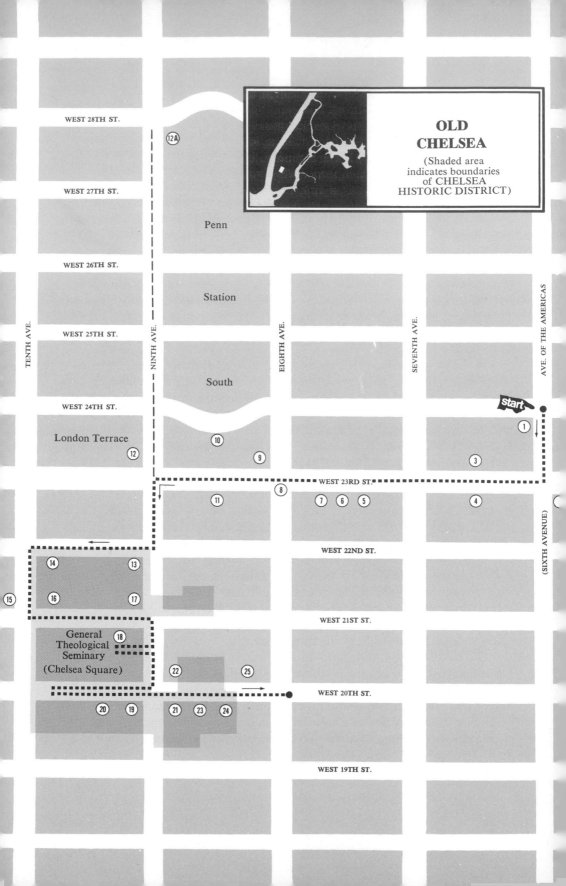

OLD
CHELSEA

(Shaded area
indicates boundaries
of CHELSEA
HISTORIC DISTRICT)

11. Old Chelsea

[*IRT Broadway-Seventh Avenue line, IND Sixth Avenue line, BMT Broadway line, PATH Line to 23rd Street stations; Broadway, Fifth, Sixth, Seventh Avenue buses to 23rd Street*]

The neighborhood now encompassed by 14th to 30th streets and Avenue of the Americas to the Hudson River, was rural farmland in 1750 when Captain Thomas Clarke bought a tract of land there and named it after the Chelsea Royal Hospital, an old soldiers' home built by Sir Christopher Wren in the Chelsea borough of London.

It was Clarke's grandson, however, who was to bring fame to Chelsea and immortality to himself. A professor of Classics and biblical literature at the General Theological Seminary, **Clement Clarke Moore** is remembered less for his scholarly *Compendious Lexicon of the Hebrew Language* than for his inspired poem, "A Visit from St. Nicholas," composed in 1822 while he was driving in a sleigh from the lower city, bringing goodies for the Christmas dinner. In addition to popularizing Santa Claus, Moore did much to influence the development and character of the neighborhood through foresight and wise urban planning. He served as vestryman at St. Luke's Church in Greenwich (Village), and was a founder of St. Peter's Church in Chelsea. He also donated the land for the General Theological Seminary and established guidelines for local residential zoning that in great measure contributed to the charming atmosphere of much of Chelsea today.

Moore is buried in uptown Trinity Church Cemetery (155th Street and Riverside Drive), where, every Christmas Eve, a candlelight procession of children carolers lays a wreath on the grave of the author of " 'Twas the night before Christmas. . . ."

By mid-19th century Chelsea had grown into a peaceful residential area. Only the chugging of the locomotives of the Hudson River Rail Road on Eleventh Avenue, and the rattling Eighth Avenue horsecar—Chelsea's first "rapid" transit, disturbed the quiet of the streets. But the tranquility of the neighborhood was shattered some 20 years later with the arrival of the city's liveliest entertainment district. Once sedate 23rd Street now echoed to the sounds of music halls and late-night revelers. The Ninth Avenue El—the city's first overhead railway, pushed through the Chelsea district in 1871, and the noisy, steam-driven trains competed with the furor of iron-tire dray wagons, horse-drawn omnibuses and clanging bells of a proliferating network of horsecar lines. Along Sixth Avenue, a new and enormous shopping center was developing, as huge, palatial department stores opened their doors in what was to be the most popular retail district in the city. A year later the Sixth Avenue El added its roar to growing clamor, and in the shadow of the El, at 30th Street, the "Haymarket" enjoyed the reputation of being the most raided den of vice in the city's history.

As the century drew to a close, a new dimension was added to Chelsea with the birth of the motion-picture industry, as studios ground out silents in enormous, barnlike buildings east of Sixth Avenue.

Chelsea has become relatively quiet again. The music halls are all gone, the theaters have moved uptown, the great department stores either folded or relocated elsewhere, the film industry discovered Hollywood, and the Els were sent as scrap iron to Japan. And with the departure of commerce, the neighborhood began to decline. The lovely row houses deteriorated, and the area took on an air of neglect and decay. Then, at the last minute, Chelsea received a reprieve. With the shortage of housing and skyrocketing real-estate values, a new population entered the scene. Writers, actors, advertising executives, teachers, and other professionals discovered Chelsea and began buying up the aging town houses, restoring them with loving care. Overnight a "restoration revolution" began and the neighborhood is once again becoming an eminently desirable place to live—and just minutes from the heart of town. The designation by the Landmarks Commission of a part of Chelsea as a Historic District has added even greater impetus to maintaining the appearance and traditions of this charming quarter.

Many vestiges of the past are still to be seen: the old department store buildings, bits and pieces of the old theater district, several lovely churches, the delightful campus of the General Theological Seminary, and the row upon row of splendid town houses. But the special quality of Chelsea—still very much in evidence on almost every block—is the charming 19th-century atmosphere, all within the shadow of midtown Manhattan.

The tour begins at the corner of Avenue of the Americas (formerly Sixth Avenue) and West 24th Street.

1. The small, red brick building on the southwest corner (best seen from across the street) is all that remains of one of the most popular entertainment spots of the gaslit era, Koster & Bial's Concert Hall. The Hall itself used to face 23rd Street, and is long since gone, but this structure, once the beer-garden annex, was known as **The Corner.** Its name still survives in the upper cornice, and is the sole reminder of a once frenetic entertainment career.

Koster & Bial's opened in 1879, and was probably the liveliest vaudeville house in town. Here Victor Herbert conducted his 40-piece orchestra, and between the music, the free-flowing liquor, and imported talent, the Concert Hall became *the* place during the "Naughty '90s." Seeking a larger theater and anticipating another uptown move by the entertainment district, Koster & Bial closed their popular establishment and entered into a short-lived partnership with impresario-composer Oscar Hammerstein at his 34th Street Manhattan Opera House (on the present site of Macy's). The relationship was tempestuous at best, and ended in a court battle that saw the exit from "show biz" of Koster & Bial, while Hammerstein's star continued to rise.

2. On the southeast corner of 23rd Street and Avenue of the Americas from 1869 to 1883 stood the **Edwin Booth Theater,** with Booth himself as manager and frequent star performer. In spite of brother John Wilkes Booth's assassination of President Lincoln, Edwin remained one of the country's most popular actors. When James W. McCreery, known as the "Dean of the Retail Trade," acquired the site, he demolished the theater and erected his second department store. (The first still stands at Broadway and 11th Street, a cast-iron building converted into an apartment house.) In 1907 the firm moved uptown again, but his building remained until 1975. [For a detailed description of the department stores of the gaslit era, *see* Ladies' Mile.]

Across the Avenue, on the southwest corner, is a small cast-iron building that once housed **Riker's Drug Company** and was later absorbed into the

Des Morgens schmeckt der Brandewein,
Desgleichen am Mittage,
Doch wer ihn Abends trinken thut,
Ist frei von jeder Plage;
Hingegen soll ein Brandewein,
Um Mitternacht
nicht schädlich
sein.

Koster & Bial's "The Corner," a beer hall annex to the famous 23rd Street Music Hall, still stands at the southwest corner of Sixth Avenue and 24th Street. This photo was taken in 1904. (Museum of the City of New York)

Liggett Drug chain. The Riker's name can still be distinguished on the Avenue of the Americas side, underneath a coat of paint on a panel below the second story.

Similarly, the name of **Ehrich Brothers,** another of the great emporiums, can barely be made out on a rusting iron panel on the adjoining building on 23rd Street. The huge store, which faced both 23rd Street and Sixth Avenue, surrounding Riker's corner, gave up the ghost in 1911.

Cross to the north side of 23rd Street and walk west.

3. Imbedded in the sidewalk in front of what was once No. 141 West is an advertisement in brass letters of **Proctor's Twenty-Third Street Music Hall.** Another of the great vaudeville showplaces, Proctor's opened in 1888, in a large, Flemish-style building, packing them in wih such top-flight stars as "Jersey Lily" Langtry, the inimitable Lillian Russell, Scotland's idol Harry Lauder, female impersonator Julian Eltinge, Eva Tanguay, the "I Don't Care" girl, and sparkling Lottie Collins, who never failed to stop the show cold with her rendition of "Ta Ra Ra BOOM De Ay!" E. F. Proctor later

Proctor's became the most famous music hall in the city when it opened in 1888, and featured only topflight entertainers. In this Byron photograph, taken c. 1910, Lillian Russell is the starred performer. (The J. Clarence Davies Collection. Museum of the City of New York)

opened other theaters throughout the city as well as out of town, and when he died, his chain was sold to R.K.O. for a reported $16 million.

4. Continue west on 23rd Street, noting **No. 148–156,** a large Gothic Revival-style commercial building on the south side of the street. Again on the north side, fanciful **Nos. 167** and **169,** a curious pair, which resemble the backdrop for a comic opera, were originally residences. Their date of construction is uncertain, but in 1898 they received a dramatic face-lifting. To a full cast-iron façade was added a sheet-metal cornice, and atop No. 167, a Disneylike tower. Farther down the street at No. 209 is the **Muhlenberg Branch of the New York Public Library,** named for the first pastor of the nearby Church of the Holy Communion (Avenue of the Americas and West 20th Street). Two doors beyond is the busy **McBurney Branch of the Y.M.C.A.,** built in 1904.

5. On the south side of the street, midway between Seventh and Eighth avenues, is a proud survivor of the quarter's Golden Age—the striking **Hotel Chelsea.** When opened in 1884 as a cooperative apartment house, it was a most luxurious address for those well-to-do artists who sought a quiet and elegant atmosphere to inspire creativity. In 1905 it became a hotel, and its guest register through the years reads like an artistic and literary *Who's Who.* Notice the bronze plaques honoring such greats as Mark Twain, Thomas Wolfe, Dylan Thomas, and Brendan Behan. Other notables who have graced the Hotel Chelsea are O. Henry, Sarah Bernhardt, Lillian Russell, Edgar Lee Masters,[*] John Sloan, Larry Rivers, James T. Farrell, Arthur Miller, Tennessee Williams, Virgil Thomson, Jackson Pollock, and Yevgeny Yevtushenko.

Built by Hubert, Pirsson & Company in a style that has been described as Queen Anne or Victorian Gothic, its outstanding architectural features are its exuberant roofline with dormer and tall chimneys, and its richly ornamented iron balconies and interior grand staircase. The labels at the base show that the iron was cast by the J. B. & J. M. Cornell Iron Works. When built, its 11 stories made it one of the tallest structures in the city. Studios were added on the roof, making it the first such building to have duplexes. The hotel also boasted the first penthouse in town. The lobby has been altered considerably and now doubles as a contemporary art gallery, presided over by owner-manager Stanley Bard, himself a patron of the arts. The broad iron staircase, which used to open with a broad sweep into the lobby, has been closed off at the ground-floor level because of fire laws. Its ten-story circular ascent to the roof can, however, be admired from the second floor. Time has been kind to the old dowager. Its Edwardian charm still remains,

---

[*] Edgar Lee Masters, known mainly for his *Spoon River Anthology* (1915), also wrote a short poem entitled "The Hotel Chelsea":

> Today will pass as currents of the air that veer and die.
> Tell me how souls can be
> Such flames of suffering and of ecstasy,
> Then fare as the winds fare?

The Grand Opera House, on the northwest corner of 23rd Street and Eighth Avenue, was not only a theater, but the headquarters of Jim Fisk's Erie Railway. After Fisk was shot by Edward S. Stokes over a lover's quarrel and lawsuit in 1872, the Opera House was taken over by Jay Gould. The Grand Opera House later featured silent films and degenerated into a second-rate movie house, falling under the wrecker's ball in 1960. (The J. Clarence Davies Collection. Museum of the City of New York)

just as faithfully as its devoted clientele. Because of the hotel's historic and architectural merit, it has been designated a New York City Landmark.

6. The synagogue **Congregation Emunath Israel,** at No. 236–238, occupies the former house of worship of the Third Reformed Presbyterian Church.

7. No. 256 was the **site of Cavanagh's Restaurant,** which opened in 1876. A favorite dining spot for the elite in the heyday of Chelsea's entertainment era, it hosted such personalities as Lillian Russell, "Diamond Jim" Brady, and John L. Sullivan. It was also the hangout of powerful turn-of-the-century Tammany Hall politicians. The exclusive establishment fell on hard times and had to close its gaslit-era dining room in 1970.

8. The intersection of Eighth Avenue and West 23rd Street marks the approximate **site of the original Thomas Clarke house.** The farm, named "Chelsea," was situated between the Fitzroy Road (which ran parallel to and just west of 8th Avenue) and the Hudson River, from 19th to 24th streets. The Fitzroy Road was the principal north-south thoroughfare and began about two blocks south, at Love Lane, between the present 21st and 22nd streets. Love Lane ran east to the Albany Post Road (later Bloomingdale Road; now Broadway), the only route to the lower city. When the Clarke house burned down in 1777, his widow had it rebuilt farther west, on a bluff overlooking the Hudson, between the present Ninth and Tenth avenues. Two years later, a grandson, Clement Clarke Moore, was born there.

9. When Pike's Opera House opened on the northwest corner in 1868 with a performance of Verdi's *Il Trovatore,* it was an instant success . . . so successful that financiers Jay Gould and Jim Fisk bought it within the year. They changed its name to **The Grand Opera-House** and enlarged its repertoire to include all kinds of theatrical entertainment. Some of the productions were tailor-made for the talents of Josie Mansfield, Fisk's mistress. Josie lived in an adjacent mansion, connected to the Opera-House by an underground tunnel. The two partners even moved the offices of their Erie Railway into the theater. That year, when Fisk and Gould attempted to corner the gold market, causing the "Black Friday" panic, it is said that Fisk, himself in a panic, hid in the vault of the Opera-House to avoid the wrath of the surging crowds. In the meantime, Josie, tiring of "Jubilee" Jim, began taking up with a former partner of his, Edward S. Stokes. This led to a series of lovers' quarrels and a sensational lawsuit, all paraded across the front pages of New York's dailies. A chance meeting on January 6, 1872, between Fisk and Stokes on a stairway of the old Grand Central Hotel resulted in Stokes drawing a revolver and shooting Fisk to death. Jay Gould continued to operate the theater for a number of years. During the first decade of the 20th century, the Opera-House inaugurated the "Subway Circuit," offering first-run productions shortly after their initial Broadway openings. By World War I, the theater, like so many of its contemporaries, switched to silent films with vaudeville, and continued as a movie house until 1960, when it was demolished to make way for the sprawling Penn Station South housing development.

10. Penn Station South (Eighth to Ninth avenues, 23rd to 29th streets) was built in 1962 by the ILGWU (International Ladies' Garment Workers Union) as a middle-income housing co-op. Appropriately close to the Garment District, this mammoth urban-renewal project occupies 12 square blocks of former tenements, injecting new life into the Chelsea area.

11. The very solid-looking building across 23rd Street, at **No. 322–324,** is an office of the T. E. Conklin Brass & Copper Company. The building was formerly the American Jersey Cattle Club.

The **James N. Wells Real Estate Company,** at No. 340, is the oldest of its kind in Chelsea and dates back to 1845 when Wells, the manager of Clement Clarke Moore's estate, helped Dr. Moore with his plans for the residential development of Chelsea. He was also a skillful builder and was responsible for the construction of St. Luke's Church in Greenwich Village (where Moore served as vestryman). (More about James N. Wells later.)

12. Before the construction of the present **London Terrace Apartments** (occupying the entire block, Ninth to Tenth avenues, 23rd to 24th streets) in 1930, an earlier "London Terrace" stood on the site. Designed by famed architect Alexander Jackson Davis in 1845, the original row of Greek Revival buildings was set back from the street behind a shady garden and protected by an iron fence. A three-story high colonnade ran the entire length of the row, giving the town houses an air of stately elegence. With the wealth of its prominent tenants, London Terrace was soon known as "Millionaires' Row." On the 24th Street side was a similar row of town houses, but only two stories high, called the Chelsea Cottages.

The new complex, built by Farrar & Watmaugh, is in reality two separate rows of interconnecting apartment buildings surrounding a central garden. In addition to the 1670 units, there is a swimming pool, solarium, a number of stores, a bank, and a post office. When the new London Terrace first opened, the doormen were uniformed as London "bobbies"—a touch of charming snobbery. After all, Chelsea was a London suburb, and this was thought to add upliftment to the area.

The Clement Clarke Moore residence stood alone in the block to the south until 1854 when land development forced the demolition of the large, three-story house. Dr. Moore spent his summers at Chelsea, his winters on Charlton Street in Greenwich Village, and occasionally stayed at a third

The original London Terrace, designed by architect Alexander Jackson Davis in 1854 and known as "Millionaire's Row." A year after this photo was taken in 1929 the new 1670-unit London Terrace apartments were erected. (The Consolidated Edison Company of New York)

The house of Clement Clarke Moore, author of " 'Twas the Night before Christmas . . . ," which stood alone on high ground between Ninth and Tenth avenues, 22nd to 23rd Street until 1854. This is a lithograph from Valentine's Manual *of the same year. (Museum of the City of New York)*

home in the village of Newtown (now Elmhurst) in what is now the Borough of Queens.

12A. An optional side trip may be made to the landmark **Church of the Holy Apostles,** at Ninth Avenue and 28th Street. The church, designed by noted architect Minard Lafever in 1846–48, is quite handsome but fits into no particular architectural style; although some say it was a forerunner of the Italianate style. Dominating the structure is the greatly oversized bronze and slate steeple, yet it is not incongruous among the towering apartment houses that surround it. Most attractive are the splendid stained-glass windows by William Jay Bolton, America's greatest stained-glass artisan of the time. The square glass panels with delicately painted circular medallions present a dazzling spectacle when brightened by the rays of a late afternoon sun. The transepts were added in 1858, and were designed by another well known architect, Richard Upjohn (& Sons).

Return to 23rd Street and continue south. Turn west (right) on 22nd Street. The tour route now enters the officially designated Chelsea Historic District.

13. Nos. 400–412, built in 1856 in the Italianate style, are known as the **James N. Wells Row.** These narrow houses were each designed with an English basement and small entranceways, and form a harmonious unit with their original roof cornice. All but one still retain their dormer windows. No. 408 is probably the best in the row, except for its modified windows and lintels (which are original in No. 406); however, only No. 404 has its original doors.

No. 419–421, on the north side, also dates from 1856.

No. 414–416 (1835) dates from the decade of the Greek Revival, and was the residence of James N. Wells. An elegant mansion, it is the last surviving Greek Revival house with five bays (windows) in Manhattan. Some remodeling took place in the 1860s, and in 1875 it was sold to the Samaritan Home for the Aged. In the 1930s the Salvation Army acquired it for a women's shelter. It is now a rooming house.

No. 436–438 was the **residence of actor Edwin Forrest** [*see* East Village, 16, for more about Edwin Forrest and the Astor Place Riot]. Built in 1835 in Greek Revival style, it was bought by Forrest in 1839 together with the adjoining properties, Nos. 430–434. It was rumored that Forrest wanted the house as a sanctuary from his numerous in-laws who had moved in with him and his new bride when he lived downtown. Some years later the house was

Actor Edwin Forrest purchased this stately town house (No. 436 West 22nd Street) four years after it was built in 1835, allegedly as a sanctuary from bothersome in-laws. In more recent times it was the home of former Secretary of State Christian Herter. Unfortunately, a series of mindless "modernizations" have all but obscured its original appearance. (Museum of the City of New York)

The interior of No. 436 West 22nd Street after Edwin Forrest's death, when it was owned by I. W. Drummond at the turn of the century. (Museum of the City of New York)

acquired by Christian Herter of the famous interior decorating firm of Herter Brothers. Sadly, the house has suffered too many "modernizations" through the years and is now a shadow of its former self.

No. 444 (1835–36) is a rather well preserved Greek Revival-style house, and was the property of Clement Clarke Moore. Note particularly the charming attic windows set in a wooden frieze (fascia) board below the cornice.

Nos. 446 and 448, the Berrian-Walker Houses, were built in 1854 in the popular Italianate style of the middle decade of the 19th century. No. 448 unfortunately suffered a major renovation when its front wall was reconstructed with the addition of two bays per floor, instead of one, as with No. 446.

No. 453, across the street, is from the mid-1850s and has interesting, ornate hooded lintels over the windows.

The L. Monette apartment building, **No. 454,** was built in 1897 in a neo-Renaissance style, and although a multifamily tenement house, is not an unpleasant addition to the street.

14. Clement Clarke Moore Park on the southeast corner of Tenth Avenue, was designed by Paul M. Friedberg, a landscape architect, as a multilevel play park, and was opened in 1968.

Turn left (south) on Tenth Avenue.

Before the progressive landfill projects of the 19th century, the Hudson River shoreline extended to where the east side of Tenth Avenue is now. As the streets and avenues were pushed through, the hills were leveled, and the earth was used to reclaim the land to the west.

15. The Guardian Angel Roman Catholic Church, known familiarly as the Shrine Church of the Sea, was built in 1910 when the port of New York was much busier than it is now, when much of the church's constituency came from the ships from far-flung parts of the world. It still serves a sea-oriented community.

On the east side of the avenue, **No. 188–192** is a small apartment house built in 1891 in the Queen Anne style.

Turn east (left) on West 21st Street.

A pleasant feature of the north side of the street is the set-back arrangement of the houses, with a lush front yard complementing the dignified "halls of ivy" of the General Theological Seminary, across the street.

16. Nos. 473–465 are a well preserved row of brick and brownstone Italianate houses, all built in the year 1853. **No. 471** is the best in the group, closest to the original design. Note the following architectural features of the houses: the bracketed entablature over the doorways, bracketed roof cornices, double-hung windows, the window lintels and window guards, cruciform paneled doors, and low stoops with cast-iron railings.

No. 463 was the first to be built on the block (1836) and dates from the Greek Revival period. Its brickwork is laid in Flemish bond (alternating short and long bricks, called "headers" and "stretchers"). Pedimented lintels cap the windows, and the attic windows are set in a wooden fascia board.

Nos. 461–459, now joined together as one house, were built separately in 1854. The pair is called the William Cummings House after a descendant of the original owner of No. 461, Thomas Cummings, and both are typical brownstones in the Italianate style. Compare them with adjacent **457 and 455.** The latter two, built in the same year, are of a somewhat different style. Note the difference in height of the stoops. Thoughtless renovations over the years have destroyed the symmetry of the row of houses.

No. 453 (1857) still preserves its splendid entranceway. Crowning the stoop with its cast-iron railings is an arched doorway, above which a huge cornice slab rests on stuccoed consoles.

No. 445 (1898) is another neo-Renaissance-style apartment house. Built of Roman brick and stone, it is typical of the so-called Eclectic Period of the late 1890s.

The brownstone doorway of **No. 407** (1852), is one of the best preserved in the neighborhood, and is also quite unique in design. Note the carved head in the keystone of the arch, the doorway pediment supported by a pair of consoles, the ornate moldings of the brownstone enframement around the doorway, and the doors themselves, with hexagonal panels.

Another fine example of the Italianate style is **No. 405,** the last in the row of set-back houses, built the same year as No. 407. The Landmarks Commission, in its designation report for the Historic District, calls it "one of the purest examples of this style in Chelsea." All the original elements remain intact, with the single exception of the entrance doors.

17. Delightful No. 401, listed officially as **No. 183 Ninth Avenue,** was built in 1831–32, and is the second oldest house in the Historic District. It still preserves much of its original Federal-style appearance, and can best be viewed from across the street. The four-sided pitched roof, dormer windows, simple cornice above an equally simple fascia board, and side entrance are typical elements of the Federal style. The brickwork is in Flemish bond, the more expensive way of laying bricks, evidence of a wealthy original owner. Look up at the painted sign on adjacent No. 191 Ninth Avenue, advertising the James N. Wells & Son Real Estate firm. Wells lived here for a time (1833–34) and maintained his office on the second floor, where his descendants carried on for many years. The sign itself is probably over 80 years old. The ground-floor store was incorporated into the building very early in 1835.

The three small wooden houses to the right, **Nos. 185, 187, and 189** were all built for Wells, No. 185 in 1856, the other pair in 1868. Wooden

The Gothic-style General Theological Seminary on Chelsea Square in an 1841 lithograph, as seen from Ninth Avenue between 20th and 21st streets. (New-York Historical Society)

houses are now a rarity in Manhattan, and these three, while not as old as they appear, add a bit of old-time flavor.

18. The General Theological Seminary, No. 175 Ninth Avenue, occupies the entire block from Ninth to Tenth avenues, and 21st to 20th streets. The plot, known as Chelsea Square, was donated to the Seminary by Dr. Clement Clarke Moore, himself a professor of Biblical Learning at the institution. The lovely campus with its shady lawns and small-town college atmosphere is a veritable oasis in the city; it is open to the public on Sundays (and at other times by appointment).

The modern building facing Ninth Avenue houses the administrative offices and the excellent St. Mark's Library; but one must first pass through the large entranceway into the inner quadrangle to appreciate the old-world quality of the campus.

Construction of the Episcopal Seminary began in 1825 with a Gothic-style East Building (now demolished), and was followed in 1836 by a counterpart on the west side, which still remains as a fine academic building. Early seminarians had an unobstructed view of the Hudson as the riverbank reached the western edge of Chelsea Square. The completion of most of the Seminary complex was accomplished during the brief period 1883–1902, when Eugene Augustus Hoffman, the third dean of the school, revolutionized the physical setting by engaging architect Charles Coolidge Haight to create a master plan for a campus equal to that of most American colleges of the day. Through Hoffman's own financial contributions and his ability to interest wealthy laymen, an endowment was established for professorships and the groundwork laid for the development of a great theological library.

The St. Mark's Library, which was completed in 1969, replaces Haight's original building and contains 170,000 volumes available to the public for reference. It is the nation's outstanding ecclesiastical collection and has the largest collection of Latin Bibles in the world! Among the Rare Book Room's treasures are a collection of medieval manuscripts, prayer books and psalters, and an original Gutenberg Bible—one of six in the nation, a gift of Dean Hoffman.

Haight's plan called for an arrangement of buildings roughly in the shape of a letter "E" with the spine along West 21st Street. The style of construction was one that he himself pioneered, the English Collegiate Gothic. Centrally placed is the **Chapel of the Good Shepherd,** dominated by a 161-foot-high, square **Bell Tower.** Interestingly, the interior of the Chapel is devoted mainly to choir stalls, since most of the communicants are postulants for Holy Orders. The spectacular bronze doors, by J. Massey Rhind, were executed in 1899, in memory of Dean Hoffman's son.

Sherred Hall, a three-story classroom building flanked by dormitories, was the first to be erected, and expresses beautifully the simple quality and uniform character sought by the architect. Its arched main entrance is especially noteworthy.

The culmination of the building plan came with the opening of handsome

An 1854 engraving of Gothic-revival row houses which once lined 20th Street at the corner of Sixth Avenue before the arrival of the parade of Fashion Row department stores. (Museum of the City of New York)

Hoffman Hall, the refectory-gymnasium building. The enormous dining hall, like a medieval knights' council chamber, re-creates an atmosphere of the Middle Ages. The huge fireplaces at each end, a musicians' gallery, a coffered barrel-vaulted ceiling, and a stained-glass bay window, combine to make it one of New York City's most beautiful interior spaces.

On leaving the Seminary grounds, turn right, and right again into West 20th Street.

19. No. 402, a neo-Colonial-style apartment house, was designed in 1897 by C. P. H. Gilbert, the architect of the Warburg Mansion (now the Jewish Museum), the former National Democratic Club, the Convent of the Sacred Heart, and a host of other fine buildings. The name "DONAC" is an acronym for the original land owner, Don Alonzo Cushman. Tenants have a pleasant view down West 20th Street through their large concave bay windows.

No. 404 is the oldest house in the Historic District. Built in 1829–30, it still retains one clapboard side wall. A Federal-style house, it later received a Greek Revival doorway, had its roof raised one story, and in the 1850s was modified with Italianate parlor-floor windows.

20. Nos. 406–418, built for Don Alonzo Cushman in 1839–40, ranks among the most beautiful Greek Revival rows of town houses in the country. Equal in many respects to "The Row" on Washington Square North [*see* Greenwich Village, 3, 5], this group of seven pristine houses, called **"Cushman Row,"** displays a wealth of architectural detail. The 10-foot front yards are a most agreeable complement to the greenery of the Seminary across the street. Nos. 408 and 414 are unchanged since the day they were built, except for the cast-iron newel posts. Notice the pineapples, a traditional symbol of welcome, atop the newels in front of Nos. 416 and 418. Exceptional are the charming attic windows encircled by cast-iron wreaths. Note, too, the well proportioned entablatures over the doorways, set on Doric pilasters; the molded window lintels and the six-over-six windows, typical elements of the Greek Revival style.

Don Alonzo Cushman (1792–1875) was a successful dry-goods merchant ("Don" *was* his first name, and not a title) who became associated with Clement Clarke Moore and James N. Wells. He was a founder of the Greenwich Savings Bank—one of the oldest savings institutions in the city. With his later involvement in real estate, he helped influence the development and shape the character of the Chelsea neighborhood.

Return to Ninth Avenue.

21. The large Greek Revival-style house on the southeast corner, **No. 162 Ninth Avenue,** was the long-time residence of James N. Wells (he lived briefly at No. 414–416 West 22nd Street, and his offices were seen earlier at No. 183 Ninth Avenue). Built in 1834, it was one of the most imposing residences in Chelsea. Although somewhat modified, it still retains its original wide doorway, fluted Doric columns topped by a large entablature, and pedimented window lintels. The rambling, former *one*-family mansion is now occupied by 12!

Continue east on West 20th Street.

22. The group of four Italianate buildings on the north side of West 20th Street **(Nos. 361–355),** were built for Don Alonzo Cushman. No. 361 was built in 1860, the other three in 1858. Although somewhat altered, they present a fine row of houses. The late 19th-century ironwork on the stoops is very attractive, as is the rope moldings on the inner doorways. No. 353 still preserves its original, ornate cast-iron railings.

23. On the south side, another Italianate row **(Nos. 348–358),** was built in 1853–54 for the six children of James N. Wells. Each house is only two bays wide and set behind a small front yard. The Landmarks Commission describes it as "one of the longest and most charming of the rows of English basement houses to be found in Chelsea." It is unfortunate that each house has suffered some alteration; however, Nos. 348 and 352 are probably closest to the original design. Note the "ear panels" on the doors of No. 358. The entire row of buildings is unified by its original cornice line, which has survived unscathed.

24. The **St. Peter's Church group,** consisting of Rectory, Church, and Parish Hall, was, like its nearby neighbor the General Theological Seminary, built on land donated to the institution by Dr. Clement Clarke Moore. The cornerstone for the original Chapel, which is now the **Rectory Building,** was laid in 1832, making it the oldest church building in Chelsea, and one of the oldest Greek Revival-style buildings in the city. It once had full-height Doric columns, but these were removed and replaced with unusual brick pilasters.

The **church building** was completed in 1838 in Gothic Revival style, and is considered a prototype of the English parish Gothic Church—the first of its style in this country. Dr. Moore served as vestryman and organist for a number of years, and it is said that he was responsible for the selection of the church's design. Among the names on the cornerstone are those of Dr. Moore, James N. Wells, and architect-builder, James W. Smith, himself a resident of Chelsea. The church building is virtually unchanged except for the loss of its beautiful Gothic wooden porches, which had to be removed because of rotting. The marks left by the old porches can still be seen on the church walls. Unlike the usual Gothic church built in cruciform shape, St. Peter's is built on the plan of a Greek temple. The pulpit, chancel rail, and lectern were presented as a memorial to Don Alonzo Cushman by members of his family.

The **Parish Hall,** called St. Peter's Hall, completes the group. It was completed in 1871 in the so-called Victorian Gothic style. The ornamental **wrought-iron fence** that embraces the three buildings is from St. Paul's Chapel downtown and was a gift in 1837 from the mother church, Trinity Church.

25. No. 331, on the north side of the street, was a rather late Greek Revival house, built in 1846. Notice its passageway leading to a rear building. Although it is the only one in the Historic District with such a passageway, nearby Nos. 307 and 305 have similar features. Occasionally called "horsewalks," they sometimes served as an access-way to a rear stable.

End of tour.

12. Forty-Second Street

Come and meet those dancing feet,
On the Avenue I'm taking you to,
Forty-Second Street.
Hear the beat of dancing feet,
It's the song I love the melody of,
Forty-Second Street.

Little "nifties" from the Fifties, innocent and sweet,
Sexy ladies from the Eighties, who are indiscreet.
They're side by side,
They're glorified.
Where the underworld can meet the elite,
Naughty, bawdy, gawdy, sporty,
*Forty-Second Street.**

[Words by Al Dubin, Music by Harry Warren]

[IND A, AA, E lines to 42nd Street station; BMT Broadway line, IRT Broadway-Seventh Avenue line, or IRT #7 Flushing line, to Times Square; 42nd Street Crosstown bus to Eighth Avenue]

Few thoroughfares in the world are as well known or as widely diversified as 42nd Street—New York's major crosstown artery for almost three-quarters of a century. Considered by New Yorkers as the center of the city and, at its intersection with Broadway, the center of the world, it slices the middle of

---

Construction of the Ninth Avenue El (the New York Elevated Railroad) station at 42nd Street, 1875–76. (Museum of the City of New York)

Manhattan horizontally from the Hudson to the East rivers. Although the street was opened officially in 1836 with the removal of squatters' shanties and the filling in of the *Grote Kil* (Big Stream), the real history of 42nd Street begins late in the 19th century, and will be discussed block by block on the tour.

The tour begins in front of the old McGraw-Hill Building, 330 West 42nd Street, west of 8th Avenue.

1. New York's "green skyscraper," the **former McGraw-Hill Building,** was completed in 1931 from plans by architect Raymond M. Hood, in collaboration with Fouilhoux & Godley, in a unique variation of the Art Deco theme. The building's shape, with its series of setbacks, was dictated by the Zoning Law of 1916, and architect Hood exploited these requirements boldly and effectively. Unusual are the metallic bands of green, silver, and gold that encircle the ground floor and continue into the lobby; while on the façade above, row upon row of bluish-green terra-cotta bands continue the motif. Two other examples of Hood's ingenuity will be seen later. When the McGraw-Hill Publishing Company opened its new office skyscraper at 1221 Avenue of the Americas, fear was expressed for the future of the lovely green tower. However, in late 1974, Group Health Incorporated (GHI) took possession of it for its own corporate headquarters.

2. The Holy Cross Roman Catholic Church, across the street, dates from 1868, and hearkens back to the time when the neighborhood was predominantly Irish, and known as "Hell's Kitchen." An area of small factories and blocks of festering slums, it was one of the most notorious sections of the city, where even the police walked in fear and only in broad daylight. The church now ministers to a somewhat smaller, if more peaceful community. The simple exterior, in an early Romanesque Revival style, belies the ornateness of the spacious interior. In a mixture of styles, primarily Italian Baroque, the architect has created an impressive nave and sanctuary. Observe the high, barrel-vaulted ceiling, the wooden balcony, the fine paintings of Peter, Paul, and Jesus in the apse, and the surprisingly high-quality stained glass. The adjacent Rectory building is interesting for the semicircular hoods (or labels) above the windows. This was famous Father Duffy's Church for many years—Francis P. Duffy, who worked so hard to uplift the old "Hell's Kitchen" neighborhood and break up the tough gangs that gave it such an unsavory reputation. It was Father Duffy who was closely associated with many theater personalities, and who served as chaplain of the "Fighting 69th" Division (actually the 165th Infantry Regiment) in the trenches of France during World War I. He served until his death in 1932, and an appreciative Broadway community erected a statue of him in Times Square.

3. A surviving row of tenement houses (c. 1875) ends at No. 319 West, which is painted in "patriotic" colors to advertise the **Kaufman Surplus Company.** A local landmark for years, its pair of World War I French Hotchkiss cannons guarding the door are about the only war surplus items not for sale.

4. At the northwest corner of 8th Avenue is the new home of the **Franklin Savings Bank,** completed in 1974 after its earlier building on the southwest corner was demolished. Although not eye-catching from without, the interior presents an unexpected sight. Rising from the center of the hall to the tall ceiling is a massive column, from the top of which, like a gigantic open umbrella, radiate 16 "ribs" of bare pre-cast concrete reaching across to the far walls. The innovative architects were Poor and Sewanke & Partners, with Richard Hayden. It is a pity, though, that the former bank building, located diagonally across the street—a lovely Classic Revival-style edifice, with superb bronze doors, designed in 1899 by York & Sawyer, could not be preserved.

5. Directly south, the busy **Port Authority Bus Terminal,** at West 41st Street, completed in 1950, is the world's largest, with twin levels of bus ramps serving tens of thousands of daily commuters from New Jersey as well as long-distance bus riders. Above the sprawling terminal is an immense multi-level parking garage.

6. The block between 8th and 7th avenues is commonly referred to as New York's **"Sin Street."** More seedy than sinful, it boasts no fewer than 15 movie houses (count 'em!)—possibly a world record. The theaters offer a wide range of films, including first-runs, foreign films, "oldies," and X-rated. Most of the older movie houses were once legitimate or vaudeville theaters and still show some architectural traces of their more glamorous past: the Empire, New Amsterdam, Lyric, Apollo, and Times Square—the latter two sharing the same Classic front. Peek into the ornate lobby of the New

Amsterdam Theater, built just after the turn of the century. Crowded cheek by jowl among the "flicks" are a dismal aggregation of penny arcades, "bargain" clothing shops, "porno" book dealers, and "going-out-of-business" stores. The block has grown to be a popular promenade with the more earthy elements of New York society and is regularly the target of (unsuccessful) clean-up campaigns by City Hall.

From the south side of 42nd Street, look north to the fancifully ornate building which rises above 43rd Street with a black, peaked roof perforated with little dormer windows, and surmounted by a lantern. Built in 1913 for the *New York Times* when it shifted operations from its Tower on Times Square, it is a handsome structure in German Renaissance style, virtually hidden by newer neighbors.

Of some architectural interest is the way-out-of-scale **Candler Building** (No. 220 West), rising high above its sleazy surroundings, and best viewed from across the street. Designed by Willauer, Shape & Bready, and completed in 1916, it represents no particular architectural style (some might call it Eclectic) but it does have a pleasing, if somewhat grimy, façade flanked by its slanted parapet "shoulder" buildings. The building is named for the owner of the Coca Cola Company, Asa G. Candler, who in 1912 acquired the property and had the structure built for his offices. The ground floor was occupied by the Bryant Park Bank; and below, a branch of the Exchange Buffet, New York's pioneer chain of "honor system" cafeterias, in which patrons merely informed the cashier on leaving what they had

The north side of 42nd Street just west of Times Square, c. 1910, showing the Lyric and Belasco theaters. Oscar Hammerstein's Victoria faces Times Square at right. (Photograph by Byron. The Byron Collection. Museum of the City of New York)

The picturesque Casino Theater was built in 1882 on the southeast corner of Broadway and 39th Street as a concert hall, but played mostly comic operas. In this Byron photograph taken around 1900, shortly before it was acquired by the Shuberts, the Arabesque style building is covered with advertisements for a long-forgotten musical. The Casino Theater survived until 1930. (The Byron Collection. Museum of the City of New York)

The height of satiety was reached in 1903 when C. K. G. Billings gave his famous Dinner on Horseback at Sherry's for a group of friends from his riding club. Diners were served on trays fastened to the horses' pommels by waiters in footman's livery. (Photograph by Byron. The Byron Collection. Museum of the City of New York)

The Latting Observatory Tower burned to the ground on August 30, 1856, a harbinger of the fate of the nearby Crystal Palace two years later. (New-York Historical Society)

The ruins of the Crystal Palace as depicted in Harper's Weekly, October 16, 1858. (New-York Historical Society)

The transept of the cast-iron-and-glass Crystal Palace Exhibition Hall as seen from the Gallery. Many nations were represented in this first American world's fair of science, industry, and art. (New-York Historical Society)

Posing for an unknown photographer in front of the Casino Theater entrance in 1924, is stage-door tender William Reilly. The gas lamp once stood in front of the Hoffman House Cafe, at Broadway and 26th Street; and was placed at the theater to recognize the 72-year-old Reilly's former career as a member of the City's once vast army of lamplighters. (The Consolidated Edison Company of New York)

Looking west on 42nd Street from in front of the original Grand Central Terminal in the early 1890s. Just beyond is the brand new Hotel Manhattan, at the corner of Madison Avenue, now the site of the Sperry & Hutchinson Building. (Museum of the City of New York)

eaten, and were charged accordingly. To the left, the **New Amsterdam Theater** (1903) is a fanciful building with a sculpture grouping in high relief in each of three tympani high on the façade. Notice, too, the old advertisements painted on the side walls—the east side proclaiming 42nd Street "The Movie Street of the World."

Walk to the north end of the old Times Tower [see map] between 42nd and 43rd streets.

7. Known universally as "The Crossroads of the World," **Times Square** is the heart of the entertainment district, and has been for almost a century. In the 1880s and 1890s, the two vertical triangles forming the "square" were lined with carriage dealers and called Long Acre Square, after a London district (the name lives on in the nearby *Longacre Theater* and in the *LOngacre* telephone exchange). Then the Rialto arrived! The Metropolitan Opera House opened just to the south, at 39th Street and Broadway, in 1893; Charles Frohman built his large Empire Theater across the street in 1894; Oscar Hammerstein (*père*) moved up from his 34th Street Manhattan Opera House site to open the dazzling Olympia Music Hall in 1895. The Olympia, looking for all the world like a Renaissance palace, occupied the entire Broadway block front from 44th to 45th streets, had a roof garden, café, concert hall, and theater, and was the talk of the town. Hammerstein also built the lavish Victoria Theater on the northwest corner of 42nd Street, where the Rialto Theater is now. Others soon followed, one more grandiose than the other, offering not only legitimate theater, but vauderville, cabaret, and music-hall entertainment. Many even had roof gardens with luxurious restaurants. And to further satisfy the appetites of the new theater crowds came such establishments as Shanley's, Rector's, Churchill's, and the Café de l'Opéra. Broadway is still synonymous with the Stage, but only about two dozen legitimate theaters survive in the Times Square area; and only one new theater has been built in the last 25 years. Most are clustered in the one block west of Broadway, between 44th and 52nd streets. Little Shubert Alley, connecting 44th and 45th streets, still evokes the glamor of "show biz," surrounded as it is by a number of theaters with brightly illuminated marquees.

With the rise of the film industry in the 1920s, enormous and opulent movie palaces opened along Broadway, displacing the "legit" theaters to the west. Who can forget such names as the Palace, Strand, Capitol, Paramount, Rialto, Rivoli, Warner (where in 1927 New Yorkers were treated to the first sound film, Al Jolson in *The Jazz Singer*), and the most lavish of them all, the Roxy? Some still remain, but mostly in name only. The Paramount Film Corporation (now swallowed up by the Gulf+Western conglomerate) erected the massive theater and office building on the west side of the Square, between 43rd and 44th streets, a unique addition to the cityscape. Designed in 1926 by Warren & Wetmore, the architects of Grand Central Terminal, the incredible shape of the **New York Paramount Building** with nine ascend-

Times Square in 1900—then called Longacre Square, looking south from 45th Street, with the New York and Criterion theaters at left, and Rector's famous restaurant in the next block. (Photograph by Byron. The Byron Collection. Museum of the City of New York)

ing setbacks on each side gives it the appearance of a symmetrical pile of gargantuan children's building blocks assembled by some young Gulliver. The setback style resulted from the Zoning Law of 1916. The tower clocks and black glass globe top off this Art Deco landmark.

With the arrival of New York's first subway line in 1904, *New York Times* publisher Adolph Ochs astonished his contemporaries by moving out of "Newspaper Row" downtown and erecting his famous wedge-shaped **Times Tower** at the intersection of 42nd Street, Broadway, and 7th Avenue. Ochs persuaded the city fathers to name the new subway station after the *Times,* and with that, the name of the Square soon followed. Built of pink granite in Italian Renaissance style, and decorated with glazed terra cotta, the Times Tower became the dominant landmark on the Square. When the *Times* moved in on New Year's Eve of 1904, its fireworks display was to start a tradition with New Yorkers. Each December 31, since 1908, enormous throngs of revelers have massed before the Tower awaiting the descent of the famous illuminated sphere announcing the arrival of the New Year. Even after the newspaper moved all of its operations into its former annex on West

43rd Street, and the Times Tower was rebuilt as the Allied Chemical Tower, the old custom was preserved. Another hallmark of the former building is the electric news "ribbon" with its 12,408 bulbs that flashes headlines around the building. When Allied Chemical vacated the old Times Tower in 1975, the building was purchased by real estate developer Alex Parker, and temporarily renamed **No. One Times Square.** A more appropriate name will be selected in a contest after a major renovation is completed. Plans by architects Charles Gwathmey and Robert Siegel call for sheathing the east and west walls with 5-by-7-foot mirrors—mirrors through which tenants can see out, but which, according to Parker, "will turn the outside of the structure into a constantly changing collage of Times Square with its lights, signs, and movement." The building is to include an upper area of clear glass to serve as an exposition hall, as well as a three-level arcade at ground level connected by escalators.

In front of No. One Times Square is a newsstand selling papers from major cities throughout the country, while just inside, *Hotaling's* has foreign

The Pabst Hotel, on 42nd Street, facing away from Longacre Square. The hotel and adjoining four-story buildings were demolished in 1903 to make way for the Times Tower. (Photograph by Byron. The Byron Collection. Museum of the City of New York)

periodicals from around the world. In the small structure to the north, operated by the City's Department of Commerce and Industry, the **Times Square Information Center** offers helpful advice to visitors.

Hotels also were built in the new theater district. For some 60 years the *grande dame* of them all, the **Hotel Astor,** was a familiar site on Times Square. Commissioned by Col. John Jacob Astor, it was built in a florid Classic style with a huge mansard roof, opening its doors in 1904 on the block between 44th and 45th streets. The modern 50-story office tower built on the site in 1969 keeps the name alive with its address, One Astor Plaza. An equally fashionable hostelry of the past was the **Knickerbocker Hotel.** It still stands, but has been converted into an office building. Situated on the southeast corner of 42nd Street and Broadway, it was also commissioned by Colonel Astor and built in somewhat the same style. Observe the three-story

The changing faces of the Times Tower (left) as it appeared when built for the New York Times in 1904; (center) as the Allied Chemical Building in 1964; (right) as it will look, sheathed in mirrors as One Times Square in 1976. (Alex Parker)

mansard roof and classic detail so popular with hotel construction in the first decade of the 20th century. Its much frequented King Cole Bar sported a Maxfield Parrish mural that now adorns the equally venerable (but still elegant) St. Regis-Sheraton Hotel uptown. Enrico Caruso lived for some time at the Knickerbocker, as did George M. Cohan.

The traffic pattern in Times Square is much saner since the one-way routing was established. Before World War II, the scene was always one of bedlam, or at least total chaos. Adding to the confusion created by the number of intersecting streets were the trolley lines that criss-crossed Times Square on both Broadway and Seventh Avenue. The 42nd Street Crosstown car, which either went west to the 42nd Street Ferry or turned north on Broadway, contributed further to the disorder.

The upper "V" of Times Square is known as **Father Duffy Square.** His statue in front of a Celtic cross stands close by that of **George M. Cohan,** "giving his regards to Broadway."

The new office tower on the east side of Times Square between 43rd and 44th streets (No. 1500 Broadway) is typical of what is slowly happening to the famous Square. Some fear that in a few short years, all the bright lights and glamor will be gone as commercialism moves in, and the Great White Way will be but a memory. In fact, much of the spectacular "sound and light" show is already gone. The block-long waterfall, the smoke-ring blower, and many other glittering cascades of neon have long since vanished. Nonetheless, Times Square continues to be a major nightly attraction; and its role as herald of the New Year seems unshakable.

Continue east on 42nd Street.

8. Midway down the block, on the south side, stands the cathedral-like **Bush Terminal Building** (No. 130 West). Although the structure was built in 1918, architects Helmle & Corbett seemed to have had a more recent tenant in mind—the Wurlitzer Music Company—formerly a next-door neighbor until No. 120 was demolished. The neo-Gothic-style building looks very

Looking north from the top of the just-completed Times Tower, 1905. To the left is the then brand new Hotel Astor with its fashionable roof garden. (Museum of the City of New York)

appropriate to a company that sells organs—actually, it is the largest key-board manufacturing company in the country, making pianos as well. Soon after Rudolph Wurlitzer founded the firm in 1856, he was called upon to produce musical instruments for the Union Army bands. Later the company specialized in keyboard instruments exclusively, producing in the early 1930s the largest organ in the city, the "Mighty Wurlitzer" for the Radio City Music Hall. For a time they made juke boxes too. Wurlitzer has been on 42nd Street for over 50 years and has resisted all temptation to move to a more "posh" location uptown, claiming that the company is unalterably rooted in this famous street.

Notice the *trompe l'oeil* effect on the side walls of the building, where vertical bands of tan and brown bricks are paired to give an illusion of depth. The sheer verticality of the structure is emphasized by its 480-foot height on a plot of ground only 50 feet wide.

Across the street, the building that houses the Love Theater was formerly the American Savings Bank, and its name is still emblazoned across the parapet. Farther east, the small decaying Art Deco building (No. 115) was another branch of the same bank.

9. The gleaming white marble and black glass **New York Telephone Company Building,** at the southwest corner of Avenue of the Americas, is one of the newest skyscraper office towers erected by "Ma Bell" for local corporate headquarters. Completed in 1974 from plans by Kahn & Jacobs, it serves as the "anchor" for a growing line of new "glass boxes" springing up along the Avenue north of 42nd Street. The narrow plaza to the west of the building with its mini-waterfalls and tree plantings is a pleasant oasis between the tall towers—a concession to the zoning laws that require open space in proportion to building height. Above the new subway entrance in the west lobby is an attractive and colorful mosaic mural by Richard Kirk (but why hidden away from the main entrance?).

Avenue of the Americas, formerly called Sixth Avenue, was renamed by former Mayor Fiorello H. LaGuardia. In spite of the decorative coats of arms of the Latin American nations mounted on the Avenue's lampposts, most New Yorkers rejected the mayor's flamboyant gesture, and still refer to the thoroughfare by its original name.

From 1878 until 1938 the Sixth Avenue El rattled overhead, keeping the busy Avenue in perpetual twilight. The broad vistas from the old wooden platform cars, however, were superb.

10. One of the newest additions to the city's ever growing skyline is the slope-fronted **W. R. Grace & Company Building** (No. 43 West), completed in 1974. The revolutionary profile derives from the architects' (Skidmore, Owings & Merrill) interpretation of the zoning regulations, which stipulate the ratio of a building's verticality to the amount of horizontal setback. The façade is covered with travertine, and although the shape is controversial, it is a relief from the endless rows of unimaginative glassy boxlike towers springing up all over town. What is objectionable to many is the resultant

The Avenue of the Americas today is a far cry from the dark and dingy Sixth Avenue (as it was then called) of 75 years ago. Looking north from 42nd Street, the Manhattan Elevated Railroad seems to cast a pall of gloom over the Avenue. (New-York Historical Society)

destruction of the 42nd Street "street wall," considered an essential element in urban design. Also unsuccessful is the rear plaza, designed like an enormous checkerboard. The addition of trees (in boxes) has not helped much. To enter from the 43rd Street side, one is forced to cross the full length of the plaza. The two-story private reception area on the 47th and 48th floors (unfortunately, not open to the public) is impressive, with a spiral staircase set against broad expanses of city panorama. A similar building (by the same architectural firm) was built simultaneously at 9 West 57th Street.

The Grace Building occupies the **site of the Stern Brothers Department Store,** which stood on the L-shaped plot from 1913 to 1970. (Interestingly, Stern's first store, an immense cast-iron building still in pristine condition, stands on the south side of West 23rd Street, between Fifth and Sixth avenues [see Ladies' Mile, 21].)

11. Adjacent No. 33 West, formerly a commercial office building, is now the **Graduate Center of the City University of New York.** The most striking feature is the renovation of the ground floor, with its concrete cantilevered "canopy" and the open passageway to 43rd Street. The split-faced concrete walls of the passage are in sharp contrast to the exterior—one can almost forget that the building was erected in 1912. Access is by a glassed-in bank of elevators in the passageway. Pleasant and convenient for pedestrians, the mall is used for exhibitions and has been tastefully planted with shrubbery (although one wonders how they can survive in the cavernous darkness). In the 1920s the building was famous for its third-floor concert hall, Aeolian Hall (note the lyres on the façade), and witnessed the premiere of George Gershwin's *Rhapsody in Blue.* The Graduate Center was dedicated in 1970 after a three-year renovation, and has been the recipient of many awards for excellence in design. The Municipal Art Society awarded it a special prize "for improvement of the aesthetic quality of life in New York City," and *New York Times* architecture critic Ada Louise Huxtable describes the Center as "one of New York's most successfully recycled buildings."

12. No. 11 West, the **Salmon Tower,** is distinguished only in its elaborate entrance and luxurious lobby. Around the ornate arched entrance on both 42nd and 43rd streets are bas-relief sculptures of the months plus a row of Classic figures above, representing the professions. Through the vaulted passage are marble walls and decorative bronze fixtures. Even the two mailboxes are adorned with similar low-relief sculpture in bronze. The "tower" actually faces Fifth Avenue, as **No. 500 Fifth,** the two buildings being connected by a second-floor passageway. No. 500, completed in 1931 from plans by Shreve, Lamb & Harmon, is the second tallest building on the Avenue, eclipsed only by the Empire State Building at 34th Street (built the same year by the same architectural firm). Known also as the Transportation Building, it formerly housed the New York offices of virtually every important railroad in the country. In their stead today are numerous foreign airlines.

Cross 42nd Street and return to Avenue of the Americas, turn left at the corner, and enter Bryant Park.

13. The entrance to **Bryant Park** is marked by a small square accommodating the memorial to José Bonifacio de Andrada e Silva, a Brazilian scientist and patriot. The statue, by José Lima, was executed in 1889 and presented by the United States of Brazil in 1954. To the right, dominating the western end of the landscaped park, is the Josephine Shaw Lowell Memorial Fountain. The pink Stoney Creek granite fountain honoring the pioneer social worker and philanthropist was designed by Charles A. Platt and presented to the City in 1912.

Bryant Park occupies the **site of the Crystal Palace Exhibition of 1853–54,** America's first World's Fair. Modeled after London's famous exhibition of two years earlier, it was an enormous domed iron-and-glass pavilion, designed to display fine arts and industrial products from around the world. Like a gargantuan greenhouse built with Victorian elegance, its pinnacles rose 76 feet above what was then called Reservoir Square. Although it was one of the most spectacular attractions ever to be presented in New York, it was a financial failure, and in 1858 it was destroyed by a tragic fire. Although no one was injured, many priceless works of art were lost. Across 42nd

The burning of the Crystal Palace, October 5, 1858. The Exposition which was held in 1853–54 is now the site of Bryant Park. (New-York Historical Society)

Street, near the northeast corner, stood the tall, conical **Latting Observatory.** Built of timbers reinforced with iron girders, and equipped with steam elevators to the second landing, the tower provided excellent views of the Crystal Palace, the adjacent reservoir, and the growing city farther downtown. In 1856 it, too, was consumed by fire. During the Civil War, the park site was used as a drill field by Union troops.

Bryant Park was dedicated in 1934 after the successful entry in a competition for its design was won by Lusby Simpson, an unemployed architect from Queens. Walk down the flagstone path shaded by London plane trees to the east end, where the beautiful New York Public Library serves as an appropriate backdrop. To the left is the statue of William Earl Dodge by John Quincy Adams Ward. Dodge (1805–1883) was a merchant and philanthropist, and a founder of the Y.M.C.A. In the center of the north-south axis, protected by a Roman-style arch, is the **statue of William Cullen Bryant** (1794–1878), poet, journalist, and orator. The sculpture was executed by Henry Adams in 1911, and dominates the eastern end of the Park. To the right is a bust of Johann Wolfgang von Goethe by Karl Fischer, presented to the City by the Goethe Society in 1932.

14. **The skyscraper panorama** surrounding Bryant Park is striking. Look particularly to the West 40th Street side where, left to right, the following interesting buildings can be seen to good advantage:

The Republic National Bank Building, formerly the Knox Building (at the corner of Fifth Avenue). This 1902 ornate Classical showpiece was built for the Knox Hat Company. It suffered some modifications in 1965 (note the "picture windows" punched into the mansard roof), but it still retains much of its charm.

Freedom House (No. 20 West), the memorial to Wendell Willkie, is dedicated to gathering information on the status of human freedom throughout the world. A mixture of Classic and Flemish Renaissance styles it is a pleasant addition to the block.

The Engineers Club (No. 32 West) is a Classic-style building of pleasing proportions.

The American Radiator Building, designed in a bold, cubic massing of forms by architect Raymond M. Hood in 1923, is the undisputed beauty of the block. With its unique black-and-gold color scheme, it is most impressive. It has been said that its striking color combination, illuminated at night, gives it the appearance of an enormous glowing coal—ideal for the corporate offices of the American Radiator Company. In 1926 Talbot Hamlin, the noted architectural historian, described it as "the most daring experiment in color in modern buildings yet made in America." Note how the tower's setbacks terminate in gold-colored cubistic masses—forms often associated with the Art Deco style. The arched and pinnacled form at the top of the tower is a delightful crown to this artistic skyscraper. Recognizing its daring departure in architectural style, its colors, and its imaginative adaptation to the 1916 Zoning Law, the building was designated a New York City Landmark in 1974.

No. 50 West 40th Street, now used by Daytop Village, is interesting for its massive, segmented column shafts. At the corner of Avenue of the Americas is a typical Classic Eclectic building of the turn of the century.

Note, too, the Beaux Arts-style former comfort stations at each end of the path, in complement to the style of the Library. Bryant Park, because of the high quality of its landscape architecture, its historical and aesthetic interest, and its splendid urban location has been designated an official Scenic Landmark by the New York City Landmarks Preservation Commission.

On exiting from the Park at West 40th Street, note the bronze plaque to Wendell Willkie, mounted on the retaining wall.

Walk left to Fifth Avenue, then left to the main entrance to the Library.

15. The New York Public Library building is considered the finest example of the Beaux Arts style in America. A majestic, delicate, and supremely aesthetic structure, its location at Fifth Avenue and 42nd Street is ideal. The site in the early 19th century was a potter's field, but with the opening of the Croton Aqueduct and water supply system for the city in 1842, a distributing reservoir was erected—a huge Egyptian-style enclosure with walls 50 feet high and 25 feet thick, surmounted by a promenade. With the construction of the Croton Dam, the reservoir was no longer needed, and was demolished in 1899 to make way for the new Library.

In a competition to select the architect, winning plans were submitted by the firm of Carrère & Hastings, and the building was inaugurated in 1911. Attending the ceremonies were the President of the United States, the governor, and the mayor. Completed at a cost of $9 million, it is one of the truly great libraries of the world. The New York Public Library was the result of the merger in 1895 of the three largest private libraries in the city: the Astor, Tilden, and Lenox libraries, with endowments from each of the trusts, plus a building grant from Andrew Carnegie of $5.2 million. The New York Free Circulating Library joined the consolidation in 1901.

The exterior is built of Vermont marble, and the building, in the traditional Louis XVI Renaissance form, presents an ingratiating rather than imposing appearance. It is built around two inner courts with an immense central reading room occupying a half-acre of floor space. Dominating the grand entrance are the two famous lions designed by Edward C. Potter. The style of the majestic lions is from standard architectural forms, but they have been the source of humorous criticism since their installation, even to the unspeakable pun of "reading between the lions." The 95-foot tapered steel flagpoles are set on exquisite bronze bases designed by Thomas Hastings and were installed in 1941 as a memorial to former reform Mayor John Purroy Mitchell. The sculptured figures on either side of the main entrance are by Frederick MacMonnies: The man seated on a sphinx on the northern side represents *Truth;* the woman seated on Pegasus on the south side represents *Beauty*. The six figures on the attic wall over the main entrance are by Paul Bartlett and are executed in Georgia marble for contrast. They depict, from left to right, *Philosophy, Romance, Religion, Poetry, Drama,* and *History*. The two groups in the pediment by George Gray Bernard represent *Art* and *History*.

The main lobby is reached by a flight of stairs to a triple-arched portico. The entire monumental space is of stone with barrel-vaulted arches, flanked by twin grand staircases supported on flying arches leading to the upper floors. Statues of John Merven Carrère and Thomas Hastings are set in niches on the first landing. The walls of the third-floor Central Hall are of dark wood, above which are plaster-paneled barrel vaults. Notice how the ceiling extends over the cornice line at each end to permit light to enter from segmental arch windows. An illusionistic painting above creates the impression of an open sky. The fine murals were painted by Edward Laning, under the auspices of the Artists Program of the WPA, and were completed in 1940. The four arched murals represent the four stages in the development of the recorded word: *Moses with the Tablets of the Law, The Medieval Scribe, Gutenberg Showing a Proof to the Elector of Mainz,* and *The Linotype— Mergenthaler and Whitelaw Reid.* The murals in the lunettes above the square-headed doors are *Learning to Read* (west side), and *The Student* (east side). The aerial mural on the ceiling, with its *trompe l'oeil* effect, tells the story of *Prometheus Bringing Fire to Men.*

Both the exterior and interior of the New York Public Library have been designated as landmarks.

Continue north on Fifth Avenue to the corner of 43rd Street.

16. The Manufacturers Hanover Trust Company Building (No. 510), on the southwest corner, was designed in 1954 by Skidmore, Owings & Merrill, and is a good example of the early use of the "glass cage" as a building style. Look through the broad glass pane at the exposed bank vault door.

Turn left (west) on West 43rd Street.

17. The former Columbia University Club (No. 4 West), is an example of Italian Renaissance style, but a much finer representation can be seen across the street in **the Century Association** (No. 7 West). A superb example of the Florentine Renaissance style so characteristic of Stanford White's architectural firm of McKim, Mead & White, it was begun in 1889 and took two years to complete. Typical Renaissance features are the monumental arched doorway and Palladian window above, the rusticated base, and the wreathed round windows above the third-floor windows, which are skilfully joined to those below. Topping the building is a balustrade and ornate cornice. The Association dates from 1847 and was established "to promote the advancement of art and literature." The name "Century" refers to the original 100 members, among whom was William Cullen Bryant.

Return to Fifth Avenue, turn left, stopping in front of the Morgan Guaranty Trust Company.

18. The 20-foot-high **Seth Thomas street clock** is probably the oldest artifact on the block. Built of cast iron, these sturdy timepieces were prevalent throughout the country from the 1880s until World War I, when the popularity of the wristwatch eliminated the need of a public clock. Most served as advertising gimmicks for the shops in front of which they were erected. Seth Thomas is still in business—the last survivor of dozens of 19th-century American clockmakers.

The southwest corner of 44th Street was the site of famed **Sherry's,** one of the most lavish and fashionable establishments at the turn of the century. A combination restaurant and residential apartments, it catered to New York's most affluent clientele for 21 years. The building, erected for owner Louis Sherry, was subsequently remodeled by McKim, Mead & White for the Guaranty Trust Company, and remained until the early 1950s when it was demolished to make way for the present successor bank.

No less extravagant was **Delmonico's,** Sherry's arch rival, which, just six months before, moved up from its Madison Square location into an ornate Beaux Arts building designed by James Brown Lord on the northeast corner.

The restaurant with its ballrooms and bachelor residences was closed in 1923, four years after the demise of Sherry's.

Turn left (west) on West 44th Street (walk on the south side of the street).

19. [The points of interest can best be viewed from across the street.]

The Harvard Club (No. 27 West) is a modest neo-Georgian style building, designed by Charles Follen McKim, and completed in 1894. The red Harvard brick is laid in Flemish bond and the trim is in Indiana limestone. The Club was extended through to West 45th Street in 1905 from plans by McKim, Mead & White, and was again enlarged in 1915. The interior Harvard Hall is an immense 3-story Florentine-inspired "knights' chamber" with two great fireplaces. The Harvard Club is a designated New York City Landmark.

The New York Yacht Club (No. 37 West) is one of the city's most romantic buildings. The sculptured design of three 17th century sailing ships' sterns, complete with waves and dolphins, built into the bay windows is both innovative and aesthetic. The Beaux Arts Eclectic building was designed by Warren & Wetmore (who helped create Grand Central Terminal) in 1901. Founded in 1844 the New York Yacht Club is the patriarch of all American sailing clubs, and sponsors the internationally famous "America's Cup Race" held every four years. It was first won by the schooner *America* in 1851, and the coveted trophy has never been lost. The next race is scheduled for 1978. This is the sixth home of the Club—a much earlier clubhouse built as a private mansion in 1846 still stands in Rosebank, Staten Island, overlooking the bay.

The Hotel Iroquois (No. 49 West) as well as the just passed **Hotel Mansfield** and **Hotel Royalton** are typical of the turn-of-the-century Classic Eclectic style hotels that sprung up in the midtown area.

The Hotel Algonquin (No. 59 West) built c. 1902, is of the same architectural school, but has managed to maintain its *fin de siècle* elegance and is still a favorite haunt for stage and literary personalities. It is remembered for its "Round Table," where Robert Benchley, James Thurber, Franklin P. Adams, Dorothy Parker, and others would gather for lunch in the 1920s. The Algonquin has always been known as "the writers' and actors' hotel." Note the vertical rows of cast-iron bay windows.

Return to Fifth Avenue on the north side of the street.

The Association of the Bar (No. 42 West, adjacent to the Hotel Royalton) is a majestic structure, appropriate to its distinguished function. Two magnificent fluted Doric columns guard the portico of this Classic Eclectic limestone building, above which rise four pairs of Corinthian pilasters to an ornate cornice supported by finely detailed brackets. The Bar Association was founded in 1870 "for the purpose of maintaining the honor and dignity of the profession of the Law, of cultivating social relations among its members and increasing its usefulness in promoting the due administration of justice." The building was designed by Cyrus L. W. Eidlitz, and completed in 1895. It contains one of the largest law libraries in the country. The Association of the Bar is a designated landmark.

The General Society of Mechanics and Tradesmen of the City of New York (No. 20 West) was founded in 1785. It began as a technical institute offering free courses in the mechanical trades. The present building, formerly the Berkeley Preparatory School, was erected in 1891 from plans by Lamb & Rich. Note the equestrian frieze above the row of Ionic columns, and the very decorative wrought-iron balconies at each end of this restrained Classic-style building.

Cross Fifth Avenue and turn right to the southeast corner of 43rd Street.

20. The Israel Discount Bank (511 Fifth Avenue) remodeled the ground-floor space, preserving the remarkable Renaissance character of the Palladian façade and interior. Observe the splendid coffered ceiling. The building was originally the Postal Life Insurance Company, and the previous tenant was the Manufacturers Trust Company. The renovation in 1962 was designed by Luss, Kaplan & Associates.

Across 43rd Street on the northeast corner, from 1868 to 1927, stood

Temple Emanu-El, at the northeast corner of Fifth Avenue and 43rd Street, with its twin moorish towers, was the largest synagogue in the world when it occupied the corner from 1868 to 1927. It still maintains the distinction at its present site at 65th Street. (New-York Historical Society)

Looking across the intersection of Fifth Avenue and 42nd Street, c. 1903, at the soon-to-be-razed Croton Reservoir. Within 10 years, New Yorkers were to have the finest research library in the world on this site. (New-York Historical Society)

As late as 1902, Fifth Avenue and 44th Street still looked almost rural, with Henry H. Tyson's Fifth Avenue Market and Ye Olde Willow Cottage tavern. Temple Emanu-El is barely visible to the right. The photo was taken from in front of Sherry's. (New-York Historical Society)

Temple Emanu-El, the largest synagogue in the world. Its twin "Moorish" towers were conspicuous landmarks on Fifth Avenue for over half a century, until rising land values and the northward push of the business district forced relocation to the present site, 22 blocks north. Its new synagogue building is again the world's largest.

    21. The c. 1875 building on the northeast corner of 42nd Street (No. 503) is interesting only for the fact that it is still there. Although partially hidden by an enormous sign, a close look reveals heavy window enframements with semicicular shapes on the 3rd and 4th floors, and simple curved shapes above. The *raison d'être* for this anachronism is probably its narrow width, making a high-rise uneconomical to erect.

Turn left (east) on 42nd Street.

    The system of designating streets east and west of Fifth Avenue was inaugurated in 1838.

    22. The Sperry & Hutchinson Building, on the northwest corner of Madison Avenue, is the home of (S & H) Green Stamps. The company was the first to introduce trading stamps as another way for merchants to encourage customer loyalty by giving them a little something extra. The company has

---

The same intersection seven years later shows a new type of Fifth Avenue omnibus. The "double decker" was to last until the end of World War II (and may someday be brought back again). The building on the northeast corner still stands. (Photograph by Alice Austen. Staten Island Historical Society)

Commodore Vanderbilt's Grand Central Station gave New York its first direct rail link. The sprawling Second Empire building, built in 1871, hides an enormous ground-level train shed. The station was enlarged in 1899 and replaced by the present multi-level terminal in 1913. (Museum of the City of New York)

been in business since 1896. The present building, which S. & H. leases, was built in 1964 from plans by Kahn & Jacobs. On the site previously was the former Hotel Manhattan, and later the National City Bank.

23. The Lincoln Building (No. 60 East) towers 53 stories above 42nd Street, and was built in 1929–30 from plans by the architectural firm of J. E. R. Carpenter. A product of the skyscraper building boom of the late 1920s, it was designed according to the setback requirements of the Zoning Law. In the 1929 prospectus it claimed that "No other office structure has ever been created where clear fresh air is more abundant or where radiant sunlight is more plentiful. . . . Other buildings are far enough away to give unimpeded ventilation to all floors." On the walls of the vestibule are quotes from speeches by Abraham Lincoln, and in the center of the lobby a miniature bronze sculpture fashioned from Daniel Chester French's original model for the Seated Lincoln at Washington's Lincoln Memorial.

The adjacent **Airline Building** was built in the late 1930s in Art Deco style to serve as the in-town terminal for the newly opened LaGuardia Field. The three-story concave map of the world with chrome details against a black background is most attractive. The functions of the building were suspended in 1974, and its future is uncertain. The site was formerly occupied by the Hotel Belmont, built at the turn of the century by financier and father of the New York subways, August Belmont. The magnate had a spur of the IRT subway built into the hotel, where his private car *Mineola* was always kept in readiness for a trip to his racetrack, Belmont Park.

24. Grand Central Terminal, a magnificent Beaux Arts Eclectic structure of mammoth proportions, has provided a dramatic gateway into New York City since its completion in 1913. Designed by Whitney Warren and James A. Wetmore together with engineers Reed and Stem, the master plan combined function, accessibility, and aesthetics, which resulted in a monumentally successful architectural achievement.

The broad south façade, with its triple arches, provides broad expanses of glass to illuminate the interior. Crowning the center arch is the imposing sculpture group by Jules Coutan, representing *Mercury, Hercules,* and *Minerva,* set above a 13-foot high clock. Below is a statue of the founder of the original railroad empire, Cornelius "Commodore" Vanderbilt (the statue is visible from the south side of 42nd Street). The Terminal covers the three blocks to 45th Street, but below ground are 33.7 miles of track on two levels —66 tracks on the upper, and 57 on the lower level—an ingenious plan devised by railroad engineer William J. Wilgus. Reed and Stem's ingenious series of ramps connect the two levels with streets, subways, adjacent office buildings, and hotels, separating pedestrian from vehicular traffic. The main concourse, one of the most awe-inspiring interior spaces in the country, is covered with a vaulted ceiling supported by 125-foot-high piers and hung

The enormous cast-iron-and-glass train shed of Grand Central Station, c. 1872. Electrification did not come until 1902. (Museum of the City of New York)

from steel trusses. On the ceiling are illuminated constellations of the zodiac (the ecliptic line, through a designer's error, runs the wrong way). Sunlight entering through the 75-foot-high windows casts long rays across the marble floor, augmenting the feeling of height and grandeur. The upper level was formerly used primarily for long-distance trains and the lower for the hundreds of commuter trains, but with the decrease in passenger business, the lower level is restricted to weekday rush-hour service only. Particularly attractive are the Guastavino hollow tile vaultings in the lower level.

Who can forget the names of such great trains as the "Empire State Express," the "North Shore Limited," or the "Commodore Vanderbilt"? Or the rolling out of the red carpet for the daily departure to Chicago of the "Twentieth-Century Limited"? The Terminal is still heavily used, however, with over 40 million passengers a year and about 120,000 daily commuters. Many physical changes over the years have not enhanced the appearance of the interior. The proliferation of small shops in the open spaces, the exhibition galleries, and the gaudy displays, have virtually destroyed it. Unused ticket windows are now used for off-track betting.

The New York & Harlem Railroad, which began chugging down Fourth Avenue in 1832, used a depot at 26th Street [the site of the first Madison Square Garden; *see* Madison Square, 11]. It then used horses to pull the coaches the rest of the way to the end of the line near City Hall. In 1854 the Common Council banned steam locomotives below 42nd Street because of the air and noise pollution, and in 1871 Commodore Vanderbilt had a huge cast-iron and glass terminal built at the present site. The former route down Fourth Avenue (now Park Avenue) cut through Murray Hill to 32nd Street. This "cut" was taken over by the Metropolitan Street Railway for use by its horsecars and later trolleys, and was covered over and converted into a tunnel. Today it is used by automobiles only and connects with an elevated viaduct that encircles the station on its way to upper Park Avenue. The viaduct also bypasses the huge Pan Am Building and passes through the former New York Central Office Building (now the New York General Building). A short spur of the 3rd Avenue El that connected with Grand Central Terminal was demolished when the viaduct was built in 1919.

The old station was enlarged in 1899, but with the 1902 regulation banning steam trains altogether from the city, the company—now the New York Central—had the choice of either relocating outside the city limits, or doing what it so wisely did, electrify its lines. The railroad then acquired the subsurface land rights for an underground terminal and yards, and began building the huge station. With the new land and air rights, the Central was able to build itself an attractive office building and two hotels, the Commodore and the Biltmore. The new terminal also served the former New York, New Haven & Hartford Railroad, allowing trains from New England direct access into the heart of the city.

Cross the main concourse and take the escalator for a brief visit to the lobby of the **Pan Am Building.** Built in 1963 and designed by Walter Gropius,

Emery Roth & Sons, and Pietro Belluschi, it did much to destroy the scale of Grand Central Terminal. The enormous office building provided more floor space than any other in the world, until the construction of the World Trade Center, adding additional traffic and congestion to an already overcrowded area. Its precast curtain-wall construction made it one of the first of its kind in the city. Its construction created an outpouring of discontent, not diminished by the helicopter landing pad on the roof (since discontinued). Former Landmarks Commissioner Harmon H. Goldstone, in his book *History Preserved—A Guide to New York City Landmarks and Historic Districts,* refers to the Pan Am Building's interruption of the broad view of Grand Central Terminal from Park Avenue as "a monstrous bland blanket."

Several years ago the Penn Central Transportation Company (a result of the merger of the New York Central, New Haven, and Pennsylvania railroads) sought to obtain permission to construct a 55-story tower *above* Grand Central Terminal. Permission was denied by the Landmarks Commission, since the Terminal is a designated landmark (it is also listed on the National Register of Historic Places). The Commission felt that such a tall tower would in effect destroy the landmark, reducing it to the status of a "curiosity." The Penn Central then had the temerity to suggest that the front of the Terminal should be demolished altogether! The Commission, of course, did not agree that this was an appropriate means of preserving the landmark. The Penn Central and its developers have taken the matter to court, and at this writing, no decision has been reached. If as you pass by, the Terminal is no longer there, we will have lost irretrievably another of our great landmarks; and its replacement will be a monument to avarice, shortsightedness, and insensitivity!

Under the viaduct is the **New York City Convention & Visitors' Bureau,** which functions similarly to the office on Times Square. A battery of obliging staff members is ready to answer any questions about the city.

25. Although the name **Pershing Square** appears on the Park Avenue Viaduct, the square really no longer exists. A rectangular piece of land on the southeast corner of Park Avenue and East 42nd Street was cleared in 1914 after the demolition of the imposing Grand Union Hotel. Named for the Commander-in-Chief of the American Expeditionary Forces in World War I, the plot was acquired by the City for an open plaza. In 1920, it was sold to a developer who three years later erected No. 100 East 42nd Street, naming it the Pershing Square Building. A large plaque in the lobby relates the history of the site.

The main office of **The Bowery Savings Bank** (No. 110 East) was built in 1923 from plans by York & Sawyer. Designed in a Romanesque basilica style, the imposing arch leads into the huge banking room, 160 feet long and 65 feet high. The walls are of variegated limestone, interspersed with blocks of Ohio sandstone. On each side wall are six columns of different-colored marble, carrying five stone arches. Between the columns are panels of unpolished marble mosaic from quarries in France and Italy. The mosaic marble floors add to the artistic effect. The former massive bronze doors are hung for ornamentation on the east and west walls. Another dramatic interior space, it was cited for architectural merit by the Municipal Art Society and the Society of Architectural Historians. The Bowery Savings Bank, founded in 1834, is one of the city's oldest and boasts a magnificent Classic-style McKim, Mead & White landmark building in its 130 Bowery office downtown [see Lower East Side, 24]. The rich architectural detail has many lovely motifs, including the bull and bear of Wall Street, a rooster representing punctuality, a squirrel for thrift, and a lion for power. Many consider this the finest work of architects York & Sawyer.

26. The 56-story **Chanin Building** is another pleasant addition to the city's panorama. Built in 1929 from designs by Sloan & Robertson, it came at a period when decoration was still considered an essential element of the architectural whole. Note the wide ornate bronze band on the third floor, with motifs of birds and fish running the full length of the façade. The lobby is a gem of Art Deco styling. Bronze is used tastefully and artistically in the amazing convector grills, the low reliefs on the elevator doors and mailboxes, the "jeweled" clocks, and even in the "waves" on the floor at the 42nd Street entrance. One cannot help but rejoice at the excellent building maintenance and the lack of "modernization" which has helped keep the Chanin Building in pristine condition. Unfortunately, the top floor observation deck is now closed. A theater on the 50th floor is also closed, as is the former basement bus station of the Baltimore & Ohio Railroad.

27. Perhaps the most unusually shaped building, and certainly one of the most beautiful, is the 1048-foot-high **Chrysler Building,** on the northeast corner of Lexington Avenue. Its graceful vertical shaft tapering into a fine stainless steel point gives it a distinctive and artistic position in New York's skyline. Designed by William Van Alen in 1929, it became, upon completion a year later, the tallest building in the world, only to be relegated to second place a few months later by the Empire State Building. Close examination of the lovely Art Deco façade readily indicates that this was planned as the automotive tower of the city. At each setback are stylized "motor" designs. The building flares out sharply at the fourth setback into what appears to be shiny radiator caps—for a 1929 Chrysler! At other levels are basket-weave designs and abstract modern automobiles. The Chrylser Building was one of the first to have exposed metal as an essential part of the design. An interesting event in the history of its construction was the deception of a rival architect by Van Alen as the building neared completion. When they reached a height of 925 feet, everyone assumed that was the maximum; and when the downtown "40 Wall Tower" (40 Wall Street) also reached that height, architects H. Craig Severance and Yasuo Matsui added another two feet to make their building "the tallest in the world." To the consternation of all, the stainless-steel spire of the Chrysler Building was secretly assembled, raised through the dome, and bolted into place, adding a victorious 123 feet. The elegant lobby is faced with African marble, with transportation motifs on the ceiling, and for years served as a showroom for Chrysler Motors products. The lavish observation deck has been closed and now houses electronic equipment.

Around the corner on 42nd Street (best viewed from the south side of the street), it will be noted that the east wall of the Chrysler Building's lower setback is not parallel to the north-south avenues. This is because the property line follows the route of the former East Post Road, which in the 18th century ran approximately between Lexington and Third avenues, wending its way up Manhattan Island.

28. The massive **Mobil Oil Building** occupies the entire block to Third Avenue. Unusual are the embossed stainless-steel panels that cover the entire building. Originally the Socony-Mobil Building, it was built in 1955 from plans by Harrison & Abramovitz.

29. Third Avenue has changed drastically since World War II. For over 70 years the avenue was darkened by the rattling Third Avenue El and, like so many of the El-covered thoroughfares, was lined with dingy tenements, saloons, and cheap little shops. When the El came down in 1955—the last survivor of Manhattan's once-extensive overhead railway network—Third Avenue underwent a complete transformation. From 38th Street to 57th Street, modern office buildings were erected; and typical of the 1950s and early '60s, most were boxlike carbon copies of each other. There is little relief in the homogeneous and monotonous streetscape. **Second Avenue** was also relieved of its overhead El and enjoyed a similar renaissance, albeit somewhat later.

30. Central Commercial High School, in the middle of the block, was built in 1906–07 from plans by C. B. J. Snyder, and is typical of the Tudor Gothic Revival style used on most public schools built between 1905 and 1920 in New York City.

Across the street, No. 219 East is not particularly distinguished except that the **REA Building** is not new! An entirely modernized façade was applied in 1962 to a building erected in 1900.

31. The New York Daily News Building (No. 220 East) was completed in 1930, a year before architect Raymond M. Hood's opposite outpost, the McGraw-Hill Building. Differing sharply from it and from his American Radiator Building of seven years earlier, the News Building uses other means to stress its verticality. In cooperation with John Mead Howells, Hood resorted to rows of brown brick spandrels and windows to create an up-and-down stripe effect. In 1958, an addition was added by Harrison & Abramovitz, wisely following the original style. Not to be missed is the spectacular lobby—designed as an educational exhibition. In the center is the world's largest interior globe, illuminated from within, and rotating slowly on a recessed platform. An excellent geography lesson, the globe's details are constantly kept up to date. On the lobby floor are bronze lines pointing to cities around the world and to the relative positions of the planets. The back wall

In the late 1920s, many rows of brownstones at the east end of 42nd Street were leveled to make way for Tudor City. This group of houses stood on the south side of 42nd Street near the present Tudor City Place before the thoroughfare was widened. (Fred F. French Investing Company)

has various meteorological instruments. The *News,* which is printed in this building and in an annex to the south, has the largest circulation of any newspaper in the country. The attractive building was cited by the Municipal Art Society and the Society of Architectural Historians for "originality in design and influence on later work."

32. The Ford Foundation Building, midway down the north side of 42nd Street, stands as a significant contribution to the quality of life in the city. The L-shaped building arranged around a 130-foot-high "greenhouse" was designed by Kevin Roche, John Dinkeloo Associates, and was completed in 1967. The architects' plan was "to provide a proper environment for the building's staff—a space that would allow them to enjoy the view, but at the same time, allow them to be aware of the existence of other members of the Foundation, people who share their common aims and purposes." They also felt that their building should contribute something to the city, maintaining a low profile and observing "the lines and planes created by other buildings which form the surrounding street." The result was eminently successful.

The 12-story glassed-in area is anchored by granite piers and side walls, and shelters a one-third-acre lush garden. The shrubbery is frequently changed and is centered about a terraced garden with 17 full-grown trees, thousands of ground-cover plants, and aquatic plants in a still pool. Each season brings its own bloomings, and the entire area is floodlit, adding to the natural effect of filtered sunlight. The "greenhouse" also serves the additional purpose of a waste air chamber and thermal buffer. Ada Louise Huxtable, architecture critic of the *New York Times,* in praising its successful design, refers to the Ford Foundation Building as "a splendid, shimmering Crystal Palace . . . one of the Foundation's more valid contributions to the arts." (The garden may be visited on weekdays.)

33. Across 42nd Street are the Church of the Covenant and the Hotel Tudor, forming part of the broad **Tudor City** complex. (*Climb the stairs on the north side of the street to Tudor City Place.*)

Tudor City was developed in 1925–28 by the Fred F. French Company as a "self-contained city" within walking distance of the city itself. There are 12 apartment houses with a total of 3000 apartments, a 600-room hotel, stores, restaurant, church, and private park—all designed in a Tudor Gothic, or English Cottage style. From the north end of Tudor City Place, there is a superb view of the United Nations.

The site has had a checkered history, beginning with the rural Winthrop Mansion, "Dutch Hill," in the 18th century. The house was later converted into a tavern and rest stop for the stagecoaches of the old East Post Road. By mid-19th century the area deteriorated badly and became the hangout for gangs of criminals. In the early 20th century, the rocky crags were taken over by the notorious "Rag Gang," led by archfelon Paddy Corcoran. The neighborhood surrounding "Corcoran's Roost" became industrialized with breweries, slaughterhouses, glue factories and a gas works (this explains why there are no windows in the east side of the Tudor City apartment houses which might provide unattractive views or admit unsavory odors). Tudor City remained a staid and tranquil enclave, enhanced by the arrival of the U.N. in the early 1950s. A recent proposal by a land developer to build a high-rise on the site of the little park was vigorously opposed by tenants and city planners alike, but it almost succeeded—which proves that the preservation of a decent environment demands constant vigilance and a ready willingness to do battle against those who would put profit ahead of humanism.

[The United Nations is described in the tour East River Panoramas.]

End of tour. The 42nd Street crosstown bus stops at the foot of the stairs to Tudor City Place.

EAST RIVER PANORAMAS

United Nations (Turtle Bay)
to Beekman Place

E. 53RD ST.

E. 52ND ST.

E. 51ST ST.

E. 50TH ST.

E. 49TH ST.

E. 48TH ST.

E. 47TH ST.

E. 46TH ST.

E. 45TH ST.

E. 44TH ST.

E. 43RD ST.

E. 42ND ST.

LEXINGTON AVENUE

THIRD AVENUE

(EAST POST ROAD)

SECOND AVENUE

UNITED NATIONS PLAZA

(First Avenue Tunnel)

TUDOR CITY PL.

FIRST AVENUE

BEEKMAN PLACE

F.D.R. (EAST RIVER) DRIVE

Orig. site
"Mt. Pleasant"
Beekman House

2nd site

MITCHELL PL.

Boundary: Beekman Estate
Turtle Bay Farm

Turtle Bay
Gardens
Historic District

De Voor's Mill Stream
(Turtle Creek)

start

(Site of
Turtle Bay)

United
Nations

East River

10

9

8

5

6

7

4

3

2

1

13. East River Panoramas

[49th/50th Street crosstown bus (M-27) to Dag Hammarskjöld Plaza; First/ Second Avenue bus (M-15) to East 47th Street; 42nd Street crosstown bus (M-104 or 106). Nearest subway: IRT Lexington Avenue line local to 51st Street station; or local, express, or 42nd Street Shuttle to Grand Central]

The walking tour begins at the United Nations and follows the East River shoreline (with some detours) to Gracie Mansion, ending at the Henderson Place Historic District at East 86th Street.

Cross United Nations Plaza (First Avenue and East 47th Street) and pass through the Visitors' Gate to the United Nations.

1. The United Nations. After several years in temporary quarters on Long Island, at the City of New York Building in the Flushing Meadow Park World's Fair Grounds, and at the Sperry Gyroscope Plant at Lake Success, the U.N. moved into its permanent headquarters on this Manhattan East River shorefront site in 1952. Technically outside the territorial jurisdiction of the United States, the U.N. complex consists of three main buildings: the 544-foot-high Secretariat, completed in 1950, the General Assembly Building (1952), and the Dag Hammarskjöld Library (1963).

The site that now appears so ideal for the location of the world body was formerly a depressing aggregation of slums, coal docks, factories, slaughterhouses, and breweries. The original plan called for a site north of the city in Westchester County, but a grant of $8.5 million from John D. Rockefeller made it possible to purchase a parcel of land that had already been accumulated by William Zeckendorf for private development. In the earlier Zeckendorf plan, all buildings east of Third Avenue between 46th and 49th streets were to be razed. The revised proposal proved more practical and saved

View of the United Nations site taken from Tudor City, looking north, December 1946. In the distance, the graceful Queensboro Bridge leaps across Welfare (now Roosevelt) Island. (Official United Nations Photo)

many beautiful houses from demolition, including the historic Turtle Bay Gardens.

The new plan was approved by Congress in record time and the City rushed through all the enabling legislation, which included the waterfront rights and tax-exempt status. An international team of renowned architects, led by America's Wallace K. Harrison, drew up the designs. Among the planners were Le Corbusier (France), Sven Markelius (Sweden), Oscar Niemeyer (Brazil), plus representatives from ten other countries. The Library was designed by Harrison, Abramovitz & Harris. The pool was a gift from American schoolchildren, its freestanding stone sculpture by England's Barbara Hepworth, and the Council Chambers a gift from Norway, Sweden, and Denmark. The buildings and grounds display many beautiful art objects, with such items as a Peace Bell and Shrine from Japan, mosaics from Tunisia, and even a model of Sputnik from the Soviet Union. At the same time, New York City diverted busy First Avenue into a five-block-long tunnel and widened East 47th Street into Dag Hammarskjöld Plaza. The flags of the approximately 140 member nations line the east side of what was formerly First Avenue, now renamed United Nations Plaza.

Broad views of the East River can be enjoyed from the formal gardens north of the General Assembly Buildings. (Free guided tours of the United Nations are given daily from 9 A.M. to 4:45 P.M., except on Christmas and New Year's and when special security measures are in effect.)

2. The west side of **United Nations Plaza** has its own panorama of modern architecture:

No. 771, the Herbert Hoover Building, headquarters of the **Boys Clubs of America.**

No. 777, the **Church Center for the United Nations** (1962, William Lascaze). The impressive stained glass in the sanctuary of this Methodist church represents *Man's Struggle for Peace and Brotherhood,* by Henry L. Willet.

No. 799, the **United States Permanent Mission to the United Nations** (1959, Kelly & Gruzen and Kahn & Jacobs).

No. 809, the **Institute of International Education** (1964, Harrison, Abramovitz & Harris). Architect Alvar Aalto designed the Edgar J. Kaufmann Conference Room in the penthouse.

No. 345 East 46th Street, the **Carnegie Endowment International Center** (1953, Harrison, Abramovitz & Harris).

On Dag Hammarskjöld Plaza:

No. 345 East 47th Street, the **United Engineering Center** (1961, Shreve, Lamb & Harmon).

No. 333 East 47th Street, the **Japan Society Building** (1971, Junzo Yoshimuro and Gruzen & Partners; Turner Construction Company). Funded by John D. Rockefeller III to the tune of $4.3 million, this striking example of modern Japanese architecture was inaugurated by Prince and Princess Hitachi, and is the U.S. headquarters of the Society.

The Holy Family Roman Catholic Church (rebuilt in 1964 by George J. Sole) is dominated by its gray granite and aluminum bell tower. The Church was built on the site of a brewery stable.

Return to United Nations Plaza.

In the mid-17th century, the area along the river below the present East 49th Street was the **site of the Turtle Bay Farm.** The origin of "Turtle" is uncertain. Some claim it to come from the many turtles that were once common along the shore of Turtle Bay (where the U.N. is now); others attribute it to the early Dutch word *deutal,* a farm implement, which was later corrupted into "turtle." The original farm dated from 1639. Just before the Revolutionary War, the neighborhood figured in a bold act by a group of "Liberty Boys," under Marinus Willett, who sailed down from Greenwich, Connecticut, in a small sloop, seized a cache of arms from a British storehouse in the lower city, then attacked a small stone fort that stood at the foot of East 45th Street, surprising the guards and making off to Boston with a boatload of supplies for the new Continental Army.

The "Old Store House at Turtle Bay, N.Y., 1852" in a lithograph from Valentine's Manual, 1857. The house was the site of a Liberty Boys' raid led by Marinus Willett, on the King's stores, just before the American Revolution. (Museum of the City of New York)

Flowing deep below East 48th Street is **De Voor's Mill Stream,** later called Turtle Creek, which once emptied into Turtle Bay. Because of a cholera epidemic in 1854, the city fathers blocked the now polluted creek and channeled it into a culvert, which still empties into the East River under the present United Nations site.

3. The twin monoliths of **Nos. 860 and 870 United Nations Plaza** are luxury cooperative apartment houses. Originally, they were planned to be the IBM World Trade Center, but now only the lower floors are used for commercial purposes.

4. **The Beekman Towers,** a residential hotel (1929), at First Avenue and East 49th Street, offers a spectacular nighttime view of the surrounding city from the top-floor cocktail lounge.

5. **Beekman Hill.** The high ground that dominated the area between 50th and 51st streets was the site of the James Beekman house, *Mount Pleasant*. Built in 1766, the beautiful Colonial mansion stood near East 51st Street, but was later moved one block south when First Avenue was opened. During the American Revolution the house was used by the British for their military headquarters. Patriot Nathan Hale, captured on September 21, 1776, at the Dove Tavern (at the present site of Third Avenue and East 66th Street) was brought to the Beekman House, tried, and returned to the tavern where he was hanged as a spy. And it was here four years later that Major

John André received his instructions to meet General Benedict Arnold and obtain the plans to the fort at West Point. Intercepted by patriots in Tarrytown, André, too, was hanged for the same offense. With the signing of the Treaty of Paris in 1783, the British Commandant, Sir Guy Carlton, was permitted to rent the mansion to carry out the plans for the British evacuation of the port of New York. A frequent visitor in the following years was newly elected President George Washington. The Beekman family continued to occupy the house until the cholera epidemic of 1854, and it was demolished 20 years later. Fortunately, a number of furnishings were saved and the reconstructed parlor, a bedroom, and three mantelpieces can be seen in the museum of the New-York Historical Society (Central Park West at West 77th Street).

Turn right on East 50th Street to Beekman Place.

6. The Beekman Place District. The two blocks, East 50th Street to Beekman Place, and Beekman Place between 50th and 51st streets, were formerly cobblestoned, and consist mainly of town houses, remodeled in the

The Abigail Adams Smith House, a museum maintained by the Colonial Dames of America, was built originally in 1799 as a stable for Col. William Stephens Smith. The site has been much improved with the removal in the 1930s of the gas tanks. (Museum of the City of New York)

1920s. This delightful group of luxury residences has a unique atmosphere of charm and tranquility, in striking contrast to the surrounding neighborhood. Although not startling architecturally, each house has a character of its own, reflecting the individual taste of the original owner and the imagination of its builder.

The town houses were favored particularly by great theater personalities. Alfred Lunt and Lynn Fontanne lived in the house on the northeast corner of East 50th Street and Beekman Place. Among others who enjoyed Beekman Place addresses were Ethel Barrymore, Katharine Cornell, and Irving Berlin. It was also home for members of the Rockefeller family and for former Secretary of the Navy and Defense James Forrestal.

Some of the more interesting houses are **Nos. 416–420, 417,** and **419 East 50th Street; Nos. 17, 25, 27, 29,** and **33 Beekman Place.** Note the lovely attic and twisted, bronze rainspout on the latter.

Turn right (east) on East 51st Street, pass through the little nameless park and out onto the footbridge over the East River Drive.

7. An excellent vantage point for a rear view of the Beekman Place District, the bridge is also a perfect site from which to view Cannon Point just to the north, where the Drive disappears under Sutton Place. Just to the south was a pleasant beach, where swimming was frequently enjoyed in the "altogether," and where Edgar Allan Poe came in 1846 to live with his young, sick wife, the former Virginia Clemm. Horace Greeley, the illustrious editor of the *Tribune,* came here to seek solace from the tragic loss of several children. Author Thomas Wolfe lived for a time on nearby First Avenue, and Yiddish novelist Sholem Asch described the neighborhood of the East 40s very vividly in his *East River,* published in 1946.

To the north is the picturesque **Queensboro Bridge,** leapfrogging over Roosevelt Island. Completed in 1909, this ornate cantilevered bridge connects Manhattan with Long Island City in Queens. The upper roadway once carried the wooden railway cars of the Second Avenue El, and a trolley line shared the lower level with vehicular traffic. The trolley, the last of the city's once-extensive network, shuttled back and forth at a five-cent fare, and was finally removed in 1955. The bridge also provided the backdrop for a number of movies in the 1930s and '40s, particularly the classic *Dead End,* which dealt with the conflicts between the wealthy of Beekman Place and the very poor of the tenements on adjoining dead-end streets.

The East River or Franklin D. Roosevelt Drive, begun in the late 1930s during the administration of New York's colorful mayor Fiorello H. La-Guardia, was planned as a link in a projected "Circumferential Belt Parkway." It is built on landfill provided by the rubble of buildings destroyed during the World War II blitz on London and Bristol. Convoys of cargo ships returning from England during the war carried the broken masonry in their holds as ballast.

Return to East 51st Street and First Avenue.

8. No. 455 East 51st Street is built on the **original site of the Beekman Mansion,** *Mount Pleasant.*

Turn north one block to dead-end East 52nd Street.

9. "River House," 435 East 52nd Street, enjoys one of the best panoramic views of the East River. A luxury cooperative apartment house, its facilities include tennis courts, a squash court, swimming pool, and ballroom, and at one time included a private dock for the convenience of visiting millionaires' yachts.

Return to First Avenue, and turn west (left) on East 53rd Street.

10. Nos. 314 and 312 East 53rd Street are surprising survivors from the days when the neighborhood was still semirural in character. The pair of wooden houses with their round-topped dormer windows and corbeled entrance hoods were built in 1866 and reflect the influence of the French Second Empire style, which became popular in this country after the Civil War. No. 312 has been designated a New York City Landmark.

Return to First Avenue, turn left (north) to East 57th Street, and right (east) to Sutton Place.

11. Sutton Place, named for late-19th-century land developer Effingham B. Sutton, was formerly called Avenue A (which now exists only between Houston and 14th streets). Lined with luxury apartment houses, the street is another riverside bastion of the "upper crust," and continues north under the Queensboro Bridge approach, where it changes its name again, this time to York Avenue. Reminiscent of the Beekman Place district are the charming town houses along the short dead-ends on East 57th and 58th streets. No. 1 Sutton Place North was the residence of the Secretary General of the United Nations.

12. Walk into little **East River Park** with its endearing bronze statue of the friendly wild boar and its tiny animal friends. The original, from Ancient Greece, is in the Uffizi Gallery in Florence, Italy. Sculptor Pietro Tacca made two other copies—one stands in Florence's Straw Market, and the other in Kansas City's Country Club Plaza. Years of children's caressing fingers have brightened the protruding parts.

Return to Sutton Place, walk north one block, then east into East 58th Street.

13. At the end of the East 58th Street cul-de-sac called "Sutton Square," is another of New York City's seemingly endless source of surprises—secluded **Riverview Terrace,** one of the city's few remaining private streets. With its protective fence and entrance gates, and fronted by lush sculptured gardens, the fortunate town house residents are quite removed from the bustle of city life. The little cobblestoned lane extends north only to East 59th Street where a stockade fence keeps out the "injuns."

Continue north on Sutton Place (now York Avenue), and turn west (left) on East 61st Street.

To the north is the modern and imaginatively designed **Tower Building of Rockefeller University,** a pleasant departure from the steel and glass cube so often identified with institutional architecture. No. 425 East 61st Street (extending through to East 62nd Street) is also somewhat of a change from the unadorned modern "boxy" style. Unsuccessful in its plan to attract commercial tenants exclusively, it is now a multiple-use building with medical offices and residences.

14. Another delightful surprise tucked away in this commercial district is the 1799 **Abigail Adams Smith House,** Headquarters of the Colonial Dames of America, and a designated New York City Landmark. The property dates from a patent granted in 1676 and passed through many hands until 1795, when 23 acres were deeded to Col. William Stephens Smith. Nine years before, Col. Smith had married Abigail Adams, daughter of John Adams, who later became the second president of the United States. The elegant mansion they planned to build, *Mount Vernon,* was never completed, and they lived instead in the present stone building, which was then a stable and carriage house.

After remaining only a few short years the Smiths departed, and the Federal-style house was sold to William T. Robinson, who enlarged it and completed the structure in 1799 (the date can be seen in the gable on the south façade). Passing into new ownership, it was converted into a hotel, which boasted having "excellent facilities for fishing, shooting, and salt water bathing" (the East River was then only about 50 feet from the door). According to an advertisement of the time reproduced in the *New-York Historical Society Quarterly,* the hotel offered "every day in season soup made from the fine green turtles fattening in a crawl made for that purpose in the East River."

In 1823 the building became "an academy for young ladies and gentlemen," but three years later suffered a disastrous fire. Rebuilt as the Mount Vernon Hotel, and named for the former Col. Smith's ill-starred mansion, it served a distinguished clientele for a number of years. The house subsequently came into the hands of the Jeremiah Towle family, who retained it until 1905, when the property was sold to the Standard Gas Light Company.

The lovely old house now began to suffer from the encroachment of urban blight as the once-fashionable rural neighborhood declined into a dismal commercial backwater. Three enormous, ugly gas tanks were erected on the property, blocking the formerly uninterrupted view of the river. And

EAST
RIVER
PANORAMAS

Sutton Place to
Henderson Place

the proud house, now subdivided into cheap apartments, suffered the additional indignity during World War I of becoming a Salvation Army soup kitchen. But in 1919 the house was rescued by Miss Jane Teller, president of the Society of American Antiquarians, who rented it from the Gas Company and painstakingly restored it, furnishing it with her collection of early American furniture. In 1924, the Colonial Dames of America, the nation's first patriotic women's organization, purchased the Abigail Adams Smith House for their headquarters and made it a museum.

Although the beautiful and extensive collection of antiques in the restored rooms is not original with the house, it is quite authentic to the periods of its occupancy, and represents virtually every style from the late 18th through the mid-19th centuries. Time should be allowed for a leisurely visit to the historic house and charming garden. (Open weekdays, except legal holidays, from 10 A.M. to 4 P.M. Admission $1.00, 50¢ for Senior Citizens.)

The adjoining building, No. 417 East 61st Street, has been remodeled in neo-Federal style and serves as the office. It has a recently built auditorium and exhibit rooms, and facilities for group orientation lectures.

Turn north on First Avenue.

The ornate Third Avenue Car Barns, on Third Avenue between 65th and 66th Streets, built in 1896 from plans by Henry J. Hardenbergh. (Photograph by Berenice Abbott for Federal Art Project "Changing New York." Museum of the City of New York)

15. On the north side of East 62nd Street, just west of First Avenue, is the building that once housed the Swedish Bethesda Methodist Church. It was acquired in 1969 for the office and studios of **WBAI,** New York City's only listener-supported non-commercial radio station (99.5 khz FM).

16. First Avenue in the East 60s and 70s, once quietly residential and later a decaying commercial thoroughfare, has since the early 1960s enjoyed a renaissance as New York's "swingles" district. With upbeat bars and restaurants attracting the young (and not-so-young) "unattached" from all over town, the Avenue "swings" every night, reaching a crescendo by Saturday evening, as lines form in front of the more popular spots. The rebirth of First Avenue has also encouraged an influx of boutiques, antique shops, plant stores, and exotic food emporiums.

17. Between East 64th and 65th streets, on the east side of First Avenue, are the **City & Suburban Homes,** designed by architect Ernest Flagg in 1915 as a low-cost multiple-dwelling complex. One of three mammoth (for the time) housing developments on the Upper East Side, these multifamily units were planned by Flagg to have as much light and air as possible in those days before air conditioning. Walk through the alley between the buildings to East 65th Street, noting how the architect used the areaways both economically and practically for the comfort of the tenants and the services for the buildings.

Turn right on East 65th Street to York Avenue.

18. Rockefeller University, a research center for medical and related sciences, was founded by John D. Rockefeller in 1901 on the site of the former Schermerhorn estate. The shady campus is dominated by the Classic-style **Founders' Hall,** opened as a laboratory in 1903. Formerly known as the Rockefeller Institute for Medical Research, the name was changed in 1965, and in 1974 the institution was designated a National Historic Landmark by the National Park Service.

Ask permission of the guard at the 66th Street main entrance, and walk up the tree-lined hill. To the left, the incongruous hemisphere is the **Caspary Auditorium,** built in 1957 by the firm of Harrison & Abramovitz. Flanking Founders' Hall is the Hospital Building and Flexner Hall. Turn right and walk to the ramp overlooking the peaceful **Berlin Memorial Garden.** Descend the spiral staircase to the Garden and walk north along the beautifully landscaped path, past the main entrance walk, exiting at the gate just beyond 67th Street.

Continue north on York Avenue.

19. York Avenue from Rockefeller University to East 72nd Street is devoted mainly to medical institutions:

Facing the University, between East 66th and 67th streets is the "glassy"

Nurses' Residence of New York Hospital-Cornell Medical Center (1965, Harrison & Abramovitz).

Between East 67th and 68th streets is the **James Ewing Memorial Building of the Memorial Sloan-Kettering Cancer Center** (1950, Skidmore, Owings & Merrill); and around the corner at 444 East 68th Street, the main building of the **Memorial Sloan-Kettering Center** (1935, James Gamble Rogers, Inc.).

For the next two blocks, the cityscape is overwhelmed by the massive complex of **New York Hospital-Cornell Medical Center,** designed in 1933 by the firm of Coolidge, Shepley, Bulfinch & Abbott.

At the northwest corner of East 70th Street stands the towering **Lawrence G. Payson House** (1966, Frederick G. Frost, Jr. & Associates), a residence of the Medical Center; and at 515 East 71st Street, around the corner, **the Institute for Muscle Disease** (1961, Skidmore, Owings & Merrill).

20. On the south side of East 72nd Street, just west of York Avenue, is the bold, multicolumned **Murry and Leonie Guggenheim Children's Dental Clinic,** built in 1930. The heavily ornate façade can best be appreciated from the north side of the street.

A reminder of the commercial past of the neighborhood is the **former Purepac Pharmaceuticals Company factory,** a rambling hodgepodge of Romanesque Revival-style buildings on the north side of East 72nd Street, just east of York Avenue. The firm, whose name is clearly visible on the buildings, moved its operations long ago to Elizabeth, New Jersey.

Continue north on York Avenue to East 77th Street, and turn right one block to Cherokee Place.

21. The Cherokee Apartments, another enormous multifamily project designed by architect Ernest Flagg, are particularly interesting. Walk into one of the vaulted tunnels leading to a central courtyard. Notice the separate entranceways grouped around the court, each with a semienclosed stairway leading five flights to the top. The exterior wrought-iron French balconies add a touch of elegance, as do the ornate overhanging cornices. The large windows are all triple-hung, making each apartment light and cheerful. The entire design is living-oriented—an incredible concept for the year 1900!

22. John Jay Park, named for the nation's first Chief Justice, is the most popular recreational spot in the neighborhood. The swimming pool and athletic facilities on a site overlooking the river add up to one of the most heavily used parks in the city.

Return to York Avenue on East 78th Street.

23. Observe the old carved stone street sign on the wall of Public School 158, hearkening back to the days when this was still **Avenue A.**

Across York Avenue, at No. 1465, is the **Webster Branch of the New York Public Library.** Built in 1905, it resembles a modest Italian Renaissance palace.

Crossing York Avenue, and continuing a few steps farther west on East 78th Street, one is again surprised by a pair of old survivors—two aging wooden buildings, numbered **450a and 450b,** of c. 1850, which were once residences and a short time later converted into shops.

On the north side of East 78th Street, No. 425, **The Multi-Level Apartments,** is a reconversion to end them all! Formerly a tenement, it was completely gutted and rebuilt with broad balconies (or levels), duplexes, and a rather unusual entranceway and lobby. The whole has been stuccoed over, giving it a somewhat Mediterranean look.

Return to York Avenue and walk north to East 79th Street. Turn right to East End Avenue, and north to East 81st Street.

East End Avenue developed as an apartment-house row for the affluent at about the same time as Sutton Place, and looks rather similar. Before the street became fashionable in the 1920s, it was named simply Avenue B.

At East 81st Street, turn right and enter the Promenade, called John Finley Walk.

24. This splendid promenade, built over the East River Drive, is one of the great pedestrian walkways of the city. It is named most appropriately for **John Huston Finley** (1863–1940), past president of the City College of New York, state commissioner of education, and editor-in-chief of the *New York Times.* He was, in addition, a *great pedestrian,* who believed that "a good walk clears the mind and stimulates thinking." Finley walked to work daily until past the age of 70, and frequently hiked the 32 miles around Manhattan Island, declaring that he enjoyed the sights of the crowded city as much as the scenery of the open country.

Roosevelt Island, directly opposite, was for many years called Welfare Island. Prior to that, it was Blackwell's Island, and in Dutch Colonial times, Varcken Eylandt (Hog Island). Two miles in length by no more than 750 feet wide, it was first acquired by Dutch Governor Van Twiller and used for pasturage for hogs. Some years later it was purchased by Captain John Manning, a British officer who surrendered New York back to the Dutch in 1673. It is said that he retired here in disgrace after having had his sword broken over his head for not resisting the invasion with more enthusiasm. Robert Blackwell took title to the island in 1686 after marrying Manning's stepdaughter, and lived there until his death in 1717. The old Blackwell House has been restored as part of the Roosevelt Island Development. In the 19th and early 20th centuries, as Blackwell's Island, it was a City property used for a hospital, penitentiary, lunatic asylum, and "poor house." The notoriety of these institutions was so widespread that an investigation was conducted in 1921, with the result that the prison was moved to Riker's Island, and the name changed to Welfare Island. Two city hospitals (Goldwater and Bird S. Coler) are still in service, and several old landmarks, the

A Currier & Ives lithograph, 1862, showing Blackwell's (now Roosevelt) Island and the East River from 86th Street. (Museum of the City of New York)

The eighteenth century Blackwell farmhouse on Roosevelt Island has been carefully restored as part of the new development project for the island. (New York City Landmarks Preservation Commission)

octagonal Victorian building of the old lunatic asylum, the old Nurses' Residence, the Strecker Laboratory, the Church of the Good Shepherd, and the lighthouse, will all be preserved.

The new Roosevelt Island Development is a city within a city, combining low-, middle-, and high-income housing in a dense massing of multistory apartment buildings. By 1982 it is planned that 5000 families will live on the island. Connection to the city proper is by a vehicular lift bridge to Ravenswood in Queens. Cars are not permitted to drive on the island and must be parked in a central garage near the bridge, where mini-buses pick up passengers and make frequent trips on a fixed route around Roosevelt Island. A subway station near the Queensboro Bridge will provide access to Manhattan and Queens when the new 63rd Street tunnel is put into operation. The most revolutionary connection, however, is an aerial tramway which carries commuters in small cabins suspended from an overhead cable—much like a ski lift—to a terminal at Second Avenue and East 60th Street.

Follow Finley Walk to Carl Schurz Park.

25. Carl Schurz Park, dramatically situated on rocky bluffs overlooking

Among the many municipal institutions on Blackwell's Island was the Hospital for Consumptives. Doctors, nurses, and patients pose for Percy C. Byron's camera on a summer afternoon in 1903. (The Byron Collection. Museum of the City of New York)

The ferry Welfare *making its regular three-minute crossing between East 78th Street and Welfare Island, 1948. The elimination of this convenient service shortly thereafter virtually isolated the island for many years.* (*Gibbs Marine Photos*)

a bend in the East River, offers unsurpassed views of the Triborough and Hell Gate bridges (the latter, a magnificent arch bridge of great architectural merit), Randall's and Ward's islands, Astoria in Queens, plus an exciting parade of ships sailing close by in the river's deep-water channel. Just off 96th Street, is treacherous Mill Rock.

The site during the Dutch Colonial period was known as Hoek van Hoorn ("Hoorn's Corner"), named for the Hanseatic town on the Zuyder Zee. Just before the American Revolution, Jacob Walton built himself a house on the promontory, but his tenancy was short-lived, as the Continental Army set up a battery of nine guns and took over the house as part of the fortifications. Known as Thompson's Battery, it was knocked out of action by a cannonade from British men-of-war seeking to isolate the island of Manhattan as the War began in earnest in 1776. The Americans fled and the site became a British Army outpost. In more peaceful times it became East End Park, and was renamed in honor of Schurz in 1911.

Carl Schurz (1829–1906) is considered the most notable German immigrant of the 19th century. Fleeing the unsuccessful Revolution of 1848, he came to America, learned the language in an astonishingly brief time, and involved himself in politics. Winning the confidence and respect of President Abraham Lincoln, he was appointed minister to Spain and, soon thereafter, a major general in the Union Army. He was also responsible for helping to shape the new liberal Republican party. After the War he was elected senator from Missouri, and in 1877 was named secretary of the interior in the Hayes administration. Returning to New York he assumed the editorship of the *New York Evening Post* and *Harper's Weekly*. Schurz settled in the nearby German community of Yorkville, where he remained until his death.

The Park has a wide range of recreational facilities distributed about the wooded and hilly terrain, and provides a verdant backdrop to New York City's most famous residence:

26. Gracie Mansion. Built as a country manor house in 1799 by wealthy merchant Archibald Gracie, it is one of the best preserved and most striking examples of the Federal style and is a place of gracious living. The Gracies entertained many famous guests, including Louis Philippe, later King of France; President John Quincy Adams; the Marquis de Lafayette; Alexander Hamilton; James Fenimore Cooper; Washington Irving; and John Jacob Astor.

In 1887 Gracie Mansion was purchased by the City. It was restored by the Parks Department in 1927 with early 19th-century antiques, and became the Museum of the City of New York, under the directorship of great New York historian Henry Collins Brown. When the Museum's new building was opened on Fifth Avenue and 103rd Street in 1930, the Mansion lay dormant for a few years until selected by Mayor Fiorello H. LaGuardia to be the official Mayor's Residence. It now holds the distinction of being the only original country seat in Manhattan still occupied as a home. A ballroom and reception wing were added in 1966 in perfect harmony with the architectural style. Gracie Mansion is a designated City Landmark and is listed on the National Register of Historic Places.

Unfortunately it is not possible to enjoy the broad river views from the colonnaded front porch, nor is the public permitted to study the exquisite entrance door with its fanlight and leaded-glass sidelights, so characteristic of the Federal style—unless, that is, one receives a special invitation from "hizzoner."

East 86th Street Park (now Carl Schurz Park) c. 1890. Barren of trees, Gracie Mansion stands out predominantly at the far end. (Photograph by Jacob A. Riis. The Jacob A. Riis Collection. Museum of the City of New York)

Exit from the Park opposite East 87th Street.

27. Occupying less than a half acre between East 87th and 86th streets is the charming **Henderson Place Historic District,** a group of 24 homogeneneously designed town houses. Begun in 1881 from plans by Hugo Lamb and Charles A. Rich, the quaint little houses are built in what is described as the Queen Anne style.

Originally farmland, the property was acquired at the turn of the 18th century by Archibald Gracie and John Jacob Astor (who also had an estate nearby). After some years it passed into the hands of John C. Henderson, a fur importer and hat manufacturer, who decided to expand into the real-estate business and build homes for "persons of moderate means."

Until the 1830s, the section had been part of the remote hamlet of **Yorkville,** surrounded by large country estates. With the arrival in 1834 of the New York & Harlem Railroad, and a stagecoach line a year later, rapid development took place. Since the 1790s the neighborhood has been predominantly German, and has been swelled by periodic waves of immigration —the largest group moving up just after 1900 from the Tompkins Square

A view of Gracie Mansion seen only by invited guests. The north side porch of this 1799 manor house, now the mayor's residence, enjoys a splendid East River panorama. (Museum of the City of New York)

area downtown. It has also been popular with immigrants from Austria, Hungary, and Czechoslovakia, and much evidence still survives throughout Yorkville of this intermingling of nationalities.

A walk around the Historic District takes but a few minutes.

Observe how the design of the individual houses combines to create a uniform effect. A turret marks the corner of each block; roof gables, pediments, parapets, chimneys, and dormer windows are arranged symmetrically; doorways, stoops, and basement entrances are paired under broad arches. The building walls are of smooth red brick, joined by black mortar, rising to meet sloping gray slate roofs. Note, too, the typical bay windows and the double-hung sash, in which the lower is a solid pane, while the upper is divided into small squares. In its *Designation Report* for the Henderson Place Historic District, the Landmarks Commission describes the dwellings as having been "designed with the characteristics of the Elizabethan manor house combined with Flemish classic detail in a style developed in England between the years 1870 and 1910, principally by Norman Shaw." Although having little to do with Queen Anne who reigned from 1702 to 1714, Shaw developed the design to create a "comfortable and romantic domestic style." The so-called Queen Anne style achieved its greatest popularity here in the 1880s and '90s.

The scale of little Henderson Place is totally destroyed by the towering apartment house on the west side, for which eight of these picturesque town houses were sacrificed.

End of tour.

A walk west along 86th Street, the *Hauptstrasse* of Yorkville, is quite interesting. The 86th Street crosstown bus connects with the IRT Lexington Avenue subway at Lexington Avenue, with the IND subway at Central Park West, and at Broadway with the IRT Broadway-Seventh Avenue subway.

14. West of Central Park

[*IND AA Line to 72nd Street station; IRT Broadway-Seventh Avenue line to 72nd Street station; Eighth Avenue-Central Park West bus to 70th Street*]

The tour begins at Central Park West and West 70th Street.

Central Park, 59th Street to 110th Street, Fifth Avenue to Central Park West, is a tribute to the foresight of our early city fathers, and particularly to poet William Cullen Bryant, who pleaded the cause of a public park and recreation area close to the inner city. The land was acquired by the city in 1856, and a contest announced for the best plan of development. The winning entry, entitled "Greensward," was submitted by landscape architects Frederick Law Olmsted and Calvert Vaux, who spent the next 20 years supervising the creation of one of the most successful landscaped areas anywhere.

This charming piece of picturesque "country" includes several lakes, forest land, rocky hills, open meadows, secluded glens, a bird sanctuary, footpaths, bridle paths, extensive recreational facilities, an excellent zoo, and an array of artistic public sculpture.* Central Park is listed in the National Register of Historic Places, and has been designated a Scenic Landmark by the New York City Landmarks Preservation Commission.

1. The Spanish & Portuguese Synagogue (Congregation Shearith Israel), at the southwest corner of West 70th Street, represents the oldest Jewish congregation in the United States. Its first house of worship was erected in

---

* Since Central Park is not included in this tour, detailed information, including a map and list of Park activities, can be obtained from the organization that is dedicated to preserving and protecting it: The Greensward Foundation, Lenox Hill P.O. Box 610, New York, N.Y. 10021.

Central Park West (then called Eighth Avenue) in 1895, looking north toward the Hotel Majestic on 71st Street, and the Hotel San Remo two blocks further. The hotels have long since been replaced by luxury apartment houses which retain the old names. (Museum of the City of New York)

1730 by the descendants of a group of 23 men, women, and children who arrived in Nieuw Amsterdam in 1654—refugees from the Inquisition in Brazil. After three successive moves uptown, this Classic Revival building was built in 1897 from plans by Brunner & Tryon. The interior is very impressive, and can be visited Sunday mornings or during services on Friday evenings or Saturday mornings. The auditorium is arranged according to orthodox tradition with the reading desk in the center. The Little Synagogue, a small room in the rear of the building, is an accurate reconstruction of the Mill Street temple of 1730, with many of the original artifacts as well as some from subsequent buildings. Two huge millstones in the hall are from the old Dutch mill, which stood at the corner of Mill Lane and Mill Street (now South William Street), where services were conducted before the construction of the first synagogue. The congregation maintains the three Spanish & Portuguese cemeteries described on other tours [*see* Lower East Side, Supplementary Tour A; Greenwich Village, 33; and Ladies' Mile, 16]. The Synagogue still follows the Sephardic tradition handed down from the Jews of Spain and Portugal, and the ritual and Hebrew pronunciation differs somewhat from that of the Ashkenazic Jews, although Sephardic Hebrew is now the official language of Israel.

2. The Majestic Apartments, 115 Central Park West, was built in 1930 from plans by Jacques Delamarre of the architectural firm of Irwin S. Chanin, and is a fine example of the Art Deco style that became the rage in the late 1920s and '30s. The avant-garde brickwork is particularly attractive, as are the pair of roof towers. One of four twin-tower apartment houses that enliven the cityscape of Central Park West, the Majestic is named for a French Renaissance-style hotel that once occupied the site. (One of the towers hides unsightly water tanks.) The Majestic was originally planned as a 53-story apartment hotel, but the newly enacted multiple-dwelling law, with its severe height restrictions, limited the number of stories to three times the width.

3. The Dakota, on the northwest corner of West 72nd Street, is the West Side's most prestigious address, and has been since it was completed in 1884. Designed by famed architect Henry Janeway Hardenbergh (Plaza Hotel, Con Edison Building, Hotel Martinique, Art Students' League Building, etc.) in a German Renaissance style, its picturesque setting facing Central Park has been the subject of many prints and photographs. The Dakota was the city's first luxury apartment house. Built of yellow brick with brownstone and terra-cotta trim, this massive eight-story edifice is considered one of the most notable buildings of its kind in the country. True to the architect's

The Dakota forms a backdrop for the throngs of skaters on Central Park Lake, c. 1890. (New-York Historical Society)

conception of a château, it is surrounded by a "moat," with access to the interior through a dramatic two-story segmental arch, guarded by a sentry box. The entranceways to the building are in the four corners of the spacious courtyard, formerly a carriageway. On the south façade of the building are two end pavilions with semicircular oriel windows that extend from the ground floor to the roof. The fanciful roof, with huge gables at each corner and in the center, is perforated with symmetrical dormer windows. The Dakota is indeed a fortress, as the load-bearing walls are several feet thick, and each floor is separated by layers of thick concrete. When completed, it had extensive facilities for an army of servants, and boasted a private restaurant for the exclusive tenants. The eight hydraulic elevators, although modernized, are still in use and are operated from a huge pump room in the basement.

The Dakota was built by Edward S. Clark, heir to the vast Singer Sewing Machine empire. Clark's friends ridiculed the idea of his constructing a luxury house so far uptown, and remarked that "it might just as well be in Dakota," which was then Indian Territory. The name stuck, but "Clark's Folly" proved to be a sound investment. The Dakota, with its atmosphere of brooding hauteur, was the setting for the film *Rosemary's Baby,* and for

In splendid isolation, the Dakota rises above Central Park West and 72nd Street, c. 1890. Completed in 1884 from plans by Henry J. Hardenbergh, the huge apartment building was the subject of jibes for being "so far out of town . . . it might just as well be in the Dakotas!" (And the name stuck!) (Museum of the City of New York)

the historical science-fiction novel *Time and Again,* by Jack Finney. It is a designated New York City Landmark.

Clark's Dakota added great impetus to the growth of the neighborhood. Coinciding with its completion, the City changed the name of Eighth Avenue above 59th Street to Central Park West. Until that time the Eighth Avenue Horsecar Line and a stagecoach on the Bloomingdale Road (now Broadway) provided the only "rapid" transit, but in 1879 the Ninth Avenue El was pushed north on what is now Columbus Avenue, as far as 81st Street, affording quick access from downtown. However, it was not until the late 1880s that the great building boom began on the West Side.

Continue west on West 72nd Street.

4. Until the late 1940s **West 72nd Street** was one of the better addresses on the West Side. Some vestiges of former elegance can be seen in the building that was formerly the Hotel Margrave **(No. 110),** built in the typical Classic Revival style of architecture so favored during the so-called Eclectic Period of the Gay '90s and first few years of the 20th century. **Nos. 129, 137, 139,** and **141** were former town houses, and **No. 166,** with its ornate, projecting cornice, was once an opulent apartment house.

Turn south on Broadway to West 71st Street.

5. No. 171 West 71st Street, **the Dorilton,** still maintains some pretense of luxury. Built in 1900 from designs by Janes & Leo, it is a grandiose French Second Empire-style structure. The original copper sheathing that adorned the roof has been replaced by shingles. Note the pair of sculptured figures on the Broadway façade, as well as the very ornate lobby.

6. Farther down West 71st Street is the neo-Gothic-style **Church of the Blessed Sacrament,** built in 1917. It is more noteworthy for its interior than for its somewhat disproportionately styled exterior. Note how the cleverly designed vaulted ceilings give the nave an impression of great height.

Return to Broadway and turn south to West 70th Street.

7. The Borough of Manhattan Community College branch at 135–145 W. 70th Street was built in 1926 as the **Temple of the Knights of Pythias.** Architect Thomas W. Lamb drew on Ancient Egyptian motifs for the styling of this fraternal organization's Grand Lodge. The polychrome designs, seated Pharaohs, ornate columns, and upper "temple" are straight out of Karnak! An Egyptian Revival style in architecture achieved brief popularity after the discovery in 1922 of the tomb of King Tutankhamen in Thebes.

Return to Broadway, cross to the west side, and turn west (left) into West 71st Street.

8. Christ Church, designed in Romanesque Revival style by Charles C.

The Boulevard, now Broadway, looking north from 70th Street in 1907, showing every mode of transportation available at the time. Somewhat blurred in the background is the newly completed Ansonia Hotel. (Photograph by Byron. The Byron Collection. Museum of the City of New York)

Haight, was completed in 1890. Built of orange brick with terra-cotta trim, the Episcopal church is laid out in the form of a Greek cross parallel to the street, rather than perpendicular to it. Architect Haight is best known for his building plans for the General Theological Seminary [*see* Old Chelsea, 18].

The trio of adjacent town houses **(Nos. 215–219)** were built in 1891 in the Italianate style. Note how these brownstones are deceivingly painted to resemble marble.

9. At the intersection of Broadway and West 72nd Street, the **IRT subway entrance** on the center "island" is one of the last of such structures remaining in the city. It dates from the original subway line built in 1904, when many touches of elegance were included in our first underground railroad. The line's route began at City Hall, ran north to 42nd Street, crosstown to Times Square, then north on Broadway to 145th Street.

The intersection is divided into **Sherman Square** to the south of West 72nd Street, and **Verdi Square** to the north.

At the beginning of the 19th century this busy confluence of major thoroughfares was the sleepy **hamlet of Harsenville,** named for farmer Jacob Harsen, whose house stood approximately at the present intersection. When the Bloomingdale Road was opened in 1816 from the lower city to the Harlem River, the area began to lose its bucolic flavor. Toward the end of the century, the Bloomingdale Road was renamed the Boulevard, north of 59th Street. Moses King, in his *Handbook of New York City,* 1893 edition, described the Boulevard as "two capital roadways, separated by a central strip of lawns, trees, and flowers. When finished it will be one of the most beautiful driveways in the world, traversing as it does, the remarkably picturesque region between Central Park and the Hudson River, much of the way over high ground, commanding beautiful views." The Boulevard was joined officially to Broadway early in this century, making it Manhattan's longest traffic artery.

10. Verdi Square, named for the great Italian composer, provides a small patch of green along busy Broadway. The benches are usually filled with older adults from the neighborhood who meet to gossip, reminisce, or take in the sun in warmer weather. The **Statue of Giuseppe Verdi,** commissioned by New York's Italian community in 1906, and executed in marble by Pasquale Civiletti, stands on a granite pedestal over four life-size figures representing characters from Verdi's operas *Otello, Aida, Falstaff,* and *La Forza del Destino.* The Square is an officially designated New York City Scenic Landmark.

Backyard of the Jacob Harsen homestead at the corner of Tenth Avenue (now Amsterdam Avenue) and 70th Street, c. 1888. The present intersection of Broadway and 72nd Street was the site of the hamlet of Harsenville during the eighteenth century. The house was built in 1701 for the Dyckman family, and survived until 1893. (New-York Historical Society)

Dominating the north side of Verdi Square is the massive **Central Savings Bank Building.** Its limestone façade, designed in the style of an enormous Renaissance palace by York & Sawyer in 1928, creates an atmosphere of solid financial security—no doubt the intention of the builders. The wrought-iron window grilles and the large lanterns (by Samuel Yellin) add an artistic touch, while a handsome clock flanked by two lions decorates the 73rd Street entrance. The bank, built on a trapezoidal plot, is a well designed and dignified structure—a fitting backdrop to Verdi Square. Central Savings Bank was declared a landmark in 1975.

11. One of the city's truly magnificent buildings is the French Beaux Arts-style **Ansonia Hotel** on the northwest corner of Broadway and 73rd Street. Begun in 1899 and completed five years later, it is the dominant landmark of the West Side. When the Ansonia opened, it was one of the most opulent hostelries in town. The builder, William Earl Dodge Stokes, a wealthy land developer and inheritor of the Phelps Dodge Company fortune, brought architect-sculptor Paul DuBoy from France to carry out his grandiose plans for a sumptuous hotel in the style of the elegant palaces along the Parisian *grands boulevards.* Although its 17 stories would have made it second only to the Eiffel Tower in Paris, its dramatic setting here on Broadway is quite appropriate.

The corner round towers surmounted by cupolas and railings in harmony with the convex mansard roof, are the most striking feature of the building. Rows of delicately ornate balconies break up the overwhelming verticality caused by tier upon tier of windows, while a series of recessed courts on the Broadway and West 73rd Street sides gives a feeling of depth and also provides a maximum of light and air.

Stokes, who owned the construction company, supervised every step in the building of the hotel. Thick masonry walls made it completely fireproof. The building also featured a roof garden, shops in the basement, and *two* swimming pools. The Ansonia is named indirectly for Stokes's maternal grandfather, Anson Greene Phelps, who founded the Ansonia Brass & Copper Company in his namesake town of Ansonia, Connecticut. In 1879, a subsidiary of the firm, the famous Ansonia Clock Company, moved its operations from the Connecticut town to Brooklyn, bringing the Ansonia name to the city 20 years ahead of the hotel. Stokes's most illustrious relative, however, was I. N. (Isaac Newton) Phelps Stokes, the architect-historian who wrote the definitive six-volume *Iconography of Manhattan Island.*

The fine reputation of the Ansonia through the years was due to its world-renowned clientele. Much the same way that the downtown Hotel Chelsea was the favorite of the *literati,* the Ansonia was the bastion of the musical world. The thick walls provided soundproofing that proved a most attractive feature. Among the "greats" who have stayed at the hotel were Enrico Caruso, Leopold Auer, Feodor Chaliapin, Mischa Elman, Geraldine Farrar, Lauritz Melchior, Ezio Pinza, Lily Pons, Yehudi Menuhin, Tito Schipa, Igor Stravinsky, and Arturo Toscanini. It was for a time the favorite of Sol Hurok, Billie Burke, Florenz Ziegfeld, and Theodore Dreiser. The Ansonia was designated a New York City Landmark in 1972.

Much of the early splendor of the hotel has now vanished. Several of the crowning cupolas and lanterns are missing, a number of the decorative railings and balconies have been removed, the immense ground floor archways have either been blocked up or converted into small stores, the spacious lobby has been partitioned into unrecognizability, and the close-up appearance of the whole establishment smacks of crass commercialism and neglect . . . but from a distance, the Hotel Ansonia is still a great lady!

Continue north on Broadway.

12. The Astor Apartments, between 75th and 76th streets, once a luxurious apartment house, was built just after the turn of the century and named for capitalist William Waldorf Astor, who owned much of the land in the neighborhood.

Turn west (left) on West 77th Street to West End Avenue.

John C. Vandenheuvel's country estate, c. 1819, occupied the entire block now bounded by Broadway, West End Avenue, 78th and 79th Streets. (The J. Clarence Davies Collection. Museum of the City of New York)

Pushed by a diminutive donkey engine, a train of the newly-opened New York Elevated Railroad (later the Ninth Avenue El) enters the 59th Street station. The name of "Ninth Avenue" above 59th Street was later changed to Columbus Avenue. (Museum of the City of New York)

13. West End Avenue was a "millionaires row" of town houses until the early 20th century. When the New York Central Rail Road freight line, one block to the west, was covered over and Riverside Drive opened, the affluent residents were lured away to the new street with its unrivaled vistas of the Hudson River. An apartment-house building boom on West End Avenue after World War I and through the 1930s again attracted the wealthy (and near-wealthy); and the street, although somewhat declined, is still a holdout of the upper middle class.

The West End Collegiate Church and Collegiate School incorporate both Dutch and Flemish features. Architect Robert W. Gibson created a charming "Netherlandisch" grouping with typical step-gables, pinnacles, and ornate dormer windows. This "Collegiate" church, built in 1891–92, is a descendant of the original Dutch Reformed Church, organized in 1628—the oldest Protestant congregation in America; and the Collegiate School is the country's oldest independent secondary school.

14. The entire block, West End Avenue to Broadway and West 78th to West 79th streets, is occupied by the **Apthorp Apartments.** A dignified luxury apartment house, it still preserves its original old-world elegance, despite the encroaching decrepitude of some of its neighboring streets. Built for William Waldorf Astor in 1906–08 from plans by Clinton & Russell, the enormous limestone structure is set around a broad central courtyard with fountain, access to which is through high vaulted passageways. The Broadway entrance is the grandest—a former carriageway whose bronze gates are reminiscent of the portcullis of some medieval castle. At each entrance, set in the spandrels of the façade, are two winged figures, and around the building runs a lovely, ornate frieze. A cast-iron portico marks the entrance to each of the four separate units. Except for the addition of ground-floor shops on the Broadway side, the building remains virtually unchanged.

The apartment house is named for Charles Ward Apthorpe (*with an "e"*), who purchased the land in 1763. The property was passed to Apthorpe's son-in-law, Baron John C. van den Heuvel in 1792, and ultimately came into the Astor family in 1879. The Apthorp Apartments is a designated New York City Landmark.

Turn north (left) on Broadway.

15. The First Baptist Church, on the northwest corner of West 79th Street, was built in 1891 in the Romanesque Revival style. The asymmetry of its twin towers is puzzling, as is the incompleteness of the right member. Contrary to expectation, the auditorium is semicircular in shape, with a quality of intimacy contrasting strongly with the austerity of the exterior.

16. Zabar's, at 2245 Broadway, is a *gourmet* landmark. Known throughout the West Side (and by *cognoscenti* in all boroughs), it is a unique emporium whose mind-boggling variety of gustatory temptations defies description.

Continue north on Broadway to West 86th Street, and cross to the east side.

Broadway and West 86th Street marks the **site of the village of Bloomingdale,** the largest settlement on the west side of Manhattan Island in the late 18th century. Its counterpart on the east side was the village of Haarlem (which subsequently dropped an "a" from the spelling).

17. Another massive luxury residence is the **Belnord Apartments,** located between Broadway and Amsterdam Avenue, from West 86th to West 87th streets, in a setting quite similar to that of its "cousin," the Apthorp. Completed in 1908, architect H. Hobart Weeks designed it for gracious living. Its porte-cochere, formal central garden, cast-iron lampposts, and ornate separate entranceways are reminders of the affluent life-style of its former tenants. The Belnord Apartments is also a designated Landmark.

Cross Broadway again and walk west on West 86th Street to West End Avenue.

18. On the northeast corner is the Romanesque Revival-style **Church of St. Paul & St. Andrew,** built in 1895. Two architects shared the design,

R. H. Robertson and W. A. Potter. (Local wags claim that a church dedicated to two saints required the talents of two architects!) Note the sculptured angels in the spandrels of the façade.

Turn north (right) on West End Avenue.

19. Adjacent **St. Ignatius Church** (1902) is another house of worship designed by architect Charles C. Haight. This "ecclesiastical block" provides a pleasant break in the monotony of the seemingly endless rows of apartment houses along West End Avenue. Some of the apartment houses are rather attractive, however. Note the typical Art Deco style of No. 565 on the northwest corner of 87th Street.

Turn east (right) on West 88th Street.

20. Dominating the middle of the block is **Congregation B'nai Jeshurun,** designed by Henry B. Herts and Walter Schneider in 1918. A broad Moorish façade of orange granite and a highly ornate, carved limestone portal in Romanesque Revival style give this synagogue a stately and imposing appearance. The richly polychromed interior is well worth a visit. B'nai Jeshurun, established in 1825, is the oldest Ashkenazic congregation in the city. It was

The original building (1869) of the American Museum of Natural History at 77th Street and Central Park West. This photo, taken ten years later, shows a broad wasteland which was soon to be covered by many new wings of the Museum. (Museum of the City of New York)

An artist's conception of the completed American Museum of Natural History was not too far amiss when drawn for Moses King's Views of New York *in 1908. The central tower, however, was never built. (Author's collection)*

founded by a group of German and English Jews who split with the Spanish & Portuguese Synagogue, adopting the German ritual and language as opposed to the Sephardic Spanish-Portuguese.

Return to West End Avenue, turn north to West 89th Street, and east to Broadway.

21. Another of the immense luxury multiple dwellings is the **Astor Court Apartments** (89th to 90th streets), designed by Charles A. Platt in 1916. The interior garden courtyard and ornate balconies add grace and charm, but its crowning glory is the superb decorative cornice.

Continue north on Broadway to West 94th Street and turn west (left). About 50 yards down the north side of the block is the entrance to Pomander Walk.

22. New York City presents an almost inexhaustible supply of architectural surprises, and delightful **Pomander Walk** is no exception. Constructed in 1921, this diminutive double row of charming town houses was designed to imitate a small street in "Merrie England." The idea originated with the stage setting for the English play *Pomander Walk,* which opened in New York in 1911. In the play, the Walk was a small mews in the London suburb of Chiswick.

Although posted signs discourage visitors, walk in anyway, passing through to the West 95th Street exit. (Be sure to close the iron gate securely to avoid the wrath of the residents!)

Proceed to Broadway and West 96th Street, and turn west (left) to Riverside Drive. Cross to the northeast corner.

23. For the past hundred years or so, New Yorkers have been called "cliff dwellers" for reasons that are obvious. The architect of this otherwise undistinguished apartment house displayed a keen sense of humor in the frieze that depicts motifs from the lives of the ancient Arizona Cliff Dwellers, with buffalo skulls, mountain lions, and rattlesnakes. It is doubtful that the building will ever be designated a landmark, but the interesting designs are more than symbolic to our contemporary "cliff dwellers."

Turn south on Riverside Drive.

24. Tree-lined **Riverside Drive** is one of the city's loveliest streets. Much of the dignity and elegance of yesteryear are gone, but the broad panoramic vistas are still unspoiled. As mentioned previously, the Drive began to flourish with the covering-over of the railroad that parallels the river. It was not long before Riverside Drive challenged Fifth Avenue as one of the most fashionable street addresses in town. Adding further to its beauty was the construction in 1937 of Riverside Park, and the subsequent spiriting away of vehicular traffic to the new Henry Hudson Parkway close to the riverbank. Along the Drive can be seen the former opulent town houses and the newer luxury apartment houses that made it so attractive to New York's wealthier citizens.

25. At West 93rd Street, on a slight crest overlooking Riverside Park, is the heroic **Joan of Arc Memorial Statue,** executed in 1915 by famed American sculptor, Anna Vaughn Hyatt. The statue was commissioned by the Joan of Arc Statue Committee to commemorate the 500th anniversary of the birth of the Maid of Orleans, presumed to be in 1412. Her armor is historically accurate, having been researched by the Metropolitan Museum of Art's curator of armor. Sculptor Hyatt has succeeded in capturing Joan of Arc's expression of intense fervor and sense of mission as she rode forth to lead the French troops in battle against the English and Burgundians. The bronze statue was cast by the well known Gorham Company, which is still in business, but no longer casting huge statues. The Gothic-style pedestal of the monument was designed by architect John V. Van Pelt.

26. At the corner of West 89th Street stands one of the West Side's most significant public sculptures, **The Soldiers' and Sailors' Monument.** Sculptor Paul E. DuBoy completed the marble Civil War memorial in 1902 (just after putting the final touches to his work on the Ansonia Hotel), patterning it after the choragic Monument of Lysicrates in Athens.

27. The majestic mansion on the southeast corner, opposite the Monument, was the **former residence of Bishop Henry Codman Potter,** built in

1902. It now serves as an orthodox Hebrew school, the Yeshiva Chofetz Chaim. Very few freestanding town houses now remain from the great array that lined the Drive in the early 20th century.

Although this is the end of the Walking Tour, a pleasant stroll back to the starting point can be made as follows:

Continue south on Riverside Drive [*see* map] to West 79th Street; east to Columbus Avenue; north to West 81st Street; east to Central Park West; then south to West 72nd Street. (Or, alternately, walk down Broadway to the Lincoln Center for the Performing Arts, West 66th to West 62nd streets.)

Following the first itinerary given above, the block between Columbus Avenue and Central Park West is quite attractive and faces the **Hayden Planetarium.** Along Central Park West to West 77th Street is the outstanding **American Museum of Natural History,** which houses one of the world's greatest scientific collections, and is one of the most frequently visited places in town. The equestrian statue of Theodore Roosevelt flanked by an Indian chief and a Bantu was sculpted in 1939 by J. E. Frazer. The red granite Romanesque Revival south building at the corner of West 77th Street is the original Museum building (1877) and is one of the finest examples of the style in the country. The American Museum of Natural History is a designated landmark.

The New-York Historical Society, on the southwest corner of West 77th Street (York & Sawyer, 1908; with wings added in 1937–38), was built in a classic style and is a designated New York City Landmark. The Society, founded in 1804, possesses a superb collection of books, prints, manuscripts, and other historical memorabilia, including the original Audubon *Birds of America*. There are also many interesting exhibitions and displays.

The two blocks between West 77th and West 75th streets mark the eastern edge of the **Central Park West-76th Street Historic District,** a grouping of 40 town houses of unified scale and general design; the New-York Historical Society Building; the neo-Gothic **Universalist Church of New York** (formerly called Church of the Divine Paternity, built in 1897); and the Beaux Arts-style **Kenilworth Apartments** (1905–06). The Church presents a varied and interesting façade with its pointed arch windows, buttresses, finials, and gables, plus two magnificent stained-glass windows. Take a brief detour along quiet, tree-lined **West 76th Street,** and notice the variety of architectural styles with their handsome details—so typical of the late 19th-century period of eclecticism.

Continuing south, the two succeeding blocks are occupied respectively by the mammoth **San Remo Apartments** (Emery Roth, 1930), and the stately **Langham** (Clinton & Russell, 1907).

15. Brooklyn Heights and the Old Fulton Ferry District

[*IND A line to High Street-Brooklyn Bridge station (use the rear exit, and walk through Whitman Close town houses to Henry Street, turn left one block); IRT Broadway-Seventh Avenue line to Clark Street Brooklyn Heights. On exiting from St. George Hotel, turn left to Henry Street, and left again two blocks to Orange Street*]

The section of Brooklyn known as Brooklyn Heights was New York City's first suburb. Situated on bluffs that rise steeply above New York Bay, the "Heights" was for over 250 years a relatively remote and rural area, undisturbed by the growth of the burgeoning port city across the East River. Before the arrival of the Dutch in 1626, the western portion of Long Island was inhabited by several tribes of the Algonkian Nation, particularly the Canarsies, who lived in long houses—some actually several blocks in length —on the high promontory facing Manhattan Island. When the first Dutch settlements were built, the Indians abandoned their village of Ihpetonga ("Silver Birches"), and in 1646 the the village of Breuckelen (named for a town in the Dutch province of Utrecht) was established by Dutch settlers from Manhattan. When the British captured New York, they changed the name to Brookland. The beginning of the Revolutionary War saw the crucial Battle of Long Island lost by the patriots on August 27, 1776, as Washington's meager forces were overwhelmed by a superior British and Hessian army under Lord Howe. After their defeat at the Flatbush Pass (in the present Prospect Park), and the threat of total annihilation through a flank-

The Plymouth Church in a Civil War era engraving, showing crowds gathering to hear the fiery oratory of abolitionist minister Henry Ward Beecher. Except for the Tuscan-style porch, the barnlike building is unchanged. (Long Island Historical Society)

ing maneuver, a small regiment of Maryland Continentals fought a desperate delaying action at nearby Gowanus, as Washington successfully withdrew the army to Manhattan under cover of a heavy night fog. In 1816 the name was again changed, this time to the Village of Brooklyn Ferry. Since Dutch colonial days, a small sail ferry operated to the foot of the Old Ferry Road (now Fulton Street) from Peck Slip, in Manhattan. A bell hung at each landing so that prospective "commuters" could summon the boat. However, the opening in 1814 of Robert Fulton's steam ferry *Nassau* signaled the beginning of the area's development as a residential community. Brooklyn Heights by 1820 was thickly settled, with much the same street layout as today. In 1834 the State Legislature granted a charter to the City of Brooklyn, and with its rapid growth and subsequent annexation of several other independent villages, Brooklyn by mid-19th century became the third largest city in the nation, with a population exceeding 85,000. Laid out at right angles to the waterfront, the shady streets provided easy access to the river, and as late as the 20th century, there were no fewer than three ferries operating to lower Manhattan (Wall Street to Montague Street, South Ferry to Atlantic Avenue, and the Fulton Ferry connecting both Brooklyn's and Manhattan's Fulton streets). With the rapid development of the City of Brooklyn (which did not merge with the City of New York until 1898) the "Heights" was bypassed, and left undisturbed as land speculators and builders moved south and east. Thus, Brooklyn Heights today remains strikingly similar to its early appearance of more than 150 years ago. Of the approximately 1100 houses in the neighborhood, more than 600 were built before 1860! The only major physical change was made in 1950 when the City of New York built the Brooklyn-Queens Expressway along the Brooklyn Heights waterfront, removing a number of old houses, but substituting the magnificent Esplanade over the roadway, which provided residents with one of the most scenic views of New York Harbor. However, with the abandonment of the ferries and the construction of the new highway, the Heights is now permanently separated from the water. Its ties to Manhattan were greatly increased with the opening in 1883 of the Brooklyn Bridge; and by 1908 the first of several subway tunnels reached the Heights, although elevated trains had already been using the Bridge for more than a decade. The arrival of the subway caused many of the patrician inhabitants to flee, and a number of their stately mansions were divided into small apartments. The neighborhood is still characterized by rows of lovely brick and brownstone houses—most with a uniform 50-foot height, representing virtually every architectural style of the 19th century. The Heights is also noted for several of its landmark churches designed by famous architects; but it is mainly regarded as one of the most charming and desirable residential sections of the city. In recognition of its aesthetic and historic value, Brooklyn Heights was designated in 1965 as the city's first Historic District.

The tour begins at the corner of Henry and Orange streets (one block west of Cadman Plaza).

Orange Street, and its two adjacent neighbors, Cranberry and Pineapple streets, were named by developers John and Jacob Middagh Hicks; or as a story goes, by one of their relatives, a Miss Middagh. Irked by wealthy neighbors who named the streets after themselves, she ripped down the immodest signs and replaced them with ones with botanical names. The city fathers promptly removed them, but after a protracted battle, the Board of Aldermen gave in and allowed her choices to remain. She is also credited with naming Poplar, Willow, and Cranberry streets.

No. 69 Orange Street is one of the oldest houses in Brooklyn Heights. Built c. 1829, it is typical of the wooden clapboard residences erected during the early development of the neighborhood. The mansard roof was added after 1870.

Just down the street is the famous **Plymouth Church of the Pilgrims.** Founded in 1847 by the fiery Henry Ward Beecher, its first minister, it was designed by architect Joseph C. Wells in an Italianate style and completed two years later. An austere, barnlike structure, it became one of the most influential churches in the nation. Beecher, an outspoken abolitionist, preached for many years and invited many noted public figures to share his pulpit. Among the antislavery agitators who shared his pulpit in passionate oratory were William Lloyd Garrison, Charles Sumner, and John Greenleaf Whittier. Abraham Lincoln worshiped here, and his pew, No. 89, is marked with a silver plaque. In 1867 Charles Dickens delivered an address on the occasion of his second visit to America; and through the years such greats as Horace Greeley, Mark Twain, and Booker T. Washington attended services here. In dramatic outpourings of rhetoric, Henry Ward Beecher fought with uncompromising vigor against slavery, and with equal grandiloquence campaigned for women's suffrage, temperance, and general reform. With typical dramatic flair, he once auctioned off a mulatto slave girl named Pinkie before an aghast congregation, using the money to purchase her freedom and arouse the attention of the entire country. Pinkie, actually Mrs. James Hunt, subsequently returned in 1927 to address the congregation from the very same platform where she had been "sold" almost 70 years before. Local Union Army units on their way to southern battlefronts would stop for services at the Plymouth Church, and at the height of the Civil War, Beecher made a trip to England to win sympathy away from the Confederate cause. President Lincoln later honored Beecher by having him deliver a speech at the symbolic raising of the flag at Fort Sumter. (Incidentally, Beecher's sister, novelist Harriet Beecher Stowe, will always be remembered for her very influential, but overimaginative *Uncle Tom's Cabin.*) Beecher, who in a few short years had become a national hero, was later involved in a sensational "page-one scandal," accused of having committed adultery with the wife of a former associate. Although the minister was subsequently acquitted by the jury, that was the Victorian era, and his reputation and career suffered irreparable damage.

The exterior of the church is virtually without ornamentation, in the tradition of the New England Congregational Church—even lacking the usual steeple. Inside, the auditorium is simple, with white walls and woodwork. A balcony supported by cast-iron columns surrounds the hall, connecting with the organ in front. There are 19 stained-glass windows designed by Frederick Stymetz Lamb representing the "History of Puritanism and Its Influence Upon the Institutions and People of the Republic," with the broader theme of political, intellectual, and religious liberty. The pulpit furniture is made from an olive tree brought from the Mount of Olives in 1868 by members of a trip to the Holy Land, the occasion made famous by Mark Twain in his *Innocents Abroad.* Adjoining the sanctuary is **Hillis Hall,** a social center. Its middle stained-glass window on the north side, is a magnificent representation from the life of Christ, one of five from the Tiffany Studios. Hillis Hall was a gift of coffee merchant John Arbuckle, and was built in 1913 from plans by Woodruff Leeming. In the arcade is a fragment of the Plymouth Rock brought from Massachusetts in 1840, and paintings of Abraham Lincoln, Beecher with Pinkie, and Harriet Beecher Stowe. In the lovely arcade garden is a statue of Beecher by sculptor Gutzon Borglum. The church was seriously damaged by fire in 1850, and in the early 20th century a Tuscan

Sixty-eight Hicks Street, southwest corner of Cranberry Street, in 1920. Built 100 years before, most changes seem to have occurred in recent years. (Long Island Historical Society)

porch was added, otherwise the structure is in original condition. The Plymouth Church was merged in 1934 with the Congregational Church of the Pilgrims (which still stands on the corner of Henry and Remsen streets, but is now Our Lady of Lebanon Roman Catholic Church). Honoring its historic past, the Plymouth Church of the Pilgrims has been listed on the National Register of Historic Places.

Turn right (north) on Hicks Street.

No. 68 Hicks Street, at the southwest corner of Cranberry Street, is a two-and-a-half-story frame house topped by a curb roof, and was built c. 1820. It was originally a grocery store and tavern. The clapboard walls have since been replaced with imitations. Note the Ionic colonnettes at the entrance-way.

Brooklyn Heights was intimately involved in the life of poet **Walt Whitman.** In his childhood he lived on Cranberry Street almost directly behind the Plymouth Church, and some 30 years later his *Leaves of Grass* was printed in a shop just down the street at the corner of Fulton (the approximate site of the IND subway exit). "The Good Gray Poet" also served for a time as editor of the Brooklyn *Daily Eagle,* whose offices were located a few steps farther north, close to the Fulton Ferry.

No. 59, another frame house of c. 1820, was the residence and shop of a cooper (barrel maker). The building has also suffered the ravages of modernization, with a stucco front and replacement entrance door. Adjacent **No. 57,** built about five years later, was the home of a merchant. The mansard roof came in during the period of the popular French Second Empire style in the 1870s. Actually, the mansard roof fit rather harmoniously with a number of the revival styles, and, as will be seen later, lent itself quite well to the Italianate brownstone row house.

No. 51, with arched dormer windows, belonged to a sea captain, and was built c. 1831. The low front stoop was removed and the entrance door installed on the basement level.

Across the street, **Nos. 60** and **56** have been altered considerably. No. 60, a two-and-a-half-story frame house with a curb roof has dormer windows similar to No. 51. The arch of a former fanlight doorway is still visible. No. 56, a three-story frame building, was probably a boardinghouse when built, and has subsequently had an additional floor added. Both houses were constructed before 1829.

Turn left (west) into Middagh Street.

Middagh Street was probably named after early resident John Middagh, either by himself or by relatives John and Jacob Middagh Hicks. One speculates on what the cantankerous Miss Middagh would have said after her successful campaign for botanical street names, only to see the street named after *her* family.

Typical residences of middle-class merchants and artisans of the early 19th century are **Nos. 33–25** Middagh Street. **No. 33–31** is a dual house, erected before 1847. The latter was a hairdressing salon; the former, a paint store. Doubtless, the rear and upper floors served as living quarters. **No. 29,** built c. 1830, was the home of an engineer; the profession of **No. 27**'s occupant is unknown, but the house dates from 1829; and **No. 25,** a laborer's house, and smaller than the others, was built in 1824. It has suffered so many physical changes as to be almost unrecognizable (stuccoed front, lowered entrance, etc.).

Across Middagh Street, **No. 30,** a three-story frame house, was built in 1824, and has a street level entranceway in Greek Revival style. Alas, the front wall has been defaced with asphalt shingles. Adjoining **No. 28** was erected c. 1829 for a sea captain. Another unfortunate modernization has rendered this old house an aesthetic nonentity.

As if to make up for the architectural desecrations committed on its neighbors, **No. 24 Middagh Street** is a delightful gem of a house! An amazingly well preserved example of the Federal style, the **former Eugene Boisselet House,** built around 1829, is referred to by the *AIA Guide to New York City* as "The Queen of Brooklyn Heights," and is said to be the oldest house in the neighborhood. The brickwork basement is laid in typical Flemish bond (alternating rows of long bricks, called "stretchers," and short bricks, called "headers"), while the walls are built of clapboard. Two stories plus an attic with dormers is very characteristic of the Federal style, although the roof of this house, rather than peaked, is gambrel. The doorway is artistically carved and flanked by Ionic colonnettes, with leaded glass side lights (small windows), and surmounted by a transom and sculptured panel. On the attic level, twin quarter-round windows enframe an arched window, and twin chimneys strike a harmonious balance. A board fence connects the house with a smaller garden cottage, probably a former carriage house. The missing back porch would likely complete the beautifully proportioned building.

Turn left (south) on Willow Street.

Nos. 20 through 26 Willow Street form a pleasing row of simple Greek Revival-style houses, built 1846–48. **No. 22** was the residence of Henry Ward Beecher. The entranceways are quite handsome, approached by stone stairs with ornate wrought-iron railings that terminate in a vertical swirl. Note the "Greek ears" on the door enframements, which are topped by a low-pitched pediment, and the recessed doors flanked by pilasters and side lights and surmounted by a transom. At the rear (not visible from Willow Street) are two-story open galleries facing the harbor, a typical and delightful addition to Brooklyn Heights houses facing the river.

Nos. 28 and **30** are a pair of Italianate brownstones, four stories high with a common cornice supported by brackets, and arched entranceways. No. 28 was built in 1858, its neighbor a year later.

At the corner of Cranberry and Willow streets stands one of the earliest apartment houses in the city, **"The Willows"** (No. 37). Elements of the Queen Anne style are evident in the high bay window with its classical swags and small broken pediment. This early multiple dwelling house was designed by architect A. F. Norris and erected in 1886.

Turn right (west) into Cranberry Street.

Nos. 13, 15, and **17** Cranberry Street show most of their original Federal style details. No. 17 (sometimes numbered No. 19), at the corner of Willow Street, was built c. 1834, and still retains its paneled window lintels and fanlight doorway as well as part of the original fence (with Greek Revival anthemion motifs) on the Willow Street side. The cast-iron balustrade on the stoop and the romantic mansard roof were added later. The entrance to No. 13, flanked by paneled blocks, probably supported ornate cast-iron basket newels. The fanlight doorway is enframed by a lovely archway with matching panel blocks; and the cornice, typical of the Federal style, is supported by rows of consoles above a bead-and-reel board. The house dates from about 1829.

Return to Willow Street and turn right (south).

Nos. 55 and **57** Willow Street, two-and-a-half-story Federal-style houses, were built c. 1832 and 1825, respectively. Both have Flemish bond brickwork, indicative of more expensive construction. No. 57, at the northeast corner of Orange Street, is known as the Robert White House, after the merchant who first occupied it. Note the handsome dormer windows, which luckily escaped the improvements that ravaged the entrance, railings, and windows. The original size of the windows can be seen in the "blind windows" on the Orange Street side. A lovely frieze with Greek key motif, and tooled stone lintels above the windows and doors, add to the charm.

Turn right (west) on Orange Street to the corner of Columbia Heights.

The rather incongruous **Hotel Margaret** sits like an old dowager overlooking the harbor, completely out of scale with its small row-house neighbors. Constructed in 1889 from designs by architect Frank Freeman, the towering structure is an interesting example of the Romanesque Revival style applied to a hotel. Exposed rivet heads on the broad expanses of sheet metal create a nautical theme appropriate for the site. Former residents of the hotel were etcher Joseph Pennell and novelists Sigrid Undset (Norwegian-born winner of the 1928 Nobel Prize) and Lillian Smith (*A Tree Grows in Brooklyn*).

Turn left (south) on Columbia Heights to Pineapple Street then left again.

Halfway down the block on the north side is a peaceful country-style house, charming **No. 13 Pineapple Street.** Built around 1830, it is a large residence with an interior central transverse stair hall, whose rooms are arranged on either side. A third floor was added to the building in the mid-19th century, requiring a new, bracketed cornice; and the front windows were then also enlarged. The stoop, too, is relatively new, as is the reproduction fanlight over the entrance. Nonetheless, it is a pleasant reminder of the past, enhanced by a spacious plot that breaks the monotony of the row houses.

Return to Columbia Heights and turn left (south).

On the southeast corner is the **World Headquarters of the Watchtower Bible and Tract Society,** commonly called Jehovah's Witnesses. Erected in 1968, the building's design won the approval of the Landmarks Commission only after several previous submissions had been rejected. The successful plans for the present structure were accepted only because the Commission found them compatible with the style of the surroundings. (One of the rejected designs called for a 12-story tower, which the Landmarks Commission felt would have been totally out of scale with neighboring buildings.) An appealing aspect of the plan is the adaptation of the house fronts of the three adjacent brownstones to the south into the overall design, and the repetition of their bay-window motif in the theme of the office building's façade.

Across the street, **No. 138 Columbia Heights** is a town house built c.

1860 in the Renaissance Revival style. Renaissance details are evident in the delicate cornice consoles, the segmental arch windows, the frieze and cornice over the window and door enframements, and the curved pediment set on consoles over the doorway.

Columbia Heights is named for the estate of early landowner Hezekiah Beers Pierrepont, whose mansion "Four Chimneys" and extensive property overlooked the harbor in the early 19th century. Pierrepont owned the Anchor Gin Distillery at the foot of Joralemon Street, which was operated by a large windmill and was conveniently close to the ferry. The wealthy merchant was also Robert Fulton's chief financial backer, helping him establish the first steam ferry in the world. By mid-19th century, Columbia Heights (then Columbia Street) became one of the most fashionable strips in Brooklyn. A row of eight three-story, wooden Greek Revival-style houses connected by a common colonnaded portico was erected in 1835 on the most prominent point on the Heights, between Cranberry and Middagh streets. Known as General Underhill's Colonnade Row, or simply, **Underhill's Colonnade,** it was the area's most significant landmark until one cold December morning

Underhill's Colonnade on the Heights, overlooking the harbor in the late 1830s. The engraving is from the letterhead of a fire insurance company, showing a house on fire (fanciful or otherwise), which was doubtless intended to serve as a graphic warning to those not insured. The Colonnade itself was consumed by fire in 1853. (Long Island Historical Society)

in 1853, when it was consumed in a spectacular conflagration. Occupying the east side of Columbia Heights between Pineapple and Clark streets from 1844 to 1904 was the sumptuous **Leavitt-Bowen Mansion** with a monumental Corinthian portico facing the harbor. Another long-vanished landmark was **Dr. Charles H. Shephard's Turkish Bath,** which occupied a Greek Revival house on the corner of Cranberry Street from 1863 until 1913.

Turn left (east) at Clark Street to Willow Street.

The **former Towers Hotel,** on the northeast corner of Clark and Willow streets was purchased by the Watchtower Bible and Tract Society to house staff members of its expanding world headquarters office. The Towers, a prominent feature of the Heights skyline since its opening in 1928, was one of Brooklyn's last luxury hotels. Designed by architects Starrett & Van Vleck, the building's four octagonal towers, illuminated at night, were a familiar landmark. Perhaps the Jehovah's Witnesses will maintain the tradition.

Continue east on Clark Street to Hicks Street and turn right (south).

Nos. 131 and 135 Hicks Street, on the east side, are rare examples of brownstones in the Gothic Revival style. No. 131 is by far the better preserved of the pair, with its elaborate cornice still intact, and without the abominable penthouse that surmounts its twin. It is referred to as the **Henry C. Bowen House,** after the original merchant-owner who had the house built around 1848. Bowen was a founder of the Plymouth Church as well as the abolitionist newspaper, *The Independent,* which Henry Ward Beecher edited. Both houses share Tudor Gothic arched doorways and ornately carved spandrels, square-topped windows with sash in imitation of casements, hood (or label) moldings over the windows, cast-iron railings with traceries, and the original iron fence. The cornice of No. 131 is set above a bead-and-reel molding, and only the missing cast-iron finials from the newel posts would complete this lovely house. (Perhaps the owner could make a deal with his neighbor in No. 135 to obtain his finials). The Gothic Revival style was in vogue in Brooklyn Heights between 1844 and 1865.

Returning to Clark Street, the **Hotel St. George,** in a massing of several buildings of different styles and eras, occupies the entire block from Hicks to Henry, and Clark to Pineapple streets. Built piecemeal from 1889 to 1929, it became the largest hotel in the city. The original section is still visible a few steps east of Hicks Street, split into two wings, surmounted by a mansard roof, and capped by a pediment inscribed with a rusting date, "188–". Few old-timers will forget the once-famous Grand Ballroom; and just about anyone who grew up in Brooklyn in the '30s remembers swimming in the enormous saltwater pool and watching his floating reflection in the room-length ceiling mirrors. And it was the favorite hotel of the old Brooklyn Dodgers. Those were the halcyon days of the St. George, for it has now reached its dotage. The ballroom no longer echoes to the strains of nightly society music,

The Congregational Church of the Pilgrims on Remsen and Henry steets still had its steeple in this c. 1880 engraving. In 1934, the congregation moved to the Plymouth Church and the building now houses Our Lady of Lebanon Maronite Roman Catholic Church. (Long Island Historical Society)

Of these five unusual row houses on Clinton Street and Aitken Place, only two survive (Nos. 140 and 142). Most unusual are the cast-iron lintels, moldings and cornices. (Long Island Historical Society)

Hezekiah Beers Pierrepont's Anchor Gin Distillery in 1823, near the present site of Joralemon and Furman Streets, in a painting by an unknown artist. The windmill and boats are reminiscent of a seventeenth-century Dutch landscape. (Brooklyn Collection. Brooklyn Public Library)

The Fulton Ferry slip in 1746, showing the step-gabled Dutch-style house of the ferrymaster, at right. (Author's collection)

Map showing the five Dutch towns and the one English town (Gravesend) which during the seventeenth century constituted Kings County. The original names of the Dutch towns are in parentheses. (The Williamsburgh Savings Bank)

The first village map of Brooklyn showing the street patterns which are virtually the same today, and the estates of the land owners, many of whom were not averse to having their names perpetuated in street designations. (Author's collection)

City dignitaries gathered to inspect the cables of the Brooklyn Bridge in 1873. Judging from engineer Roebling's warning sign, the terrifying hike on the Bridge's catwalk across the river must have been fairly commonplace. (*Brooklyn Union Gas Company*)

The Bridge Promenade has always been a popular attraction. In warm weather hundreds of commuters from Brooklyn Heights still use it daily. (*Long Island Historical Society*)

A two-cent ticket to walk across the Brooklyn Bridge after it was opened to the public in 1883. (Brooklyn Union Gas Company)

Traffic was already heavy on the Brooklyn Bridge in 1905. (Long Island Historical Society)

New-York and Brooklyn Ferry.

SUCH persons are inclined to compound, agreeable to law, in the Steam Ferry-Boat, Barges, or common Horse Boats, will be pleased to apply to the subscribers, who are authorized to settle the same.

GEORGE HICKS, Brooklyn,
JOHN PINTARD, 52 Wall-st

Commutation for a single person not
transferable, for 12 months, $10 00
Do. do. 8 months, 6 67
May 3, 1814. 6m.

The ferry from the tip of lower Manhattan entering its slip at the foot of Atlantic Avenue, Brooklyn, c. 1830. (South Street Seaport Museum)

Brooklyn Union Gas Company emergency wagon leaving on a call for assistance, c. 1900. (Brooklyn Union Gas Company)

Pierrepont Street is piled high in snow drifts after a near-record blizzard on February 14, 1899. (Long Island Historical Society)

Brooklyn's Romanesque Revival-style General Post Office is a designated landmark. Completed in 1891, it represents an unusually high standard of government-sponsored architecture. The tree-lined plot to the right was the site of the Brooklyn Eagle. (*Brooklyn Union Gas Company*)

Opening day of the Brooklyn Elevated Railroad with its special trainload of city officials, May 13, 1885, from an engraving in Leslie's Illustrated Newspaper *of the following week.* (*Long Island Historical Society*)

the pool lies darkened and empty, and more than half the building has been sealed off. The once lavish Art Deco public rooms and corridors have been allowed to go to seed, becoming gathering places for undesirables, as an indifferent and greedy management seems to promote the growth of this, the biggest and ugliest blight in Brooklyn Heights. The rear of the oldest section, facing Pineapple Street, is surprisingly intact (from the outside), preserved almost museumlike between two more modern wings. Sporting a flaking black-and-silver coat of paint, its elaborate Second Empire roof re-creates the Victorian atmosphere of earlier days.

(For a quick look, walk north on Hicks Street and turn right (east) on Pineapple Street.)

Return to Clark and Willow streets and turn left (south).

Nos. 101 and 103 Willow Street are a pair of Greek Revival-style houses, both with an added fourth story. No. 101, built c. 1839, displays the characteristic (for Brooklyn Heights) pedestal blocks flanking the stairway with an ornate wrought-iron railing adorned with cast-iron rosettes rising to an elaborate swirl. On No. 103, dating from c. 1848, look for the "Greek ears" at the corners of the entrance door enframement.

Across the street is the **Danish Seamen's Church,** 102 Willow Street, a

This charming residence, the Peck House, stood on the southwest corner of Clark and Willow Streets until it was demolished c. 1905. (Long Island Historical Society)

The lavish Bowen-Leavitt mansion was one of the area's most elegant. Razed over a half-century ago, it faced Columbia Heights at the northwest corner of Clark Street. (Long Island Historical Society)

reminder of earlier days when the busy Brooklyn waterfront was crowded with sailors from many nations, and Brooklyn Heights and adjacent Cobble Hill had a large Scandinavian population. Its neighbor, **No. 104,** was built c. 1829. A frame house, it has a rather high basement laid in Flemish bond, and was the home of a baker.

The best example of the Queen Anne style in the Heights are the three houses **Nos. 108- 112.** More a fashion than a revival, the basic characteristics of "Queen Anne' are the picturesque massing of different building materials (stone, brick, terra cotta, shingles, and slate) in a harmonious potpourri of gables, chimneys, bay windows, dormers, towers, rectangular and arched windows and entrances, balconies, and porches—combining elements of the Romanesque, Gothic, and Renaissance styles. The major advocate of the so-called Queen Anne style was English architect Richard Norman Shaw. Its popularity in America became fairly widespread after its introduction at the British Pavilion during the Philadelphia Centennial Exposition in Philadelphia in 1876, and lasted for about 20 years. Actually, Queen Anne of England died in 1714; however, some of the Gothic and Renaissance elements popular during the reign of the last Stuart queen are evident in the design motifs.

A charming trio of Federal-style houses are **Nos. 155, 157, and 159** (the latter having lost its dormers to a third-floor addition). All were built before 1829 and retain much of their original appearance. The articulated stone lintels above the windows and doorways are somewhat unusual. The trim buildings are laid in Flemish bond, have handsome entranceways framed by Ionic colonnettes and leaded-glass side lights and transom, and are topped by a peaked, or curb roof with twin arched dormers set over a simple cornice. Note that the houses are not parallel to the street, as they were built in accordance with an earlier street pattern. (Love Lane [*see* map] formerly extended to Willow Street and emerged adjacent to No. 155.) A tunnel leads from No. 159 to a former stable that was located at the site of No. 151. Look for the skylight imbedded in the pavement near the gate to house No. 157.

Turn left (east) on Pierrepont Street.

(Resist for the moment the temptation to visit the harborfront area—it will be seen later in the tour.)

Pierrepont Street, opened in 1832 and named for Hezekiah Beers Pierrepont, whose estate occupied the surrounding area, extends from Fulton Street to the Esplanade. Before the construction of the Brooklyn-Queens Expressway, the western end dipped down to the waterfront. The two oldest houses on the street are Nos. 27 (at the corner of Willow Street) and 58, farther down the block. **No. 27,** one of the oldest Greek Revival houses in Brooklyn Heights, has suffered many alterations, including a dropped entrance and an added mansard roof. The ornate frieze over the parlor floor is based on a design by famed architect Minard Lafever [*see* page 346].

At the southwest corner of Hicks Street, 36 Pierrepont Street, is the **George Hastings House,** an attractive Gothic Revival-style residence. Built c. 1844, it features the typical hood molds over lancet arches, trefoil and quatrefoil motifs, traceries, a handsome wrought-iron side balcony replete with Gothic designs, and a fence to match.

No. 55, the **Hotel Pierrepont,** was designed in 1928 by Herman I. Feldman and completed just before ornamentation on commercial buildings became, unfortunately, passé. Look up at the griffin gargoyles and lion finials! The hotel ceased operations in 1975, joining the Towers in a growing list of hotel closings.

Across the street, **No. 58** (previously mentioned), shares with No. 27 the distinction of being the oldest house on Pierrepont Street. Adjacent **No. 60** (c. 1849) has a Greek Revival-style doorway with "Greek ears."

No. 62 presents a very lavish façade above the first floor. The *AIA Guide to New York City* describes it with some imagination as "Edwardian French architecture." Whatever it is, it does add spice to the streetscape, with its florid sheet-metal bay windows, ornate fire escapes, and ten-story tower.

The Herman Behr House, at the southwest corner of Henry Street, is an exquisite Romanesque Revival mansion, designed in 1890 by the architect of the Hotel Margaret, Frank Freeman. This massive style was popularized by Boston architect Henry Hobson Richardson in the early 1880s, and is characterized by heavy masonry walls, usually of rough-faced sandstone; low-relief carvings; a fortresslike design; restrained terra-cotta ornamentation, usually in wide bands or courses; tan-colored upper brickwork; tile or slate roofs with gables and chimneys; arched openings; rounded bays; substantial stone entranceways; and an overall pleasantly asymmetrical composition. This "Richardsonian Romanesque" was applied not only to large residences, but to public buildings as well—banks, offices, city halls, courthouses, and even railroad stations. The style remained popular until the turn of the century. The Behr house was enlarged with a six-story addition in 1919 and became the Hotel Palm. Declining fortunes compromised its former elegance, and, according to local legend, "the Behr *House* was no longer a *Home.*" As if to redeem it from its life of sin, the mansion recently was acquired by nearby St. Francis College as the Franciscan House of Studies—a residence for novitiates—and is again a respectable landmark on Pierrepont Street.

Turn left (north) on Henry Street to Love Lane.

Love Lane was, as its name implies, a favorite path in Colonial times for young swains to promenade with their maidens fair. Earlier, it had been an Indian trail leading from a village to the water's edge. In 1822, the Brooklyn Collegiate Institute for Young Ladies was built on the site between Henry Street and the present **College Place.** The Institute later became a hotel called the *Mansion House,* and the former hotel stables on College Place now serve "horseless carriages."

Return to Pierrepont Street and turn left (east).

No. 104 Pierrepont Street is a handsome four-story brownstone row mansion, built c. 1857. The roof cornice is supported by ornate console brackets, with hoods similarly set on brackets over the windows and doorway. The verdigris bronze stoop railing was added later.

Nos. 108 and **114** must be compared from across the street. The two were built as an identical pair around 1840 in Greek Revival style for Messrs. P. C. Cornell and George Cornell. Clay Lancaster, in his *Old Brooklyn Heights,* calls the pair "the noblest residential building ever to grace Pierrepont Street." Today, only the right-hand half bears any semblance to the original appearance, as No. 114 was completely remodeled in Romanesque Revival style around 1877 for Alfred C. Barnes. No. 108, the **P. C. Cornell House,** still retains many of its Greek Revival elements: the pedimented entranceway with anthemion motif as an acroterium, a high stoop, corniced lintels over the windows, and a high stone basement. Note, too, the line of quoins on the right side. In a 1907 remodeling, the neo-Colonial doorway and adjacent bay window were added. Its former look-alike twin, No. 114, is now sheathed with brownstone, brick, and terra cotta, with typical Romanesque Revival features, including rounded bays, gables, a turret, and carved reliefs. In 1912, the George Cornell (or Alfred C. Barnes) House became the Headquarters of the Brooklyn Women's Club.

Across Pierrepont Street is architect Minard Lafever's **Church of the**

Saviour, now the First Unitarian Church. The lovely Gothic Revival-style church is the home of the oldest Unitarian Society in Brooklyn, organized in 1833. The tall pinnacles and high central gable emphasize the verticality of the sandstone edifice, while a broad roof extends beyond the nave over the side aisles, with small skylights illuminating the interior. In 1890 a new set of windows was installed from the studios of Louis Comfort Tiffany. Lafever, whose residential architecture was executed almost always in the Greek Revival style, used the *Gothic* Revival exclusively for his many churches. (Another of his fine churches will be seen shortly.) This was the approximate site of a British fort built here between 1780 and 1781.

On the northwest corner stands the **Appellate Division of the New York State Supreme Court,** designed by Slee & Bryson, and built in 1938 in a simple Classic Revival-style.

Walk up Monroe Place to **No. 46,** on the right side of the street. Set on paneled pedestal blocks are a lovely pair of wrought-iron basket urns, once fairly prevalent throughout the Heights, and now reduced to this last surviving pair. The pineapples atop the urns were a traditional symbol of hospitality. Both No. 46 and its neighbor No. 44 are Greek Revival-style houses laid in Flemish bond, and, like the trio of houses on Willow Place (Nos. 155–159), are built askew from the street line. The houses were originally aligned with Love Lane, which in the early 19th century extended through to Fulton Street.

Monroe Place is the widest street in Brooklyn Heights, and, unlike others in the Heights, has the even-numbered houses on the *east* side. It also retains the original house-numbering system, which was abandoned on all other streets in 1871. The street is named for James Monroe, fifth president of the United States, who spent the last years of his retirement in New York City.

Continue east on Pierrepont Street to Clinton Street.

The handsome **Long Island Historical Society Building** is best viewed from the diagonally opposite corner. Built for the Society between 1878 and 1880 from plans by George B. Post (architect of the New York Stock Exchange), it is a pleasing combination of Richardsonian Romanesque and Classical styles, which properly should be called Eclectic. Since its organization in 1863, the Society has amassed one of the finest historical collections in the country. Although primarily concerned with the four counties that comprise Long Island, it has extensive source material on New York City and New York State. The library contains over 125,000 volumes plus a collection of manuscripts, periodicals, pamphlets, newspapers, maps, paintings, photographs, prints, and other Long Island memorabilia. The library is considered one of the three best in the nation in the field of genealogy. Many paintings by famous American artists are displayed in the hall and reference room, and so extensive and valuable are its historical holdings that it has earned the sobriquet "Long Island's strongbox." The building is open to the

There is now a vacant lot where the Frank Freeman-designed Brooklyn Savings Bank stood at the northeast corner of Pierrepont and Clinton streets. A delightful Classic Eclectic building erected in 1893, it was taken down in 1962 when the bank built a modern structure around the corner on Montague Street. (The Brooklyn Savings Bank)

public Tuesday through Saturday, 9 A.M. to 5 P.M., and a visit is a "must" (be sure to pick up a membership application!). On exiting, note the high-relief sculptures of the Viking and Indian in the spandrels of the entrance arch, as well as the rich façade with busts of Columbus and Franklin, and its earthy tones of red and brown in the terra-cotta adornments and Philadelphia pressed brick. The Latin inscription on the Clinton Street side is from Cicero, and means "History is Witness of the Times."

On the northwest corner, **St. Ann's Episcopal School** occupies the building of the **former Crescent Club,** one of a number of private athletic clubs that prevailed around the turn of the century. Designed in 1906 by architect Frank Freeman (of the Behr Mansion and the Hotel Margaret), it was the Club's second building. Find the little stone crescents set in the upper section of the façade. Across Clinton Street on the northeast corner stood another Frank Freeman building—the Brooklyn Savings Bank—a splendid Classic Eclectic edifice with an extravagant oval interior. Built in 1893, it was lost to the wrecker's ball in 1962, and the Bank moved into more modern quarters at Montague and Court streets.

Diagonally across the street, and extending to Montague Street, is the old

Brooklyn Trust Company Building, now a branch of the Manufacturers Hanover Trust Company. Designed in 1915 by the noted architects York & Sawyer, the exterior is said to be patterned after the Palazzo della Gran Guardia in Verona, and the interior possibly after the Tepidarium of the Roman Baths of Caracalla. The impressive granite-and-limestone Renaissance Revival-style *palazzo* was the home office of the Brooklyn Trust Company until it was absorbed by the present bank in 1950. Don't miss the splendid bronze lamp standards in whose delicately sculptured bases are griffins and turtles.

Turn right on Clinton Street to Montague Street.

Back to back with the Long Island Historical Society is the **Diocesan Church of St. Ann and the Holy Trinity, formerly the Holy Trinity Protestant Episcopal Church,** and another fine example of architect Minard Lafever's ecclesiastical work. Completed in 1847 in his customary Gothic Revival style, it is reminiscent, in its dark-red color, of an old English church. Unfortunately, the porous brownstone has weathered very badly. The interior is constructed of cast and painted terra cotta, a departure from the usual carved stone or plaster. The lovely windows were designed by William Jay Bolton, America's foremost stained-glass artist of the time. The reredos are by Frank Freeman, and a bust of John Howard Melish by sculptor William Zorach is mounted in the vestibule. The church's tall spire was dismantled early in the century when blasting for the new Montague Street tunnel of the BMT Subway made it unsafe. St. Ann's Holy Trinity Church is now headquarters of the Episcopal Diocese of Brooklyn.

Just to the east of the Manufacturers Hanover Trust Company, on the north side of Montague Street, is the old **People's Trust Company Building,** now a branch of the First National City Bank. Designed in the style of a Classic temple by Mowbray & Uffinger in 1904, it is an attractive if somewhat pretentious structure, technically described as having an engaged tetrastyle portico with Roman Ionic columns. The *AIA Guide to New York City* describes the marble bank building as being more appropriate to a D. W. Griffith "spectacular." Note the odd effect created in the pediment by the antipigeon spikes. The addition to the building was erected in 1929 by Shreve, Lamb & Harmon, architects of the Empire State Building.

The adjacent **American Bank and Trust Company Building** was considered quite avant-garde when completed in 1929. Its somewhat cubistic massing is straight out of the Paris Arts Décoratifs Exposition of 1925, and was designed by Corbett, Harrison & MacMurray. The Art Deco style was to remain extremely popular until World War II.

The next member of Brooklyn Heights' "Bank Row" is the modern **Brooklyn Savings Bank** at the corner of Court Street, which moved from its Pierrepont and Clinton streets site in 1962 (architects: Carson, Lundin & Shaw).

Return to the corner of Clinton Street.

Completing the row of banks is the picturesque **Franklin Trust Company Building** on the southwest corner. With the invention of the elevator, the skyscraper came into its own, and this charming Romanesque Revival "tower," complete with moat, is an outstanding example of the style applied to commercial buildings. Built in 1888 from plans by George L. Morse, the Bank presents a striking façade of limestone arches on a granite base, brick and terra-cotta piers, columns topped by arches, and a charming red tile roof with dormer windows.

Continue west on Montague Street.

Montague Street is named for Lady Mary Wortley Montagu, née Pierrepont, the English author of wit and letters who died in 1762. (No one seems to know how Montague Street got its final "e"). It is the principal commercial thoroughfare of Brooklyn Heights and an appropriate place to stop for some refreshment. When the street was opened through to the river front around 1850, ferry service was begun to Wall Street in Manhattan. The street has a varied assortment of shops, including some interesting book stores. Along the south side, cast-iron stoops lead up to raised first-floor retail establishments whose wares are displayed in large, triple bay windows. There is a gay, relaxed atmosphere which adds charm and seems almost anomalous on such a busy street.

At Henry Street, turn left (south) one block to Remsen Street.

Our Lady of Lebanon Roman Catholic Church, formerly the Congregational Church of the Pilgrims, was a radical departure for architect Richard Upjohn, renowned for his Gothic Revival-style churches, particularly Trinity Church in Manhattan; and this early Romanesque Revival church, built in 1846, is thought to be the first building of that style in this country. When the church merged with the Plymouth Church on Orange Street in 1934, the fragment of Plymouth Rock imbedded in the tower was bronught along. The new church acquired the building in 1944. It practices the Maronite Rite, serving a large and long-established Lebanese community, much of which is clustered along Atlantic Avenue in "Brooklyn's Middle East" [*see* Cobble Hill walking tour]. The interior of the church is surprisingly delicate, with widely spaced slender columns and semicircular arches supporting the ceiling. Unfortunately, the steeple deteriorated and was removed. Newly installed windows detract from the overall effect. Incongruous are the west and south portals made from metal panels with nautical motifs, rescued from the *Normandie,* which burned and capsized at its Hudson River pier in 1942 during World War II.

Return to Montague Street and turn left (west).

The "Penny Bridge" over Montague Street, c. 1922, when the street sloped downhill to the Wall Street Ferry. In the background are the side-by-side Low and White Mansions (Nos. 3 and 2 Pierrepont Place) and the now-demolished Pierrepont Mansion. (Long Island Historical Society)

Nos. 111–115 Montague Street are an interesting pair of Queen Anne-style apartment houses with a particularly engaging upper façade. The *Berkeley* and *Grosvenor* were built in 1885 in a combination of brownstone, brick, and terra cotta. The Hotel Montague (No. 105) is of the same vintage. Note the sculptured figure in the ornate pedimented gable.

The Hotel Bossert, at the corner of Hicks Street, was built for lumber merchant Louis Bossert in 1909–12. Designed by architects Helmle & Huberty, the Bossert was a center of Brooklyn social life for many years; and its Marine Roof, decorated like a yacht, provided an unsurpassed view of the harbor. In spite of the demise of virtually all of its competitors, the Bossert steadfastly hangs on as the last luxury hotel in Brooklyn Heights, perhaps following the tradition of its predecessor hotel on the site, the elegant Pierrepont House, which was here in the mid-19th century.

The Heights Casino, 75 Montague Street, an exclusive tennis and squash club, was designed by William Alciphron Baring, Jr., and opened in 1905. In front of the site of the Casino stood the H. B. Pierrepont Mansion, "Four Chimneys," built before the American Revolution and used briefly by General Washington as headquarters before the retreat to Manhattan. The mansion was razed in the mid-19th century when Montague Street was extended to the water's edge. At about the site of No. 63, the street began its descent to the harbor. The street was elevated in the late 1940s when the Esplanade was built.

At the end of Montague Street, turn right into Pierrepont Place.

Facing the end of Montague Street are **Nos. 3 and 2 Pierrepont Place,** considered to be the most elegant brownstone dwelling houses in the city. Designed by noted architect Richard Upjohn [*see* page 343] and built in 1856–57, they form a splendid pair of Italianate mansions situated in an ideal location. A third house, No. 1, whose empty plot now serves as an accessway to the Esplanade, was built for Henry E. Pierrepont, and was demolished in 1946. The twin mini-*palazzi* were built for Abiel Abbott Low, a tea merchant (No. 3), and for Alexander M. White, a fur dealer (No. 2). A. A. Low's son, Seth Low, served as mayor of Brooklyn from 1882 to 1886, then as president of Columbia University, and in 1901 was elected mayor of the City of New York. He is remembered for his vigorous campaigns to reform the police, finance, and education departments, and for his donation of the Library to Columbia. No. 2 was later occupied by Alfred Tredway White, a wealthy businessman and philanthropist, and president of the Brooklyn Bureau of Charities. It was White who believed in "philanthropy plus 5%" when he built the Riverside Houses on Columbia Place (to be seen shortly) and the Tower and Home Apartments in the Cobble Hill section [*see* Cobble Hill, page 340]. A few yards to the east on Montague Street was the site

The Brooklyn Heights Esplanade provides one of the finest views in the country. This photo was taken in the early 1960s before the construction of the huge boxlike office buildings which now obscure much of the traditional skyline. The Singer Tower is visible to the left of the tree. (Brooklyn Union Gas Company)

of a charming, but short-lived stone arch built by architect Minard Lafever around 1855 to span the street. Connecting Pierrepont Place with Montague Terrace over the Montague Street cut was the "Penny Bridge," an iron footbridge that survived until the demolition of the Pierrepont Mansion. Walk around the north side of No. 2 to the Esplanade for a rear view of the lavish mansions and a 100-year-old gingko tree behind No. 3. The film *No Way to Treat a Lady* was filmed here some years ago.

The Esplanade provides one of the most unforgettable harbor panoramas, which can be enjoyed while relaxing on one of the convenient benches. Considered by many to be New York City's most spectacular vantage point, its design is a commendable attempt at separation of vehicular and pedestrian traffic, and a tribute to the planning of our city fathers. Local civic groups such as the Brooklyn Heights Association cooperated with Parks Commissioner Robert Moses in the planning, and the resultant cantilevered Esplanade over the Brooklyn-Queens Connecting Highway, completed in 1950, gave sudden impetus to the redevelopment of Brooklyn Heights. A somewhat better design would have duplicated the almost total separation of roadway from pedestrian mall as was achieved with the East River Drive on the Upper East Side, where traffic noise and fumes were completely eliminated. Spend a few minutes enjoying the magnificent view of the unique Lower Manhattan skyline.

Leave the Esplanade at the exit to the south of the two Pierrepont Place mansions (the extension of Montague Street), noting the "Four Chimneys" plaque, and turn right into Montague Terrace.

Nos. 1–13 Montague Terrace, built c. 1886, is a charming English style "terrace row" in almost pristine condition. Author Thomas Wolfe, while living at No. 5 in 1935, wrote *Of Time and the River*. Wolfe spent a number of years in the Heights and nearby Cobble Hill, and his novels are drawn from personal experiences. The last house on the west side has its Remsen Street wall completely covered with ivy.

Turn left into Remsen Street.

Named for Henry Remsen, who lived nearby and opened the street in 1825, this shady, quiet thoroughfare is lined with interesting mid- and late-19th-century residences. The houses on the south side to Hicks Street date mostly from the pre-Civil War period, while those on the north were built in the 1880s and '90s.

Turn right (south) into Hicks Street.

Grace Court Alley, a charming little mews running eastward to a dead end, was formerly the stable alley for the patrician residents of Remsen Street. The stables and carriage houses, now considered very chic, have been converted into luxurious duplexes. Note particularly the solidly built **Nos. 2, 4, 12,** and **14.**

Grace (Protestant Episcopal) Church of Brooklyn Heights is another Richard Upjohn work, completed in 1847. In style it is typical Gothic Revival, much like an English parish church but rather low, long, and narrow. The side entrance court offers a delightful spot of repose, tucked under a magnificent 85-foot-high elm. The boldly carved moldings, capitals, and brackets are highlighted against the textured wall surface with its pattern of varied tooled groovings. Inside, open wood-vaulted trusses support the roof, but matching wooden piers were replaced by stone during a 1909 restoration. At that time, the handsome Pierrepont Morgan Memorial Doorway was installed. In the sanctuary are an alabaster altar and reredos surmounted by an artistic stained-glass window. The Church boasts three Tiffany stained-glass windows in the nave and aisles.

Walk a few yards down **Grace Court** and look through the tall iron fence into the spacious backyards of the houses that face Remsen Street.

Turn right (west) into Joralemon Street.

Joralemon Street is named for Teunis Joralemon who purchased the Philip Livingston estate in 1803.

Nos. 29–75 Joralemon Street are 24 modified Greek Revival-style houses, built from 1844 to 1848 in neatly descending pairs, each about 30 inches lower than the next. They were owned by merchants and professionals when the street was opened in the 1840s after the break-up of the Remsen farm. Although most of the houses retain their pilastered entranceways and original iron fences, many are in a sad state of disrepair; nonetheless, the overall view of the descending three-story row houses is quite picturesque.

At the southwest corner of Columbia Place are the remarkable **Riverside Houses,** model tenements built for Alfred Tredway White in 1890 by William Field & Son. These multiple dwellings followed on the heels of his revolutionary Tower and Home Apartments in Cobble Hill [*see* page 340], the first such project in America and a rare example (in public housing, anyway) of enlightened self-interest. His motto "Philanthropy plus 5%" actually did bring him a profit. These houses were aptly named, but in the construction of the Expressway, the "river side" was demolished, along with a superb view of the harbor. A remnant of the original central garden, which was a major part of the plan to provide as much light and air as possible for the 280 apartments, is still visible between the remaining building and the Expressway. Such is progress!

Turn south into Columbia Place.

Across from Riverside Houses is a charming row of four clapboard frame houses, **Nos. 7–13 Columbia Place,** which were once part of the nine-unit "Cottage Row" built in the late 1840s.

Return to Joralemon Street, turn right one block into Willow Place.

Nos. 2–8 Willow Place are a most unusual row of Gothic Revival-style duplex houses, built about 1847. Among their interesting features are the coupled porches with clustered colonnettes, diamond-paned side lights and transoms in the entranceways, Tudor arches with trefoils in the spandrels, recessed panels connecting the second and third floors with wooden "chevron" moldings (forerunners of the spandrels used on tall modern buildings), hood labels over the third-floor windows, and an appropriate iron fence and stoop railings.

Farther down the street is a small former Gothic Revival church now used as a community center for the immediate neighborhood. The passionate civic spirit of this block association has earned the section the nickname **"Willow Town."**

Buildings **Nos. 38, 40, 44,** and **48,** erected in 1966, are an excellent example of the use of modern materials and techniques applied harmoniously in a more traditional environment. Designed by Joseph and Mary Merz, the arrangement of garage space and the use of special 8-by-8-inch cement blocks gives the houses a simple dignity and helps them blend well with their venerable neighbors.

Across the street is the **last surviving "Colonnade Row" in Brooklyn Heights, Nos. 43–49 Willow Place.** Designed c. 1846 as a middle-class imitation of the elegant multicolumned row houses such as Underhill's Colonnade or the very sumptuous marble Colonnade Row on Manhattan's Lafayette Place, it is now rather down at the heels and reminiscent of a decaying antebellum Southern mansion. The two-story brick houses are revealed behind the twin-story porches whose square wooden columns support the entablature and cornice. Although the continuous portico is only a foot above ground level, the total effect is undiminished—even enhanced by the simple Greek Revival doorways flanked by pilasters. (Across Willow Street are two remnants of a similar four-house colonnade, **Nos. 42** and **46**—of which only the latter bears any semblance to its original appearance.) In *Bricks and Brownstone,* author Charles Lockwood refers to the dignified wooden porch of the Willow Place Colonnade Row as "an easily forgivable architectural fraud . . . [which] holds great appeal today because of its modest scale and the naïveté of its conception and execution."

Turn left (east) on State Street to Hicks Street, then left again.

The exterior **cast-iron spiral staircase** on the former St. Charles Orthopaedic Clinic (281 Hicks Street), is an interesting addition to the streetscape. The Clinic buildings are now the Alhambra Center, a Catholic Charities' senior citizens' center and school for retarded adults. This is the approximate site of the Philip Livingston house, built c. 1764.

Across the street, **Nos. 284–276,** are a row of five former carriage houses. Note the round and elliptical arches, and the carved woman's head on the dormer of **No. 276,** formerly the home of sculptor William Zorach. Adjacent No. 274 is a very pleasing **fire house** (Engine Co. 224) with Renaissance Revival-style details plus dormer windows. The building, in scale with its neighbors, was designed in 1903 by Adams & Warren. **Nos. 270–262,** built in 1887, add to the variety of the street with their romantic Queen Anne-style grouping of picturesque details.

Turn right (east) on Joralemon Street to Garden Place.

Take a brief detour down **Garden Place,** laid out in 1842 and named for the garden that once graced the Philip Livingston estate. The back fence of the houses on the east side of the street from Nos. 29 to 41 incorporate part of the brownstone retaining wall that once separated the terraced garden from the orchard. (Livingston was one of the signers of the Declaration of Independence.) Note the Queen Anne style of **No. 26,** and the storybook converted carriage house at **No. 21;** note also the atmosphere created by the addition of trees, in this case, the row of London planes, which since their planting in the early 1940s have grown to provide a charming umbrella for the street.

Continue east on Joralemon Street to Henry Street, and turn left (north) to Hunts Lane.

Hunts Lane is another former stable alley, whose brick carriage houses were converted to duplexes, and which, like nearby Grace Court Alley, served the affluent homeowners on Remsen Street whose backyards abutted the Lane.

Return to Joralemon Street and continue east.

No. 129 Joralemon Street, the David Chauncey Mansion, was built around 1890 by Harvey Murdock in an odd combination of Romanesque Revival and Colonial Revival details. A massive stone and yellow-brick mansion, it gives the impression, nonetheless, of being a "bungalow." It is now subdivided into apartments.

No. 135 always astonishes the visitor. Almost hidden between two over-powering neighbors, this delightful gem of a house is reminiscent of No. 24 Middagh Street, its "cousin" seen at the beginning of the tour. Built c. 1833, and known as the **John Haslet House** (after its first owner, a U.S. Navy surgeon), it is the sole survivor of a row of similar residences that once lined the street, and is a remarkably well preserved example of Federal-style architecture. The ornate cast-iron porch was added in the mid-19th century and the parlor-floor windows were lowered, but otherwise the house is in virtually pristine condition. Note the Flemish bond brickwork of the basement, the handsome entranceway with Ionic colonnettes (alas, the door has an unauthentic glass panel in it!), the neat clapboarding, simple cornice, twin dormers, and gambrel roof.

Turn right into Sidney Place.

Sidney Place is even more varied than its neighbor Garden Place. It is named after Sir Philip Sidney, or Sydney (1554–1586), an English author, statesman, and soldier who was a distinguished figure in the court of Queen Elizabeth. Most of the houses on the west side date from the 1840s. **No. 2,** the corner house, built about 1848, has a peculiar appendage facing Sidney Place in the form of a wooden two-story-high vestibule, with—lo and behold! —a delicate Federal-style entryway. Twin Ionic colonnettes and wreathed side lights flank the door, with a transom and carved plaque above. It is said that the entranceway originally belonged to a house that was demolished to make way for the construction of the Towers Hotel. **No. 18,** a Greek Revival house of about 1838, has an attractive recessed doorway flanked by Doric columns. Some years later, three additional floors were added, making this, doubtless, the tallest Greek Revival house in the City.

Beyond Aitken Place, the row of houses on the east side is set back behind lush gardens and iron fences, adding to the charm of the shady street. **Nos. 31–49,** a continuous row of Greek Revival-style houses, were all built about 1845. Most have suffered modifications, but **No. 35** is closest to the original appearance.

Framing the entrance to Aitken Place are the **St. Charles Borromeo (Roman Catholic) Church** (1869), and across the street, the Rectory (1929) and adjacent parish school (1916). The church is a simple modified Gothic Revival-style structure in dark-red painted brick, but in scale with its surrounding neighbors. Inside, the supporting arches and trim are in a delicate "carpenter Gothic" style. The plain, light-colored walls contrast strongly with the dark-brown ceiling. Rev. Ambrose S. Aitken was a recent pastor of the congregation, and the adjoining street is named for him.

Follow Aitken Place to Clinton Street.

At the corner, look south down **Clinton Street.** Except for some modifications to the exteriors of the row houses, little has changed in the past 100 years. On the southeast corner is a row of four red-brick houses, **Nos. 133– 139 Clinton Street,** built c. 1850, whose appearance is enhanced by the trio of gaslights, which burn continuously. The corner house was once the home of the *Excelsiors,* an early Brooklyn baseball team, and champions of the world in 1860.

Clinton Street is named for De Witt Clinton (1769–1828) who served ten annual terms as mayor of New York City and two terms as governor. He was the guiding spirit behind the construction of the Erie Canal, ran unsuccessfully for president, was an amateur naturalist, and for his entire career a dedicated public servant.

The **former St. Ann's Episcopal Church** was closed in 1966 and merged with the Holy Trinity Church, three blocks north. In a move to cut costs and help maintain their parochial school, the Episcopal Diocese of Brooklyn sold the church to the nearby Packer Collegiate Institute, and moved its headquarters along with its congregation to Holy Trinity. Designed by famed architect James Renwick, Jr., who planned St. Patrick's Cathedral as well as Manhattan's Grace Church, this is the only example in Brooklyn of the Ruskinian or Venetian Gothic style. Where this style differs from the more conventional Gothic Revival is in the use of polychromy in the façade. The arch blocks (voussoirs) are in alternating white and dark brown, while horizontal bands of white stone run across the full width of the exterior. The church was completed in 1869.

Nos. 142 and **140,** across the street from the church, are survivors of a row of five similar houses. Most unusual are the bracketed gables and the highly ornate black-painted hoods, made of cast iron, and set over the windows and entrances.

Walk north on Clinton Street to Joralemon Street and turn right (east).

The Packer Collegiate Institute, designed in the "Collegiate" Gothic Revival style by Minard Lafever in 1854, was built on the site of the Brooklyn Female Academy destroyed by fire two years earlier. These lovely "halls of ivy" were endowed by Mrs. William S. Packer to honor her late husband's interest in women's education. The delightful exterior was published by

Brooklyn's Civic Center at the turn of the century. To the left rear of Brooklyn's City Hall is the Court House (now the site of the Brooklyn Law School). Also gone are the trolley lines and the Brooklyn Rapid Transit Elevated on curving Fulton Street. The statue of Henry Ward Beecher in front of City Hall has been moved several hundred yards farther north. (Author's collection)

Lafever in his *Architectural Instructor* and reflected his belief that churches as well as schools should be constructed in the medieval Gothic tradition.

Continue to Court Street.

The tall commercial structure on the northwest corner, the **Temple Bar Building** (44 Court Street), was the tallest in Brooklyn when completed in 1901. Interesting are the ogee-shaped twin cupolas (the one on the right has lost its copper sheathing) and the Classic Eclectic details of the façade. Court Street between Livingston and Pierrepont streets is the major axis of the Brooklyn "Financial District," conveniently located opposite the Borough Hall (former City Hall), the Brooklyn Municipal Building, and the various city, state, and federal courthouses. Within just a few blocks are six colleges and universities, the main Brooklyn post office, the Transit Authority headquarters, the Brooklyn Heights branch of the Brooklyn Public Library, the New York City Board of Education, and Fulton Street, Brooklyn's major retail center.

End of tour. At Borough Hall are the IRT Lexington and Broadway-7th Avenue lines, and the BMT RR line. Follow Joralemon Street into Fulton Street two blocks east to Jay Street for the IND A line.

A BRIEF LOOK AT BROOKLYN'S CIVIC CENTER

The Brooklyn Municipal Building, an immense and functional Indiana limestone structure, was designed in a modified Roman Eclectic style by McKenzie, Voorhees & Gmelin, and completed in 1926. The granite for the base came from Deer Island, Maine, and the interior marble was quarried in Vermont and Tennessee. The building houses most of the offices of borough government, including the files from the demolished Court House and Hall of Records, which stood just to the east.

Directly in front, and facing Cadman Plaza, is **Borough Hall, formerly the Brooklyn City Hall.** Said to be one of the most beautiful public buildings in the entire city, the old City Hall was built in 1836–49 in Greek Revival style, although its cupola is strictly Victorian and was added in 1898. The Hall was originally planned to be a replica of Manhattan's City Hall, but instead the Greek Revival style was selected. The architect, Gamaliel King, was in fact a grocer and carpenter! An excellent view is from the Plaza where the splendid façade with its broad staircase gracefully ascending to the Ionic colonnade is seen to best advantage. Borough Hall, a designated Landmark, houses the offices of the president of the Borough of Brooklyn.

From the colonnade of Borough Hall there is a broad perspective of **Cadman Plaza.** Named for Rev. S. Parkes Cadman, an active community leader and America's first radio preacher [*see* Clinton Hill, 8], the Plaza was

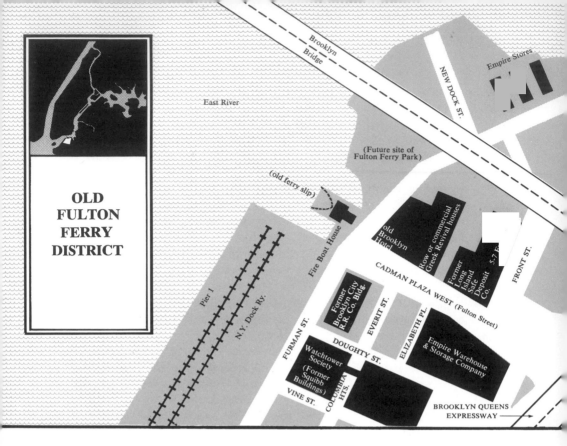

OLD
FULTON
FERRY
DISTRICT

East River

Brooklyn
Bridge

NEW DOCK ST.

Empire Stores

(Future site of
Fulton Ferry Park)

(old ferry slip)

Fire Boat House

old
Brooklyn
Hotel

Row or commercial
Greek Revival houses

Former
Long
Island
Safe
Deposit
Co.

5-7 F

FRONT ST.

Pier 1

N.Y. Dock Ry.

Former
Brooklyn City
R.R. Co. Bldg.

CADMAN PLAZA WEST (Fulton Street)

EVERIT ST.

ELIZABETH PL.

Empire Warehouse
& Storage Company

DOUGHTY ST.

FURMAN ST.

Watchtower
Society
(Former
Squibb
Buildings)

COLUMBIA HTS.

VINE ST.

BROOKLYN QUEENS
EXPRESSWAY

the result of major urban renewing in the 1950s, including the razing of the Fulton Street El, which came over the Brooklyn Bridge and darkened Fulton Street for miles, the removal of trolley tracks, and the rebuilding of major traffic arteries. A pleasant park resulted, which acts as a "buffer zone" between Brooklyn Heights and the rest of the borough.

To the right is the modern **New York State Supreme Court,** designed in 1957 by Shreve, Lamb & Harmon (architects of the Empire State Building). At the south end are **lamp standards from the old Hall of Records;** and to the rear, the **Federal Building and Court House,** completed in 1961 from plans by Carson, Lundin & Shaw.

In the background, rising like a medieval chateau, is **Brooklyn's General Post Office,** a designated New York City Landmark. Designed in 1885 in Romanesque Revival style by Mifflin E. Bell, the work was later assumed by William A. Freret, supervising architect for the Treasury Department, and completed in 1891. A north section, in harmonious style, was created by James A. Wetmore in 1933. The Post Office, built of granite while Brooklyn was still an independent city, represents a high standard of government-sponsored architecture, and with the great advances in stone-cutting techniques achieved late in the 19th century, it was possible to produce masonry buildings of great beauty. To the south of the Post Office stood the Brooklyn

Eagle Building, built in 1893 and demolished in the late 1950s as part of the civic center redevelopment plan.

Directly in front of Borough Hall is a **Memorial to John Cashmore,** former Brooklyn Borough President under whose administration the Cadman Plaza project was realized. Near the entrance to the Supreme Court is a bronze plaque honoring **Washington Augustus Roebling** and his marvelous Brooklyn Bridge. When completed in 1883, it was the longest suspension bridge in the world. To the west is a **bust of Senator Robert F. Kennedy,** by sculptor A. Ottavino. Farther to the north is a **monument to Christopher Columbus,** reminiscent on a small scale of the statue in Columbus Circle.

The best piece of sculpture in the Plaza, and one of the finest in the city, is the extraordinary bronze **statue of Henry Ward Beecher,** by John Quincy Adams Ward, unveiled in 1891; with a black granite pedestal designed by Richard Morris Hunt. When Beecher died on March 8, 1887, Ward received a telegram urgently requesting that he make a death mask within four hours. Complying, he then received the commission for the 8-foot-high statue. In the completed monument, an austere Beecher, in a simple, knee-length Inverness cape, stands above three intimate figures of youngsters, a young black girl placing a palm frond in gratitude at the abolitionist's feet, and a young boy helping a girl climb the base to lay flowers at Beecher's feet—all three representing his love and devotion to children. The statue was originally placed in Borough Hall Park, but was moved to its present site in 1959. The Metropolitan Museum of Art in its *New York City Public Sculpture by 19th Century American Artists* praises the Beecher Monument and calls it "public statuary at its best."

End of tour.

THE FULTON FERRY HISTORIC DISTRICT

Walk down Cadman Plaza to the waterfront (about a half mile) or take the B-41 bus to the end of the line at Furman Street. (Fulton Street to the river has been renamed Cadman Plaza West.)

The modern history of Brooklyn began at the waterfront hamlet of Fulton Ferry, which after the introduction of Robert Fulton's steam ferry in 1814, became the gateway not only to Brooklyn but to Long Island as well. Other ferries subsequently linked Manhattan with Brooklyn, and in 1872 as many as 1200 daily crossings were recorded, but the Fulton Ferry was by far the most important. The little village grew rapidly and soon boasted several hotels, a newspaper (the Brooklyn *Daily Eagle*), a bank, law offices, and a stagecoach terminal. With the opening of the Brooklyn Bridge in 1883, the Fulton Ferry district began a gradual decline, becoming an almost forgotten backwater by the 20th century. The ferry hung on, however, until 1924, after 110 years of service. Plans are now underway to restore many of the old landmarks and to re-create much of the early 19th-century atmosphere of the Village of Fulton Ferry.

Behind the picturesque former **Fire Boat House** is the old decaying **pier of the former Fulton Ferry.** The Fulton Ferry House, built in 1871 in an ornate French Second Empire style, is long since gone, and stood about on the site of the present fire boat house. This is the site of Washington's near miraculous escape to Manhattan from the disastrous Battle of Long Island, August 29, 1776. The land to the right of the pier along the water's edge is being developed as **Fulton Ferry Park** and, when completed, will offer a magnificent panorama of lower Manhattan, with a floating restaurant and a museum in the fireboat house. The tower of the house was not a lighthouse but a fire hose drying shaft.

At 8 Fulton Street (or Cadman Plaza West) is the **former headquarters of the Brooklyn City Railroad Company,** the horsecar enterprise that replaced the stages and built ribbons of track throughout most of the city of Brooklyn. (A track is still visible on the west side, to the rear.) The structure was designed in Second Empire tradition and is constructed of brick with granite trim. Completed in 1861 it occupies the site of the former Judge

The Fulton Ferry terminal, built in 1871 in Victorian style, continued in operation until 1924. This 1891 view shows a steam train of the Brooklyn Elevated Railroad about to leave from the adjacent el station to join the main line crossing the Brooklyn Bridge from Manhattan, on its way to various points in Brooklyn. (Long Island Historical Society)

Looking northeast on Fulton Street (now Cadman Plaza) in 1954, toward the old Brooklyn Eagle Building and the still-standing General Post Office Building. (Brooklyn Picture Collection. Brooklyn Public Library)

William Furman residence. From 1910 until recently, the building housed a manufacturer of toilet seats and it is now being converted to an apartment house by imaginative architect David Morton. In recognition of its historical role and architectural merit, the building has been designated an official New York City Landmark.

Across Fulton Street—which in the early 19th century was called Old Ferry Road—is a **row of commercial structures in Greek Revival style,** built in the 1830s. The corner building once housed the Franklin Hotel, the others comprised a variety of merchandising establishments. Note the remains of the old sidewalk awnings toward the end of the row—a fairly common physical adjunct 100 years ago.

Directly opposite, and dominating the block, is the massive Romanesque Revival-style **Eagle Warehouse & Storage Company,** designed in 1870 by noted architect Frank Freeman. The somber "fortress" stands on the site of the original *Daily Eagle* building, and displays the newspaper's old **zinc eagle** conspicuously near the entrance. The impressive brick arch with bronze lettering is screened by an ornate bronze gate, complete with a griffin lamp-post.

Behind the warehouse rise the yellow-painted twin factory buildings that were once the **Squibb Pharmaceutical Company plant.** Connected by a "Bridge of Sighs" over Everit Street (whose name changes to Columbia

Heights after one block), the once-busy drug manufacturing facility is now one of a number of facilities of the Watchtower Bible & Tract Society, the Jehovah's Witnesses. The Squibb name in brick lettering is still visible on the tall chimney on the Furman Street side.

At the northeast corner of Fulton and Front streets is a highly ornate cast-iron-front building erected in 1869 for the **Long Island Safe Deposit Company.** Designed by William Mundell at a time when cast iron had come into vogue as a successful building medium, the highly decorative façade is modeled after a Venetian Renaissance palace. The company's safety-deposit vaults were once visible on the first floor of the bank, set in their own granite foundations. The bank closed in 1891 and the building has since served a wide variety of owners; and through good fortune remains in relatively good condition. At this writing, no plans have been advanced for its participation in the area's restoration. It is hoped that the Office of Downtown Brooklyn Development, which is the foremost proponent of the project, will come up with some acceptable plan of adaptive reuse for the old bank.

Around the corner, **No. 5–7 Front Street** is an even older neighbor, dating from 1834. It was once the law offices of a number of firms and even housed the Long Island Bank, Brooklyn's first such institution. A similar structure, the Law Building, occupied the corner site, but was razed to make way for the cast-iron bank building. Note the Greek Revival details, particularly the cap-molded lintels, the diminutive granite stoop, and the entranceway enframed by pilasters.

Follow Front Street to Dock Street, turn left, and right at Water Street.

Directly ahead and ranged along the waterfront are several abandoned warehouses built at the time of the Civil War, the **Empire Stores.** Owned by Con Edison, these solid buildings with arched windows and steel doors may again come to life as a complex of shops and small businesses. The dense undergrowth of weeds hides an old railroad roadbed, whose tracks once led to the water's edge for the transfer of freight cars by car float to points in New Jersey and the Bronx.

A BRIEF NOTE ABOUT THE BROOKLYN BRIDGE. Construction began on January 3, 1870, and was completed 13 years later, providing the vital link to Manhattan that ultimately led to the consolidation of Brooklyn into the City of New York in 1898. The monumental bridge represented the largest leap across an open space to that date—1595.5 feet—and is still considered by many to be the most beautiful span ever built. Engineer John Augustus Roebling had few architectural precedents to draw upon and had to test his designs on the spot. He had built three smaller previous bridges—the Suspension Bridge at Niagara Falls, in 1852, the still-extant Delaware & Hudson Aqueduct Bridge at Lackawaxen, Pennsylvania, and the Ohio River Bridge in Cincinnati. The Delaware bridge originally carried canal boats across the Delaware River and now is used by vehicular traffic. The Cincinnati bridge is also still in service. In planning the bridge, Roebling wisely anticipated the oscillation caused by aerodynamic instability and was a great pioneer in the use of structural steel. He is ranked with Joseph Paxton, who designed London's Crystal Palace Exposition Hall in 1851, and with Gustav Eiffel, whose great Tower was erected in Paris in 1889. The Brooklyn Bridge cost in excess of $16 million, some of which ended up in the pockets of "Boss" Tweed and his Ring. Roebling suffered a fatal accident in the early stages of the bridge's construction. His foot was crushed by a wooden piling as the Fulton ferry-boat was docking, and he died of tetanus a few weeks later. His son, Washington Augustus Roebling, carried on the project, and proved himself as capable an engineer as his father. He, too, was struck down by the bridge, suffering a disabling attack of caisson disease (the bends) from a too-rapid ascent from the underwater pressure chambers, and he directed the remaining work from the window of his sickroom, several blocks away. Little was known then of nitrogen narcosis, and the dangerous construction job took the lives of many workers. Opening day caused some furor among the Irish population of the city, as the date coincided with Queen Victoria's birthday. Shortly thereafter, a tragedy occurred that took the lives of a number of bridge pedestrians caught in an unexplained panic at the Manhattan end. Newspaper accounts attributed the crush to an organization of pickpockets who spread confusion to facilitate their criminal activities. To date 45 people have leaped from the bridge, of whom only 11 survived, including a Bowery saloonkeeper named Steve Brodie, whose claim of having survived the plunge may have been a publicity stunt. For many years the bridge carried the trains of the Brooklyn Elevated Railway as well as trolley cars. These were removed in the early 1940s and replaced by additional traffic lanes. More supporting cables were added later, but the strength and beauty of the bridge remains an enduring monument to the genius and skill of the Roeblings. A few years ago the twin Gothic style stone piers were sandblasted, and to everyone's surprise, the original color of the granite was revealed to be pink!

The view of the Manhattan skyline at dusk, framed in the dark arches and gossamerlike cables of the great span, is a never-to-be-forgotten experience. Thomas Wolfe, in *Of Time and the River,* extolled the beauty of the bridge "whose wing-like sweep" reached across to the "shining city, far-flung and blazing into tiers of jeweled light."

Follow Water Street back to Fulton Street. To reach the IND A line, continue along Fulton Street (Cadman Plaza West) about four blocks. The station entrance is opposite Cranberry Street, adjacent to the Whitman Close town houses, where the Brooklyn Heights tour began. Or take the B-41 bus at its turnaround, at the corner of Furman Street, to Borough Hall for the IRT or BMT subways.

COBBLE HILL

Shaded area indicates
boundaries of
Cobble Hill Historic District

STATE ST.

ATLANTIC AVE.

start

PACIFIC ST.

AMITY ST.

CONGRESS ST.

Cobble Hill
Park

VERANDAH PL.

COURT ST.

BROOKLYN-QUEENS EXPRESSWAY

WARREN ST.

WARREN PL.

BALTIC ST.

KANE ST.

HICKS ST.

CHEEVER PL.

HENRY ST.

STRONG PL.

CLINTON ST.

TOMPKINS PL.

DEGRAW ST.

To
Carroll
Gardens

To subway

16. Cobble Hill and Carroll Gardens

[*IRT Lexington Avenue and Broadway-Seventh Avenue lines to Borough Hall station, walk south on Court Street four blocks to Atlantic Avenue; IND F, GG lines to Bergen Street station, walk back (north) three blocks to Atlantic Avenue and left (west) two blocks to Court Street*]

The history of Cobble Hill began in the mid-17th century when Dutch colonists were granted patents to farm the land between the Gowanus * valley and the East River shore. The hilly terrain was very fertile and the area remained a bucolic suburb for over 10 years.

At the outbreak of the Revolutionary War, Cobble Hill figured in the Battle of Long Island, when the garrison of a small fort built on a promontory known as "Cobbleshill" fired a prearranged two-gun signal to warn General Washington's Continental Army that the British had landed at Gravesend, down the bay. It was from this redoubt—one of several strong points along the heights of Brooklyn—that Washington and his generals on August 27, 1776, observed the massive forces of Lord Howe gradually overwhelm the patriot defenders and force them into a strategic withdrawal across the East River to Manhattan. The British Army subsequently destroyed the fort and painstakingly cut away the commanding high ground on which it was built.

During the War of 1812, another fortification was erected nearby, and named Fort Swift; however, no invading forces attacked New York, and the defending cannon remained silent.

In 1834 Cobble Hill was annexed by the newly incorporated City of

---

* *Gowanus* derives from the name of the Indian sachem, Gouwane, who sold the first land to the Dutch in 1636.

Brooklyn, joining adjacent Brooklyn Heights, which earlier comprised most of the original Village of Brooklyn. Many of the old Dutch land holdings were broken up into smaller lots for residential development, and with the opening two years later of the South Ferry connecting District Street (now Atlantic Avenue) with the southern tip of Manhattan, the area grew rapidly. The street pattern of Cobble Hill was laid out from Atlantic Avenue south to what is now Kane Street and Strong Place, and row-house construction began in earnest. By the mid-19th century, the district referred to as "South Brooklyn" had lost all of its rural character and become largely a residential suburb of mostly wealthy merchants and a completely self-contained community with its own shops, churches, school, and bank, and some light manufacturing. The growing population was swelled by an influx of immigrants, particularly from Germany and Italy; and with the opening in 1879 of Alfred T. White's famous "model tenements," other nationality groups—Irish, English, Swedes, and Norwegians—settled in Cobble Hill. After World War I, the neighborhood attracted large numbers of Syrians and Lebanese, and today Atlantic Avenue is known as New York's Middle East. In more recent times, new immigrants from Latin America have joined the proverbial "melting pot"; while young families of all backgrounds, in search of lower-cost housing, have been buying up row houses, carefully restoring them, and putting Cobble Hill into the front ranks of New York's "Brownstone Revolution." And what was at the turn of the century merely a "workingman's district" has become a very desirable place to live. Cobble Hill has a unique quality of its own, with 19th-century moderate-income houses, much well preserved iron work, a uniform skyline punctuated only by occasional churches—many of them architectural gems—tree-lined streets, and a surprising small-town atmosphere. Twenty-two blocks were designated by the New York City Landmarks Commission as the **Cobble Hill Historic District.**

The walking tour begins at Atlantic Avenue and Court Street.

In 1836 ferry service was inaugurated between **Atlantic Avenue** (then Atlantic Street) and the southern tip of Manhattan. The same year, the Brooklyn & Jamaica Railroad constructed a right of way along Atlantic Street, connecting the South Ferry with the town of Jamaica and the Long Island Rail Road, and the thoroughfare developed quickly as one of the major commercial arteries of Long Island. The grade up Atlantic Street proved to be too steep for the tiny wood-burning locomotives, so in 1836 construction was begun on a half-mile-long tunnel under the street, extending from Columbia Street almost to Boerum Place. Seven years later, New York's first underground railroad began operation, with trains preceded through the tunnel by a man on horseback. It remained in service for only 16 years, as a group of merchants and politicians pushed through legislation banning all steam railroad operations from the City of Brooklyn. The tunnel was closed, and the reorganized Brooklyn Central & Jamaica Railroad moved its terminal to Flatbush Avenue, where it was forced to use horsecars as far as the city line. The tunnel is still in existence under Atlantic Avenue and has been the subject of much speculation for many years. In 1911 the Brooklyn *Daily Eagle* reported at length on a fruitless search for an entrance to the tunnel, as rumors were rampant on its use by counterfeiters, smugglers, bootleggers, and white slavers. Ultimately, access was obtained, but the search was called off prematurely because of the large river rats and an inadequate

The Long Island Rail Road tunnel under Atlantic Avenue, from an engraving, c. 1844. The tunnel was used for only 16 years, before being forced to close by a City of Brooklyn ordinance against steam locomotives. (Long Island Historical Society)

means of illuminating the tunnel. Stories still persist about the mysterious underground passage, and it is even claimed that a complete train with locomotive and string of wooden coaches lies hidden in the dark recesses under the avenue. One merchant swears that late at night he occasionally hears the muffled blast of a steam whistle beneath the streets (the Long Island *was* the first railroad to use the steam whistle).

At the turn of the century, Atlantic Avenue was heavily Swedish and was known locally as "Swedish Broadway." The Avenue is now famous for its variety of Middle Eastern establishments that line the street almost to the river. As you walk along the avenue, notice the restaurants and souvenir stores; but more importantly, the Syrian-Lebanese groceries and specialty food shops, stocked with their special hollow, flat bread, twisted cheese, halvah, baklava, pistachio nuts, stuffed grape leaves, yoghurt, and a thousand other taste-tempting delicacies. Take a pocketful of goodies with you, as there are few places of refreshment along the way.

The Independence Savings Bank, formerly the South Brooklyn Savings Bank, at the corner of Atlantic Avenue and Court Street, is reminiscent of a Florentine *palazzo*. Typical is the heavily rusticated façade and the highly ornamental door frame with sculpture above (on the Court Street side). The roof cornice is rather unusual with its row of carved stone eagles supporting it. The Bank building was completed in 1922 from plans by McKenzie, Voorhees & Gmellin. An addition (No. 136 Court Street) was built in 1936, also in Italian Renaissance style. This was **the site of "Cobbleshill,"** the conical-shaped hill on which the Revolutionary War fort was built. The little promontory was also called "Ponkiesbergh." Nearby, and roughly following the present route of Court Street, was the old Red Hook Lane, laid out in 1760. When the Cobble Hill street grid was laid out, the ancient road was de-mapped.

No. 180 Atlantic Avenue is a commercial cast-iron-front building, erected in 1873. Except for the storefront, the structure is in pristine condition. Cast iron was a very popular medium of building-front construction during the period 1860–90 (for detailed information, *see* introduction to the SoHo Cast-Iron District walking tour). The roof cornice shows the typical neo-Grec design of that period.

Nos. 170–178 are the last survivors of a row of Gothic Revival-style buildings, built during the famous 1840s decade of the "Gothic" popularity. Look for the traces of the window label moldings on Nos. 170–174. Only the end houses are of the original three-story height, and just two buildings still retain their stoops.

Although **Nos. 164–168** would seem to have been built in 1859, according to the date set in the gable, the two houses were each built at a different time, but joined together with a common roof cornice. No. 166–168 was erected in 1860, and No. 164 in 1864. The house is somewhat representative of the Italianate style, especially in the bracketed cornice and the stone quoins. Sadly, the ground floor was "modernized" with no understanding of the architectural style of the whole, and mars the elegant appearance of the building.

The building at the southeast corner of Clinton Street was **the original home of the South Brooklyn Savings Bank,** built in 1871. Constructed of Tuckahoe marble and designed by E. L. Roberts, what is left of this once-magnificent Italian Renaissance-style structure is still impressive. The roof balustrade has been removed and the street level has also been "modernized" into incongruity. In its description of the building for the *Cobble Hill Historic District Designation Report,* the Landmarks Commission mentions that "the vault (of the old bank) was constructed of granite blocks mortised out to receive cannon balls between each pair, so that the stones could not be forced out of alignment without demolishing the entire wall." There was once "an imposing central doorway flanked by columns that supported the balcony of a pedimented window which was also enframed by columns."

Beyond Clinton Street is a **group of houses that still show traces of the Greek Revival period.** Most were erected during the years 1848–52. Many still retain their original roof cornices. Note the cap moldings above the second- and third-floor windows on Nos. 152 and 154, and the wood panels under the parlor windows of No. 140. Although all were residences, the first-floor stores are original.

No. 130, a much altered Italianate brownstone, was built in the 1850s as Brooklyn's branch office of the City Bank, later the National City Bank, and now the First National City Bank. Observe the typically Italianate pedimented windows and the roof cornice with its dentils ("toothlike" blocks) and supporting brackets.

No. 124–128 was once the most important dry-goods emporium in the neighborhood, **the former Journeay & Burnham Store.** The firm began in 1851, at No. 126, and was so successful that new quarters were built in 1884, adding to an already large annex on Court Street built five years before.

Return to Clinton Street and turn right (south).

Nos. **197** and **199** on the east side, near the corner of Pacific Street, are the only two surviving Italianate row houses of the group of four that still have any character left. Look for the following typical features: high stoops, round- and segmental-arch entranceways, floor-length parlor windows, and a bracketed roof cornice. The brownstone facing, a type of sandstone, was usually quarried in Connecticut or New Jersey.

The apartment houses across the street, **Nos. 214–220,** were erected in 1892 and reflect the style of multiple-dwelling house construction of the 1890s. Decorated with classical motifs and some Romanesque Revival influence, they are representative of the so-called "transitional period." The sheet-metal bay windows serve two purposes: to admit more light and air, and to add a decorative facet to the broad façade of the building. Note, too, the ornamental doorway with its round-arch and carvings, surmounted by a pediment. The same type of entrance is repeated around the corner on Pacific Street.

Turn left (east) into Pacific Street.

The change in atmosphere from bustling Atlantic Avenue to quiet residential **Pacific Street** is immediately evident. The feeling of remoteness and tranquility increases with each block. The architecture of this block is varied, with fine examples of Victorian and Romanesque Revival styles. The diversity is due to the former role of Pacific Street (particularly the north side) as the stable row for the establishments on Atlantic Avenue.

No. 172, built in an early Romanesque Revival style of the 1850s, was formerly a stable, and has been remodeled as a residence. A rather handsome building with its three arches and gable, it is an interesting counterpart for its neighbor across the street, **No. 173.** Built about ten years later, it is also an example of the Romanesque Revival-style stable converted to residential use. The center wagon entrance is now the garage door, and the old hayloft above embraces a picture window. Oddly, a reconverted stable is now much more desirable than an original house.

Old Public School No. 78, now the Louis Hirsch Memorial Jewish Education Center, was built in 1888–89 in the tradition of the small neighborhood public school and designed in early Victorian style. The roof line presents a dramatic profile with its elaborate cornice, gables, and central tower. A truncated slate roof crowns the projecting entrance tower.

A fine example of the Romanesque Revival style is **No. 162,** with its *rundbogenstil,* or round-arch windows and doors on each floor. A divided stoop climbs to a central landing in an eye-catching effect. Notice the blind bull's-eye on the stepped gable, which was added later, and the massiveness of the first floor with its piers and corbeled arches. Typical, too, is the extensive use of red brick.

Return to Clinton Street, and continue west on Pacific Street.

The **south side of Pacific Street** reveals row houses built in groups of two or three, many in the Greek Revival style. Particularly attractive is the wrought ironwork of the stoops' handrailings, with their swirls in Greek motifs. **No. 122 is the oldest house in the neighborhood,** built before 1833. The mansard roof was added later, but the Greek Revival-style doorway with sidelights still remains. The doorways at **Nos. 126–130** and **116–120** are framed by stone pilasters supporting entablatures. Note the yard railings in front of **Nos. 118–120** with anthemion-motif finials.

Four Greek Revival-style houses on the north side of the block near Henry Street **(Nos. 115–119)** are quite simple in design, but the eye is drawn to the very ornate stoop and yard iron railings. The adjacent building, **Nos. 121–125,** was an extension of the Journeay & Burnham Dry-Goods Store on Atlantic Avenue. It was completed in 1881 and was designed by architect

John A. Raymond in neo-Grec style. Note the typical incised floral motifs on the window lintels.

Turn left (south) on Henry Street.

The **Long Island College Hospital** occupies several blocks, and dates back to 1857, when it was organized by a group of German immigrants who fled persecution in Europe in 1848. None of the original buildings remain. Interestingly, according to hospital records, the original medical staff included a leecher and cupper. Across the street, the Main Building dates from 1905. At the southeast corner of Pacific and Henry streets stood the Hoagland Laboratory, the first private bacteriological laboratory in the country, built in 1888. The magnificent Romanesque Revival building was destroyed by fire several years ago, and the hospital could not afford the exorbitant reconstruction costs. **The Nurses' Residence** at the northeast corner of Amity Street is a modern addition to the campus, completed in 1963. Diagonally across the street is the **Polhemus Clinic,** built in 1897, a good example of the Classical Eclectic style, representing the transition from the so-called "Romantic Era" to the more functional and less ornate modern style.

Turn left (east) on Amity Street.

The **Dudley Memorial** (110 Amity Street) was built in the style of a small French Renaissance château. The roof deck contains a small loggia with Doric columns, and the roof cornice, constructed of sheet metal, is painted to simulate stone and is set on very elaborate brackets. Named for the Hospital's original council member, Dr. William H. Dudley, it was originally built as a nurses' residence in 1902 and now serves as a Pediatric Disabilities Center.

No. 130 is a most interesting French Second Empire-style house. Forming part of a row of Italianate houses (Nos. 126–142), it was built in the 1850s for a wealthy merchant. Ornate foliated brackets can be seen under the lintel cornices of the parlor-floor windows. Individual window balconies with balusters add a touch of grace; while the wide, graceful stoop is adorned with iron balustrades that glide down to octagonal newel posts (only the left one is original). The splendid mansard roof with its delicate wrought-iron cresting was added in the early 1860s. Typical, too, of the Second Empire style are the double inner and outer doors, elaborately carved and crowned by arched transoms, while twisted floral-design moldings frame the entranceway.

Along the north side of Amity Street are several **rows of neo-Grec-style houses,** dating from the period of popularity of the style, 1875–81. Note **No. 141** with its triangular bay which runs four stories high, and also **Nos. 129–133.** A group of Italianate houses (Nos. 137–139) interrupts the neo-Grec theme. **Nos. 143–153** again show the neo-Grec style, especially in the delicate design of the cornice brackets. All have mansard roofs with hexagonal tiles and pedimented dormer windows. This row dates from 1875–76, and was built by E. L. Patchen, a descendant of the Patchens who were prominent landowners in the area at the beginning of the 19th century.

No. 155 is a very late Queen Anne-style building, so late in fact (1903!) that it is almost an anachronism. The treatment of the windows is the interesting element—wooden two-story polygonal bays made of wood and supported on basket-shaped corbels, with a cartouche design.

Before turning the corner at Clinton Street, step back and admire the magnificent **Degraw Mansion** across the street at the southeast corner (actually **219 Clinton Street**). Built in 1844, and enlarged in 1891, it occupies a beautiful setting on ample grounds with lush plantings. The Landmarks Commission considers it "without a doubt the most imposing property in the Cobble Hill Historic District." The original house, in Greek Revival style, was built for Abraham J. S. Degraw, a Manhattan commission merchant. The major remodeling of the building was planned by the architects D'Oench and Simon for the second owners, Laura and Ralph Cutter. Mr. Cutter was a dry-goods merchant and treasurer of the nearby First Presbyterian Church on Henry Street. The Romanesque touches on the ground floor and the Flemish stepped gable roof stem from the 1891 reconstruction, as well as the lofty tower, which was equipped with the first private passenger elevator in Brooklyn! The sideways-facing brownstone stoop was also added, giving a feeling of elegance and dignity. The house was acquired in 1924 by its third owner, A. N. Saab, who has wisely made no exterior changes in this lovely mansion. It is indeed rare for such an old house to have been owned by only three families. The view of the harbor from the tower is probably reminiscent of the broad panoramas enjoyed by the early landholders whose large houses overlooked the Upper New York Bay in the early 19th century.

(Although not on the itinerary of the tour, No. 197 Amity Street, one block farther, near the corner of Court Street, is the birthplace of Jennie Jerome [January 9, 1854], mother of Winston Churchill. The house was built five years earlier in Greek Revival style, but except for some attractive ironwork on the stoop, little remains of the original, the façade having been "modernized" with a fake stone siding. Her father, Leonard Jerome, was a wealthy financier and race-horse fancier who built Jerome Avenue in the Bronx as a direct route to his race track. Jenny grew up to marry Lord Randolph Churchill in 1874. Incidentally, it was commonly believed that Jennie Jerome was born at 426 Henry Street, and a plaque on that house makes the claim; however, it is incorrect—she was indeed born here.)

At the southwest corner of Amity and Clinton streets is the **Church of St. Mary the Virgin.** Built in 1922, it was planned as a much larger house of worship, but was never completed, as the Syrian congregation acquired the former Congregational Church of the Pilgrims in Brooklyn Heights, now renamed Our Lady of Lebanon.

Turn right (south) on Clinton Street to Congress Street.

The rather large three-story house on the northeast corner **(No. 235)** was built in the 1840s. Originally a Greek Revival house, it was remodeled in the late 19th century with neo-Grec motifs (pedimented lintels); on the Congress Street side, it was given rectangular bay windows of stained glass. It is now the Convent of the Sisters of Charity of nearby St. Paul's Roman Catholic Church.

Turn right (west) on Congress Street.

Cobble Hill Park, a pleasant open space, will become even more attractive as the recently planted trees and shrubbery grow in height. Much more could have been done with the little park to maintain harmony with the surrounding neighborhood. How much nicer it would look with old cast-iron lamp standards instead of the garish modern pylons. In the city's haste to remove the old Bishop's Crook lampposts from all our thoroughfares, a few might have been kept for just such a place as this. The Park was not planned, but resulted when the Second Unitarian Church was demolished. Built in 1857–58, from plans by J. Wrey Mould, it was fondly referred to as "The Church of the Holy Turtle." Built by New Englanders, its first pastor was Samuel Longfellow, a brother of the famous poet and an active abolitionist. Until its removal, the Second Unitarian Church was considered an important center of cultural and community activity.

Midway down Congress Street, **Nos. 159–163** form an interesting Anglo-Italianate-style group (the "Anglo-" refers to the English custom of having lower stoops of only two or three steps). Compare this trio with **Nos. 166–170,** across the street. At first glance they appear identical, but differences can be seen in the window treatment. The former, being older, has square-headed windows on the upper floors, rather than the segmental-arched windows of the later groups on the south side. Both groups, however, share a common cornice in the shape of a low gable. The low first stories are called "English basements."

The last house on the north side facing Congress Street, **No. 147,** is also the newest on the block, built around the turn of the century. It is another anachronistic Queen Anne building, but it is, nonetheless, quite charming. Note how the entry tower, like a medieval *donjon,* culminates in a high pyramidal roof. Note, too, the cast-iron newel posts and the ornate daisies on the handrails.

Reverse direction toward Clinton Street, and enter the Park.

Spend another minute examining the buildings on the north side of Congress Street from a more distant vantage point. Compare **Nos. 173** and **175.** Both were at one time identical, having been constructed the same year, 1877, by the same builder. But there the similarity ends, for No. 173 has been preserved in its fine neo-Grec appearance, whereas its twin has suffered the ravages of "modernization." Focus on the roof line of the various buildings extending to Clinton Street. No Landmarks Commission was around to dictate procedures for arriving at a common solution of uniform building height. Each owner did "his own thing" with no regard to the harmony of the block, and the result is only too evident. And what is a Colonial-style doorway doing on No. 177?

Walk through the Park to Verandah Place.

Charming **Verandah Place,** which extends for only a block-and-a-half, was probably built as an alley for carriage houses and stables, and dates from the 1840s and 1850s. The owners of the carriages and horses no doubt lived in the large row houses on Clinton, Henry, Congress, and Warren streets. Before the construction of the park, the little mews must have been much less inviting than it is today. **Thomas Wolfe,** who lived for a brief time at No. 40, described his little basement apartment in _No Door:_

> _The place is shaped like a Pullman car, except that it is not so long and has only one window at each end. There are bars over the window that your landlady has put there to keep the thugs in that sweet neighborhood from breaking in; in winter the place is cold and dark, and sweats with clammy water, in the summer you do all the sweating yourself._

The little "railroad flats" are now much sought after, and the "sweet neighborhood" is much more peaceful than during Wolfe's Depression years sojourn. He later moved a mile north to Brooklyn Heights where he finished _Of Time and the River._

Explore Verandah Place (including the short cul-de-sac on the other side of Clinton Street dating from 1876–78), noting how the new owners have used their imagination to convert their little two-and-a-half and three-story houses into handsome dwellings. The upstairs hayloft doors are now large windows, and some even retain the old iron hoist in the gable. At the Henry Street end, a little 19th-century corner store adds a nostalgic touch.

Turn left (south) on Henry Street.

On the west side of Henry Street are the **Congress Nursing Home** and **St. Peter's Roman Catholic Church.** The Nursing Home, rebuilt in 1963, was formerly St. Peter's Hospital, erected in 1888. The original Romanesque Revival building lost all of its distinguishing features when it was remodeled.

Turn right (west) on Warren Street to Warren Place.

One of the most remarkable housing developments in the city, and probably the earliest, are the **Warren Place Workingmen's Cottages** and adjacent **Tower and Home Apartments.** The "cottages" and apartment houses were built in 1878–79 by businessman Alfred Tredway White who believed in

"Philanthropy plus 5%." White was also president of the Brooklyn Bureau of Charities, and after a visit to the slums of London, he returned convinced that "No European city suffers so much and so unnecessarily from the evils of overcrowding as does New York today." Deciding to help remedy the evil, he engaged the firm of William Field & Son to build the Cottages and Towers, to give the workingmen of the city "the chance to live decently, and to bring up their children to be decent men and women. . . ."

Of the 44 brick cottages, the 26 that face the pedestrian walkway are "triplexes" 24 feet high—precisely the width of the common garden. Only 11½ feet wide, they are small by modern standards, but in 1879 they were revolutionary. The flanking cottages at the Warren and Baltic Street ends of the walk are four stories high, neatly framing the garden and its twin row of charming row houses. In White's time, they rented for $18 per month. Each cottage cost $1100 to build, but at today's prices the purchase price would be at least 25 times that amount (if one ever became available).

Walk around the Tower Apartments to Hicks Street. (For the best view, cross to the west side of the Brooklyn-Queens Expressway.)

Between Warren and Baltic streets are the **Tower Buildings,** and between Baltic and Kane streets, the **Home Buildings.** The architecture of these Victorian-inspired tenement houses is both innovative and attractive. White's aim of supplying each tenant with sunshine and air is admirably accomplished through the use of outside recessed balconies and three open stair towers, providing tenants with separate entrances and cheerful apartments. The buildings are U-shaped to allow for more light and ventilation. (Compare these buildings with the thousands of dismal "dumbbell" tenements built in the following 20 years throughout the city's poor neighborhoods, in which millions lived in squalor and misery.) The bold towers and decorative iron balconies create a dramatic effect. A central courtyard around which the six-story buildings are grouped was designed as a recreational area for the residents of the 226 apartment units. Shortly after opening, a four-room apartment could be rented for $1.93 per week, or $7.00 per month if paid for in advance. Three rooms rented for $1.48 per week, or $6.00 per month. And White still made his 5 percent profit!

Return to the corner of Warren and Hicks streets.

St. Peter's Roman Catholic Church, now called Our Lady of Pilar in deference to the growing Hispanic congregation, was built in 1859–60 from plans by Patrick Charles Keely. Keely is noted for the number of Catholic churches he designed throughout Brooklyn, and the Church, an interesting example of early Romanesque Revival style, has some unusual details. Note the crenelated effect of the round-arched window heads, and the little gables above the front side doors. Unfortunately, the tall octagonal spire has disappeared from the steeple. Beneath the louvered belfry are attractive brick corbels extending around the sides of the steeple. The adjacent **St. Peter's Academy** (now School) was founded by the Church's first pastor, Father Fransioli, in 1866. The architectural style, with its round-arched windows and crenelated doorway, is quite similar to the Church.

Walk south on Hicks Street, past the Tower and Home Buildings, and turn left (east) on Kane Street.

The street pattern between Kane Street and Degraw Street (one block south) is interrupted by an additional street between each of the major north-south thoroughfares: Cheever Place, Strong Place, and Tompkins Place [*see* map].

On the south side of Kane Street between Hicks Street and Cheever Place are an engaging **group of c. 1850 town houses** that ascend in pairs to conform to the slope of the street. A corner store at each end enframes the row, but more interesting is the Greek fret design cast into the iron railings on the stoops of each house.

No. 139, across the street, also has attractive ironwork on the stoop and areaway. **Nos. 147–149** are a fine example of Greek Revival-style architecture, and have survived since their building date of 1845–46 in a relatively good state of preservation. Note particularly the doorway of No. 149 with its sidelights and five-paned transom. An unusual oval floralwork motif can be seen in the pair of rectangular panels at the stoop, and also on No. 147. It is believed that the ironwork gate and railing of No. 147 is original.

At the southwest corner of Henry Street, the house (actually No. 424 Henry Street) has a little attic room built in between the chimneys. Beyond the back yard is an **unusual two-story brick garage** which was erected in 1892 by owner-architect Owen McShane as a soda water factory, with space for horse stables. Above, the hayloft doors can still be distinguished.

Turn right to 426 Henry Street.

Although the plaque proclaims this as the birthplace of Winston Churchill's mother, Jennie Jerome, it is the incorrect location. As previously mentioned, the site is at 197 Amity Street. Before Jennie was born, however, her parents did stay briefly at this address with uncle Addison G. Jerome.

At the northeast corner of Kane and Henry streets is **Public School 29,** built in 1919 in the so-called Collegiate Gothic style of the period. The school blends well with the neighboring brick houses, and is a good example of a modern building complementing its more traditional surroundings.

Standing alone at the southeast corner of Strong Place is **No. 176,** an imposing residence built in the late 1840s in largely Italianate style. It is believed that the house once served as the rectory for Christ Church at the corner of Clinton Street.

Across the street, the five-story **Romanesque Revival apartment house,** built just before the turn of the century, breaks up a row of Greek Revival-style town houses dating from the mid-1840s. **No. 201,** to the east, was formerly a stable, now a combination garage and private dwelling. Its dentiled brick arch and toothed fascia are very typical of the 1880s and '90s.

Christ Church (Episcopal), the first religious organization in Cobble Hill, was designed by architect Richard Upjohn,* and built in 1841–42. Its imposing tower rises 117 feet above the street, adding graceful punctuation to the Cobble Hill skyline. The church is built of varying color sandstone blocks that give the building a venerable and elegant appearance. Typical of the English Gothic style are the pointed windows on the main body of the church, on the chancel, and on the tower; the polygonal turrets above the crenelated tower, and the drip moldings above the windows. The tower itself is divided into several sections: the pointed-arch entrance with drip molding, a triple-pointed window, the clock faces, a belfry with louvered "windows" under pointed arches, and the four turrets. In 1917 the church acquired a number of furnishings designed by Louis Comfort Tiffany (son of the founder of Tiffany & Company, and himself a distinguished artist and noted stained-glass designer), including the altar, altar railings, pulpit, reredos, lectern, and chairs—all damaged in a 1939 fire, but meticulously restored. Upjohn lived nearby in a house at 295 Clinton Street (near Baltic Street, one block north). Take a moment to visit the attractive interior.

The adjacent **rectory** (No. 326 Clinton Street) is in Greek Revival style. Its most notable feature, and one which is almost unique to the Cobble Hill section, is the splendid ironwork design in the form of a **swirl** at both top and bottom of the hand railings. Notice also the wrought-iron Gothic designs on **No. 328,** and its lovely Gothic Revival twin, **No. 330,** with quatrefoil motifs at the pediments over the parlor windows and doorway. The pair of houses was built in the mid-1840s.

No. 334 has a Queen Anne-style façade, added in 1888. The details in brick, stone, and terra cotta were designed and assembled with great care, creating the impression of more building width than is there. One of the characteristics of the style is the quaintness caused by asymmetry, very evident in the relative positions of the entrance tower and bay window. The top floor is built into both the mansard roof and the tower, adding to the storybook effect. Incidentally, its neighbor, **No. 336,** was also its twin when built in the mid-19th century. It might have been interesting to compare the original appearance with the remodeled Queen Anne house, but alas, a "Howard Johnson" doorway and an imitation stone façade deny us the pleasure.

No. 340, built in the early 1860s is a one-family Victorian-style house.

---

* Richard Upjohn designed many beautiful Episcopal churches in New York City: Grace Church in Brooklyn Heights, Christ Church in the Riverdale section of the Bronx, St. Alban's Church in Staten Island, The Church of the Holy Communion and The Church of the Ascension in Manhattan, and many others. His most celebrated is Trinity Church, at Wall Street and Broadway. Upjohn's churches were virtually all built in the Gothic Revival style so popular in the 1840s.

The widest in the Historic District, it has exceptionally high stories and an attic built into the mansard roof.

Cross Clinton Street and walk back toward Kane Street.

Nos. 301–311, reaching to the corner of Kane Street, represent an early example of community planning. The row is part of a group, some of which are immediately around the corner on Kane Street, and some one block farther on Tompkins Place. Built during the period 1849–54, they are interesting for their doorways, which are paired in projecting sections, and for their ironwork with Gothic trefoil motif.

Turn right (east) into Kane Street.

Nos. 206–224 Kane Street are a continuation of the development just seen on Clinton Street. The group, built by Gerard W. Morris, a New York lawyer, consists of 18 Italianate row houses on three adjoining blocks. The effect of the paired projecting entranceways with their joined pediments gives an impression of spaciousness and charm, eliminating the monotony sometimes associated with row-house construction. Fortunately, the ironwork with its Gothic trefoil motifs is still intact on most of the houses.

The ironwork across the street is also worthy of mention. Almost all have ornate swirling stoop railings. Note, too, the Italianate ironwork on the balconies of **Nos. 219, 223,** and **225**—the latter two with palm-leaf motifs; and the railings on **Nos. 231, 239,** and **241.**

Congregation Baith Israel Anshei Emes, at the corner of Tompkins Place, was organized in 1856, and is the oldest Jewish congregation in Brooklyn. The so-called "Mother Synagogue" acquired the building from the Trinity German Lutheran Church in 1905, which in turn had purchased it in 1887 from the original Middle Dutch Reformed Church. The early Romanesque Revival-style church building dates from 1855. Originally trimmed with brownstone, it is now stuccoed. The main entrance is enframed by round-arches supported by clustered columns, between which is a handsome triple doorway. The round-arch motif can also be seen above windows, arcades, and the traceries of the stained-glass windows. On the side, pointed buttresses alternate with the windows, and towers of different dimensions rise at the front corners. The changes in congregation through the years reflect the shifting population of the Cobble Hill area.

Turn right (south) on Tompkins Place.

Nos. 10 and **12** Tompkins Place belong to the same development as Nos. 206–224 Kane Street and 301–311 Clinton Street.

Tompkins Place is a particularly attractive street because of the narrow row-house arrangement as well as its outstanding and varied ironwork.

Unusual, too, is the profusion of ornate window lintels over doorways and parlor-floor windows.

On the east side of the street are two rows of Greek Revival houses, **Nos. 11–25,** built in the 1840s. The splendid line of stoop railings with their ornamental vertical scrolls and paneled pedestals can best be appreciated by standing alongside the first house and looking down the row at the diminishing perspective of the line of railings. This angle of view also enhances the third-dimensional effect of the façades, intended by builders of row houses.

Back across the street, a pleasant feature of these houses is the setback arrangement that allows for small gardens and extensive use of yard railings and gates. Note the elaborate curved lintels above the doorways and windows of **No. 42** and **Nos. 48–52,** built in the early 1850s by two owners who wisely decided to share the common design. A passing glance across the street reveals fake Federal-style façades on Nos. 41–47, although they do have nicely landscaped front gardens. **Nos. 60** and **62** still retain their original Anglo-Italianate ironwork and low three-step stoops.

The visual effect of **Nos. 53–61** on the east side, in which alternate houses project and are crowned by a pediment, is very striking. Since small houses were very much in demand in this neighborhood, such an architectural procedure compensated for the 15-foot widths of each row house. **No. 61** is probably the best example of the style, with its low stoop and Italianate curved ironwork both on the railings and on the oversize newel posts. **Nos. 53 and 55** in the row have similar ironwork enclosing their front yards. It was not unusual for the builder to live in one of his row houses, and No. 55 was the home of Thomas Sullivan, after Nos. 53–61 were completed in the early 1850s.

A brief detour to the east on Degraw Street reveals three charming houses in the middle of the block. **No. 271** is a Gothic Revival-style house of unusual richness, built in 1850. Notice the characteristic pointed arches of the ironwork designs and the drip moldings over the windows, and don't miss the miniature pointed arches that support the roof cornice. Only 21½ feet wide, it has no room for a window in its angular bay. Above the entranceway, a molding ends in ornate impost blocks.

Nos. 273 and **275** display Romanesque Revival touches, particularly in their arcades supporting the dentiled brick roof cornice. Both have a paired entranceway flanked by masonry bays that climb to the full height of the houses, giving an appearance of more than their 42-foot combined width. These lovely forerunners of the Romanesque Revival period were constructed in 1847–48.

Now walk west on Degraw Street.

Degraw Street is named for Abraham J. S. Degraw, who in 1844 built the only remaining freestanding house with spacious grounds in Cobble Hill, at 219 Clinton Street (seen earlier on the tour). The Cobble Hill Historic District extends only to the north side of Degraw Street.

The church in the middle of the block, in a Gothic Revival style, was built in 1905 for the Trinity German Lutheran Church, which had just moved from its earlier site at Kane Street and Tompkins Place. Much of the early German population has gone, and the building is now the house of worship of the **South Brooklyn Seventh Day Adventist Church.** Worthy of note is the ogee arch over the central doorway, the corniced pointed arches over the windows, and the church's high railing.

Continue beyond Clinton Street to the church at the corner of Strong Place.

Formerly the **Strong Place Baptist Church,** this handsome Gothic Revival-style edifice since 1969 has been the St. Frances Cabrini Roman Catholic Chapel. Erected in 1851–52 from plans by famed architect Minard Lafever,* its massive corner tower dominates the site. At the west aisle, a small turret with lancet windows rises asymmetrically. The main section of the church is designed with a gabled façade and a triple-pointed arched window, while triple-arched belfry openings in the tower are flanked by high stepped buttresses. A solid iron railing with tall gateposts surrounds the church.

Adjoining the church, around the corner on Strong Place, is the Lafever-designed **chapel,** where the church held its first services in 1849. It then became the church's Sunday school and is said to have been one of the most popular in Brooklyn. The chapel with its adjacent building (No. 56–58 Strong Place) is now the Strong Place Day Care Center. The Catholic church now caters mostly to the Italian community of Cobble Hill and the contiguous Carroll Gardens section.

Return to Clinton Street. End of tour.

Although the Cobble Hill walking tour ends at Clinton and Degraw streets, a short optional walking tour can be made into the Carroll Gardens section, ending conveniently close to subway transportation (*see* below).

To return directly, walk east on Degraw Street two blocks to Smith Street, where the B-75 bus goes north to Fulton Street near the IRT subway Borough Hall station as well as the Jay Street-Borough Hall station of the IND A and F lines. Or turn south on Smith Street and walk four short blocks to the Carroll Street station of the IND F and GG lines.

---

* Minard Lafever designed many churches and a number of private residences in the decade of the 1840s. Among his works are two churches in Brooklyn Heights, the Church of the Saviour and the Holy Trinity Protestant Episcopal Church; and in Manhattan, the Church of the Holy Apostles, St. James Roman Catholic Church, and the Mariners' Temple. He remodeled the Bartow-Pell Mansion in the Bronx, and is believed to be the architect of the Old Merchant's House on East 4th Street in Manhattan's East Village.

A WALK THROUGH CARROLL GARDENS

Continue south on Clinton Street.

No. 363 was formerly a livery stable, where before the advent of the automobile, a horse and carriage could be rented, or your own horse boarded. Those who could not afford the luxury of their own stable used such facilities. Before the turn of the century, livery stables were as common as today's public garages.

Crossing Sackett Street, observe the exposed rails of the former Hoyt-Sackett trolley line. Until World War II, Brooklyn had one of the most extensive trolley networks of any city in the world, where, for a five-cent fare and free transfers, one could ride almost indefinitely.

No. 396 is the handsome **Carroll Park Branch of the Brooklyn Public Library.** Still an independent library system, the Brooklyn Public Library began lending books in 1897, antedating the New York Public Library by several years. The building, designed in a modified Renaissance Revival style, was opened in 1905.

Continue south on Clinton Street to Carroll Street.

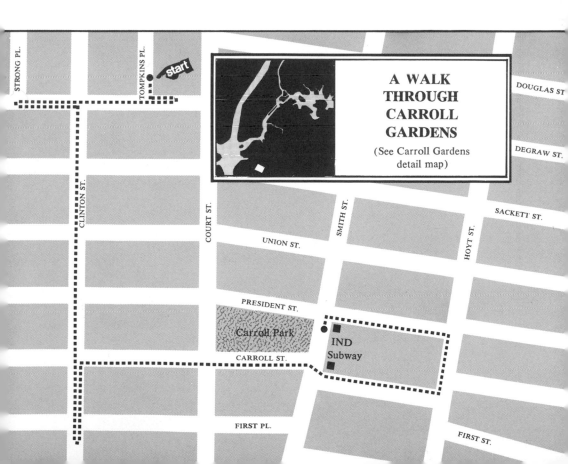

At the northeast corner is **St. Paul's Episcopal Church of Brooklyn,** another Richard Upjohn church, this one designed together with son Richard W. Upjohn. Completed in 1884, it is a simple, but rather heavy English Gothic Revival-style building. Enter the church and notice the unusual treatment of the interior. The transepts are extremely narrow because of the shape of the lot, and the supporting columns, instead of rising to the cleristory, terminate in capitals under large arches. The arrangement of the pulpit is said to be French in style, set halfway down the nave, together with a *banque* (a row of double pews directly in front of the pulpit to seat clergy and servers who would be too far back in the sanctuary to hear the sermon). The church is constructed of dark-brown sandstone and has no spire. St. Paul's adds "of Brooklyn" to its name to distinguish it from St. Paul's of Flatbush, as the two Episcopal houses of worship were originally in separate towns. The town of Flatbush was not annexed by the City of Brooklyn until 1894.

Although **Carroll Gardens** is a veritable "melting pot," the largest group are the Italians. Mainly from southern Italy and Sicily, they began arriving in the late 19th century, and their influence is clearly visible in the names of so many commercial establishments along adjacent Court Street.

No. 440 Clinton Street, on the southwest corner, is considered the finest

CARROLL GARDENS

(Shaded Area Indicates Historic District)

UNION ST.

HOYT ST.

Public School 32

PRESIDENT ST.

B-75 Bus

IND Subway

from Cobble Hill →

CARROLL ST.

Carroll School (Public School 58)

FIRST PL.

SMITH ST.

First Place looking west from Clinton Street, in 1896. Few changes have occurred through the years, giving Carroll Gardens a very special atmosphere not often found in a big city. (Long Island Historical Society)

Greek Revival town house in the city. Built c. 1840 for a well-to-do merchant, it is in a superb state of preservation in its adaptive reuse as the Guido Funeral Home. The salmon-colored brick façade is flanked by pilasters that rise to the full height of the house, and are crowned by granite capitals. The stoop, on a slightly projecting central section, is also made of granite, as are the cap-molded window lintels, the sills, newel posts, and basement facings. The Guido family which lives in the house as well as uses it as a funeral parlor, takes pride in maintaining the elegant mansion, and will on special occasions trot out an ornate horse-drawn hearse to re-create a dignified 19th-century funeral. The lovely house has been designated a New York City Landmark.

One block south, at the corner of Clinton Street and 1st Place, is the **Norwegian Seamen's Church,** built c. 1865 for an earlier Presbyterian congregation. When the present group acquired the church in 1929, an imposing Norwegian-style wood pulpit was installed, and an old sailing-ship anchor placed on the lawn. Although most of this Scandinavian community has moved to the Bay Ridge section of Brooklyn, a substantial number of older members still come here to worship.

Return to Carroll Street and turn right (east) past Court Street to Carroll Park.

The Park and street are named for Charles Carroll of Maryland, a signer of the Declaration of Independence. It was a Maryland regiment under General Stirling that during the Battle of Long Island fought a desperate delaying action at the "Old Stone House at Gowanus" * on August 27, 1776—an act of bravery by a small, outnumbered garrison that permitted General Washington to evacuate the entire Continental Army safely to Manhattan. The Park was originally a private garden, but was acquired by the State of New York in 1850 and made into a public park 20 years later.

The Carroll Gardens Historic District (*see* map) is a small, quiet residential district, and very much a separate enclave within the city.

---

* The "Old Stone House at Gowanus," known now as the Vechte-Cortelyou House, was reconstructed in 1935 by the Department of Parks with the original stones. The 1699 Dutch farmhouse is located in the James J. Byrne Memorial Plaground, at 3rd Street, west of Fifth Avenue, five blocks east and three blocks south. Cross the Gowanus Canal on the 3rd Street Bridge.

The Vechte-Cortelyou House, known familiarly as the Old Stone House at Gowanus, was built in 1699 and figured importantly in the Battle of Long Island. The house has been reconstructed with the original stones and can be seen in a playground at 3rd Street, west of Fifth Avenue in Brooklyn. (Long Island Historical Society)

Because of the peculiar street pattern, Carroll and President streets both appear to be dead-end streets, probably a contributory factor to the feeling of separateness of these two blocks. The pleasant appearance of the district is the fortunate result of foresighted 19th-century planning. Immediately evident is the row of setback front yards, ranging from 25 to 39 feet. The uniform pattern of two- and three-story brick and brownstone houses built in long rows on shady, tree-lined streets, each with a well tended garden, creates a sense of open space and architectural harmony. The houses date mostly from the late 1860s to the early 1880s, and represent a spirit of cooperation among the various builders. The row houses, built for middle-class merchants, were designed in two of the popular styles of the late 19th century: late Italianate and French neo-Grec. In spite of some building modifications, most of the neighborhood remains uniquely homogeneous.

Space does not permit a detailed house-by-house description, but do make a circuit of the District by walking east on Carroll Street, north on Hoyt Street, and west on President Street (_see_ map).

The dominant building and most striking architectural landmark is the **Church of the South Brooklyn Christian Assembly,** Nos. 297–299 Carroll Street. Built in 1872–73 as the Carroll Park Methodist Church, it was acquired in 1891 by the Norwegian Methodist Episcopal Church, reflecting the influx of many Norwegians into the neighborhood. The present congregation purchased it in 1949. Differing in style from the adjoining residences, the brick church was designed in a flamboyant Victorian Gothic. Note, too, the **former parsonage** at No. 295, completed in 1878, and stylistically similar to the church.

The IND Carroll Street station is at the corner of Smith Street, with another entrance on President Street.

17. Park Slope

[*IRT Broadway-Seventh Avenue or Lexington Avenue lines to Nevins Street (Brooklyn), change for local to Bergen Street station*]

The "Slope" rises gradually eastward from the Gowanus Canal to Prospect Park in a several-square-mile sweep; however, the Park Slope neighborhood is usually defined as the area encompassed by Flatbush Avenue and Prospect Park on the east, St. Marks Avenue south to 15th Street, and Fifth or Sixth Avenue on the west. The New York City Landmarks Preservation Commission designated a section of Park Slope as a Historic District in 1973 (*see* map). From Dutch colonial times until the last quarter of the 19th century, the area remained largely rural in character—a hilly terrain of farms, fields, and pastures—bypassed by the developers of the nearby towns of Flatbush and Brooklyn. Flatbush, from the Dutch *Vlacke Bos* (Flat Woods), was not annexed by the City of Brooklyn until 1894.

At the outbreak of the Revolutionary War, the Park Slope area was the scene of the retreat of the Continental Army after the battle of Flatbush Pass. Outnumbered and overwhelmed by the combined British and Hessian forces that had made an amphibious landing on August 26, 1776, at Gravesend, the patriots pulled back along the Port Road, located approximately parallel to the present 1st Street. A brilliant delaying maneuver was executed by General William Alexander, Lord Stirling with a small Maryland regiment about a mile west at the "Old Stone House at Gowanus," at the present corner of Fifth Avenue and 3rd Street [*see* Cobble Hill, page 350]. Although his brave defending force was decimated and he, himself, was captured, Stirling's action permitted General Washington to withdraw safely across the East River to Manhattan.

Development came relatively late to Park Slope, in spite of the proximity of the heavily traveled Flatbush Road (now Avenue) and the opening of Prospect Park in the late 1860s. It was not until the mid-1880s that its potential was really discovered. While it is true that adjacent Prospect Park was a major influence in the growth of Park Slope, the completion in 1883 of the great Brooklyn Bridge was the catalyst. Within a decade, rows of brownstones, like parades of caterpillars, inched their way up the gentle hill. In the blocks closest to the park, wealthy merchants and professionals built lavish town houses and opulent mansions. So many imposing residences were constructed that the section came to be called the "Gold Coast." And so it remained for almost half a century, rivaling Manhattan's Fifth Avenue in grandeur. The Park Slope neighborhood still retains much of its charm in the tree-lined streets, uniform row houses, attractive churches, tranquil atmosphere, and the exciting variety of architectural styles of its once-rich mansions. It remains a stable, family community with a deep sense of civic pride, strongly dedicated to preserving the very special quality of the neighborhood.

The tour begins at the corner of Flatbush Avenue and St. Marks Place.

Until late in the 19th century, **Flatbush Avenue** was the main thoroughfare connecting the City of Brooklyn with the towns to the south (Flatbush, Gravesend, New Utrecht, and Flatlands). Stagecoaches gave way to horsecars, then trolleys, and finally buses, while, below the street, came the subway—built as the Interborough Rapid Transit and now part of the municipally owned Metropolitan Transit Authority. Even before the mid-19th century, the Long Island Rail Road had its Brooklyn terminal on Flatbush Avenue, one mile north.

The opening in 1909 of the Manhattan Bridge with its direct connection with Flatbush Avenue made it for a time the busiest thoroughfare in the entire city. Until after World War II, it was a bustling and important commercial street, but as population patterns shifted, it declined rapidly, yielding to the effects of urban blight. Yet surprisingly, little of this very contagious decay seems to have seeped across into the Park Slope neighborhood. Looking up Flatbush Avenue, the Brooklyn skyline is dominated by the lofty **Williamsburgh Savings Bank Building** with its 512-foot, gold-domed tower. Built the same year as Manhattan's Chrysler and Empire State buildings (1929–30), it is Brooklyn's only real skyscraper.

In all directions are gaily painted buildings advertising Pintchik's Paint Store. The bizarre assemblage includes so many painted house fronts that the *AIA Guide to New York* refers to it as **"Pintchikville."** Gleaming through the asphalt of Flatbush Avenue are traces of the rails of the once wide network of Brooklyn trolley lines.

Walk south on Flatbush Avenue and turn half-right into Sixth Avenue.

At the northwest corner of St. Marks Place is the **Cathedral Club of Brooklyn.** Built in 1890 as the Carlton Club, it was one of several exclusive clubs for the wealthy. It later became the Monroe Club, followed by the Royal Arcanum Club, ending in 1907 as a Roman Catholic fraternal club

Brooklyn Union Gas Company's "Cinderella of Prospect Place" project—a trio of decaying, abandoned stores before their conversion to town houses and the revitalization of the street in 1971. (Brooklyn Union Gas Company)

organized by a young priest, George Mundelein, who ultimately became Cardinal of Chicago.

Turn left on Prospect Place.

On the left side of the street are three neo-Colonial-style houses, completed in 1971. Called the **"Cinderella of Prospect Place,"** they were formerly one-story boarded-up and abandoned stores—an eyesore on the block and a symptom of the growing deterioration of the periphery of Park Slope. The success of the transformation, using the original strong framework of the stores instead of demolishing them and starting from scratch, was the innovative plan of the Brooklyn Union Gas Company, and a joint endeavor with builders Asen Bros. and Brook. Such projects demonstrate the feasibility of restoring decrepit and abandoned buildings, and serve to encourage neighborhood improvement and revitalization.

Return to Sixth Avenue and turn left.

The rows of brownstones on both sides of **Sixth Avenue** are typical of middle-class row-house architecture of the late 1870s to mid-1880s. Most are built in the earlier Italianate or contemporary neo-Grec styles. Look for these characteristics of the *Italianate style:* high stoops with cast-iron railings, usually in the form of a baluster; round-arched doorways with double entrance doors; a pedimented entranceway supported by foliate brackets; segmental (curved) arches over windows; rusticated basements; and a roof cornice above foliate brackets. The original brownstone facing may be disguised with ill-conceived coats of paint. At first glance, the *neo-Grec style* may appear similar, but observe the curvilinear, incised ornamentation (carved by machine, rather than hand-carved as in the Italianate); triple vertical grooves on the brackets; door and window lintels with acroteria ("ears" that protrude at the ends)—all Greek elements introduced at the Ecole des Beaux Arts in Paris. The neo-Grec houses are also much more angular, having three-sided, full-height bays up to the roof, and rather massive newel posts (usually in cast iron, but occasionally in stone) at the tall stoops. It is apparent that many of the minority groups that have moved into this part of Park Slope take great pride in the appearance of their new brownstones. Sometimes, however, enthusiasm for appearance has resulted in the installation of aluminum siding, fake carriage lamps, or garish adornments.

St. Augustine's Roman Catholic Church, between Sterling and Park places, is considered one of Brooklyn's finest church buildings. Designed in 1888 by the English-born Brooklyn architects Parfitt Brothers, it was completed four years later. Built in Victorian Gothic style of a mottled sandstone, it rises dramatically above the uniform rows of houses. The interior is almost as elaborate as the exterior, with excellent stained glass and ornate sculpture work. The tall tower virtually overwhelms in its mass and detail. Spend a few minutes inside and examine the well proportioned and majestic nave.

Look east down **Sterling Place** at the large garage on the left side. Unless is has since been repainted, a 75-year-old sign is still visible above, reading "Fleetwood Stables." Before the advent of the automobile, livery stables were as common as public garages are today—the local "rent-a-horse" agency of the neighborhood. Horse owners could also board them at the livery stable, or rent an appropriate rig: a victoria, landau, brougham, or, in winter, a cutter. Sterling Place is named for Revolutionary War General William Alexander, Lord Sti*r*ling, mentioned earlier.

At this point, the walking tour enters the **Park Slope Historic District.**

Continue on Sixth Avenue to Lincoln Place.

The Sixth Avenue Baptist Church was designed in Victorian Gothic style by Laurence B. Valk. Built in 1880, this picturesque church unfortunately lost its steeple in the hurricane of 1938. Unusual is the massive main tower, its attached polygonal turret, and the cupola over the transept. The horizontal stone band courses, which contrast with the red brick façade, are typical of the style, while the buttresses with stepped sandstone shoulders add another interesting touch. Look, too, at the ornamentation on the arches above the doors and on the corbels of the main gables.

Turn left on Lincoln Place.

Named for Abraham Lincoln in 1873, **Lincoln Place** is an extension of Degraw Street, an important street at the bottom of the "slope," in the Cobble Hill section.

Lincoln Place, between Sixth and Seventh avenues, has an interesting and varied collection of row houses. **Nos. 96–110** present an engaging combination of Queen Anne and Romanesque Revival styles, while **Nos. 99–113** show delicately incised neo-Grec detailing on the doors, cornices, and window lintels, including the characteristic "ears" on the lintels. The first two have French Second Empire mansard roofs. All have two-sided bays and are two stories high. The neo-Grec style is personified across the street in **Nos. 114, 116,** and **118.** Note their cast-iron balustrades and lovely newel posts, and the attractive yard railings with spikelike motif. Back on the north side is another row of handsome neo-Grec houses, **Nos. 127–135.**

No. 139, an individual town house, was built in 1881. Observe how the treatment of the bay with its pyramidal slate roof creates the impression of a tower, balanced at the right by a third-story mansard roof. Note the sunflower designs in cut brick below the second-floor windows, and the entrance-door panels—both are typical Queen Anne features. Other little touches are the miniature Ionic capitals on the brackets below the mansard roof and the delicately designed stained-glass transom.

No. 151–155 is a massive Romanesque Revival town house with ample grounds. Now a hotel, it was built in 1886–87 by the architectural firm of Lamb & Rich as the residence of Frank L. Babbott. Typical of the Romanesque Revival style is the asymmetry of the façade. At the front, a three-sided bay at the corner, topped by a peaked roof, emphasizes the sweeping line of the whole roof. A large gable on the east side emphasizes the corner bay. The chimney rises high above a lion's head corbel at the second-story level. Note, too, the rough-cut lintel blocks above the first-floor windows, tied together below the chimney with lozenges; and the fret pattern beneath the eaves, combining brick, stone, and terra cotta. Money went to money, as they say, for Babbott's wife was a member of the Pratt family (discussed in the Clinton Hill walking tour) which made its fortune in kerosene, later merging with John D. Rockefeller's Standard Oil Company.

Turn left on Seventh Avenue.

The corner mansion, now the **Brooklyn Conservatory of Music,** was erected in 1881 as a private residence. Before becoming a music school it housed the Park Slope Masonic Club. The attractive Victorian Gothic-style house with some Queen Anne elements, built of brick, and trimmed with brownstone and terra cotta, is in an excellent state of preservation. Notice

Looking north on Seventh Avenue toward St. John's Place in 1896. To the left rises the spire of Memorial Presbyterian Church, and across the Avenue, Grace Methodist Church. Both were built in 1882 in Gothic Revival style, but Grace Church lost its steeple in the Hurricane of 1944. (Long Island Historical Society)

the decorative cast-iron crestings above the first floor of the projecting corner bay. An interesting roof line, with gable, chimney, and dormer windows tops this fine mansion.

Across Seventh Avenue is the **only complete blockfront of French Second Empire houses** in Park Slope. The row was built in 1871–72.

At the corner of St. John's Place are two Victorian Gothic churches. **Memorial Presbyterian Church,** on the southwest corner, dominates the site with its octagonal spire rising from a square tower. Considered late Victorian Gothic (1882), it was designed by the firm of Pugin & Walter. The building is constructed entirely of rough Belleville (New Jersey) sandstone, with little of the polychromy so characteristic of most Victorian Gothic structures. Quatrefoils pierce the parapet above, adding a decorative element. The adjacent **Chapel** on St. John's Place was added in 1888. A charming decorative feature is the quatrefoil with a carving of three children being comforted by an angel. Only close inspection reveals that the Chapel and Church are separate entities, so well integrated are they architecturally. A number of the stained-glass windows in the chapel and church are from the Tiffany Studios.

Before returning to the corner, walk briefly down St. John's Place, beyond the Chapel of Memorial Presbyterian Church.

Nos. 176 and **178** St. John's Place are two charming Queen Anne houses. Built for a pair of physicians in 1887–88, they present a fanciful array of gables, finials, dormer windows, Romanesque and Gothic arches, a conical roof, and even a tower. Although two separate buildings—No. 178 is wider —they blend together as a single unit. Note the caduceus in the ornate gable of No. 178, announcing to all that Edward Bunker, M.D., was in residence. A few minutes must be spent to take in all the delightful details of both houses' façades.

Across the street is the lovely **St. John's Protestant Episcopal Church**— one of the oldest in Park Slope, and built in 1869 in the style of an English country parish church. With its setback position on a grassy plot, it presents a harmonious grouping with its adjacent **Rectory** (No. 139), terminating the uniform line of row houses to the left. The Church and Rectory are fine examples of the Victorian Gothic style, and are built of rough-faced, random ashlar sandstone. The main gable includes seven narrow lancet windows, stepped over the pointed-arch doorway, and surmounted by a bell cote. The Rectory has a Gothic cast-iron porch facing the yard, and an interesting colonnette set in a chamfered recess between paired windows on the southeast corner. St. John's Place, formerly Douglass Street, was renamed in 1870 in honor of the church.

Return to Seventh Avenue.

The third member of the trio of Victorian Gothic churches is **Grace United Methodist Episcopal Church,** on the northeast corner, built from plans by the ubiquitous Parfitt Brothers in 1882. Constructed of a more vari-colored stone than its neighbor diagonally across the street, the church presents a very picturesque addition to the cityscape. A rather large window and gable face Seventh Avenue, while a large tower dominates the corner. Its graceful brownstone spire, however, fell victim to the hurricane of 1944. Look for the ornate "diaper" pattern in terra cotta around the nave's circular windows, and the foliate capitals on banded columns of the side windows.

To the left of the church, the **Parsonage and Sunday School** are an architectural transition to the row of town houses to the north. Completed five years after the Church, also from Parfitt Brothers plans, it is a rough-faced building in a late Romanesque Revival style. Interesting is the two-story bay —curve ended—with transom bars and stone mullions at both levels. Notice the stained glass in the first-floor transoms. In harmony with the turret at the Ward Mansion farther up the block, the Parsonage has a third-floor oriel on the south corner, providing visual balance to the blockfront.

The exceptionally fine row of four Romanesque Revival houses from the Parsonage to Sterling Place, **Nos. 21–27 Seventh Avenue,** were built in 1887 from designs by the architect of the Sixth Avenue Baptist Church, Laurence B. Valk. The row can best be appreciated by viewing it from the southeast corner of Sterling Place. **No. 21** was for a time the residence of opera singer Lillian Ward and, as the first house in the row, is the most handsome. Mounted on a second-floor corbel is an imposing projecting turret with a curvilinear peaked roof. Typical of the Romanesque Revival style are the contrasts in color, details, and materials, and although each house has its own particular details (as in the individual arched porches), the group gives an impression of unity. Note how the brick, brownstone, terra cotta, and slate were employed, with even some ornate wrought-iron work. Try to find the Queen Anne "sunburst" motifs on some of the little dormer window gables. The entrance to No. 21 is on Sterling Place. Its handsome arched porch has dwarf columns protecting the original doorway, with wrought-iron work highlighting the transom and sidelights, and a bizarre cast-iron animal figure serves as the newel post for the entrance to the offset stoop. Look up at the Queen Anne-style ornamental band course just below the roof, and the profusion of gables and finials in the steep, hip-shaped slate roof.

The corner of Seventh Avenue and Sterling Place was the **site of a tragic plane crash,** when on the cold, misty morning of December 16, 1960, two commercial airliners collided over Brooklyn. One of the large planes fell on Staten Island; the other, in a vain attempt to reach the open ground of

A light covering of snow blanketed the Grand Army Plaza when this picture was taken in 1898. The triumphal arch by John H. Duncan was still to be adorned by the monumental sculpture groupings by Frederick W. MacMonnies three years later. The Soldiers' and Sailors' Memorial was paid for by the citizens of Brooklyn and dedicated to the defenders of the Union in the Civil War. (Brooklyn Union Gas Company)

Prospect Park, careened into Sterling Place, the nose of the broken fuselage coming to rest against the doorstep of the Ward Mansion. A number of buildings were destroyed by the ensuing fire, including the appropriately named Pillar of Fire Church (which stood on the vacant lot on the north side of Sterling Place, just west of Seventh Avenue), an adjacent building (now a one-story funeral home), and the house that occupied the southwest corner—part of a row of 1873 residences. A large piece of the parapet of No. 116 Sterling Place was sheared off, and its replacement brick is of a noticeably different color. None of the passengers survived the crash, but astonishingly, there were no fatalities on the ground.

Cross Seventh Avenue and continue east on Sterling Place.

Just beyond the beautiful Lillian Ward Mansion is charming **No. 146,** a Queen Anne-style house designed by Laurence B. Valk in 1887, and built at the same time as his handsome Romanesque Revival row around the corner on Seventh Avenue. On the west side are three lovely chimneys; while the main entrance has a pair of unusual wrought-iron hand railings mounted on wing-walls. The distinguishing feature of the house is its asymmetry. Adjoining the arched doorway is a wide-arched parlor-floor window, Romanesque Revival style in character, divided in three sections. Above is a bay window, sheathed in sheet metal, with a pedimented central arched window. A wide dormer rises on the third story, surmounted by a gable adorned with terra-cotta tile.

The tour departs briefly from the Park Slope Historic District for a visit to Grand Army Plaza.

Continue ahead to Flatbush Avenue, turn right one block to the mall of Grand Army Plaza.

GRAND ARMY PLAZA

The enormous oval plaza was designed by Frederick Law Olmsted and Calvert Vaux (the landscape architects of Central and Prospect parks) as a grandiose approach to Prospect Park. The Plaza was designed in 1862, but the monumental arch and the accompanying groups of sculpture were not added until much later. At the time of the plan, the City of Brooklyn lay almost a mile to the north.

Enter from the north and, passing through a formal circle of sycamores, mount the terrace to see New York's only official **monument to President John F. Kennedy.** The latest addition to the Plaza, the bust is the work of sculptor Neil Estern. The monument, with its unusually placed bust, was designed by Morris Ketchum, Jr., & Associates, and was installed in 1965.

The original plan called for a marble cube with eternal flame, but was rejected as being too similar to the monument in Arlington National Cemetery.

The Bailey Fountain, built in 1932 and named for donor Frank Bailey, was designed by architect Edgerton Swarthout, with the central sculpture group by Eugene Savage. Male and female figures representing Wisdom and Felicity stand on the prow of a ship, while Neptune and his Tritons, together with a young boy grasping a cornucopia, present a humorous backdrop.

Ahead is one of the world's most magnificent triumphal arches,* **the Soldiers' and Sailors' Memorial Arch,** erected in 1892. Its prizewinning design was won by John Hemingway Duncan (the architect five years later of Grant's Tomb) who planned it as an "armature" for patriotic sculpture dedicated to the Union forces of the Civil War. Several distinguished American sculptors designed the various groups that adorn the 80-foot-high granite arch. Topping the monument is a magnificent **triumphal quadriga** in bronze by Frederick MacMonnies, depicting a female figure carrying a banner and sword, flanked by two winged figures of Victory. The south pedestals display military **groupings representing the Army** (left) **and the Navy** (right)—both by sculptor MacMonnies. (Frederick MacMonnies was a pupil of Augustus Saint Gaudens and a resident of Brooklyn.) The cornerstone of the Arch, incidentally, was laid by General William Tecumseh Sherman in 1889. The **inner bas-reliefs of Lincoln and Grant** were executed by William R. O'Donovan, and their horses by Thomas Eakins (Eakins is best known as one of the great "realist" painters of the late 19th and early 20th centuries). The width of the arch is also 80 feet, and the aperture, 50 feet, with a span of 35 feet. Unfortunately, no sculpture was designed for the north pedestals, so the only view is from the park rather than from the approach. Framing the circular plot is a necklace of stanchions. The Soldiers' and Sailors' Memorial Arch is Brooklyn's most splendid monument, and has been designated an official New York City Landmark.

Prospect Park is not within the purview of this walking tour, but should not be missed. At least a day is required for even a superficial visit. With the brief stop at the Litchfield Villa at the end of the tour, more details will be given,† including a suggested walk through the Park.

Cross Grand Army Plaza (carefully!) to Plaza Street, on the west side.

An earth mound along Plaza Street—part of Olmsted & Vaux's foresighted design for the Plaza—shields the residential street from the noise

---

* New York City has two other triumphal arches, the Washington Memorial Arch, designed by Stanford White, and erected in 1892 in Washington Square Park [for a description, *see* Greenwich Village, 4]; and Carrère & Hastings's Arch at the approach to the Manhattan Bridge, constructed in 1905.

† Information on Prospect Park, including a map and list of activities, can be obtained from the organization dedicated to its preservation and protection: the Greensward Foundation, Lenox Hill P.O. Box 610, New York, N.Y. 10021.

and congestion of traffic. **Nos. 1–5 Plaza Street,** neo-Classic-style limestone town houses built in 1901, may be considered the beginning of the former "Gold Coast." At the turn of the century, elegant mansions lined both sides of the Plaza; however, all but these four residences have been replaced by apartment houses. (The tour has now reentered the Park Slope Historic District.)

Turn right on Lincoln Place to Eighth Avenue.

The spectacular **Montauk Club** is one of Brooklyn's architectural treasures. One of the last of the many private clubs that abounded in Park Slope, the building's elegance is indicative of the affluent and influential membership. Completed in 1891 from plans by Francis H. Kimball,* it was inspired by the Cà d'Oro, a Venetian *palazzo* on the Grand Canal, whose glittering gold-painted façade was symbolic of the glory of the Italian Renaissance. The best view of the building is from the end of Plaza Street at the head

---

* Architect Kimball also designed the landmark Emmanuel Baptist Church in the Clinton Hill section of Brooklyn, the Trinity and U.S. Realty buildings on lower Broadway in Manhattan, and a number of other office buildings, theaters, and churches.

The house of Guido Plessner, designed by architect Frank Freeman, at the corner of Lincoln Place and Plaza Street c. 1900. An apartment house now occupies the site. (Long Island Historical Society)

of Lincoln Place, where two of the elaborate façades can be studied. A warm golden color is produced through the careful blending of yellow and reddish-brown bricks, brownstone, and matching terra cotta. In its *Designation Report* for the Park Slope Historic District, the Landmarks Commission emphasizes "the contrast of solids and voids" in the design for the Club. The groupings of traceried windows, the balconies and loggia, and the extravagant use of terra-cotta ornamentation engage the eye almost relentlessly. To the left of the elaborate main entrance is the separate ladies' entrance, as the Montauk Club was restricted exclusively to men. However, it was the first such club to extend the use of its facilities to women. This side entrance leads to the dining room floor, bypassing the main lobby. Above the main entrance is a band of carved Indian heads, while the spandrels between the arches depict American Indian motifs; look, too, for the little animals and birds. Above the second-floor round-arch is a frieze representing the founders and builders laying the cornerstone. (The Montauk Club is named for the tribe of Indians that inhabited most of eastern Long Island.) Above the second-floor balcony on the Plaza Street side is a relief panel illustrating the inscription: "Wyandance, Sachame of Pamanack, His Wife and Son Wiankabone Giving a Deed to Lion Gardner of Saybrook, Easthampton, Long Island, July 14, 1659." Most striking, however, is the wide terra-cotta frieze that encircles the three principal façades of the Club, presenting a continuous history of the Montauk Indians.

Spend a few minutes and examine carefully the wide variety of detail in the imaginative façade. Let the eye drift slowly upward from the ornate cast-iron fence to the soaring chimneys above, as this is truly a unique edifice, which, in its design, successfully combines European tradition with American Indian themes.

Continue south on Eighth Avenue and turn left on Berkeley Place.

Berkeley Place was renamed in 1881 for George Berkeley, an Episcopal minister and educator. It is said that many of his educational principles were adopted by King's College, later Columbia College. The original name, Sackett Street, is retained west of Fifth Avenue. The street is considered one of the finest in the "Slope."

No. 274–276, an exceptionally fine house, was built in 1890–91 by the architectural firm of Lamb & Rich for George P. Tangeman. The wealthy owner made his fortune through the Royal and Cleveland Baking Powder Companies, and his handsome residence has been much admired for its transitional quality between the Romanesque Revival style and the newly awakening neo-Classicism. At first glance the house seems to show all the characteristics of Romanesque motifs (massive rough-cut granite wall framing the open front terrace, the Roman-style brick at the second floor, the loggia-like window with columns, a large central dormer window, and the tile roof whose windows have small lights in the upper half). The roof treatment is unusual, with a Dutch step-gable effect, meeting high paneled chimneys near the top. However, on closer observation, certain Classic elements can be seen: egg-and-dart molding enframing the entranceway, the Greek anthemion motif in the frieze, Ionic capitals and shell designs in the lintel blocks, and a delicate roof cornice. To the right of the entrance is a recessed, stained-glass window.

Return to Eighth Avenue and turn left (south).

No. 52–54 Eighth Avenue, at the corner of Berkeley Place, is another attractive mansion. Originally two separate town houses, they were built in 1886 and joined together after a fire in 1914. The building is now divided into apartments. Most interesting is the quality and variety of building materials: Euclid stone at the basement and parlor floor, red brick at the upper two stories, red Spanish tile at the roof, and terra cotta for adornments. Note how the masonry is treated differently at each level: The Euclid stone is laid in rough-faced random ashlar; above the parlor floors, the stone is used to form a checkerboard design; and topping the next floor is a wide brick band of diagonal studding. At the corner of the building, the bay rises the full height of the building to a truncated, cone-shaped roof. On the Eighth Avenue side, the bay rises only two stories. Other noteworthy features are the huge chimney, the semicircular curved window, and the ornate wrought-iron work of the yard railing and the basement windows.

Nos. 64 and 66 are another pair of Parfitt Brothers houses, built in 1889 in a late Romanesque Revival style. Note how the proportions of the two houses mask the fact that No. 64 is four feet narrower than its neighbor. The stonework is excellent, providing an effective backdrop for the elaborate ornamentation. Polished granite columns at the top level support typical Romanesque Revival capitals. Both houses have L-shaped stoops with carved posts and street numbers hidden in the ornament above the doorways.

No. 70–72 is a massive Romanesque Revival mansion with some Queen Anne details, which balances the large house at the Berkeley Place end of the block. Built in 1887, it has several charming details: a Jacobean gable on the Union Street side with a brickwork design indicating the chimney flue, and a lovely corner turret with a wide band of studded brick whose design is repeated at the large gable in front of the house above the dormers. Terra-cotta ornamentation appears on the tower in sunflower panels and in the cresting of the roof ridges. Unfortunately, the wide-arched stone entrance has been filled in to accommodate a single entry door. In the early 1930s, the house was used by a bridge club and restaurant.

Make a short detour west on Union Street for a glance at the interesting rows of houses, Nos. 905–913 and 889–903. The latter dates from 1889, the former from 1895. Both display a riot of Romanesque Revival and Queen Anne details: oriels, arched windows, bull's-eye windows, crenelations, sheet-metal cornices with ball-topped spikes, dormers, gables, high pediments, and L-shaped stoops. Union Street's name reflects the national patriotic sentiment after the Civil War.

No. 860, across the street, was the carriage house for a mansion that stood at the southwest corner of Eighth Avenue until 1922. Few carriage houses exist in the neighborhood, and this small house, built originally in a Victorian Gothic style, was remodeled into a neo-Tudor residence in 1923. Its attractive leaded, four-part window is typical.

Return to Eighth Avenue and turn right to President Street. Walk down the north side of President Street.

No. 873 is one of the older houses in the neighborhood, completed in 1878. Designed as a "country villa," it has a "stick style" overhang at the front gable together with wooden supporting struts and elongated brackets. Sadly, a wood porch was removed some years ago from the east side. At the apex of the gable of this brick house is an ornate jigsaw grille. Wooden blinds once decorated the small windows under the projecting eaves. Note also the "toothed" brickwork at the parlor floor and second story.

No. 869, now the residence of the Missionary Servants of the Most Holy Trinity, was designed by architect Henry Ogden Avery for Stewart L. Woodford, ambassador to Spain, and a prominent member of the Montauk Club. The rather individualistic house was completed in 1885 and is unusually wide (36 feet). Most striking are the twin oriels at the second floor, bracketed out from the masonry wall on struts. Unusual are the three wide arches above the entrance, the wrought-iron grille and glass entrance door with Art Deco-style peacocks, and a wooden roof cornice whose outlookers are carried on brick corbels. The façade is remarkable in its simplicity and is beautifully arranged; and, although somewhat Romanesque in style, its symmetry throughout is quite atypical.

Return to Eighth Avenue.

No. 101 Eighth Avenue, on the southeast corner of President Street, is a handsome neo-Georgian style mansion built in 1909 for the president of a brewery. The stately building, set behind a wrought-iron fence with granite posts and approached by a low stoop, is a pleasant addition to elegant Eighth Avenue. Take note of the Georgian elements which give such grace to the house: the fluted Doric columns flanking the entranceway, the well detailed roof entablature, the Flemish bond brickwork, the blind limestone arches with carved swags over the windows beside the entrance, and the balustrade above the roof cornice. The building is now the home of the Unity Club, which has occupied it for more than 30 years.

To its right, **No. 105** is another imposing mansion. Built in 1912 of marble in a neo-Classic style, it was designed by architect Frank J. Helmle who is noted for the Tennis Pavilion and Boathouse on the Lullwater in Prospect Park—both designated landmarks, as well as for a number of banks.

A beautiful entablature is supported by four fluted Corinthian columns and is replete with motifs from ancient Greece, while the main entrance with its bronze and glass doors, fanlight, and imposing central arch radiates elegance.

Adjacent **Nos. 109** and **111** are also worthy of note; the former, built in 1887, is in the Queen Anne style, and the latter is a Romanesque Revival house, completed in 1892.

The entire blockfront to Carroll Street remains intact and in pristine condition. The end mansion will be discussed shortly.

Return to President Street and turn right.

Nos. 902–906 are four pleasing Queen Anne houses built in the mid-1880s. The three-sided bays are complemented by triangular pediments in which Tritons' heads and scallop shells provide the embellishment. **Nos. 908–934** are a row of 14 town houses with L-shaped stoops, erected in 1899. The angularity of the façades is reflected in the shape of the roof cornices. According to the Landmarks Commission, No. 916 was the residence of novelist Laura Jean Libbey (Mrs. Van Mater Stilwell), author of some 80 books with such romantic titles as *The Price of a Kiss; Lover Then, But Stranger Now;* and *A Fatal Wooing.* Apparently quite popular in her day, her books sold millions of copies. She died in 1924 and is buried in Green-Wood Cemetery. **Nos. 940** and **942** are another pair of interesting Queen Anne houses, built in 1886. Note the terra-cotta gable shields with the date of construction. Noteworthy are the intricate terra-cotta panels between the parlor floor and the second story and the toothed brickwork. Battered brickwork flanks the parlor-floor windows and their stained glass, and at the left side of No. 946 is an impressive tall chimney. Carl Tollefson was a noted music teacher famous for his collection of antique instruments. The house is now the Tollefson School of Music.

Turn right (south) on Prospect Park West.

Typical mansions of the "Gold Coast" are **Nos. 16 and 17 Prospect Park West.** Both were designed by Montrose W. Morris in 1899 and are representative of the "new wave" of Classical Eclecticism that began sweeping the country after its introduction at the 1893 Chicago Columbian Exposition. Architect Morris planned a number of imposing residences in Brooklyn, including Nos. 18, 19, and 22, and the soon-to-be-seen mansion occupied by the Ethical Culture Society.

Prospect Park West was called Ninth Avenue before its "elevation to elegance."

Turn right on Carroll Street.

Carroll Street was named for Charles Carroll of Maryland, a signer of the Declaration of Independence.

The block between Prospect Park West and Eighth Avenue is one of the most interesting architecturally. The north and south sides of the street are quite different in style and arrangement, and it will be necessary to zigzag back and forth to study and compare the rather unusual aggregation of houses designed by some of the best known architects in New York. (Odd-numbered houses are on the north side, even on the south.)

The house on the northwest corner **(No. 17 Prospect Park West)** has a handsome Ionic loggia on the third floor (Carroll Street side) above arched windows on the first floor. The pair of houses fronting Prospect Park West on the southwest corner (by Montrose W. Morris, 1898) were planned in neo-Italian Renaissance style. The corner residence marks the geographic high point in Park Slope with an appropriate pair of tall chimneys. A charming Palladian window emphasizes the first floor.

No. 863, with a full-height bay and unusual entablature frieze, was built in 1890 from plans by Napoleon LeBrun & Sons, architects of the Metropolitan Life Insurance Company Building and Tower on Manhattan's Madison Square, as well as many of the city's firehouses. Note the windows piercing the frieze and the lovely balustrade at the roof.

Nos. 888–880, built in 1894, are a row of late Romanesque Revival town houses. Look for the variety of window treatments: arched or flat, paired or triple. **No. 886** shows some of the Classic influence of the Columbian Exposition in its swags and dentils in the cornice; **Nos. 888, 882,** and **880** are perhaps the purest in late Romanesque Revival styling.

Adjacent **Nos. 878** and **876** were designed in 1911 by the Brooklyn firm of Chappell & Bosworth. Similar in plan except for their entrance porches and limestone bay on No. 876, they are reminiscent of the neo-Georgian style with their use of red brick and stone and their façade details. Pleasing is the modillioned roof cornice and the horizontal courses of stone at the second- and fourth-story windowsill levels.

Nos. 861–855 are a four-house row with alternate styling of each house. Built in 1892 and designed by Stanley M. Holden, they are basically Romanesque Revival with a proliferation of Italian Renaissance details. Note the polychrome effect achieved by the varying colors of the limestone, rough-cast brick, orange Roman brick, and copper and dark-red tile. The houses have alternating pyramidal and pseudo-hipped roofs, while a loggia effect is created by the columns supporting the lintels above the triple windows at the third floor on the second and fourth houses; but the dominant features are the ornamented copper oriels with tiled hip roofs at the second floor.

No. 853 is a very attractive Romanesque Revival-style house, built in 1888 by Harvey Murdoch, the developer of nearby Montgomery Place (to be discussed later). The massive structure is crowned by a peaked gable and flanked by pseudo-bartizans (small medieval castle-wall overhangs, added for defense).

No. 874, a neo-Georgian-style house built in 1904, has a pleasing Palladian window over the entranceway and a typical baluster over the roof cornice.

The five picturesque Queen Anne houses, **Nos. 864–872,** were designed in 1887 by architect William B. Tubby. Among other Tubby works in Brooklyn are the Charles Millard Pratt Residence and the Library of Pratt Institute [see Clinton Hill walking tour], as well as No. 53 Prospect Park West. The rambling quality of the roof line recalls the architectural innovations of English architect Richard Norman Shaw, who is generally credited with the so-called Queen Anne style. The fanciful profile is punctuated with gables, pseudo-hip-roofs, and dormers. Note the "eyebrow" window of No. 870 and the Flemish gable of No. 872. A typical Queen Anne feature is the treatment of the windows and bays, in which the upper sash is divided into small lights (panes). A wide selection of building materials is used for contrast: brick, tile, wood, rough-cut brownstone, and sheet metal. Note, too, the "stepping" of the party walls between the individual houses, reminiscent of the Flemish Renaissance.

No. 860 is a satisfying blend of Queen Anne and Romanesque Revival styles, contemporary with its neighbors. The twin arched windows in the tall gable and the charming hooded dormers set in the roof are delightful touches.

Nos. 858 and **856** are a lovely pair of unified town houses that combine the Romanesque Revival with a neo-Colonial style. The rough-cut brownstone basement and stoop contrast in texture and color with the upper façade's smooth, orange-colored Roman brick. Note how the first floors are treated, with paired doors and wide windows unified by their arches. The fan design in the arched lunettes above both doors and windows is typical of the Colonial style. The stained glass, however, is more appropriate to the Romanesque Revival. A garlanded sheet-metal cornice is topped by a slate roof with tall, corbeled chimneys.

No. 848 is a very narrow four-story house, most of whose façade is taken up by the two-story central bay set on fluted columns in front of the entrance. Built in 1905, it reflects the turn-of-the-century popularity of red brick and limestone trim.

Adjacent **No. 846** was completed in 1887 from plans by noted architect Charles P. H. Gilbert.* The house shows a transitional style from the late Romanesque Revival to the neo-Italian Renaissance. The stonework of the first floor—rough-hewn and light in color—and the large, arched doorway are associated with the Romanesque Revival style, as is the general asymmetry of the façade; while the treatment of the upper windows and roof cornice foretells the awakening popularity of the Italian Renaissance style.

---

* Charles P. H. Gilbert is best known for his designs for many of the finest residences in the city (the Warburg Mansion, now the Jewish Museum; the DeLamar Mansion, formerly the National Democratic Club, now the Polish Consulate General; the Burden House, now the Marymount School; plus most of the town houses on neighboring Montgomery Place).

Within a few years, such architectural firms as McKim, Mead & White would raise the style to its zenith. Note the unusual overhang at the roof cornice, with projecting rafters whose brackets end in carved animal heads.

Nos. 842 and **838** are by architect C. P. H. Gilbert, and built in 1887. Both are in the late Romanesque Revival style and are particularly fine houses. The latter has an interesting V motif in the arch over the entranceway and a curved bay at the second story. More imposing is No. 838, built for James H. Remington, a president of the United States Law Association and a distinguished member of the Montauk Club. The two houses display the usual Romanesque Revival asymmetry, but the corner tower of 838 with its conical slate roof is its prime attraction. Notice the composition formed by the arched doorway and its adjacent window, surmounted by a three-sided bay, which is in turn topped by four arched windows, the whole being crowned by a triple-window dormer with a highly ornate peaked gable and finials. (There is no No. 840—it was skipped in the street numbering system.)

Across the street, **Nos. 817–831** are an eight-house row in Romanesque Revival style, built in 1896. Contrast the shallow, two-story bays in the middle, with the polygonal bays of the pairs at each end. Look, too, for the typical Romanesque Revival ornamentation on the stoops and parlor floors.

No. 813–803 is officially designated 115–119 Eighth Avenue, and is known as the **Thomas Adams, Jr. Residence.** Designed by the ubiquitous C. P. H. Gilbert in 1888, it is considered the finest example of Romanesque Revival-style residential architecture in the city! This grand double house was the home for a number of years of the Adams Chewing Gum king, whose factory is still a well known landmark in Long Island City. Most striking is the overall use and variety of the masonry: sandstone, terra cotta, and salmon-colored brick—the smooth brick contrasting in texture with the rough-cut brownstone base. Dominating the Carroll Street façade is a massive and deep entrance arch with a swirling leaf pattern carving. Above the arch is a complementary trio of windows, enframed by the same foliate pattern, and supported on columns whose capitals have the Romanesque basket-weave design. Incidentally, note the clustered dwarf columns that support the elaborate entrance arch. The leaf design is again repeated in the peak of the gable. The huge corner tower, which is round at the first level, is polygonal above and rises to a tall, octagonal tile roof. Notice the quite beautiful stained glass in the first-floor transom bars and in the transoms above. Walking around the corner, the Eighth Avenue façade is also dominated by the corner tower, and is balanced by the two-story curved bay to the left, and the entrance arch is duplicated by a window arch to the right. Another member of the Adams family lived in this half of the house; while later, relatives of the F. W. Woolworth family occupied the other. However, the day of the single-family mansion is past, a victim of the harsh realities of economics, and the Adams Residence has been subdivided into apartments.

Across Carroll Street, on the southeast corner of Eighth Avenue, **No. 123** is another Montrose W. Morris-designed residence. Built in a restrained neo-

Classical style, its soft, off-white appearance is extremely handsome. Brick, limestone, and terra cotta, all of similar color, combine to create this mono-chromatic effect. The entrance is especially attractive with its arched tympa-num above, displaying a variety of Renaissance motifs on composite columns. The anthemion designs on the long frieze below it are repeated around the building to the Carroll Street side. "Ears" can be seen on the corners of the attic story windows, while the roof cornice displays a lovely garland motif on its convex frieze.

Cross Eighth Avenue and continue west on Carroll Street.

In the distance, the 212-foot-high spire of the **Old First Reformed Church** punctuates the skyline. The Reformed Church is the descendant of the old Dutch Reformed Church, the first religious body in America. The church, located at the corner of Seventh Avenue, was designed in 1892 by George L. Morse.

Turn left into Fiske Place.

Charming little **Fiske Place** and its equally diminutive neighbor to the west, Polhemus Place, re-create much of the late 19th-century residential atmosphere of Brooklyn. Ignoring the apartment houses on the east side of the block (whose only merit is the pleasant view for its tenants), the small scale of the row houses across the street is quite appropriate for this short block.

Nos. 12–16 form a symmetrical group of late Romanesque Revival houses that date from the middle of the last decade of the 19th century. The second-floor bays of this trio resemble an exercise in geometry with their squared, semicircular, and triangular gables; otherwise their composition is basically unified. Back-to-back on Polhemus Place are a complementing trio of houses with identical façades.

Nos. 18–20, a dissimilar pair of town houses, were designed in 1889–90 by the architectural firm of Parfitt Brothers. In common they share Roman-esque Revival and neo-Italian Renaissance elements, but the differences in detail are clearly evident, and No. 20 is much more Renaissance in style.

The two neo-Grec-style apartment houses, **Nos. 22** and **24,** were built in 1888, and designed as "twins." Note their side-by-side arched doorways, three-sided bays rising full height, heavily bracketed roof cornices, and the still-intact cast-iron railings and newel posts.

Turn left into Garfield Place.

Originally called Macomb Street, the name was changed to honor the 20th president of the United States, James A. Garfield, two years after his assassination.

Nos. 248–256 Garfield Place are another attractive row of Romanesque

The Charles L. Feltman Mansion, which stood on the southwest corner of Eighth Avenue and Carroll Street until 1950, when it gave way to an apartment house. Feltman is credited with having invented the "hot dog" at his popular beer garden in Coney Island. (Brooklyn Collection. Brooklyn Public Library)

Revival houses, each 20 feet wide, with alternating building designs (in a pattern "ABABA"). The "A" houses have full-height polygonal bays, while the "B" houses have only two-story bays, above which is a third-floor balcony with Palladian window. Compare the treatment of the doors and windows of the two types.

Across the street, on the north side, are three **eight-family apartment houses,** typical of the kind erected in many sections of the city, including the Park Slope area, during the first decade of the 20th century. Built in 1903 in the then-popular neo-Italian Renaissance style, they bear rather fanciful and enigmatic names: *Serine, Lillian,* and *Ontrinue.* (*Ontrinue?* Could the builder have possibly meant *Entre Nous?*)

Temple Beth Elohim ("House of God") is an impressive eclectic structure with many classic elements. Built in 1909–10, the synagogue was designed by Simon Eisendrath in association with B. Horwitz. Since the main entrance is at the corner of the building, the plan is pentagonal, possibly representative of the Five Books of Moses. A pair of enormous Ionic columns *in antis* flank the three-sided stairway, and are surmounted by an arched pediment with modillions, while a large dome with lantern on a polygonal drum is set above the entrance. On a pipe railing on both sides of the temple are seven-branched Menorah, or candelabrum, motifs.

Turn left on Eighth Avenue.

The apartment house numbered **140,** on the west side of Eighth Avenue, has an Art Deco entrance located in a recessed central section. Art Deco motifs appeared in great profusion on apartment houses and commercial buildings from the last few years of the 1920s till World War II. The adjacent building, **No. 130,** occupies the site of the old Feltman Mansion. Charles L. Feltman is credited with introducing the "hot dog" to the American scene at his famous beer garden in Coney Island. His opulent Romanesque Revival residence was designed by Montrose W. Morris, and dominated the corner lot until demolished to make way for the apartment house. An adjacent spacious garden is now the site of No. 140.

Turn right into Montgomery Place.

Montgomery Place, Park Slope's "Block Beautiful," is named for Revolutionary War general Richard Montgomery, who was killed in the abortive Battle of Quebec in 1775. The one-block street was developed as a single

The northeast corner of Eighth Avenue and Carroll Street was the site of the J. H. Hannan House, designed c. 1888 by C. P. H. Gilbert and built shortly before this heliotype was made. Another Gilbert-designed mansion, the Adams House, still stands across the street, while the fourth corner boasts an elegant house by Montrose W. Morris. (Long Island Historical Society)

real-estate venture by Harvey Murdoch between 1887 and 1892. According to the *AIA Guide to New York City,* Murdoch wished "to create row houses that broke away from the traditional disciplined and repetitive approach." He commissioned C. P. H. Gilbert to design 20 of the 46 houses on the street, and the visitor may judge for himself how eminently successful the master plan was.

The following houses were designed by Gilbert: (north side) 11, 17, 19, 21, and 25; (south side) 14, 16, 18, 36, 38, 40, 42, 44, 46, 48, 50, 54, 56, 58, and 60. Harvey Murdoch himself resided at No. 11, the house with the impressive Dutch stepped-gable. By now, the various architectural revival styles popular in Park Slope should be fairly familiar. Since space does not permit a building-by-building description, and the amount of time required to read it would render it impractical at this hour of the tour, the visitor should take a leisurely walk down this block, examining and comparing for himself each of the lovely houses, for nowhere else in the neighborhood is there such a picturesque assemblage of residential architecture so rich and so varied in detail and ornamentation. Don't miss a single oriel, arched window, step gable, bay window, L-shaped stoop, stained-glass transom, triangular pediment, corbel-sill, copper dormer, slate roof, or panel of ornamental brickwork.

Millionaire industrialist Henry C. Hulbert commissioned this splendid house at 49 Prospect Park West by Montrose W. Morris in 1892. When built, it commanded an unobstructed view of the harbor. The Ethical Culture Society has occupied it since 1928. (Long Island Historical Society)

Cross to the Prospect Park side of Prospect Park West.

The row of stately mansions along Prospect Park West can best be appreciated from across the street. **No. 22,** just north of the corner, was designed by Montrose W. Morris in neo-Classical style in 1899. Built of limestone with a bright-red, steep tile roof, it is an attractive, symmetrical building. **Nos. 24** and **25** also have red tile roofs, but share a façade of yellow Roman brick with limestone trim. Interesting is the frieze at the second-floor cornice of 24, with the typical Greek anthemion and palmette design, and the polygonal tower of 25, topped by a steep tile roof.

At the southwest corner of Montgomery Place stands a magnificent mansion, **No. 28,** built in 1901, and designed by Charles Brigham of Boston. Rising above smooth walls is a fanciful roof line with steep gables. Look for the fascinating sculpture work in the Indiana limestone walls: stone relief panels, bizarre human masks, grotesque animals, and finials in the shape of heraldic animals. The central gable is flanked by tall masonry chimneys as well as a pair of Flemish dormers. Note, too, the copper finial on the high dormer window to the left of the gable. Above the recessed doorway is a balcony with ornamental panels and rampant lions.

No. 32, designed in Romanesque Revival style by George W. Chappell in 1888, is approached by an imposing L-shaped stoop leading to a highly ornate entranceway. The color of the Belleville (New Jersey) rough-cut brownstone blends harmoniously with the brickwork on the upper floors. Observe how the coping, with its keystone motif, rises to form a finial, while the steep brick gable with its pair of arched windows and little slot window is highlighted by the upsweep of the stone coping.

Continue south, past First Street, the site of the old Port Road to Gowanus.

Montrose W. Morris's Park Slope masterpiece is the **Henry Carlton Hulbert Mansion** at 49 Prospect Park West. Built in 1892 for the millionaire-industrialist, it is now the Brooklyn Ethical Culture School, and one of the finest examples of residential architecture in the city. Hulbert was a paper-supply magnate and member of the board of a number of large corporations, including the Pullman Palace Car Company of Chicago and the New York Life Insurance & Trust Company. The massive fortresslike edifice is reminiscent of the work of architect Henry Hobson Richardson, one of the greatest exponents of the Romanesque Revival style. In its *Designation Report* for the Park Slope Historic District, the Landmarks Commission, in its description of the building states that "one of the most dramatic features of the mansion is its picturesque castellated profile at the skyline created by the penetration of the roofline by bays, towers, gables, dormer windows, and tall chimneys arranged in vertical clusters representing the flues within." The freestanding, light-gray limestone mansion was originally two separate houses, the larger one at the corner, the residence of Henry C. Hulbert, and the somewhat smaller one to the south, built for his daughter and son-in-law (a practice not uncommon in those days). Although apparently equal in size, they are not quite, as "papa," of course, had to have the more imposing house. The tower on the north house is much more striking because of its polygonal shape on the upper floors. The south tower is designed in just the opposite manner, polygonal below, and round above! Unifying the pair, however, is a splendid entranceway with twin arches over the doors, "so beautifully joined by a single robust column," according to the *Designation Report,* "that they form a point of focus for the front." The houses also share a common entrance staircase and a third-floor loggia. Ornamentation is also used very effectively on the façade, combining Romanesque and Byzantine motifs to provide a pleasing contrast with the rugged walls. Lovely also are the rich carvings on the third-floor loggia enframement. To the rear, a second-floor porch was erected for a panoramic view of the harbor—a vista now totally obliterated by the adjacent houses. (When built, the mansion stood in "splendid isolation" at the crest of the "Slope.") The Ethical Culture Society has maintained the building in pristine condition since its acquisition in 1928.

The adjacent mansion, **No. 53,** which now serves as the **Meeting House of the Brooklyn Ethical Culture Society,** was designed in 1900 by the noted architect William B. Tubby. The beautiful residence, whose broad entranceway is flanked by heraldic lions, was built for William H. Childs, founder of the Bon-Ami Cleansing Powder Company. The symmetrical red-brick street façade is topped by a stepped, curved gable. Contrasting with the white limestone bay window enframements and gargoyles are the red tile roof and the bright red Flemish-bond brickwork wall. Pilasters flank the front door and arched window, adding to the symmetry of the house. Above is a wide bay window surmounted by a stone balustrade in front of handsome enframed windows on the third floor. Higher in the gable, these windows are connected to an upper window by a panel, carved medallion, and a drip molding. To crown the composition, a finial adorns the top. Twin tall chimneys and a steep step-gable dominate the south façade. A balustraded wing was added by the architect in 1907 to house a sunlit morning room with basement billiard room below. The spacious garden, which lends so much charm to the mansion's setting, is surrounded by an attractive wrought-iron railing set in brick piers. The Childs Mansion is a fine example of the rather scarce neo-Jacobean style in New York City.

No. 61, whose main entrance is on 2nd Street, was also designed by William B. Tubby. A brick house with a tile roof and striking projecting copper cornice, it presents quite a contrast with Tubby's Childs Mansion across the street. Built for Childs's married daughter, it is separated from "papa" (perhaps intentionally) by 2nd street, and is also quite different in design. The architect employed the briefly popular North Italian provincial style, adding many interesting touches, such as the English crossband brick walls, the horizontal stone band courses and panels at the upper level, shallow bay windows, and the cornice brackets.

Between 4th and 5th streets, enter Prospect Park on the roadway leading to the Litchfield Villa.

Built almost a decade before the development of Prospect Park, this delightful Tuscan manor house and surrounding estate was the residence of lawyer and railroad magnate Edwin C. Litchfield. Designed in 1857 by Alexander Jackson Davis,* one of the greatest architects of the mid-19th century, it is the oldest mansion in Park Slope, and its survival (relatively) intact is a tribute to the aesthetic sensibilities of the municipal authorities of the old City of Brooklyn. Originally called "Ridgewood" and later "Grace Hill Mansion," the richly furnished villa was the center of social life of Brooklyn's high society shortly after the Civil War. The extensive grounds

---

* Alexander Jackson Davis is noted chiefly for his Greek Revival-style buildings, some remarkable examples of which still survive: the old Custom House, now Federal Hall National Memorial (designed in cooperation with Ithiel Town) and Colonnade Row, on Lafayette Street; as well as the charming Nos. 3 and 4 Gramercy Park—all described in other walking tours. He also designed Jay Gould's palatial Lyndhurst, in Tarrytown— a magnificent mansion with all its furnishings in a charming rural setting, operated by the National Trust for Historic Preservation, and open to the public.

Brooklyn south of Park Slope in the early 1860s was flat farmland with scarcely a house to be seen. Ten years later, Olmsted and Vaux's Prospect Park plan completely transformed the scene. (Brooklyn Union Gas Company)

The Battle Pass (now in Prospect Park) from a sketch made in 1791, where the Colonial Army failed to halt the advance of English and Hessian troops during the Battle of Long Island. (Long Island Historical Society)

included virtually all of today's Park Slope neighborhood, from 1st to 9th streets and all the land in between down to the Gowanus Canal. Not only did Litchfield make his fortune in Midwestern railroad development, but his Brooklyn Development Company undertook the draining of the swampland at the foot of the "Slope" and the construction of the Gowanus Canal. The Canal is still one of the city's important commercial waterways. Litchfield lived in the villa until 1882, having sold part of his estate to the City of Brooklyn for the development of Prospect Park. A year later it became the headquarters of the Brooklyn Parks Department, and is still the Brooklyn office of the Parks, Recreation & Cultural Affairs Department. The Litchfield Mansion, or Villa, is considered the finest example of Alexander Jackson Davis's Italianate style. Time and Parks Department use have taken toll of some of the building's accouterments. Of the rich household furnishings, nothing whatever remains. Only the double stairway of cast iron, the central rotunda, and a few carved mantelpieces survive. The original stucco, simulating rough-cut stone, on the exterior walls has been removed, exposing the bare brickwork beneath. Unique decorative elements that have survived, however, are the corn and wheat motifs, instead of the traditional acanthus leaves, on the Corinthian capitals. The mansion also retains its lovely frieze and cornice, and displays a delightfully romantic aggregation of towers, turrets, balconies, bay windows, and porches. In recognition of its historic significance and architectural merit, the Litchfield Villa has been designated an official landmark by the New York City Landmarks Preservation Commission.

To the rear of the villa is the handsome **Annex,** designed in an architecturally harmonious style in 1911 by Helmle & Huberty, and completed two years later.

Prospect Park, which rivals Manhattan's Central Park as the city's most beautiful park, contains 562 acres of scenic woodland, broad meadows, picturesque bluffs, exquisite plantings, several ponds, and a lake, together with extensive playing fields and recreational facilities, a zoo, a number of Classic buildings, a Quaker burial ground, and a Dutch Colonial farmhouse. The land for the Park was acquired by the City of Brooklyn beginning in 1859, with landscape architects Frederick Law Olmsted and Calvert Vaux selected to draw the plans. (Brooklyn, at the time, was the nation's third largest city.) Much of the credit for the Park's creation is due to a 24-year crusade by Parks Commissioner James S. T. Stranahan, whose statue (by sculptor Frederick MacMonnies) can be seen near the Grand Army Plaza entrance. An earlier design, known as the Viele Plan, was rejected by Olmsted and Stranahan to avoid the bisecting of the park by Flatbush Avenue; instead, land to the west was acquired for the present layout. Much of the former land to the east was subsequently used for the Brooklyn Botanic Garden, the landmark Brooklyn Museum, and the Main Branch of the Brooklyn Public Library— all suitable companions to this magnificent natural oasis. With the acceptance of the Olmsted & Vaux *Design for Prospect Park* of 1866–67, the park project gradually took shape, culminating with the monumental approach of the Grand Army Plaza in the 1890s. The Park is now a Scenic Landmark.

Those wishing to return to the Plaza through the Park can follow the paths along the West Drive. A station of the IRT subway is located at Grand Army Plaza; or, for further views of Park Slope's "Gold Coast," continue south on Prospect Park West to 14th Street, the lower end of the Park Slope Historic District. The nearest subway station is the IND F line at Seventh Avenue and 9th Street.

FORT GREENE

18. Fort Greene

[*IND B and D lines, BMT, RR, N, and QB lines to DeKalb Avenue station*]

The tour begins at DeKalb Avenue and Flatbush Avenue Extension, northeast corner (in Brooklyn).

Flatbush Avenue Extension is a major connecting artery between Canal Street in Manhattan (via the Manhattan Bridge) and the downtown and central part of Brooklyn. Before the construction of the Brooklyn-Battery Tunnel and the network of expressways, Flatbush Avenue Extension was the busiest link between the two boroughs and one of the most heavily traveled streets in the world. Beneath the roadway is the DeKalb Avenue subway station, considered the busiest in the city transit system—particularly at rush hours—as so many lines to Manhattan converge at this station.

1. Long Island University's Main Building, at 385 Flatbush Avenue Extension, was originally the famous **Brooklyn Paramount Theater.** Built in 1928, it was one of the country's grandest movie palaces, and Brooklyn's No. 1 showplace for 34 years. When LIU saved it from demolition, the theater and office tower were converted to school use in two major steps. The tower, which housed the offices of many theatrical agents, was redesigned in 1950 for classrooms and administrative offices; and when the theater closed in 1962, the auditorium was rebuilt as a gymnasium and named Founders' Hall. The heavily ornate ceiling, balcony, and statuary are preserved intact, as are several thousand red-plush orchestra seats, which surround the new basketball court. The "mighty Wurlitzer"—second only in size and sound to the Radio City Music Hall organ—is still in use, restored to its original beauty and adding excitement to home basketball games.

When the neighborhood began to decline in the 1950s and '60s and threatened to become a seedy, decaying backwater, the city and local community leaders worked together on a plan for the **Central Brooklyn Urban Renewal Project.** Evidence of its success can be seen in the extensive building boom still in progress. To the southeast of the LIU campus a new commercial district has arisen from the urban blight of slums and abandoned factories, in many ways a tribute to the University's confidence in the neighborhood. Phoenix-like, the spanking new New York Telephone and Con Edison buildings have recently been completed, the latter on the site of Fabian's Fox Theater, another of the old vaudeville and movie palaces. Barton's Candy Company and other smaller firms, plus a new housing project, have emerged to bring jobs and vitality to this underdeveloped area.

Walk east on DeKalb Avenue one block to Hudson Avenue.

2. During the Revolutionary War this was the site of the **Oblong Redoubt,** one of a series of forts and entrenchments that extended across Brooklyn from Gowanus to nearby Fort Putnam (now Fort Greene). The Battle of Brooklyn, which took place in the last week of August 1776, not far from these battlements, was the first major engagement of the War. Outnumbered and outflanked by superior British and Hessian forces, General Washington's Continental Army was forced to withdraw across the East River to Manhattan from Brooklyn Heights, about a mile-and-a-half to the west. Brooklyn was to remain in British hands until the end of the war.

3. On the corner of Rockwell Place is the over one-hundred-year-old **Goldner Building.** The "stars" on the walls are braces at the end of iron tie-

The Terrace and former Prison Ship Martyrs' Monument in Fort Greene Park before its replacement in 1908 by Stanford White's marble shaft. The landscaping for the Park was designed by Olmsted & Vaux who also planned Central and Prospect parks. (Long Island Historical Society)

rods, used to reinforce the masonry and literally hold the building together. The star was a favorite motif for tie-rod braces in the 1860s and '70s. (In the Fulton Fish Market in lower Manhattan, one can even see tie-rod braces in the shape of star*fish*.) The **Benziger Brothers Building** on the opposite side of the street is another Civil War-era commercial structure, and is reminiscent of the architecture of San Francisco's Ghiradelli Square. The firm is still in business making Catholic religious articles.

At the corner of St. Felix Street, note the old stables.

4. The Brooklyn Hospital, built in 1920 with additions and alterations in 1967, occupies the site of Brooklyn's first hospital. The original hospital was established through the efforts of Cyrus Smith, who, as mayor of Brooklyn, in 1839 started a vigorous campaign for a public hospital, only to receive a token $200 appropriation from the Board of Aldermen. He then contributed one of his own houses for the project, funding it himself. (Brooklyn was an independent city until 1898.)

5. Brooklyn Technical High School, at the corner of Fort Greene Place, is one of the city's special schools, dedicated to pre-engineering training. Brooklyn Tech has always been considered one of the city's "better" schools. The antenna on the roof broadcasts the signal of Radio Station WNYC, New York City's own municipal radio voice (830 Khz AM, 93.9 FM). The transmitter also broadcasts school programs on the educational FM station WNYE (95.5).

6. Fort Greene Park, with its commanding views of downtown Brooklyn and the Manhattan skyline, was the site of previously mentioned Fort Putnam during the Revolutionary War. When the War of 1812 brought the panic of another British invasion, the hill was fortified again and renamed Fort Greene (after Revolutionary War General Nathanael Greene). In 1868 landscape architects Frederick Law Olmsted and Calvert Vaux combined their talents to convert the 30 acres of hill and old fort into elegant Washington Park. In the early 20th century the name was changed to Fort Greene Park. (Olmsted & Vaux made their greatest contribution to the beauty of the city with their designs for Manhattan's Central Park and Brooklyn's Prospect Park.)

Enter the Park and follow the path (which appears as an extension of Fort Greene Place) along the western perimeter, as far as Myrtle Avenue.

At the crest of the hill, the distant twin spires of the **Church of St. Michael & St. Edward** can be seen among the 38 acres of towers of the Fort Greene Houses, the city's first postwar low-income housing project. The Church, built in French Renaissance style in 1890, has a new altar in which sections of steel girders from the recently demolished Myrtle Avenue El are incorporated into the design. Near the base of the hill, immediately to the left of the fence, is the **site of the former Raymond Street Jail,** a dismal gray fortress that was Brooklyn's answer to Manhattan's old "Tombs." Some of

The fortress-like Raymond Street Jail, Brooklyn's own "Tombs," stood alongside Fort Greene Park until it was demolished in the early 1960s. When it neared completion in 1880, it was discovered that an entranceway had not been designed, and a consequent rapid revision of the building plan had to be made. (Long Island Historical Society)

the prison's "no trespassing" signs are still visible. A bizarre sidelight to the history of the late and unlamented prison was the discovery when the building was almost completed in 1880 that there was no front entrance! This rather serious oversight was blamed on both the architect and the Brooklyn Board of Supervisors.

Turn right on Myrtle Avenue to the main entrance to the Park, then re-enter the Park and follow the path to the broad stairway leading up to the Monument. Climb to the top.

THE PRISON SHIP MARTYRS' MONUMENT

7. In 1780, at the height of the Revolutionary War, the British Navy anchored a flotilla of some 12 decrepit ex-men-of-war and hospital ships in Wallabout Bay (near the site of the present Navy Yard), and converted them into floating prisons for captured American seamen. They hoped that the unpleasant conditions aboard the crowded, filthy, and disease-ridden hulks would induce the captives to enlist in His Majesty's Navy. Few did, however, and the tale of privation and ultimate death of between 11,500 and

12,500 prisoners—no one will ever know for sure how many—is one of the most sorrowful events in American history. The worst of the prison ships was the H.M.S. *Jersey,* a decommissioned ship of the line, on which 1100 men were jammed together between decks in unspeakable conditions. About a dozen died each night from a variety of causes—dysentery, typhoid, small pox, yellow fever, food poisoning, starvation, and flogging. At the end of the war in 1783, there were from the whole prison fleet only 1400 sick and emaciated survivors.

At the cry each morning of "Rebels, turn out your dead!" the bodies were hauled up on deck, lowered into boats, rowed ashore, and buried in shallow graves. There the bleaching bones remained until 1808 when as much of the remains as could be recovered were unearthed and reburied on the nearby John Jackson estate. The task was performed by the Columbian Order, a patriotic society that was later to become the political Tammany Society. As for the *Jersey,* it wallowed at anchor for several years, slowly rotting away until it desintegrated and slipped beneath the waters of the bay.

Thirty-six years later, a monument to these martyrs was erected; and in 1873, the remains were transferred to a crypt under the stairway of a new monument on the present site. (On June 17, 1973, a brief public ceremony was conducted by the City commemorating the 100th anniversary of this interment.)

The British prison ship Jersey, *in an old engraving. About 12,000 American prisoners died of disease and maltreatment aboard this and 11 other prison ships anchored in Wallabout Bay. (Long Island Historical Society)*

The first Prison Ship Martyrs' Monument, built in 1844 near Hudson Avenue. (Long Island Historical Society)

When the first Martyrs' Monument (left, below) fell into decay, its state of collapse was noted by an artist for a contemporary news magazine. In the rather grisly engraving above, coffins containing the heroes' skeletons, and labelled with the names of the 13 original states, are heaped in rows in the neglected tomb. The present, more permanent crypt was built in 1873. (Long Island Historical Society)

On a cold, wet November 18 in 1908, President William Howard Taft dedicated the newest Prison Ship Martyrs' Monument. Designed by noted architect Stanford White on a 220-foot-square plaza at the top of the stairway, it consists of a simple granite shaft, topped by a large brazier, or lantern. Measuring 148 feet 8 inches, it is the tallest Doric column in the world. The bronze brazier was executed by sculptor A. A. Weinman. The base of the fluted column consists of a double platform, or stylobate, with entrances on the north and south sides (now closed). The actual entrance to the crypt (also no longer open to visitors) is located two flights below, at the first landing. The entrance is so unobtrusive that it is usually unnoticed in ascending the stairs. A planned electric elevator for the Monument was never installed, although for many years visitors were permitted to climb the interior stairway to the upper platform. In the original plans, a gas flame was to burn perpetually in the lantern. Granite standards at each corner of the plaza have

A heavy snowfall covers Fort Greene Park in this Brooklyn Eagle *photograph taken the morning of December 26, 1926. The new Martyrs' Monument rises solemnly at the top of the hill. (Brooklyn Collection. Brooklyn Public Library)*

disappeared, and the entire monument suffers from abuse and neglect . . . a parallel perhaps to the sufferings of the martyrs, but wholly inappropriate to their memory. Significantly, this was Stanford White's last commission. He was shot and killed a year-and-a-half before the monument's dedication. [*see* Madison Square, 11].

Follow the path leading down from the east end of the plaza.

Just beyond the Monument is a small white marble building designed by McKim, Mead & White as a public comfort station. The diminutive Doric "temple" has been referred to as "the most elegant outhouse in the world"!

Arriving again at DeKalb Avenue, turn left to the corner of the Park and Cumberland Street, and left again into Washington Park (the continuation of Cumberland Street facing Fort Greene Park).

8. **Washington Park** was the most fashionable street in the Fort Greene section in the 1870s and '80s, when many of the affluent residents of nearby, exclusive Clinton Hill found the newly created Olmsted & Vaux park very attractive. The row of old brownstone mansions is now but a shadow of its

former opulence. All have been carved up into small apartments, and some are now rooming houses. Here and there one does see evidence of pride of ownership, so perhaps all is not lost.

Return to DeKalb Avenue, turn right past South Oxford Street to South Portland Avenue.

9. The splendid rows of Anglo-Italianate brownstones along shady **South Portland Avenue** are typical of residential construction that became immensely popular throughout the city in the mid-19th century. Brooklyn by the 1870s had become the bastion of the brownstone row house in such neighborhoods as Brooklyn Heights, Cobble Hill, Bedford-Stuyvesant, Park Slope, Clinton Hill, and Fort Greene.

The characteristics of the style are evident in the tall stoop with cast-iron balustrades; elegant entranceway surmounted by a protruding arched pediment, supported by consoles decorated with acanthus-leaf motifs; recessed portico with round-arch double entrance doors; stone-enframed windows, usually topped by curved lintels; and an elaborate cornice supported by console brackets with the familiar acanthus-leaf design. The houses were generally four stories high above a raised basement. The front masonry bearing wall was faced with chocolate-colored sandstone, quarried in Connecticut or New Jersey. The windows on the first, or parlor, floor were almost as high as the room itself, and like all the windows, were double-hung (plate glass had become much less expensive by mid-century). Most brownstones were owned by merchants or professionals. One of the early row-house builders was Walt Whitman, editor for a time of the *Brooklyn Eagle*.

The influence of fashionable London streets can be seen in the names of so many of Fort Greene's thoroughfares: Oxford, Adelphi, Carlton, Cumberland, and Waverly. South Portland Avenue was named for once-elegant Portland Place. Other nearby avenues honor such Revolutionary War generals as Washington, Greene, DeKalb, Willoughby, Gates, and Lafayette.

With shifting populations in the 1940s and '50s, the Fort Greene neighborhood began to decline, succumbing rapidly to the effects of urban disintegration and decay. All seemed lost until the mid-1960s when a last-minute miracle occurred. A revolution broke out!—a "brownstone revolution"—which was to sweep not only Fort Greene, but virtually all the brownstone neighborhoods in Brooklyn and Manhattan as well. Armies of the middle class, beset by a growing shortage of family living space, began buying up the deteriorating row houses, which were available at bargain prices, and painstakingly renovating and restoring them to their former beauty. These new "brownstoners," banding together in brownstone-revival organizations, pooled their knowledge and experience, and set to work using every spare minute (and dollar) to restore the once-elegant houses. Paradoxically, the recent quick decline of the neighborhood spared the row houses the effects of gradual "modernization" and great numbers of Fort Greene's brownstones survive in virtually pristine architectural condition. Explore the street, noting the harmonious, uniform cornice lines of the row houses, and the effect of depth created by the block-long repetition of balustrades, entranceways, and windows. The beauty of a brownstone row can best be appreciated when viewed at an angle, rather than *en face*.

Turn left at Lafayette Avenue, and left again at South Oxford Street.

10. Although lacking some of the quality of South Portland Avenue—mostly because of fewer trees—**South Oxford Street** presents a varied panorama of architectural styles used in row-house construction. It was not unusual for an owner to add a French Second Empire mansard roof, providing an extra attic bedroom or two. The sloping mansard roof, with its dormer windows and iron cresting, is not an unpleasant addition to the Anglo-Italianate brownstone.

The Lafayette Avenue Presbyterian Church, designed in 1860 by J. C. Wells, boasts one of the finest collections of Tiffany stained glass windows. Pulitzer Prize-winning poet Marianne Moore was one of the church's most celebrated and devoted parishioners. The 200-foot steeple had to be dismantled when the IND subway construction threatened to topple it. (Long Island Historical Society)

The Roanoke (No. 69), built in the early 1890s, was one of the City of Brooklyn's first luxury apartment houses.

11. The Lafayette Avenue Presbyterian Church was designed in 1860 in a modified Gothic Revival style by Joseph C. Wells (architect Wells was also responsible for the Church of the Pilgrims, in Brooklyn Heights, and the First Presbyterian Church, on Manhattan's Fifth Avenue). The sanctuary of the Church boasts a magnificent set of Tiffany art-glass windows. All but one of the upper windows and half of the lower were made in the Tiffany Studios in 1890. In the Underwood Chapel, the large stained-glass window, installed in 1920, was the last to be produced by the firm. A towering 200-foot steeple had to be removed when blasting for the new IND Subway line beneath Lafayette Avenue threatened to topple it.

One of the Church's most celebrated and devoted parishioners in modern times was Pulitzer prize-winning poet Marianne Moore (1887–1972), a long-time resident on nearby Cumberland Street.

Visitors are welcome at 10:45 any Sunday morning.

At this point there are two alternatives:

(1) The walking tour of Fort Greene may be completed by following the remaining itinerary below, or

(2) the final portion of the Fort Greene tour may be skipped (or returned to later), and a tour made of neighboring **Clinton Hill,** by turning east (left) on Lafayette Avenue to the corner of Clermont Avenue [*see* map].

To complete the Fort Greene walking tour, continue south on South Oxford Street to Hanson Place and turn right (west).

Fulton Street is the borough's oldest thoroughfare. During the Colonial and Revolutionary periods it was known as the King's Highway (not to be confused with the present Kings Highway in Central Brooklyn), and later as the Old Ferry Road. Connecting with the first ferry to the island of Manhattan, its name was changed to honor Robert Fulton, whose steam ferry *Nassau* began regular service in 1814, opening the town of Brooklyn to an era of growth and development.

12. The Hanson Place Seventh Day Adventist Church (No. 88), a designated New York City Landmark, was built in 1857–60 as the Hanson Place Baptist Church. A pleasant combination of Greek Revival and Italianate styles, the imposing, gleaming-white church building complements the surrounding neighborhood, which despite some urban blight, still retains a good deal of its mid-19th-century charm. The dominant features of the church building are the portico with its tall Corinthian columns and pilasters, a large pediment set on a cornice supported by carved modillions, typically Greek twin doorways and surmounting windows, and a similarly typical Italianate row of arcaded windows illuminating the nave.

A helicopter view of Brooklyn's tallest skyscraper, The Williamsburgh Savings Bank Building, at 1 Hanson Place. Completed in 1929, the building's observatory commands a spectacular view of downtown Brooklyn and the Manhattan skyline. (Brooklyn Union Gas Company)

13. Brooklyn's tallest skyscraper, the **Williamsburgh Savings Bank Building,** called "The Tower of Strength," measures 512 feet to the top of its gold-domed tower. Completed in 1929 from plans by Halsey, McCormick & Helmer, this singularly conspicuous landmark with its four illuminated tower clocks is clearly visible for miles around. The builders hoped in vain that its more central location on Brooklyn's Times Square (Brooklyn had its own *Times* for many years) would attract business away from the mile-distant civic center. Apparently the management of the Long Island Rail Road had the same opinion when they built the terminal around the corner. A visit to the observatory for sweeping panoramas of Brooklyn and the rest of the city is a "must."

Turn right (north) on St. Felix Place to Lafayette Avenue, then right again.

14. The Brooklyn Academy of Music, which compares favorably in al-almost every respect with Carnegie Hall, was constructed in 1908 from plans by Herts & Tallent, and moved to this larger site from its original location on Montague Street in Brooklyn Heights. As Brooklyn's leading cultural center, it is noted for the variety and high quality of its musical programs, theater productions, lectures, and films. The main auditorium, or Opera House, with a seating capacity of 2200, was inaugurated on November 14, 1908, with a production of *Faust,* sung by Geraldine Farrar and Enrico Caruso. Caruso opened the gala evening with a rendition of the "Star Spangled Banner."

A 1400-seat Music Hall and a newly built flexible-seating Lapercq Space offer dance recitals and chamber music concerts. A Chelsea Theatre Centre on the fourth floor houses the Academy's resident professional drama company. The Brooklyn Philharmonia, conducted by musical director Lukas Foss, presents a concert series each season, and the resident Pennsylvania Ballet performs a wide spectrum of classical and modern dance. There are also regular series in chamber music, Black Theater, and films. Visiting groups from out of town and abroad are frequent, with recent performances by the Royal Shakespeare and Young Vic Companies. Some of the notables who have performed or given lectures at the Academy are: Sergei Rachmaninoff, Ignace Jan Paderewski, Ernestine Schumann-Heink, Fritz Kreisler, Jascha Heifetz, Pablo Casals, Carl Sandburg, Edna St. Vincent Millay, Sinclair Lewis, William Jennings Bryan, and Winston Churchill.

The nearest subway station is at Atlantic Avenue. Follow Ashland Place past Hanson Place to the corner of Flatbush and Atlantic avenues, for the IRT Lexington and Broadway-Seventh Avenue lines, BMT QJ and M lines, and IND D line.

MYRTLE AVE.

WILLOUGHBY AVE.

RYERSON ST.

⑮

Pratt Institute

HALL ST.

CLINTON AVE.

WAVERLY AVE.

WASHINGTON AVE.

VANDERBILT AVE.

CLERMONT AVE.

RYERSON WALK

"THE

⑭

⑬

⑫ ⑪

DeKALB AVE.

HILL"

⑯

Underwood
Park

㉓

㉒

⑲

⑳

⑰

start

①

⑦

LAFAYETTE AVE.

□ IND
Subway

⑱ CLIFTON PL.

← To Fort Greene

⑥ ⑧

⑨

㉑

⑤

⑩

②

GREENE AVE.

③

ST. JAMES PL.

CAMBRIDGE PL.

④

GATES AVE.

CLINTON HILL

FULTON ST.

19. Clinton Hill

[*IND GG Line to Clinton-Washington station*]

With Brooklyn's rapid growth of population in the mid-19th century, a boom in row-house construction began. Pushing east and west, new neighborhoods developed along the post roads that led to the suburban villages of Bushwick, Jamaica, Flatbush, New Utrecht, and Gravesend. As the Brooklyn Heights section became completely built up, prosperous merchants and professionals found the high ground to the east to be very much to their liking. By the 1840s, the "Hill" [*see* map] became second only to Brooklyn Heights in elegance. The majority of new residents worked in Manhattan, only a 20-minute ride by stagecoach or omnibus to the Fulton Ferry landing, enjoying a quiet suburban life within sight of the city. By the 1880s and '90s, Clinton Avenue became a "Millionaires' Row," lined with the mansions of industrialists. Known as the "Fifth Avenue of Brooklyn," it remains in a remarkable state of preservation. Virtually all of Clinton Hill has survived the encroachments of rapid urban growth, and to this day presents a fascinating collection of architectural styles in its residences, churches, schools, and commercial buildings.

The tour begins at the corner of Clermont and Lafayette avenues.

1. Medgar Evers College of the City University of New York was formerly the Brooklyn Masonic Temple. Built in 1909 from plans by Lord & Hewlett, it is indeed a temple. The stately Ionic columns and terra-cotta polychrome designs are reminiscent of ancient Greece of the 4th century B.C.

2. Bishop Loughlin High School, built in 1933, marks the site of the **proposed Brooklyn Cathedral,** whose cornerstone was laid in 1868. Planned to be the largest church in the city, construction was suddenly halted when the walls reached a height of 12 feet, and the entire project abandoned, with the money diverted to charitable purposes. The Roman Catholic Diocese of

Brooklyn was founded in 1853, with John Loughlin appointed the first bishop.

3. The sole surviving part of the projected cathedral is the **Bishop's Residence,** on the northwest corner of Clermont and Greene avenues, designed by architect Patrick Charles Keely in 1889.

Across the street, on the northeast corner, is the **Roman Catholic Brothers' Residence and Chancery,** built c. 1885. It is an attractive, if somewhat somber building, with a mansard roof and cleanly dressed granite blocks. The *AIA Guide to New York City* claims that its grim appearance is not unlike that of "an orphan asylum in a Charlotte Brontë novel." The grounds, however, are much less grim and forbidding.

On the southeast corner once stood the Church of the Messiah and Incarnation, built between 1865 and 1892. An enormous Romanesque Revival-style building with a 130-foot tower, it was destroyed by fire in the late 1960s.

Turn left (east) on Greene Avenue to Vanderbilt Avenue.

4. At 90 Greene Avenue, **The Clinton** was built c. 1870 as a tenement house. Coinciding with the upgrading of the area at the end of the 19th century, the house was rebuilt in 1890 as a luxury "French flats," or apartment house for the affluent. "Tenement house" in those days did not have quite the negative connotation it does today—it was merely a multiple dwelling for the poorer classes.

5. The small residence at **375 Vanderbilt Avenue** was built originally as a stable.

6. The ornate clapboard house at the southeast corner of Vanderbilt and Lafayette avenues presents something of an architectural mystery. Known officially as the **Joseph Steele House,** and locally as the Skinner House (after the family that has lived in it since 1900), its precise history is unclear. The two-story section that now serves as a wing was built in Federal style, probably in 1812 when the "Hill" area was a remote, rural farmland. In the 1840s the main section was added in Greek Revival style. The house, which was actually located about 150 yards farther east, was moved to the present site around 1853 to make way for the construction of the Clinton Avenue Congregational Church, and further alterations were made—this time in the *Italianate* style! The roof was raised and certain Renaissance features added: the elaborate cornice, a new entranceway, and pedimented lintels over the front windows. It is likely that the wooden cupola dates from this latest modification, but it could be earlier. In spite of the lack of architectural integrity, the Steele (or Skinner) House is a delightful addition to the cityscape; and in recognition of its uniqueness of style and its history, it was designated an official New York City Landmark.

7. The Cathedral Church (and School) of Our Lady Queen of Martyrs, on the northwest corner, was designed by Gustave Steinbach in 1913. An impressive edifice, its splendid collection of stained-glass windows suggests the Sainte-Chapelle in Paris, while the 36 excellent sculptures of saints are reminiscent of St. Peter's in Rome. The building of the Church was commissioned by George Mundelein, Pastor of St. John's parish, who went on to be named Cardinal of Chicago. It is still referred to locally as "Bishop Mundelein's Church."

Turn right on Lafayette Avenue to Clinton Avenue.

8. The Cadman Memorial Church is a relative newcomer to Clinton Hill. It was erected in 1923 to replace an earlier Gothic church built in 1853 which had been designed by noted architect James Renwick, Jr. Three beautiful Tiffany art-glass windows were saved from its precursor, the Clinton Avenue Congregational Church, and incorporated into the design of the new building. In 1943 the congregation was merged with the Central Congregational Church and renamed in memory of the Central Church's former minister, Dr. S. Parkes Cadman. It was the Rev. Cadman who delivered the dedicatory invocation for the Prison Ship Martyrs' Monument in nearby Fort Greene Park [*see* Fort Greene, 7]. He was also the nation's first radio preacher, and was recognized by the City of New York for his activity in community affairs by the naming of downtown Brooklyn's Cadman Plaza.

9. The Clinton Hill Apartments, Section No. 2 of the Clinton Hill Development, were built in 1955 (Harrison & Abramovitz, Irwin Clavan), for families of naval personnel and workers in the nearby New York Naval Shipyard. Each entranceway has a different nautical motif.

10. Tree-lined **Clinton Avenue** still retains its 1880-period charm in the four-block stretch between Gates and Willoughby avenues. Turn right and walk a block-and-a-half past Greene Avenue, and return noting the following mansions: **410, 405** (in fascinating Queen Anne style), **324, 330–338, 321** (note its setback position and ornate cast-iron fence), **315, 313, 307–309,** and **287–293.**

Turn right (east) on DeKalb Avenue.

11. Two imposing sets of Romanesque Revival-style (with some Queen Anne-style) town houses bracket DeKalb Avenue near the corner of Waverly Avenue: **Nos. 285–289** (c. 1890) with a highly ornate terra-cotta frieze unifying the trio of brick and brownstone buildings, and **Nos. 284–288.** When built, each was designed for one (wealthy) family. All have since been subdivided into multiple dwellings.

Turn left (north) on Waverly Avenue.

Although it is not within the purview of this guidebook to recommend restaurants, it is not unlikely that hunger has now replaced architecture and history as a primary concern. And inasmuch as there are no places of refreshment in the immediate vicinity (with but one exception), it is fortunate that **Joe's Place** offers good food at modest prices, in a converted carriage house at 264 Waverly Avenue. The interior garden is particularly pleasant in warm weather.

Observe how narrow Waverly Avenue is, compared to Clinton and Washington avenues. Originally the stables and carriage houses of the wealthy residents were located on this street between the two "fashionable" streets.

Return to DeKalb Avenue, and turn right to Clinton Avenue again.

12. No. 275 Clinton Avenue is a well preserved triple-size luxury apartment building, built c. 1890.

13. The block between DeKalb and Willoughby avenues is a living memorial to the Pratt Family, and unquestionably the most beautiful in Clinton Hill. No less than four family mansions survive, and in pristine condition. Although now in other hands, they are still lovingly preserved.

When Charles Pratt built his huge oil refinery in the Greenpoint section in 1869, he made his fortune with a successful coal-oil product called "Astral Oil." So widely used was this kerosene that it was said that "the holy lamps

Clinton Avenue between DeKalb and Willoughby avenues c. 1895, showing three mansions built by petroleum industrialist Charles Pratt for his children. Clinton Avenue justly earned the reputation of being the "Fifth Avenue of Brooklyn." The scene is virtually the same today, only the home owners are different. (Brooklyn Collection. Brooklyn Public Library)

of Tibet are primed with 'Astral Oil.' " In 1874 Pratt became associated with John D. Rockefeller, and the firm was merged with the Standard Oil Company. He settled on Clinton Avenue and subsequently built homes for three of his sons in the same block, presenting each with a lovely mansion as a wedding present.

No. 245, now occupied by a department of St. Joseph's College, was built by Pratt for son George DuPont Pratt in 1901. A large, stately mansion, it was designed by the architectural firm of Babb, Cook & Willard.

No. 241 was built for eldest son Charles Millard Pratt in 1893. Designed by William B. Tubby in the Romanesque Revival style made popular by Henry Hobson Richardson, it is probably the most elegant of all his wedding-gift houses. To the south of the building is a conservatory built in semicircular shape; while illuminating the spectacular arched porte-cochere is a decorative spherical bronze lamp (which probably burned "Astral Oil"). The mansion is now the residence of the Roman Catholic Bishop of Brooklyn.

No. 229, now the Caroline Ladd Pratt House, was built for son Frederick B. Pratt in 1898. The gray-and-white Georgian Revival-style house was designed by the same architects as No. 241, and presents a most unusual appearance, attached on its left and freestanding on the right. Atlantean figures and caryatids support a kind of pergola entraceway.

No. 232, across the street, is the "daddy" of them all—the original Charles Pratt manor house, built c. 1875. Designed in an Italianate style, the building and picturesque gardens are virtually unchanged—a credit to St. Joseph's College, the present owner. Pratt's fourth son, Harold I., chose instead to live on Manhattan's fashionable Park Avenue, building a mansion of his own at the corner of East 68th Street.

Adjacent No. 226, McEntgart Hall, is another addition to St. Joseph's rambling Clinton Avenue "campus."

Across the avenue, Nos. 221–215 are an attractive row of town houses, also originally designed for single-family occupancy.

Turn right (east) on Willoughby Avenue.

14. Nos. 112–122 Willoughby Avenue are an interesting row of middle-class town houses.

Continue east on Willoughby Avenue past Hall Street (St. James Place) to the entrance to the Pratt Institute Campus.

15. Pratt Institue was the pet project of Charles Pratt himself. Founded in 1887 and dedicated to science and art, it was directed personally by the industrialist until his death in 1891. The school has an enviable reputation in the fields of art and design, fashion, architecture, engineering and science, and food science and management.

Entering the campus on Ryerson Walk (formerly Ryerson Street—now

The Main Building of Pratt Institute on Ryerson Street in 1910, designed in an "industrial Romanesque" style. Charles Pratt founded the institution in 1887 and ran it as his own private project. The school still maintains high standards in its major fields of science and art. (Brooklyn Collection. Brooklyn Public Library)

demapped), the first building on the left is North Hall, followed by the Byzantine-style Memorial Hall. Adjacent to the right is the original 1887 **Main Building,** designed by William Wingren in an industrial Romanesque Revival style. To the right of Ryerson Walk is the Student Center.

When Pratt Institute expanded its campus in the 1950s and '60s, a number of streets were closed and several unneeded buildings demolished, resulting in a five-square-block campus area in which the remaining school buildings stand in "splendid isolation."

The Pratt Institute **Library** was built by the school's industrialist-benefactor as Brooklyn's first free public library. Completed in 1896 from plans by William E. Tubby (who designed the Charles Millard Pratt House), and later altered by John Mead Howells, it is a dramatic Romanesque Revival building with some Renaissance details. The heavy brick piers on the west façade (facing Hall Street) give the building a massive and overwhelming aspect. Interesting is the entrance portico with its diminishing arches. Since 1940 the Library serves the needs of the student body only, and is no longer open to the public.

Bear to the right, cutting diagonally across the campus, and exit at the corner of Hall Street and DeKalb Avenue. Follow Hall Street, which is now called St. James Place, to the University Terrace Apartments.

16. An unusual feature of the **University Terrace Apartments** (Kelly & Gruzen, 1963) are the rows of *recessed* balconies, rather than the usual overhanging type.

Continue to the corner of Lafayette Avenue.

17. The enormous brick building on the southeast corner, extending to Clifton Place, is **Higgins Hall** (of Pratt Institute). Built in 1887–88 for the now-defunct Adelphi Academy, the cornerstone was laid by none other than the outspoken antislavery preacher Henry Ward Beecher. The honors for the South Building's cornerstone were performed by Charles Pratt. The structure is a veritable exercise book in Romanesque Revival motifs, with its towering buttresses, corbel-tables, and round- and segmental-arches. (Brick was relatively inexpensive in those days.)

The now defunct Adelphi Academy at St. James Place and Lafayette Avenue, photographed in 1896. The building is now part of Pratt Institute and was renamed Higgins Hall. The cornerstone was laid in 1887 by Henry Ward Beecher, and is almost a textbook example of the Romanesque Revival style. (Long Island Historical Society)

18. Clifton Place, from St. James Place to Grand Avenue, is lined with middle-class row houses dating from the 1870s.

Return to Lafayette Avenue and turn left (west).

19. The Emmanuel Baptist Church, a designated New York City Landmark, was built like a French 13th-century Gothic Cathedral, and its massive square twin towers dominate the entire area. Architect Francis H. Kimball, who designed it in 1887, employed Ohio sandstone, which is by nature somewhat porous, thus creating an affect of aging. The plan of the interior is in startling contrast, with its radial seating plan spreading fanlike from the pulpit. The style is similar to that of the First Baptist Church on Broadway and West 79th Street in Manhattan [*see* West of Central Park, 15]. The Church was cited in 1957 for its architectural distinction by the Municipal Art Society and the Society of Architectural Historians.

20. The neighboring **Apostolic Faith Mission,** at the northeast corner of Lafayette and Washington avenues, was built in 1868 as the Orthodox Friends Meeting House. In restrained Northern Italian, or Lombardian Romanesque style, it has been "brightened" by coats of pastel-colored paint by the new congregation.

21. Washington Avenue, between Lafayette and Greene avenues, is an unusual block. Virtually every architectural revival style can be seen (includ-

The Graham Home for Old Ladies at the corner of Washington and DeKalb Avenues was originally named The Brooklyn Society for the Relief of Respectable Aged Indigent Females. Erected in 1851, it is little changed from the outside. (Long Island Historical Society)

The dining room of the Graham Institution for Aged and Indigent Females in the mid-nineteenth century. The building is now a hotel. (Long Island Historical Society)

ing all the imitations) in **Nos. 357–359, 361, 364** (across the street), **363, 365, 374** (again across the street), the dismal **Mohawk Hotel,** and **396–404.**

Return to Lafayette Avenue.

22. Underwood Park, at the corner of Lafayette and Washington avenues, is named for typewriter king John T. Underwood, who donated the plot to the City. His family mansion, which formerly stood on the site, was a red-brick and brownstone structure with a glass-enclosed greenhouse, and was demolished, according to his will, to make way for the park.

Turn right (north) on Washington Avenue.

23. One of the oldest structures of its kind in the city is the former **Graham Home for Old Ladies** at 320 Washington Avenue. Built in 1851 on land donated by Underwood, it served for many years as a home for the aged, and has recently been converted into a hotel. The cornerstone was laid by founder John B. Graham, and the institution named the Brooklyn Society for the Relief of Respectable Aged Indigent Females. According to its charter, it was designed "for the benefit of poor gentlewomen who had been unfitted by previous culture and refinement to accept willingly the public asylum provided by the State for the poor indiscriminately."

End of tour. The IND Subway station is around the corner at Lafayette and Waverly avenues.

137TH ST.   34TH ROAD

(Site of Prince House)

PRINCE ST.

RKO Keith's

FARRINGTON ST.

Flushing Town Hall

LINDEN PL.

LEAVITT ST.

35TH AVE.

Flushing High School

(Site of Parsons House)

NORTHERN BLVD.

Civil War Mon.

Street Clock

Cemetery

Quaker Meeting House

Armory

Masonic Temple

Old Orthodox Meeting House

(Site of Aspinwall House)

YMCA

Weeping Beech Park

Cedar of Lebanon

Kingsland House

Fox Oaks Rock

Bankers Trust Co.

37TH AVE.

109 Pct. P.D.

Bowne House

Remonstrance Monument

St. George's Church

38TH AVE.

138TH ST.

Parking Field (future bus terminal)

39TH AVE.

IRT Subway

Chamber of Commerce

Lippman Arcade

Korean Church of Queens

ROOSEVELT AVE.

start

UNION ST.

BOWNE ST.

Long Island Railroad

(Port Washington Branch)

LIRR Sta.

41ST AVE.

MAIN ST.

41ST ROAD

BARCLAY AVE.

KISSENA BLVD.

SANFORD AVE.

HISTORIC FLUSHING

MAPLE AVE.

FRANKLIN AVE.

ASH AVE.

20. Historic Flushing

[*IRT #7 Flushing line to Main Street station (travel time about 45 minutes)*;
*Long Island Railroad, Port Washington Branch, from Pennsylvania Station
to Flushing-Main Street. Travel time 17 minutes.*]

Among the earliest settlements in the Dutch colony of New Netherlands
was the town of Vlissingen, now known as Flushing. In the charter granted
by Governor William Kieft in 1645, six years after he purchased the land
from the Matinecock Indians, the original 18 freeholders were assured of
their freedom of religious worship. Although the town was named for its
Dutch counterpart in Flanders, the settlers were all English. The tiny village
on the north shore of Long Island soon figured in one of the great events
in the cause of religious freedom in America. With the arrival in 1657 of a
group of English Quakers, newly appointed Governor Peter Stuyvesant, ignoring the original charter, issued a proclamation banning all religious observance
but the official Dutch Reformed.

In angry response, 30 townspeople signed a document of protest on
December 27, 1657, known as the **"Flushing Remonstrance."** Stuyvesant's
reaction was swift. A detachment of militia was dispatched to Flushing where
all signers were arrested and fined. This did not put an end, however, to
meetings by the Religious Society of Friends, as they gathered secretly in the
house of a newly arrived Englishman, John Bowne, who invited them to
worship in his kitchen. When news of this act of disobedience reached Governor Stuyvesant, he again took punitive action, imprisoning Bowne for a
period of several months, then banishing him from the colony. Bowne, however, ultimately reached Amsterdam, where he successfully pleaded the cause
of religious freedom before the Council of the Dutch West India Company.
The Council then sent a strong letter to Peter Stuyvesant stating in no uncertain terms that all men could exercise freedom of conscience. The Quakers
continued to meet in the Bowne House until a meeting house was built in
1694. Both buildings still remain and will be visited on the tour.

Flushing prospered for almost 200 years as one of several independent towns in what is now the Borough of Queens, until 1900 when it was consolidated into the City of New York. With the opening of the Queensboro Bridge to Manhattan in 1909 and the Long Island Rail Road tunnel to Pennsylvania Station a year later, Flushing grew rapidly. In 1928 the subway arrived, opening the suburb for even more development. La Guardia Airport was built across Flushing Bay in 1939, the same year the New York World's Fair was inaugurated in Flushing Meadow Park. In 1964–65 a second World's Fair was held at the same site, and with the accompanying construction of several major expressways, Flushing became another extension of the city's urban sprawl.

So many historic landmarks remain in a relatively small area that local historical societies have designated it as Flushing's "Freedom Mile." (*Note: The best day to visit is Sunday when virtually all of the points of interest are open to the public.*)

The tour begins at the intersection of Main Street and Roosevelt Avenue.

Walk north on Main Street, the principal thoroughfare and commercial

Main Street, looking north toward Northern Boulevard from Thirty-seventh Avenue in 1914. Trolleys and horses were the major form of transportation in what still appears to be a typical small town. (Queens Borough Public Library)

A supply of beer has just been delivered by horse and wagon to Edward McCormick's "Klondyke" at 115 Main Street, c. 1910. (Wiener Collection. Queens Borough Public Library)

Part of the annual Farmers' Parade in front of the Fountain House, at the southeast corner of Main Street and Northern Boulevard, c. 1898. The Fountain House was a small hotel and saloon, on the "other side of the tracks" from the elegant Flushing Hotel. (Queens Borough Public Library)

St. George's Episcopal Church is the third structure on the site. This view of the second *building shows it on Lincoln Street (now 38th Avenue) in 1903. It was moved around the corner from Main Street in 1854, 33 years after it was built, and was used until 1930. The newer St. George's visible at the left, took over the Main Street site in 1854. (New-York Historical Society)*

John Geddes's Paint Store, at 105 Main Street, c. 1898. Note the hitching posts and stepping stone. (Wiener Collection. Queens Borough Public Library)

Battery-operated street car on Main Street, opposite the stately Flushing Hotel on Broadway (now Northern Boulevard), c. 1900. The hotel was the center of Flushing social life during the latter nineteenth and early twentieth centuries. (David G. Oats, Flushing Tribune)

district of Flushing. The **Chamber of Commerce Building**, No. 39–01 Main Street, at the northeast corner of Thirty-ninth Avenue, is an interesting example of the Art Deco style so popular in the 1930s.

Diagonally across the street, is **St. George's Episcopal Church,** occupying the entire block to Thirty-eighth Avenue. An earlier church on the site received its charter in 1761 from King George II of England. A subsequent house of worship replaced it in 1821, and the present structure dates from 1854. Built in Gothic Revival style from plans by Wills & Dudley, its graceful spire is the tallest landmark in Flushing. Francis Lewis, signer of the Declaration of Independence from New York, served here as vestryman from 1769 to 1790. Peek over the iron fence at the early churchyard, which contains the graves of many of the early residents.

On the northwest corner of Main Street and Thirty-seventh Avenue is a fine example of the Art Deco style in the **Bankers Trust Company,** Flushing branch building. Erected for the Flushing National Bank in the mid-1930s, its smooth limestone façade with low-relief "modernistic" sculpture and octagon-shaped clock are typical of the period.

Midway between Thirty-seventh Avenue and Northern Boulevard, on the west side of Main Street, is a 15-foot-high **cast-iron street clock.** Hearkening back to the days before the invention of the wristwatch, these public time-

The Prince House, located until the late 1950s, at the intersection of Northern Boulevard and Prince Street. William Prince established the first tree nursery in the country in 1737. (David G. Oats, Flushing Tribune)

pieces performed a useful service to those who could not afford a pocket watch, at the same time functioning as an advertisement for the retail establishment that erected it. Only a scant handful of street clocks survive in New York City from the thousands that decorated sidewalks from coast to coast at the turn of the century.

At the head of Main Street, on Northern Boulevard, is the **RKO Keith's** movie house. A popular vaudeville theater when it opened, its stage is said to have launched the careers of a number of Hollywood stars. The theater occupies the site of the old Flushing Hotel, a rambling wooden structure whose double tiers of broad porches and well appointed parlors made it the focal point in the '80s and '90s of Flushing's social life.

To the left of the theater, from Prince Street down to Flushing Creek, was the world famous **Prince Nursery.** Established in 1737 by William Prince, it was the first tree nursery in the country. Known later as the Linnaean Botanic Garden, it provided thousands of tree specimens from all over the world. George Washington was a guest at the Garden in 1789. Although it is now long since gone, the heritage of William Prince's old nursery lives on in the more than 200 species of trees growing throughout the country.

The "island" in the middle of Northern Boulevard marks the center of **Daniel Carter Beard Square.** "Dan" Beard, a naturalist and illustrator, and a native of Flushing, was one of the founders of the Boy Scouts of America,

The Flushing Quaker Meeting House on the south side of Northern Boulevard in the early 1930s. The building faces south, away from the winter's north winds. Built in 1694, it is New York's oldest house of worship. (Queens Borough Public Library)

In the Quaker Meeting House, a "ship's knee," removed from an old sailing vessel, helps support a 40-foot beam, hand-hewn in 1717 from a tall oak. (Office of the Borough President of Queens)

and served as National Scout Commissioner until his death in 1941 at the age of 91. The monument is Flushing's **Spanish-American War Memorial,** erected in 1950. Note the plaque cast from a piece of the battleship *Maine*. The adjacent **Washington Elm** was planted in 1932 by the American Legion to commemorate our first president's visit to Flushing on October 10, 1789.

Turn right (east) on Northern Boulevard.

The Friends Meeting House is the oldest house of worship in New York City and one of the earliest in the country. Built in 1694, with an addition in 1717, it provided a permanent place for religious observance for those who first met secretly in the home of John Bowne. Except for a period during the Revolutionary War when the occupying British forces used it as a prison, a hospital, and a storage place for hay, the Meeting House has been in continuous use for almost 300 years. The plain, rectangular building with a hip-roof faces south—away from the winter winds—towards an interior burial ground. Two doorways on the open front porch originally served as separate entrances for men and women. Devoid of ornamentation, the simple meeting room with its plastered walls and unfinished wood benches reflects the

A scene in the Flushing Town Hall's court room, c. 1895. Flushing was an independent town until 1900, when it joined the City of New York. The Town Hall then became the Court House. (Wiener Collection. Queens Borough Public Library)

Quaker spirit, which calls for undistracted devotion. Hand-hewn 40-foot oak beams, cut from a single tree, are still in place on the second story, and are as solid as the day they were installed. Timbers from a dismantled sailing ship were used in the 1717 section, and ships' "knees" can be seen supporting the ceiling beams. One of two early cast-iron heating stoves dating from 1760, and used until 1956, is on display in the Meeting House, while the original hand-wrought iron door hinges, latches, and locks are still in use. The churchyard, no longer used for interments, contains simple, low stones inscribed with the names of many prominent Long Islanders of the early 19th century. Headstones placed before 1835 bear no inscriptions. The Friends Meeting House is the oldest house of worship in the New York area and is listed in the National Register of Historic Places. It is also a designated New York City Landmark. Visitors are welcome to visit the Meeting House and grounds, and attend the hour-long Sunday worship meetings.

The **Civil War Monument** and surrounding mini-garden was erected in 1866 in memory of the young men of Flushing who died in the tragic war to preserve the Union. The funds to build the monument were raised through public subscription. Enter through the iron gate and read the fading inscriptions on the pedestal.

Across Northern Boulevard, at the corner of Linden Street, is the **Flushing Municipal Court House,** formerly the Town Hall. Saved at the last minute from the wrecker's ball, it is now well protected as a designated New York City Landmark. Built in 1862 by Cornelius Howard, a local carpenter, in an early Romanesque Revival style, the Flushing Town Hall served the community until 1900 as a center of civic, cultural, and social life. In addition to its role as a town meeting house and seat of local government while the village was still independent, it hosted a variety of public events. The Hall witnessed celebration balls, political meetings, community gatherings, and even operas and concerts. It was also the headquarters of the local Volunteer Artillery Unit. When it gave up its function as a municipal courthouse in the 1960s, it was slated for demolition. Faced with the loss of their oldest civic structure, concerned citizens and local historical societies raised a storm of protest, which ultimately convinced the city fathers of the need to preserve this picturesque and historic landmark. Plans have just been approved for appropriate adaptive reuse of the building as a 19th-century-style restaurant with office space and meeting rooms in the basement for city and community use. Note the tall, thin buttresses, paired arched windows, and brick corbels under the cornice—all typical of the early Romanesque Revival style.

Farther down the center mall is the **World War I Memorial Monument,** executed in white marble by famed sculptor Hermon MacNeil in 1920, and is best viewed from the north side of the Boulevard. Like the Civil War Monument, it was financed through public subscription.

Reminiscent of a medieval castle is the red-brick **New York State Air National Guard Armory.** With its twin turrets, crenelations, machicolations, and ramparts, it seems a holdover from the days of knighthood. Built in 1905 in the typical "armory architectural style" popular in the 19th and early 20th centuries, it still conveys an impression of strength and security. On the site stood the house of Michael Milnor, where in 1657 the Flushing Remonstrance was signed, touching off the first struggle for religious freedom in America.

To the left of the Armory, and almost hidden behind the Masonic Temple, is a two-story red-brick structure which once served as the meeting house for a breakaway group of Quakers. Objecting to the liberal tendencies of preacher Elias Hicks, a schism developed, and the more orthodox group separated itself from the "Hicksites," erecting this building in 1827 as their own house of worship. The sect has long-since disappeared.

Flushing High School, on the north side of the Boulevard, was built in 1915, in the then-popular Gothic Revival Public School style. The building replaced an earlier structure located a few blocks west, which received its first charter in 1875. Flushing High is the oldest, free public high school in the City of New York. The newer east wing was completed in 1954 and is dedicated to those students who gave their life in World War II.

The Samuel Bowne Parsons House stood on the site of Flushing High School's annex, on Broadway (now Northern Boulevard), opposite Bowne Street. Parsons maintained a tree nursery in the mid-nineteenth century and many of his plantings are still to be seen throughout Flushing, particularly the Weeping Beech and Cedar of Lebanon near the Bowne House. (Queens Borough Public Library)

A sketch of the Bowne House as it appeared c. 1790. The "salt box" was built by John Bowne in 1661 and is considered a shrine to religious freedom in America. (Bowne House Historical Society)

Directly opposite Flushing High School, and to the right of the present Y.M.C.A. Building, stood the **old Aspinwall House,** built in 1762. During the Revolutionary War it became the headquarters of the officer corps of the occupying British Army; and in the Civil War it was a station on the Underground Railroad, helping escaping slaves reach freedom. It is said that a secret tunnel connected the Aspinwall House with the nearby Bowne House, where these runaways were hidden and cared for while awaiting passage on a ship to New England. Unfortunately, the house was razed in the late 1950s.

Turn right at the Y.M.C.A. into Bowne Street.

About 100 yards down the street is a large gray boulder known as the **Fox Oaks Rock.** George Fox, who founded the Religious Society of Friends in England in 1645, came to America to preach in 1672. He intended to hold his meeting in the Bowne House, but the turnout was so great that he was forced to hold it outdoors under some tall oak trees opposite the house. The oaks have disappeared, but the site is marked with the inscription on the rock.

The **Bowne House,** built in 1661, is a landmark shrine to religious freedom. Little did John Bowne anticipate when he arrived in Flushing in 1655 that he would be the central figure in a monumental struggle for freedom of religious observance—freedom for a sect to which he did not even belong at the time! That he would defy the law, be arrested, fined, imprisoned, and banished, later to return a hero, never entered his mind.

The Quakers had been holding clandestine worship meetings in nearby woods, when Bowne built his home, embraced Quakerism, and invited the Friends to meet in his spacious kitchen. The rest is history. And the well-built house survives intact as a memorial to the accomplishments of this courageous, soft-spoken man. The House is now a museum maintained by the Bowne House Historical Society, and is open to the public on Tuesdays, Saturdays, and Sundays, 2:30 to 4:30 P.M. The furnishings of the house are all original, with additions provided by each of the successive nine generations of Bowne descendants who lived in it until 1946. A number of periods are represented in the house's fine collection of antiques. Extensions were added to the house in 1680 and 1696—the latter, a "salt box" section, with sloping roof. Additional living space was provided in 1830 when the roof on the main house was raised and an extra wing added. The kitchen is the focal point of the house, just as it was when John Bowne entertained George Fox and, later, William Penn.*

The kitchen has been restored to its original appearance and is the oldest part of the house. Not only was this the center of culinary activities, but the center of most of the family's domestic activities. The kitchen even housed overnight guests. Its enormous fireplace could easily roast an ox, and the "beehive" oven extends through the fireplace wall.

The wooden shed in the garden shelters a huge cast-iron cauldron formerly used for making soap. Across the garden is the **Remonstrance Monument** with a plaque containing the complete text and list of signers of the Flushing Remonstrance. To the rear of the house is a typical herb garden. The original Bowne property extended north for some distance and included much of the land up to where Flushing High School is now located. The Bowne House has been designated a New York City Landmark.

Exit through the rear garden and follow the path along the playground to the beginning of Thirty-seventh Avenue. To the left is the Kingsland House.

The **Kingsland House** is New York City's only building that had to be relocated to maintain its landmark status. Built by Charles Doughty in 1774 as a typical middle-sized farmhouse, it was situated about one-and-a-half miles east, at what is now the intersection of 155th Street and Northern Boulevard. "Kingsland" was named after Doughty's son-in-law, Joseph King, an English sea captain. In the early 19th century the house was acquired by William King Murray who moved the house to the site of 155th Street and Roosevelt

---

* It was William Penn, usually thought of only in connection with Pennsylvania, who in 1683 persuaded the Duke of York to grant permission to the towns of Long Island to establish their own Representative Assembly. This body then drafted its historic Charter of Liberties, almost 100 years before the Declaration of Independence!

The Kingsland House, on its former site at 155th Street near Roosevelt Avenue, is the only landmark that had to be relocated before it could be designated. The house was built in 1774 as a middle-class farm house, and has been moved twice. It is now a museum and stands adjacent to Weeping Beech Park. (Office of the Borough President of Queens)

Avenue. The Murray Hill section of Flushing is named for the family which occupied the house until 1932. An earlier relative, Robert Murray, owned a farm in the late 18th century on Manhattan's East River shore, and it is for him that the midtown Murray Hill neighborhood is named.

In 1965 "Kingsland" was scheduled for demolition to make way for a shopping center. The Kingsland Preservation Committee was organized to save the house, and after four years of painstaking effort and negotiation, the 200-year-old house was moved on a flat-bed trailer to its present site in Weeping Beech Park. The operation required the cooperation of nine city departments, plus the New York Telephone Company and Con Edison. Six hundred feet of telephone and utility wire had to be removed from the city streets before the 38-foot-high house could make the journey.

The two-story house represents both Dutch and English Colonial architectural styles, particularly in the gambrel roof, central chimney, and round-headed and quadrant window in the gables. It is the second-oldest house in Flushing and the only surviving house from the 18th century. "Kingsland" is now owned by New York City's Parks, Recreation & Cultural Affairs Depart-

The great Weeping Beech, a city landmark, in 1926. The house to the left was demolished, and in its place stands the recently relocated Kingsland House. (Office of the Borough President of Queens)

ment, and serves as a museum of local history, architecture, and decorative arts, as well as a community center. It is staffed by volunteers, and is sponsored by the Queens Historical Society, which has its headquarters in the House. The landmark is listed in the National Register of Historic Places, and is open to the public at the same hours as the Bowne House.

At the rear of "Kingsland," in diminutive **Weeping Beech Park,** is one of the most extraordinary trees in the world. The weeping beech's enormous canopy of lush foliage presents an incredible vista of long, spreading branches reaching skyward, then arching gracefully to the ground, to create a charming, enclosed bower. The tree was planted by Samuel Parsons in 1847 from a small shoot brought by his son from Belgium. Parsons, who married into the Bowne family, established his nursery in 1838 on land obtained from his in-laws. Much of the nursery was located where the playground is today. Like the earlier Prince Nursery, Parsons grew many species of trees and specialized in exotic varieties that could adapt to the local environment. The lovely beech was one of his enduring successes. In the late 19th century the nurseries were moved to the Kissena Park district; however, a number of beautiful trees scattered throughout Flushing are reminders of the extensive horticultural industry. Flushing's involvement with trees is seen in the names of so many of its streets: Ash, Quince, Hawthorn, Laburnum, Maple, etc.

Recognizing its history and unique permanent beauty, the Landmarks Preservation Commission in 1970 awarded landmark status to the weeping beech.

Another example of the legacy of the Parsons Nursery is the **Golden Larch** on the lawn of the Kingsland House, facing Thirty-seventh Avenue. According to the Queens Botanical Garden, it is a very rare species.

On returning to Bowne Street by the path alongside the playground, notice the unusual **Cedar of Lebanon** in the middle of the playground; and at curbside on Bowne Street a mighty swamp oak. Both trees remain as living evidence of Samuel Parsons's horticultural skill; his name is also immortalized by Parsons Boulevard, the next major thoroughfare to the east.

The Cedar of Lebanon tree in mid-nineteenth century stood alone in this uncultivated field. The tree, a little the worse for wear, is almost lost in the center of a playground on Bowne Street surrounded by other trees and apartment houses. (Queens Borough Public Library)

Turn left (south) on Bowne Street, past the Bowne House to the corner of Roosevelt Avenue.

On the northeast corner is the former **Reformed Church of Flushing.** Built in 1892, it belonged to the Dutch Reformed Movement—the first organized congregation in New York, dating from 1628. The massive red-brick building is built in the Romanesque Revival tradition so popular at the close of the last century. The building was recently acquired by the Korean Church of Queens.

On the northwest corner is the site of "Dan" Beard's home (coincidentally replaced by a "Dan's" Supreme supermarket).

A half-block to the south is the "cut" used by the Long Island Railroad Port Washington Branch. The ancestor of this line was the Flushing North Side Railroad, which reached Flushing in 1854.

Turn right (west) on Roosevelt Avenue to Main Street, and the end of the tour.

Daniel Carter Beard's home at the northwest corner of Roosevelt Avenue and Bowne Street in a 1941 sketch. The site, coincidentally, is occupied by a "Dan's Supreme" supermarket. (Queens Borough Public Library)

Related Bibliography

ACKERMAN, JAMES S. *Palladio*. Baltimore: Penguin, 1966.

A1A Guide to New York City. WHITE, NORVAL, and WILENSKY, ELLIOTT, eds. Sponsored by the New York Chapter, American Institute of Architects. New York: Macmillan, 1968.

ALBINO, ROBERT GREENHALGH. *The Rise of New York Port (1815–1860)*. New York: Scribner's, 1967.

ANDREWS, WAYNE. *Architecture in New York*. New York: Atheneum, 1969. (Republished 1973, Harper & Row Icon Books)

———. *Architecture, Ambition, and Americans—A Social History of American Architecture*. New York: Free Press, 1964.

ASBURY, HERBERT. *All Around the Town*. New York: Knopf, 1929.

———. *The Gangs of New York*. Garden City: Garden City Publishing Company, 1927.

ASHER, BENJAMIN. *The American Builders' Companion*. A facsimile of the 1827 edition. New York: Dover, 1969.

BAILEY, ROSALIE FELLOWS. *Pre-Revolutionary Dutch Houses and Families in Northern New Jersey and Southern New York*. New York: Morrow, 1936. (Republished 1968, Dover)

BARAL, ROBERT. *Turn West on 23rd*. New York: Fleet Press, 1965.

BARLOW, ELIZABETH. *The Forests and Wetlands of New York City*. Boston: Little, Brown, 1969.

——— and ALEX, WILLIAM. *Frederick Law Olmsted's New York*. In association with the Whitney Museum of American Art. New York: Praeger, 1972.

BEARD, JOHN, ed. *Blue Water Views of Old New York*. Barre, Mass.: Barre Publishers—Scrimshaw Press, 1970.

BERGER, MEYER, *Meyer Berger's New York*. New York: Random House. 1960.

BIXBY, WILLIAM. *South Street, New York's Seaport Museum*. New York: McKay, 1972.

BLACK, MARY, ed. *Old New York in Early Photographs*. From the collection of the New-York Historical Society. New York: Dover, 1973.

BLIVEN, BRUCE, Jr. *The Battle for Manhattan*. Baltimore: Penguin Books, 1965.

———. *Under the Guns—New York: 1775–1776*. New York: Harper & Row, 1972.

BOTKIN, B. A., ed. *New York City Folklore*. New York: Random House, 1956.

BROWN, HENRY COLLINS. *Fifth Avenue, Old and New, 1824–1924*. Publication of the Fifth Avenue Association. New York: Fifth Avenue Association, 1924.

———, ed. *Valentine's Manual of the City of New York*. New series. 12 vols. published annually, 1916–1928, including *New York in the Elegant Eighties* (vol. of 1927) and *New York in the Golden Nineties* (vol. of 1928). New York: 1916–1928.

———. *The Story of Old New York*. New York: Dutton, 1924.

BURNHAM, ALAN, ed. *New York Landmarks*. Middletown, Conn.: Wesleyan University Press, 1963.

CALLENDER, JAMES H. *Yesterdays in Brooklyn Heights*. New York: Dorland Press, 1927.

———. *Yesterdays in Little Old New York*. New York: Dorland Press, 1929.

CHRISTMAN, HENRY M., ed. *Walt Whitman's New York*. New York: Macmillan, 1963.

CLARY, MARTIN. *Mid-Manhattan*. Publication of the 42nd Street Property Owners & Merchants Association. New York: 1929.

CONDIT, CARL W. *American Building*. Chicago: University of Chicago Press, 1968.

CONDON, THOMAS J. *New York Beginnings—The Commercial Origins of New Netherland*. New York: New York University Press, 1968.

CORDASCO, FRANCESCO, ed. *Jacob Riis Revisited—Poverty and the Slums in Another Era*. Garden City: Doubleday Anchor, 1968.

Dedication of the Prison Ship Martyrs' Monument. Souvenir Dedication booklet, November 14, 1908. New York.

DELANEY, EDMUND T. *New York's Greenwich Village*. Barre, Mass.: Barre Publishers, 1965.

———. *Turtle Bay, Old and New*. Barre, Mass.: Barre Publishers, 1965.

Designation Reports of the Historic Districts: *Carroll Gardens, Central Park West —76th Street, Chelsea, Cobble Hill, Greenwich Village, Henderson Place, Park Slope, SoHo-Cast Iron*. New York City Landmarks Preservation Commission, 1966–1974.

DICKENS, CHARLES. *American Notes* (Chapter 6, "In New York"). New York: J. B. Lippincott, 1885.

DILLIARD, MAUD ESTHER. *An Album of New Netherland*. New York: Bramhall House, 1963.

DUNSHEE, KENNETH HOLCOMB. *As You Pass By*. New York: Hastings House, 1962.

The 1866 Guide to New York City. A facsimile edition of J. Miller's *New York as it is*. New York: Schocken, 1975.

ELLIS, EDWARD ROBB. *The Epic of New York City*. New York: Coward-McCann, 1966.

FABOS, JULIUS GY, MILDE, GORDON T., and WEINMAYR, V. MICHAEL. *Frederick Law Olmsted, Sr., Founder of Landscape Architecture in America*. Amherst: University of Massachusetts Press, 1968.

FEININGER, ANDREAS. *The Face of New York*. New York: Crown, 1954.

FIELD, THOMAS W. "The Battle of Long Island with Connected Preceding Events and the Subsequent American Retreat." In *Long Island Historical Society Memoirs*, Vol. II. Brooklyn: 1869.

Fifty Years on Fifth, 1907–1957. Publication of the Fifth Avenue Association. New York: Fifth Avenue Association, 1957.

FINNEY, JACK. *Time and Again.* New York: Simon & Schuster, 1970.

"The First Two Hundred Years." Selections from *Via Port of New York.* The Port Authority of New York & New Jersey. New York: undated.

FURMAN, GABRIEL. *Notes Geographical and Historical Relating to the Town of Brooklyn in Kings County on Long-Island.* A facsimile of the 1824 edition. Brooklyn: Renascence, 1968.

GAYLE, MARGOT, and GILLON, EDMUND V., Jr. *Cast Iron Architecture in New York.* New York: Dover, 1974.

The Gentle Art of Walking. A compilation from the *New York Times.* George D. Trent, ed., introduction by Hal Borland. New York: Arno Press/Random House, 1971.

GIFFORD, DON, ed. *The Literature of Architecture.* New York: Dutton, 1966.

GOLDSTONE, HARMON H., and DALRYMPLE, MARTHA. *History Preserved—A Guide to New York City Landmarks and Historic Districts.* New York: Simon & Schuster, 1974.

GOODWIN, MAUD WILDER, ROYCE, ALICE CARRINGTON, and PUTNAM, RUTH, eds. *Historic New York: First and Second Series of Half Moon Papers.* New York: G. F. Putnam's Sons, 1899.

HAMLIN, TALBOT. *Greek Revival Architecture in America* (Chapter 6, "Classic Revival in New York"). New York: Oxford, 1944. [Republished 1964, Dover]

HAPGOOD, HUTCHINS. *The Spirit of the Ghetto.* New edition with drawings by Jacob Epstein and preface by Harry Golden. New York: 1902. [Republished 1966, Schocken]

HEADLEY, JOEL TYLER. *The Great Riots of New York, 1712–1873.* New York: Dover, 1971.

The Heritage of New York. The New York Community Trust, with introduction by Whitney North Seymour. New York: Fordham University Press, 1970.

A History of Fifty Feet in New York at Wall and William Streets. The Bank of America. New York: 1926.

HITCHCOCK, HENRY-RUSSELL. *The Architecture of H. H. Richardson and His Times.* Cambridge: M.I.T. Press, 1961.

———, FEIN, ALBERT, WEISMAN, WINSTON, and SCULLY, VINCENT J., Jr. *The Rise of an American Architecture.* Published in association with the Metropolitan Museum of Art. New York: Praeger, 1970.

HONAN, WILLIAM H. ed. *The Greenwich Village Guide.* New York: The Villager, 1959.

HUXTABLE, ADA LOUISE. *Classic New York: Georgian Gentility to Greek Elegance.* Garden City: Doubleday Anchor, 1964.

IRVING, WASHINGTON. *Knickerbocker's History of New York,* New York: 1809.

IRWIN, WILL and SUYDAM, E. H. *Highlights of Manhattan,* New York: Century, 1927.

JAMES, HENRY. *Washington Square.* New York: Harper & Brothers, 1881.

JANVIER, THOMAS A. *In Old New York.* New York: Harper & Brothers, 1894.

JENKINS, STEPHEN. *The Greatest Street in the World: Broadway.* New York: G. P. Putnam's Sons, 1911.

KAHN, ALAN PAUL. *The Tracks of New York, 1907: The Metropolitan Street Railway.* New York: Electric Railroaders Association, 1973.

KIDNEY, WALTER C. *The Architecture of Choice: Eclecticism in America 1880–1930.* New York: Braziller, 1974.

KING, MOSES, ed. *King's Handbook of New York City.* New York: 1893.

———, ed. *King's Views of New York, 1908–1909.* New York: 1909.

KOUWENHOVEN, JOHN A. *The Columbia Historical Portrait of New York.* New York: Doubleday, 1953. [Republished 1972, Harper & Row Icon Books]

KRAMER, ELLEN W. "Contemporary Descriptions of New York City and Its Public Architecture, ca. 1850." In *Journal of the Society of Architectural Historians,* XXVII:4, December 1968.

———. "The Domestic Architecture of Detlef Lienau." Including a description of the A. T. Stewart Store, pp. 51–57. Published as a dissertation for the degree of Doctor of Philosophy, New York University Institute of Fine Arts, 1958.

LAAS, WILLIAM. *Crossroads of the World—The Story of Times Square.* New York: Popular Library, 1963.

LADIES OF THE MISSION. *The Old Brewery and the New Mission House at the Five Points.* New York: Stringer & Townsend, 1854.

LAMB, MARTHA J. *History of the City of New York.* 2 vols. New York: A. S. Barnes & Company, 1877.

LANCASTER, CLAY. *Old Brooklyn Heights.* Rutland, Vt.: Charles E. Tuttle, 1961.

LANIER, HENRY WYSHAM, and ABBOTT, BERENICE. *Greenwich Village Today and Yesterday.* New York: Harper & Brothers, 1949.

LEWIS, EMORY. *Cue's New York.* New York: Duell, Sloan & Pearce, 1963.

LLOYD, THOMAS, ed. *Lloyd's Pocket Companion and Guide Through New York City for 1866–67.* New York: 1866.

LOCKWOOD, CHARLES. *Bricks and Brownstone.* New York: McGraw-Hill, 1972.

LYMAN, SUSAN ELIZABETH. *The Story of New York.* New York: Crown, 1964.

MACOY, ROBERT. *Old Landmarks, or How to See New York and Its Environs.* New York: undated, but probably 1881.

Manna-hatin—The Story of New York. Introduction by Mayor James J. Walker. New York: The Manhattan Company, 1929.

MARCUSE, MAXWELL F. *This Was New York!* New York: LIM Press, 1969.

MAYER, GRACE M. *Once Upon a City.* New York: Macmillan, 1958.

MCCABE, JAMES D., Jr. *Lights and Shadows of New York Life, or The Sights and Sensations of the Great City.* A facsimile of the 1872 edition. New York: Farrar, Straus & Giroux, 1970.

MCCAUSLAND, ELIZABETH, ed. *New York in the Thirties as Photographed by Berenice Abbott.* New York: Dover, 1973. [Originally published as *Changing New York.* Guilds' Committee for Federal Writers' Publications, Works Progress Administration. New York: Random House, 1939.]

MCCULLOUGH, DAVID. *The Great Bridge.* New York: Simon & Schuster, 1972.

MORRIS, LLOYD. *Incredible New York.* New York: Random House, 1951.

MUMFORD, LEWIS. *The Brown Decades: A Study of the Arts in America, 1865–1895.* New York: Harcourt Brace, 1931. [Republished 1955, Dover]

———. *The Roots of Contemporary Architecture.* Second edition. New York: Dover, 1972.

NEVINS, ALLAN, ed. *The Diary of Philip Hone, 1828–1851.* New York: Dodd, Mead, 1936.

————, ed. *The Diary of George Templeton Strong, 1835–1875,* 4 vols. New York: Macmillan, 1952.

New York City Guide. Guilds' Committee for Federal Writers' Publications, Works Progress Administration. New York: Random House, 1939.

New York, N.Y. New York: American Heritage, 1968.

New York Public Sculpture by 19th Century American Artists. Catalog by Lewis I. Sharp, walking tours by David W. Kiehl. New York: Metropolitan Museum of Art, 1974.

The New York Subway—Its Construction and Equipment. Interborough Rapid Transit Company. New York: privately printed, 1904. [Republished Arno Press, undated]

OSBORN, GARDNER. *The Streets of Old New York.* New York: Harper & Brothers, 1939.

PAYSON, WILLIAM FARQUHAR. *Through the Lich Gate—A Biography of the Little Church Around the Corner.* New York: Church of the Transfiguration, 1931.

The Penguin Dictionary of Architecture. FLEMING, JOHN, HONOUR, HUGH, and PEVSNER, NIKOLAUS, eds. Baltimore: Penguin Books, 1966.

PHELPS, H., ed. *Phelps' Strangers' and Citizens' Guide to New-York City.* New York: 1857.

A Proposal for the Designation of Fort Greene as an Historic District. Fort Greene Landmarks Preservation Committee, 1973.

REED, HENRY HOPE. *The Golden City.* New York: Norton, 1971.

The Renaissance of City Hall. Commemorative Presentation Publication of the Rededication of City Hall. Introduction by Allan Nevins, with selections by various contributors. New York: City of New York, 1956.

RESSEGUIE, HARRY E. "A. T. Stewart's Marble Palace—The Cradle of the Department Store." *New-York Historical Society Quarterly,* XLVIII:2, April 1964.

RIDER, FREMONT, ed. *Rider's New York City: A Guide for Travelers.* New York: Macmillan, 1924.

RIIS, JACOB. *How the Other Half Lives—Studies Among the Tenements of New York.* New York: Charles Scribner's Sons, 1890. [Republished 1971, Dover]

————. *The Making of an American.* New York: Macmillan, 1924.

RISCHIN, MOSES. *The Promised City—New York's Jews, 1870–1914.* Cambridge: Harvard University Press, 1967.

ROBINSON, CERVIN and BLETTER, ROSEMARIE HAAG. *Skyscraper Style—Art Deco New York.* New York: Oxford University Press, 1975.

ROSEBROCK, ELLEN FLETCHER. *Walking Around in South Street: Discoveries in New York's Old Shipping District.* New York: South Street Seaport Museum, 1974.

————, TOWNLEY, CHRISTINE, TOWNLEY, JOHN, and WALTON, TERRY. "Fulton Ferry Brooklyn . . . Our River's Other Shore." *South Street Seaport Reporter,* VIII:4, Winter 1974–75, 2–9.

RUSKIN, JOHN. *Seven Lamps of Architecture.* Reprinted, New York: Farrar, Straus & Cudahy Noonday Books, 1969.

SANDERS, RONALD. *The Downtown Jews—Portraits of an Immigrant Generation.* New York: Harper & Row, 1969.

SCULLY, VINCENT J., Jr. *American Architecture and Urbanism.* New York: Praeger, 1968.

Silver Jubilee of Greater New York, 1898–1923. Official publication of the Exposition. Mayor's Committee of the 25th Anniversary of the Greater City of New York, 1923.

SILVER, NATHAN. *Lost New York.* New York: Houghton Mifflin, 1967. [Republished 1971, Schocken]

SMALL, VERNA. *Nineteenth Century Dwelling Houses of Greenwich Village.* New York: Association of Village Homeowners, Landmarks Committee, 1968.

SMITH, MARY ANN. "John Snook and the Design for the A. T. Stewart Store." In *New-York Historical Society Quarterly,* LVIII:1, January 1974.

SMITH, MATTHEW HALE. *Sunshine and Shadow in New York.* Hartford: J. B. Burr, 1868.

STEIN, LEON. *The Triangle Fire.* Philadelphia: Lippincott, 1962.

STILES, HENRY R., ed.-in-chief. *A History of the County of Kings and the City of Brooklyn, N.Y., 1683–1884.* 3 vols. Brooklyn: 1884.

STILL, BAYRD. *Mirror for Gotham.* New York: New York University Press, 1956.

STOKES, ISAAC NEWTON PHELPS. *The Iconography of Manhattan Island, 1498–1909.* New York: Robert H. Dodd, 1915. [Republished 1971, Arno Press]

———. *New York Past and Present, 1524–1939.* New York: New-York Historical Society, 1939.

STURGES, WALTER KNIGHT. "Cast Iron in New York." In *Architectural Review,* 114:682, October 1953.

———, ed. *Origins of Cast Iron Architecture in America.* Daniel D. Badger's "Illustrations of Iron Architecture" (1865) and James Bogardus's "Cast Iron Buildings, Their Construction and Advantages" (1856). A facsimile edition. New York: Da Capo Press, 1970.

VALENTINE, DAVID T. *History of the City of New York.* New York: G. P. Putnam, 1853.

VAN RENSSELAER, MARIANA GRISWOLD. *Henry Hobson Richardson and His Works.* New York: Houghton Mifflin, 1888. [Republished 1969, Dover]

VAN WYCK, FREDERICK. *Recollections of an Old New Yorker.* New York: Liveright, 1932.

VIALLS, CHRISTINE. *Industrial Archaeology: Cast Iron.* London: A. & C. Black, 1970.

VLACK, DON. *Art Deco Architecture in New York,* 1920–1940. New York: Harper & Row, 1974.

WAITE, JOHN G., ed. *Iron Architecture in New York City.* The Edgar Laing Stores and the Cooper Union. State Historic Trust and Society for Industrial Archaeology, 1972.

WARE, CAROLINE F. *Greenwich Village 1920–1930.* New York: Harper Colophon Books, 1965.

WHARTON, EDITH. *The Age of Innocence.* New York: Grosset & Dunlap, 1920.

WHIFFEN, MARCUS. *American Architecture Since 1780: A Guide to the Styles.* Cambridge: M.I.T. Press, 1969.

WHITEHOUSE, ROGER. *New York: Sunshine and Shadow—A Photographic Record of the City and Its People from 1850–1915.* New York: Harper & Row, 1974.

WILSON, RUFUS ROCKWELL. *New York Old and New—Its Story, Streets and Landmarks.* 2 vols. Philadelphia: B. Lippincott, 1902.

WISCHNITZER, RACHEL. *Synagogue Architecture in the United States—History and Interpretation.* Philadelphia: Jewish Publication Society of America, 1955.

Index